3/7/09

To Joe ~

May you always
with sharp hooks and
tight loops.....

Let's do it again!!

Best wishes,

Stu Apte

MW00781442

OF WIND AND TIDES

A Memoir

By

STU APTE

Hall-Of-Fame Angler,

Fighter Pilot, Pan-Am Captain—

The Incredible Story

Copyright © 2008 by Stu Apte

All rights reserved. No part of this book may be reproduced in any manner
whatsoever without written permission, except in the case of brief quotations
embodied in critical articles and reviews.

Printed by API Book Distribution, Inc.
USA

Publisher's Cataloging-In-Publication Data
(Prepared by The Donohue Group, Inc.)

Apte, Stu.
Of wind and tides : a memoir / by Stu Apte.

p. : ill. ; cm.

ISBN-13: 978-0-9821227-0-9

1. Apte, Stu. 2. Fishers--Biography. 3. Air pilots--Biography. 4. Fishing. I. Title.

SH415.A68 O5 2008
799.12/092   2008908358

FRONTISPIECE

…Though anglers are rarely surprised by a totally grim day, we nearly always maintain our optimism. We understand pessimism because our dreams are sometimes dented by the blows of fate, but always our hope returns, like a primrose after a hard winter.

–Chris Yates, "How To Fish"

I learned how to fly fish in the hit-and-miss, trial-and-error way that makes things stick, and I learned patience, persistence, acceptance and probably a few other good things, too.

–John Gierach, "Another Lousy Day in Paradise"

Oh! I have slipped the surly bonds of earth
And danced the skies on laughter-silvered wings,
Sunward I've climbed, and joined the tumbling mirth
Of sun-split clouds—and done a hundred things
You have not dreamed of—wheeled and soared and swung
High in the sunlit silence…
Put out my hand and touched the face of God.

From "Dancing the Skies"
By John Gillespie Magee, Jr.

TABLE OF CONTENTS

ACKNOWLEDGMENTS

I offer sincere thanks to all my friends who helped ensure this book's clarity and accuracy. With a special thanks to the following, whose inspiration and contributions have been a key factor in my finally pressing on to completion of this Herculean task: Allison [Ali Cat] McDonald, who helped me get started on the right foot with this project, Fred Anderson, Dave Beshara, Richard Campiola, Jim Chapralis, brothers Pete and Tim Eshelman who loaned me their "girl friday" Melanie, Greg Friedman who offered me one of his secretaries, General Bill Gorton, my old friend Lefty Kreh, Francis Pandolfi retired president and CEO of Times Mirror Publications, John Randolph Editor and Publisher Fly Fisherman Magazine, Bob Rich Jr., Dr. Neal Rogers, Jennifer Aquia the wonderful young lady artist responsible for the painting of my life on the dustcover and line drawings on the hardcover, Todd Milligan for the many hours he spent helping me upload photographs on the computer. Also I cannot thank enough my old friends Doug Kelly and Lamar Underwood, for without their guidance and editing this would end up as just another memoirs book.

Finally, words cannot express my love and sincere appreciation for my wife Jeannine, the love of my life, whose patience and proof reading and suggestions have kept me focused.

PREFACE

I'm from Miami. Born and lived there.

Not the Miami you know today. *My* Miami is long gone. Today I live in the Florida Keys.

The Miami you know today is a burgeoning, sprawling blob of concrete and construction, laced by networks of highways that are either thundering with traffic or suddenly turned into parking lots of jammed vehicles. Today's Miami has more than its share of crime, including drug trafficking, and is replete with immigration and racial strife. The familiar face of South Beach, with the bronzed glistening bodies of models and actresses, the paparazzi following them, the gawking tourists, the expensive shops, restaurants and hotels—they put a cosmetic face on the Miami of today that did not exist in my Miami.

Born in 1930, I grew up in a kinder, gentler Miami. There were no four-lane highways, there were streetcars instead of buses, and only about 20,000 people lived there. Miami was a safe town then, and with my brother Marvin, five years older, I was riding bikes and streetcars to explore the myriad waterways and canals by the time I was six. The fever to fish was already rampart within me at that early age, and Miami was filled with places a kid could go to and fish by walking, bike or streetcar.

Through the late 30s and into the early 40s, the nation was still gripped by the Great Depression. But, like everyone else, the Apte family coped and my childhood was spent surrounded by a loving, caring family—and fishing opportunities that I learned to explore more and more as I grew toward my teens.

Although I was too young to pay much attention early-on, we entered the 40s overshadowed by what an often-quoted passage from the Bible (Matthew 24:6) describes perfectly: "Ye shall hear of wars and rumors of wars."

On December 7, 1941, the day "Rumors of Wars" erupted into the real thing, the Apte family was spending a relaxing day on the sands of Miami Beach. My father worked long hours, six days a week, and treasured these Sunday outings. To this day, I recall peering through the car window on the ride home and seeing paperboys on street corners shouting, "Extra! Extra!" behind front pages proclaiming Japan had bombed Pearl Harbor.

The Apte's were a patriotic family. We had a victory garden in the back yard, and my mother worked in a large room at the Filter Center plotting plane and ship movements in the South Florida area for the Air Defense Network. Aunt Gloria, my mother's younger sister who lived with us, worked for the U.S. Censorship Bureau, reading and censoring Spanish language letters. Aunt Gloria received a letter of commendation from President Roosevelt for breaking up a spy ring above and beyond her normal duties. While waiting for her friend to finish censoring mail in Portuguese, she happened to pick up a letter her friend Maria had already passed, and detected something in it that did not seem just right. She took it to her supervisor for clarification and the U.S. military got lucky. Marvin graduated high school from Gordon Military College in Barnesville, Georgia, in 1942, and with our parent's written permission joined the Navy.

My passion for fishing and "Rumors of Wars" collided in 1942.

Early one Saturday morning, I took my bicycle and plug-casting outfit to the seawall at 25th Road and the Bay. By mid-morning I ran into another young fisherman I knew from school, who was with his parents mostly having a family day out. Fishing must have been slow, because we ended up driving to Matheson Hammock in Coconut Grove to try our luck there. Fishing was much better and we didn't leave there until 8:00 in the evening. By the time I got home, all of my immediate family and relatives from as far away as Miami Beach were at my house. As far as my parents knew, I was a missing person. They had called the police and the two local hospitals, the police had found my bicycle where I'd left it at 25th Road in the Bay, and the assumption was that I had fallen in and drowned or been abducted.

That particular Saturday, a German submarine was spotted just off Government Cut in Miami. During that time of the war, the Germans were putting spies ashore in Miami and the Florida Keys by submarine. My mother believed my disappearance had something to do with the German submarine. When I walked in the house my mother started crying, my father started scolding and all of the relatives started questioning me at the same time. "Where have I been? Why didn't I call?" Everyone believed I was dead. Evidently my friend's parents figured that because they had fed me, all was okay.

A little later in 1942, on a Sunday, we were relaxing on a blanket above the high waterline once again on Miami Beach. We heard loud reports from offshore. A German U-Boat had surfaced, shelled and sank an oil tanker that had just come out of the Port of Miami through Government Cut. The U-Boat evidently felt no need to use one of their torpedoes. We were witness to the whole episode. Each time the submarine fired its deck gun, we first saw a puff of smoke from the U-boat, then a flash of the explosion as the shell struck the tanker, and in a few moments heard the two reports as the sound drifted to shore.

It must have been an incoming tide with a strong wind from the east that pushed the ship's debris, some bodies and a few survivors along the beach where we were. It's a frightful sight that I'll never forget no matter how long I live.

The long shadows of the war had reached my beloved home town. Little could I know how those shadows, how "Wars and Rumors of Wars" would shadow my life far into the future. Through World War 11, into Korea, even Vietnam, those "Shadows" would dictate how I was to live and work and evolve. Of course, I could not perceive that in any way at that time. There on the darkening beach—what is South Beach today—I could only feel a sense of

15

dread, of uneasiness. Had I know that my love of fishing would sustain me through any crisis, war or peace, I probably could have smiled that day. But I had no such vision, no such powers of perception.

A few months later, a German U-boat surfaced one night and fired five shells at an oil storage depot near Fort Lauderdale's seaport. Censorship at that time during the war kept this from being in the newspapers and on the radios across the country. Every house and every building had blackout curtains, and used them. Gasoline and oil was rationed as was sugar and coffee.

Nobody in my family liked to fish, but I was fortunate enough to have a next-door neighbor who was a great outdoorsman. He gave me my first plug-casting outfit, a custom-made, split-bamboo rod, 5 feet long with a Shakespeare Superior level-wind casting reel. Bud James would have been in his late 50s or early 60s in 1942, and was a retired Texas Ranger. This means he would've been a Ranger near the turn-of-the-century. What a great role model for a 12-year-old boy to have as a next-door neighbor.

The James's, as my parents referred to them, would take me fishing in the 10,000 islands of the Everglades and in the Florida Keys. They were fixing up a little house they bought right on the bay on Key Largo. It's presently where the Cross Key Canal or Adams Cut goes through from Backwater Sound to Key Largo Sound. Bud painted a small sign he tacked on a palm tree, calling his place "El Retiro Lodge." The summers of 1942 through 1945 were some of the most enjoyable, memorable times I can remember. I was able to spend three or four weeks each summer with the James's at El Retiro Lodge, exploring the wonders of the upper Florida Keys.

Fishing in Miami and the Keys, growing into teen-age years with a wonderful family—that was my life. I had not yet thought of becoming a pilot, of fishing around the world. Miami and the Keys *were* my world. I worshiped every canal, creek, channel, and flat I could fish. Had I known what the years ahead had in store for Stu Apte, I suppose I would have fainted.

Now my flying logbook is finished, closed. My fishing memory bank has been stoked full, but I'm still adding to it, every chance

I get. Looking back, I can see clearly how lucky I have been and blessed by God time after time. Mine has been a life many would envy—flying a Navy jet fighter; becoming a pilot with Pan-Am; fishing literally all over the globe, often with interesting and famous people; becoming a flats guide in my beloved Keys; filming television shows; and learning, along the way, how deeply I need to love and be loved.

As a fighter pilot, I have flirted with extreme dangers and emerged to fly again. As an angler, I have fought, sometimes winning, sometimes losing, many fights with fish to dream about. But I feel today that my most courageous fight came not with a rod in my hand in some exotic fishing destination, but here in Florida at home, and in doctors' offices and hospitals. Cancer had invaded by blood cells, and had I not fought back, and been lucky at the same time, I would not be writing these words.

And writing them is something I've wanted very much to do. I want to share in some small way, if I can, glimpses into my journey. From Florida's legendary waters, into the skies, and into boats and skiffs around the world with people like Ted Williams, Curt Gowdy, John "Hondo" Havlicek, Dick Butkus and many, many other famous and infamous characters.

If you don't care a thing about fishing and flying and living life to the hilt, you've got the wrong book in your hands. But if you do, you're in for a heck of a ride—just like I was!

And, even though it's been said before in other places, I can say here that the strangest thing of all about my story is that it really happened.

Stu Apte
Islamorada, Florida,
November, 2007

17

CHAPTER

ONE

CRISIS IN THE COCKPIT:

Three Narrow Escapes,

And a Fishing Revelation

Aviation in itself is not inherently dangerous. But to an even greater degree than the sea, it is terribly unforgiving of any carelessness, incapacity or neglect.

–Captain A.G. Lamplugh, British Aviator, Circa 1930s

As in fishing, where "the big ones always get away," flying has more than its share of little clichés that hang around forever. One you've no doubt heard goes, "Any landing you can walk away from is a *good* landing." To which some wise-cracking pilots add, "Any landing you can *taxi* away from is a *great* landing."

Another popular aviation homily goes, "He bought the farm." That one stems from the barnstorming days of flying when crash landings damaged farm properties and compensation had to be made. A pilot whose crash cost him his life was said to have "bought the farm."

In 1952 I was a 22-year-old Naval Aviation cadet when the possibility of "buying the farm"—literally and figuratively—suddenly loomed in my face. My ride into terror was provided by the Navy's SNJ, the same airplane I had been training in for weeks and had soloed in the day before, to great personal exaltation and celebration with my fellow students. I loved that airplane. Its R-1340 air-cooled engine put out 600 horsepower and could sweep me across the landscape at 205 mph max. Now that's what I call a trainer! It was the first airplane I had ever flown. With my instructor in the seat behind me, I had met the challenges of learning to fly with his approval and praise. Today, on my first solo cross-country flight, I had flown from my home field at South Whiting, just outside of Pensacola Florida, to an outlying strip called 8-Able near Brewton, Alabama. The syllabus for the day's practice menu called for flying stalls and recoveries at 5,000 feet and shooting touch-and-go landings.

After touching down on one of my practice landings, I was giving that big engine the gun, climbing straight ahead on the runway heading. At 1,000 feet, my windscreen suddenly was awash with oil, totally obscuring my view ahead. The engine shuddered, then quit. Cold turkey! The sudden silence was like a stunning blow. Only the sound of the wind could be perceived above my own thoughts, which were racing.

I'm at a dangerously low altitude with a frozen engine. I need a place to park. Fast!

My instructor had always been adamant about practicing emergency short-field landings, for situations exactly like this one. I could hear his voice now:

Don't turn back for the runway. You'll stall! Maintain airspeed, Fly the airplane! Straight ahead! Don't stall! Airspeed! Airspeed!

I slid the canopy back and peered over the side into the slipstream of rushing air.. I seemed to remember a cornfield being straight ahead, bordered by a line of trees. I had to clear those trees! I popped out full flaps, cutting my airspeed but giving me some immediate lift, precious lift to clear those trees. I left the wheels up; they would rob airspeed if lowered.

My thoughts were screaming: Stay level, stick and rudder. Nose down. Airspeed. Airspeed. Ease her down. Don't stall!

Suddenly the trees sweep past, just barely cleared, and I'm over a cornfield, sinking slowly into it. My wheels-up landing is a good one, and I touch down with a minimum of speed. I am mowing down corn rows when my right wing slams into a tree. Yes a tree! In the middle of a cornfield! Probably the only cornfield in Alabama with a tree in the middle of it. And I've hit it!

At the crash the airplane spins around and around through the corn. At that moment I thought I was a goner. When the whirling stopped, dust and debris were so thick I could barely breathe. But I was alive and in one piece!

Instinctively, I had cut all the switches. (Later, I couldn't even remember doing that.) I unbuckled my seat belt and shoulder harness and jumped out of what was left of the airplane, my thoughts telling me, "She's going to blow in a second." I must have set some kind of record for a 100-yard dash, all the time thinking my back was broken. When I couldn't run any farther and fell flat on my face, I rolled over and discovered to great relief that my back was not broken. I couldn't run in an upright position because I still had my parachute strapped to my butt!

As I unbuckled my parachute, a farmer pulled up in an old jeep. He wore a straw hat, and had a piece of straw hanging from his lips, the scene would have looked like Ol' MacDonald had come to my rescue. He took off his hat and scratched his head. First he surveyed me, then the airplane, and finally the mess that used to be his cornfield.

"Are you OK, son?" he said. "Looks like you had a little trouble."

Back at the Pensacola Naval Air Station Hospital, I got a complete physical and checked out fine, except for a couple of pretty badly skinned shins and an unusually high blood pressure (good old adrenaline).

Fortunately, for the Navy and me, I had not "bought the farm." But I felt that I sure as hell had made a pretty good down payment on one.

* * *

No matter how you look at it, flying in the military is a dangerous job, especially operating high-performance aircraft from aircraft carriers. Add flying combat missions to the mix, and you can believe there will be casualties. Without my realizing it, my Alabama Adventure had been a mere tune-up for what was to come.

Fast-forward, if you will, to March, 1954. I'm a jet jockey now, having worked my way through more-advanced airplanes and years of training, including carrier operations, into the cockpit of the F9F-5 Panther. I have joined an elite squadron, VF 81, which had just returned to their home base at NAAS Oceana, Virginia, after duty in Korea. Rumors were flying that VF 81 was first in line for receiving the new, highly-touted, supersonic F7U-3 Cutlass

Back in July, the previous year, a flight of four F9F-5 Panther jets dropped the last U.S. Navy bombs of the long Korean Conflict, doing so on an airfield southwest of Hungnam. It had been three years, one month and two days since the North Korean People's Army attacked South Korea in the pre-dawn hours of June 25, 1950, crossing the 38th Parallel behind a firestorm of artillery barrage equipped by the Soviets with 150 T-34 tanks. Now the War ("Conflict" it had been called!) was over, but VF 81 and its Panthers were very much on duty and I was part of the team.

Because of my background fishing in the Everglades, I was given a collateral duty in VF 81 as Aviation Equipments and Survival Officer, which put me in charge of the squadron parachute loft, oxygen equipment and survival gear.. At first as a young, brand-new Naval officer, I felt strange having a much older chief petty officer, the senior enlisted sailor in my division, calling me "Mister Apte" and "Sir."

Some months later I was assigned a three-week Temporary Additional Duty at the SAC Survival School, Stead Air Force Base in Reno, Nevada. After checking into the base, we were stripped of all our personal items except our wristwatch, a parachute and survival knife. I was issued minimum hygiene items, including a sleeping bag which evidently had not been properly fumigated and gave me a horrid case of crabs.

My group of four Naval Aviators went through five days living off the land, while escaping and evading the "aggressors" that were looking for us while at the same time having to travel 65 miles, mostly at night. When captured we were tied up, blindfolded, transported back to a very realistic mock prison camp, physically and mentally abused, sometimes experiencing days of sleep deprivation and made to do heavy calisthenics until we dropped. The aggressors next forced me to lie in a hole just long enough to cover my body length, with the ground beneath lined with rocks. A heavy wooden door placed over me almost touched my nose.

After hours of this horrific treatment, I was interrogated by the aggressors, who were dressed in North Korean/Russian uniforms. No doubt, I probably went through more than my share of this because I was slated to fly an airplane that was classified Secret (the F7U3 Cutlass), and I'd be dealing with the first Sparrow Missiles, classified Top Secret. The aggressors already knew about this and were trying to break me down because I had a Top Secret as needed clearance. This type of interrogation became so realistic, an Air Force B-45 pilot who had been interned in a German Stalag during World War II completely flipped out. *Time* magazine had a big write-up about the SAC Survival School, calling it the "Air Force Torture School."

Back at the squadron, my job was to teach all of my squadron mates everything I learned about surviving on their own while escaping and evading if shot down over enemy terrain. Of course, I was still an active pilot.

One Friday in September, after flying two rocket and bomb training hops totaling more than three hours, my home waters and fishing were very much on my mind. Visions of snook, redfish and tarpon danced through my head.

I decided to launch a most unusual fishing trip. I would "borrow" a Panther jet for the weekend, fly it down to the Naval/Marine Corps Reserve Air Station in Miami to visit my parents and get out on the water for some fishing action. My "ride" was perfectly OK with the Navy. The flight would be logged as a "cross-country proficiency flight."

I stowed my two-piece spinning outfit and a tackle box of artificial lures in one of the 20mm gun bay/radio compartments in the nose of the Panther. Little did I know that in a short time my seemingly routine "baggage handling" was to play a potentially lethal role in the skies over the Florida coast.

The weather forecasted tail winds, making it a fast flight, with relatively clear skies in route. Pilots are taught that weather forecasts are just that: *forecasts*. In the sky it doesn't matter what kind of weather you *want* to get; it doesn't matter what kind of weather the forecast said you *would* get; all that matters is what you *do get*. And what I got was not the forecast I had so eagerly received that morning.

Approaching the Jacksonville, Florida, area from 25 miles offshore at 21,000 feet, I encountered the leading edge of a fast-moving, severe cold front. While flying on instruments, I penetrated a large very active cumulus nimbus thunderstorm. The clouds were dark, towering, boiling with wind and up- and down-drafts. My Panther became a bucking bronco, and level flight became difficult, then impossible. I thought the wings could be torn off any second (in most airplanes they would have been!). Suddenly a gigantic blast of air severely flipped my airplane upside down, tossing my fishing tackle around. Making myself believe the instruments, I did a slow aileron roll the left. Now I was fighting a severe case of vertigo…my instincts telling me I was still upside down while my Gyro Horizon instrument indicated I was not. Vertigo is one of the most difficult things I've had to cope with in the cockpit of an airplane and is responsible for killing many pilots.

When I regained control of my Panther, I discovered I had lost the VOR and ADF radios—which was my only means of navigation—and one of my two VHF communication radios. My fishing tackle crashing around in the gun bay/radio compartment had obviously damaged some critical components.

I had to get my jet on the ground, out of that damned storm!

For some reason I was unable to raise Jacksonville Naval Air Station on 121.5 guard channel with the radio, but NAAS Sanford tower could hear me loud and clear and had me in radar contact. After receiving clearance to descend on a specified heading, Navy Sanford approach control was going to give me a GCA [Ground Controlled Approach] to land. This is the kind of "talk down" approach where the controller brings you right to the runway threshold.

All went well until at 50 feet above the ground, with the Panther again bucking like a rodeo bronco, in heavy rain and hail, the final approach controller lost radar contact with me, telling me to execute a missed approach and climb out to 1,000 feet straight ahead on the runway heading, and prepare to make another GCA approach. Two more approaches had the same tension-building ending. My Panther and I were vectored up and around for the fourth approach attempt.

Was I sweating now? Hell yes! And then things got even worse!

Now my hundred-pound fuel bingo light came on, necessitating my telling the approach controller that I'd have to pull up and eject if he lost me on my next approach. Luckily I was not being pitched around quite as severely as I was on the previous three approaches and managed to see runway lights through the torrential downpour just before touching down. Mother Earth had never felt so good!

Exiting the duty runway on a high-speed turnoff, I was given taxi instructions to park at a visiting aircraft designated area. Barely able to see the taxi-way lights, I advanced my throttle in order to start moving toward the tower. The jet engine started spooling up, then abruptly started winding down, out of fuel.

As I sat in the cockpit waiting for a tow truck to come out and pull me to the designated parking area, I thanked God for blessing me with that extra little bit of fuel in my tank. Without it, this "fishing trip" could have been my last.

At the BOQ, soaking wet from both rain and sweat, I took a quick shower and went downstairs to the Officer's Club lounge. There, I suddenly came down with a severe case of hives, swelling both of my eyes completely shut. The next morning I felt okay enough to continue my flight to the Naval/Marine Reserve Air Station in Miami and enjoyed a precious day and a half of fishing, before returning nonstop to my squadron at Oceana, Virginia.

That was definitely a fishing trip I would never forget!

* * *

Now it was back to our day-in, day-out training sessions of air-to-air gunnery and practicing dive bombing and rocket attacks. Even though we were designated a fighter squadron, we knew our primary duty was to provide close air support to the Marines and Army troops in addition to destroying bridges, ammunition dumps, fuel dumps and other targets of opportunity – all requiring precision flying.

The new all-delta-wing, supersonic F7U-3 Cutlass was on the way, its arrival eagerly anticipated, when suddenly the new fighter cast a dark shadow over Fighter Squadron VF-81. We lost two of our highly regarded, well-seasoned squadron mates. They were both on their third tours of duty, had been checked-out flying the F7U-3 Cutlass at Patuxent River Naval Air test facility in Maryland, and were now slated to instruct the rest of our squadron. We'd be one of the first to receive this innovative fighter.

Our pilots were doing a low altitude fly-by during the new super carrier USS Forrestal's commissioning at the Norfolk Naval Shipyard, when one of the Cutlass's went into a post-stall gyration, tumbling head-over-heels, crashing into the other one, killing both pilots instantly.

The jet crashes and losses of life drove home the fact that flying military jets is not child's play. Then came an experience which will be imbedded into my mind forever.

Follow along with me, in the cockpit of my F9F-5 Panther:

We are flying a rocket and bomb practice exercise. *Only a drill,* I assure myself, pickling [shooting] five-inch HIVARS [High Velocity Aircraft Rockets] and dropping 100-pound practice bombs in an area known as Duck and Caffy Target Range

The racetrack pattern around the target is at 10,000 feet. While maintaining radio communication with ground personnel in the target area, my wingman, John White, flies in a right echelon formation to me as we circle to the left around the target area. We await the Charlie word – an okay from the ground to make a dry pass or a firing run when the target area is hot. If other aircraft or Navy personnel are on the ground resetting the target, it's Dog – the signal to continue circling the target area.

The jet is equipped with six rockets, three on each wing, and two 100-pound water-loaded practice bombs. Each bomb has a blast cap in the nose and a load of flour that disperses upon detonation to determine if it hit on or near the target.

At the time, all American fighter planes are "stick and rudder" aircraft; the rudder pedals and the joystick are used to fly the airplane. The rudder helps keep the aircraft in balanced flight, without slipping or skidding during a turn. The joystick operates the ailerons, which roll the airplane to the right or left, and the elevators, which make the aircraft climb or descend. But, the joystick has one more important function – weaponry activated by two pickle switches. An index finger operates one switch – a trigger to fire the four 20mm cannons—and the thumb operates a trigger to fire rockets and drop bombs, depending on which are selected.

The switches that arm the rockets or release the bombs are located to the left side of the gun sight, just below the glare shield. A guard around the master-arming switch must be selected up, to the on position, in order to fire any of the ordinances. The two switches just to the right of the master switch are three-way switches, labeled GUNS, outboard or inboard for firing the 20mm cannons. The center position is off; the down position is safe and the up position ready. The next two switches are for the rockets and bombs. The first time I fired all four 20mm cannons at the same time, I was actually thrown forward in my shoulder harness – the recoil from the cannons caused that much rapid aircraft deceleration.

The bright sun is still in the eastern sky. That makes my firing run east to west; the sun slightly behind me. I double check, and then cross check that I have the correct switches in the proper arming position before starting the hot dive.

I whip the Panther Jet over into a diving left turn, out of the racetrack pattern.

Concentrate! I order myself..

I roll out into a 60-degree dive, speed brakes extended to slow down to 300 knots. As I start the firing run, I'm almost hyperventilating in the oxygen mask. With the canopy closed, my oxygen mask is on 100 percent, and the Polaroid helmet goggles almost touch the mask. I am married to this Panther Jet, virtually a part of it. We are as one.

Concentrate! Keep the airplane in balanced flight, I remind myself. *No slip or skid.* The gun-sight pip is skewed by G-forces. *Don't throw the rockets off course.* I continue the list in my mind. *Keep the pip on the target. Check and allow for windage observed by smoke in the area. Maintain a constant airspeed until you pickle the rocket on target.*

It seems like both my heartbeat and breathing slow to a bare murmur during the last few seconds prior to pickling, squeezing off a shot.

The target on the ground is a circle, and I have my eyes on it long before I start the dive. In a 60-degree dive from the 250-knot racetrack pattern, the airplane plummets like a rock and the acceleration is more rapid then I can imagine. I activate my speed brakes, but the fighter plane keeps picking up speed. I reduce my power to maintain 300 knots until pickling my ordinance at the target, and start to pull out at approximately 3,000 feet. The jet, as if it had a mind of its own, swoops to 2,000 feet before reacting to the controls and climbing back into the racetrack pattern. Occasionally, a pilot's concentration is so acutely intent on hitting the target, they fail to start their pullout in time and end up crashing; they become hypnotized by the ritual of homing in.

Flying jet fighter planes gives me the feeling of exhilaration, a high. That high is accentuated when firing rockets, shooting 20mm cannons, or dropping bombs; it becomes a form of competition, bringing out the competitive spirit. But, both of those highs pale in comparison to the thrill of flying air-to-air gunnery.

I reach nearly four G's on every pullout, which for several seconds makes my body weigh three or four times more than normal. The special G-suit I wear plugs into the airplane and inflates like a balloon around my stomach, thighs and calves, helping to keep the blood from draining out of my brain and causing unconsciousness as I pull out of the dive.

Today has been a good shoot and I am feeling pretty confident about my ability to hit the bull's eye with both rockets and bombs. I climb to 20,000 feet and head back to NAAS Oceana with my wingman.

The air is smooth, and I am almost fully relaxed, looking off to my left at the North Carolina/Virginia coastline. My thoughts briefly stray to a fishing trip I took not too long ago, looking for big, 100-pound tarpon. Every summer these fish migrate along this coast, as far north as Chesapeake Bay. As for my favorite fish to catch in my home state of Florida, it has always been tarpon.

Staring out the window of the cockpit, it looks like a calm morning along the beach – perfect conditions for catching my favorite fish.

This picture disappears in a blink.

With a start, I am brought back to reality as two fire-warning lights flash and glare at me in the cockpit. In this model Panther Jet, the emergency instruction to all pilots is: "If a fire-warning light comes on in the plenum chamber, eject. Eject immediately! The aircraft is going to blow up." The plenum is where fuel and air combine in a potentially explosive mixture.

Damn I have two fire-warning lights come on, and one of them is in the plenum chamber.

The ejection procedure words to remember in the F9F-5 Panther Jets are, PRE-POS-OX-PULL.

PRE – activate your pre-ejection lever on the right side of the cockpit, which arms the ejection seat and jettisons the canopy. POS – position your feet in the stirrups of the ejection seat to prevent your kneecaps from being painfully removed as you exit the airplane. OX – reach down and activate your bailout oxygen bottle in your parachute seat by pulling a tab in the seat portion of your parachute. PULL – reach up, grab, and smartly pull down the two rungs extending from the ejection seat that houses the face curtain, in order to fire the seat. The Navy believes that the face curtain will give the pilot some protection when he hits the high-velocity air stream.

Although I can say "Pre-Pos-Ox-Pull" faster than I can complete the procedure, for this run though, I definitely set a record.

When the airplane explodes in a massive fireball, I am already on my way out. My wingman barely misses me in his evasive maneuver to avoid hitting my airplane's debris, and probably me along with it. The last thing I recall is pulling my face curtain. I don't remember tumbling through the air, unbuckling my seat belt and shoulder harness, or kicking myself out of the seat and pulling the ripcord.

John sees the parachute open and broadcasts a Mayday on the Guard Channel, which everyone monitors. The Naval Air Station's job is to immediately dispatch a rescue helicopter.

As I float towards the Atlantic Ocean from 20,000 feet, I drift in and out of consciousness until my mind actually flashes back quite vividly to when I was five years old. We're living in a house on the corner of Southwest 4th Street and 13th Avenue, in Miami. Being just a little tyke, my next-door neighbor's goldfish pond is full of what, it seems to me, are monster-size fish. I've used some of my mother's sewing thread, a straight pin which I bent to form a hook, and some dough balls to form a makeshift fishing apparatus.

When I think no one's watching, I cautiously sneak through the hedge that separates our properties, and fish for what I perceived as giant goldfish. This is a dangerous mission, because I know full well that if captured by the enemy, there is hell to pay. If my parents get me, I'll be punished; if my neighbor catches me, I'll be thrown out of his yard by the seat of my pants and it'll be a rough landing. This is definitely a stealth mission.

I reach my destination – the "lake" of fish. My imagination runs wild as I envision pulling fish after fish out with great explosions of water, fish sailing through the air into a large growing pile of flopping trophies. Contrary to my imagination, more often than not, the pin-type hook pulls out of the mouth of the goldfish. During the few times I manage to hook a goldfish, the fish breaks my thread, keeping the pin hook. The first time it happens, I feel so bad I cry.

My family knows I love to fish and swears it's because of the "baby-can-hear" theory. My mother says that women sing, play music, and perform soothing recitals for their yet unborn baby to bond with the child and give them a love for song, music and prose. But in my case, she tells me it happened a bit differently.

On a beautiful Sunday in late April of 1930, my parents went for a day of fishing with several uncles and aunts to the sea wall near the County Causeway that extends from Miami to Miami Beach. Some of the family fished with hand lines, twirling hooks and sinkers over their heads, before releasing them for long casts. I'm told it was quite a day of fishing; my Uncle Harry even managed to hook his own finger clear through.

Eight and a half months in my mother's tummy, perhaps I did feel the happiness of family, and began to understand the camaraderie of fishing together. I got an inkling of the competitiveness between fish and man, and heard those words for the first time: "You got one!" My mother says she loved that fishing day with her family so very much that two weeks later when I came into this world, she believes I was born with her same joy and love for fishing.

Now, suddenly, I'm with my 11-year-old brother, Marvin, who is five years older than me. We are at the main streetcar transfer stop in downtown Miami, behind Burdines Department Store, on Southeast 1st Street and Miami Avenue. We search the sidewalk in hopes of finding a discarded one-cent transfer ticket each, expensive items we can't afford. Luck is with us; we find a pair of transfers just in time to catch the next streetcar that will deposit us at the Miami side of the County Causeway, which goes across Biscayne Bay to Miami Beach.

Miami in 1936 is a small town with a population of perhaps 20,000 people. It is a very safe place to live. There are no four-lane highways, no city buses. Miami is in its infancy and so is the tourist trade. Very few hotels exist on Miami Beach and even fewer hotels can be found across the bay. Most of America is mired in the Great Depression; life is a grind for many people and young families. My father and his two brothers are partners in Dade Wholesale Produce Company. And, although we always have plenty of fresh fruits and vegetables, times are tough for the Apte family, as well. Only about once or twice a week can my family have meat on the table for dinner.

It seems as though we have moved to a new place to live every few years. And suddenly, I am living in the small apartment building that is half a block from the Miami River. I have already semi-perfected a fishing outfit of thread, bent pin and dough ball, becoming addicted to my hobby of fishing. I'm so dedicated, in fact, that I am prepared to suffer for my passion.

I get punished more than once for going down to the Miami River to fish. My mother worries about the possibility of her baby falling into the water and drowning. But, there I am, once again, and it seems like there is an abundance of two- to three-inch shiners that are more than willing and eager to sample my dough-ball bait. On this day, I somehow tie my thread to an old piece of bamboo cane pole I find on the shoreline. I do pretty well catching these little fish with my homemade, super-deluxe fishing outfit. Until, out of nowhere, bigger fish – snook, tarpon, and jack crevalle – find that my hooked shiners are easy prey.

Each time one of these bigger fish grabs the shiner, it puts me out of business with a broken thread line. As young as I am, it does not take long to figure out that I need a heavy-duty fishing outfit. And I'm dreaming of the day when I'll have a real fishing rod and a great reel, and maybe even a boat, and …

As if changing TV channels, I am suddenly seeing a 300-foot ship sitting on Biscayne Boulevard around 11th Street, deposited there by the hurricane of 1926. It has become a seafood restaurant, where my parents sometimes take the family to eat.

Just as quickly, the channel changes once more, and I'm walking with my brother Marvin along the County Causeway sidewalk, [renamed in the 1940s the McArthur Causeway in General McArthur's honor]. Bait is just one more thing we kids can't afford. So, Marvin and I are looking up and down the causeway sidewalk for any old bait or pieces of fish that we can use on our hand lines. We're lucky, because we are there at just the right time, during the slack water change of tide, and catch a variety of grunts and small snappers. We use bolt nuts for sinkers …now there we are, fishing, Marvin and I; the tide is coming in strong, and I can't get my bait near the bottom where the fish are…

The next thing I remember is waking up in the Portsmouth Naval Hospital, some 40 hours later. When those hours are recalled for me secondhand, they tell me that luckily the dispatched helicopter was hovering nearby as I hit the water. The pilot of the helicopter immediately dispatched a paramedic into the water, who pulled the toggle switch on my Mae West to inflate it. The paramedic also disconnected the parachute, untangling me from the shroud lines.

At the hospital, when I felt stable enough to make a phone call, my father uttered an expression that was to stay with me all my life: "Mom's Worry." He said, "Stu, I want you to know that you really are your mom's worry." From that time on, all of my boats and my radio "handle" have been *Mom's Worry*.

I am released from the hospital with a few stitches in my head from some of the debris, a strangulated hernia, and numerous cuts and bruises – all injuries that will remind me of this adventure for the rest of my life. I look like I have been in one helluva fight. After such a close call, I feel like God is telling me that life – and fishing – should mean a whole lot more to me. I will spend the rest of my life letting my adventures fulfill that prophecy.

CHAPTER

TWO

MY MEXICO EDUCATION:

Tarpon, Snook and Adventure

In my formative years, before I joined the Navy and became a pilot, my family wanted me to be a doctor. And up until I was starting my senior year at the University of Miami, that goal certainly clicked with me. I was working toward a Bachelor of Science degree with a major in chemistry and minors in zoology and psychology for pre-med. I have to admit it was all interesting stuff, and I especially enjoyed chemistry and psychology. [Dreams of flying and aviation had not yet stirred within me; they would come later, when I joined the Navy.]

As my senior year loomed the end of 1950, one thing had become apparent to me: For all their great financial gains and opportunities, doctors did not have a shot at what I loved most in life—going fishing! Fortunately for me, the chance to take command of my future came along, and I grabbed it.

My brother, his wife, my aunt, and my uncle had been attending Mexico City College [MCC] since 1949 on the GI Bill. Uncle Sam paid for the college tuition, books and an additional subsistence of $128 a month. The rate of exchange in Mexico was 8.65 pesos for the dollar, making $128 in Mexico the equivalent of $1,107 a month in the U.S. Since you could buy just about as much in Mexico for a peso as you could at home for a dollar, $128 was big money back then.

When my relatives had returned home for Christmas vacation, they talked endlessly about Mexico. It was "Mexico this" and "Mexico that"–wonderful stories about great adventures and their lives there. In addition to describing the great times and high lives they enjoyed on their pesos, they had wonderful things to say about MCC [later to be known as the University of the Americas]. I learned that most major universities in the states accepted MCC as fully accredited, and that numerous students from schools all over the U.S. were already enrolled. So, for my senior year, off I went to seek my own brand of education and adventure in Mexico, and MCC.

My brother had a two-bedroom apartment, including living quarters on the roof for a maid. The apartment was right on a main thoroughfare, Insurgentes Boulevard, with a large Sears and Roebuck's store a block away. The monthly rent for the apartment was only 302.75 pesos per month, a meager $35 U.S. Add a full-time maid who cooked, cleaned, did the laundry and the grocery shopping – all for only $12 a month – and you can see we were living high on the hog. [Don't feel sorry for Socorro, our maid, though; at 103.80 pesos a month she was one of the highest-paid maids in the area.]

Even though Americans were really popular among Mexicans, we still have to use the same caution in some areas as you would in any large city. We had a great time in Mexico City during my senior year. Some might say I am having too good of a time; but, hey, I did manage to pull off some decent grades. One of the few A's I received at MCC was in the only course of journalism I ever took. Encouraged, I started writing a twice-weekly column in the American tabloid newspaper on hunting and fishing. My byline appeared under "Mexican Outdoor Sports." And, since I needed plenty of material for my column, a great deal of fishing was on my agenda.

On one occasion, when a three-day holiday from classes rolled around, my friend John Boudroe and I launched a "research outing." John, a wild Cajun student from New Orleans on the GI Bill and fellow hunting and fishing addict, grew up fishing for saltwater trout and largemouth bass. He had a reasonable amount of expertise casting artificial lures. He also liked imbibing rum, and sometimes went off on a toot.

Gathering our fishing tackle and camping equipment, we hopped into John's 1940 four-door Hudson automobile and headed down to the Gulf Coast of Mexico, with our sights set on Tuxpan. I had read somewhere that this small coastal town between Vera-cruz and Tampico is host to the Tuxpan River, which, in turn, draws lots of big tarpon and snook from a few miles up river all the way to where its mouth empties into the Gulf of Mexico.

Going on faith, we drove the six hours it takes to travel over the mountains on a road often pockmarked with deep holes and washed-out areas. We left the paved road near the mouth of the river and transcended onto a dirt road that was more like a path bordered with all kinds of flowering cactus. Looking off to our right, we could see a series of line squalls over the Gulf.

"Oh, please stay south of where we are heading," I prayed out loud. John and I followed the road along the river as best we could, leaving a large cloud of dust, hoping that we won't get stuck or get a flat tire from some of the ruts and small boulders that were hazards along the road. It's a good thing that John's Hudson was built like a tank because it felt like it was battling the road, at times almost losing the war.

It was nearing midday, and in this arid region of cactus, the sun was starting to take its toll on us, making our travel hot and stifling. And then there was always the dust. God forbid we should get behind someone on this trace of a road.

Eventually we pulled up to a stretch of river where three native Indians were fishing from the bank. We stopped and watched awhile. They were using hand lines and some sort of cut bait. One caught a mangrove snapper weighing about two pounds, which they immediately gutted and stashed under a pile of seaweed.

By now John and I were anxious to talk to these dudes and learn what we can about this river, so we got out of the car and walked slowly toward them along the riverbank. Just as we got to them, I spotted something that made me jump up, turn around, and run for the car. These Indians must have thought I'd seen a snake. But it had actually been a 40- to 50-pound tarpon approximately 80 feet out, rolling up for a gulp of oxygen. Reaching the car, I grabbed the first fishing outfit I can get my hands on – a bait-casting outfit with a 5½-foot Heddon-Pal two-piece tubular steel rod and a Pflueger Akron level-wind reel filled with 15-pound-test, black nylon line. The rod was already rigged with a wire leader and a Heddon Pal-O-Mine deep-swimming lure in anticipation of just this type of chance happening.

In my rush to get back to the water's edge, I almost stepped in a hole that would have sent me back to school in a cast. John was talking to one of the Indians in Spanish as I approached, but I didn't stop to catch the translation. I had nothing but that tarpon on my mind. I unlimbered a long cast out beyond where the tarpon rolled. Holding the rod tip down close to the water so that my lure would swim deep, I started a slow retrieve, wiggling my rod tip from side to side, giving the plug a bit of wounded-fish action. It hasn't traveled 20 feet when it abruptly stopped in mid wiggle. I immediately reared back sharply, setting the hook, and was answered with the kind of strong, slow head shake that I remember so well. Knowing that it was probably either a tarpon or a snook, I wound the slack out of my line and set the hook again.

Line started screaming through the guides and the handle on my reel was spinning like a whirling dervish. The only drag on this casting reel was my thumb on the spool of line that acts as a break and helps slow the fish down, plus keeps the line from back-lashing into a bird's nest.

"Hey, I've got a good one!" I shouted to John and anyone else within earshot.

I certainly had enough experience fighting that particular size fish in my home waters of South Florida to know how to apply maximum pressure, and just as important, when to apply it. The moment this critter stopped its run, I pulled back, turning its head to the shoreline where I was standing, and started a rhythmic pumping-and-winding motion, quickly bringing it toward me. After I recovered about two thirds of the line back onto my reel, a 15-pound snook broke the surface with a violent jump.

You would think that I just performed a miracle from the antics of yelling and dancing of the three Indians, who would have been hailed as heroes in their village if they had returned with such a fish.

I quickly brought the snook to the river's edge and rapidly backed up, beaching it, all in one motion. While the snook was flopping around trying to get back into the water, all three Indians pounced on it like their lives depend on it. I make three immediate friends by presenting them with my catch to take back to their village.

Three casts later, even before John has retrieved a second casting rod from his car, I hooked and land another snook that looked like the clone of the first.

After six hours of traveling the road from hell, headed into the unknown, and then the adrenaline rush of suddenly being on the river and in the fight, John and I were both hot and tired. It was time to look for a place nearby where we could camp for a couple of nights. Our new Indian friends understood our need, and probably thought, "Hell, why only bring in the miracle fish when you can also bring in the hero who caught them?" We accepted their invitation.

The Indian village was about two miles up river, alongside the deeply rutted wagon trail we were maneuvering on. What a sight we must have been: a 1940 Hudson with three people crunched into the front seat and an Indian on each front fender, each holding a big fish. The two fender jockeys must have required new kidneys after the two-mile, half-hour, *bumpity-bump* trek to their village.

When the villagers saw us coming with our huge bounty, they acted as if we were conquering heroes. The whole village of around 40 Mayan Indians strained to see the two snook, the tackle that I caught them with, and, of course, the two magic men, John and me. The chief, who spoke Spanish and a few words of English, quickly honored me with the title, "The Greatest Provider of Food." A thatched hut to sleep in came with the award. The chief had women broom it out, giving us some clean dirt to sleep on. Fortunately, since we are prepared for camping out, we had out sleeping bags.

I continued to provide large amounts of snook and big snappers, and even let them have one tarpon that was hooked too deep in its gill rakes to release. That's when I make my mistake. Already an honored man among the tribe, and considered to have powers beyond mere mortal fishermen, the gift of a tarpon somehow prompted the chief to offer me his very pretty 12-year-old daughter – as my wife!

We tried to explain to him as best we could that I am already married [even though I'm not] and that among our "tribe," it was against our laws to have two wives. He was determined to have me for a son-in-law and persisted in his offer right up until the moment we departed for Mexico City and our comparatively mundane lives as college students.

John and I left the Indian Village with new friends, a new tribe, several stories for my column, and still very much single.

CHAPTER

THREE

INTO THE WIND:

Takeoffs, Landings and Other Assorted Adventures

Of a Navy Fighter Pilot

My mother was in tears.

It's a disturbing sight for any young man or woman, but was particularly wrenching to me because I was the instigator of her distress. The news that I was about to become a Naval Aviation Cadet both surprised and saddened this gentle, patient and usually-understanding lady.

The year was 1951 and I was 21. When I had recently set out to join the Navy, my mother had been positive that I would never be accepted as an Aviation Cadet. An old family friend who happened to be a cardiologist had assured her that since the Navy gave the strictest flight physical of any military organization, "Stuart could not possibly pass the Navy's physical exams—certainly not, with his past history."

The "history" the doctor was referring to had begun when I was very young, just a few years old. I was diagnosed with rheumatic fever, which supposedly left me with an enlarged heart and a slight heart murmur. Because of this, my mother always watched over me with special concern. As a consequence, at 16, when I started boxing in the Golden Gloves representing the YMHA, my mother never knew about it. I wasn't supposed to be involved in any sport that required vigorous training. When I went off for my high school senior year at Gordon Military College, I easily made the boxing team. Then at the University of Miami, I was on the boxing team as a bantamweight at 126 pounds. I'll never forget how the Navy flight surgeon on my initial physical noted that I had "minor malnutrition." By then, I weighed 132 pounds. My body was as hard as concrete and in excellent physical condition.

My joining the Navy was not a problem for my mother, since my older brother Marvin had already served as a gunners mate in the Pacific, from 1942 through 1945. But the flying…The idea was tough for her to handle, to say the least. Nevertheless, I went ahead with my pursuit, knowing that I would have to master a lot of hard study and training before Uncle Sam let me loose in the skies with one of our taxpayers' airplanes. If I failed, "washed out" as they still say today, I would not become "an officer and a gentleman," with wings of gold on my uniform. I would remain an enlisted man for the duration of my naval service. I had never flown an airplane in my life, not even a Piper Cub, but I had made up my mind to take a crack at becoming a Navy pilot.

My decision to join the Navy had been an easy one. After being graduated from Mexico City College and returning to Miami that summer, with the Korean War raging hot and heavy, I had become 1-A for the draft. My years attending high school at Gordon Military College had given me a taste of Army life and I wanted no more. I spent a great deal of time that fall actually trying to join the Air Force as an Aviation Cadet. I passed all their physicals and weird training tests at Moody Air Force Base in Valdosta, Georgia, then waited and waited for the beauraucratic machine to spit out my acceptance papers. In December they still had not come. Meanwhile, the Draft Board was looking my way, so I visited the Naval Air Station in Opa Locka, Florida, just outside Miami. I applied for Naval Aviation Cadet Training, took the written exam, passed the flight physical, and just like that I was sworn into active duty in the U.S. Navy.

A little over a month had passed since the day I was sworn into the Navy, when the notice arrived. My preflight class was 13-52, the 13th class in 1952. The two other cadet trainees who accompanied me from Miami to Pensacola were Lenton Tyler, already a private pilot, and Admiral-to-be Jim McCormick, a graduate of Georgia Tech's School of Aeronautical Engineering. Jim and I are the only two in my class 13–52 who eventually became fighter pilots.

Later, after flight training, we were both offered the option of going into the Regular Navy instead of the Reserves. Jim opted for Regular Navy and the Navy sent him back to College, to MIT where he earned a Master's degree in Aeronautical Engineering. Further into his career, Jim was offered a training opportunity as one of the early astronauts, or test pilot training. He chose wisely, I believe, becoming a test pilot for a while, then going on to numerous Navy War Colleges, receiving promotions as they come due. Jim rose to three-star Admiral in the fleet—Vice Admiral. Years later, he became an Admiral of one of the Pacific Fleets, a feat almost unheard of for someone not a graduate of what we called "Canoe U," the U.S. Naval Academy at Annapolis, Maryland.

Strangely enough, the other Cadet-hopeful who rode with me to Pensacola, Lenton Tyler, who had his civilian pilot's license, finished preflight with flying colors, but during primary flight training washed out of the program. Sometimes, it's difficult for a pilot who learns to fly as a civilian to learn to fly the "Navy's Way." It's the Navy's Way, or it's the Way Out of the Navy. I felt sorry for Lenton at the time, but not today. After he finished his tour of duty as a Navy enlisted man, he entered the pharmaceutical business and made millions.

In pre-flight training at Pensacola there were two specific Battalions, known as Batt-1 and Batt-2. We had well-seasoned Marine Gunnery Sergeants from World War II and early Korea fame, both highly decorated with at least two Purple Hearts. The gunnery sergeant in my Batt-2 was awarded two Purple Hearts from WW-II and one Purple Heart from Korea. Now this dude was one tough sergeant. He had us all line up the first day in our new khaki uniforms. It was kind of a ragtag line up, like you see in the movies.

"Okay, youse guys," he shouted. "I don't care which one of youse guys went to what university or college, or what education youse has. All I want to know is, does we have any boxers or wrestlers in the battalion?"

The fact was that we had boxing and wrestling competitions between the Battalions. I'm sure each Gunnery Sergeant was betting on his own men. With my background in boxing, naturally, I raised my hand. You could say that because of boxing, things go a little smoother for me during Pre-Flight indoctrination, and after. Turns out that raising my hand was the best move I make during my boxing career in the Navy.

Preflight consisted of 16 weeks of vigorous mental and physical training. During the first month we are called upon big time by our marine sergeants, learning close-order drill, the manual of arms, and a lot about naval orientation. Besides understanding how to be pilots – Naval Aviators – we also have to digest the history of the U.S. Navy, dead reckoning and celestial navigation, how to be a Naval Officer, and in some cases, a gentleman. We were issued a high-top pair of boon-docker shoes that were probably meant to be worn in the swamps. They are rough and oiled. I'm sure they were never meant to be shined. Guess what? By the end of two weeks, all our shoes are spit shined, so you can see your face in them. The same goes for all of our brass buckles; you can use them instead of a mirror.

For fifteen weeks, we were hard at it, from reveille until taps. Starting Week Three, we were well into daily courses of naval orientation, engineering, learning about aircraft engines, principles of flight, navigation, and meteorology, which the Navy calls aerology.

Next it was time to learn to swim, the Navy way. This included a trip in the "Dilbert Dunker," down a rail more than two-stories high, strapped into the simulated cockpit of an SNJ trainer, the first airplane I will ever fly, and hitting the water at approximately 35 miles per hour. This mockup of an airplane's cockpit turns upside down and sinks to the bottom at the deep end of the pool. You have to wait until the bubbles clear, then unbuckle your shoulder harness and seatbelt, and swim down and out at a 45-degree angle, away from the airplane, before coming to the surface. For some, this is not an easy feat. A scuba diver waited in the water nearby, just in case a cadet became disoriented and in danger of drowning.

During my day in the Dunker, two cadets are pulled out by the safety diver. Fortunately, I was not one of them; I performed well on all the required swimming exercises, including the Dilbert Dunker, except the Australian crawl the Navy way. For that, I am rewarded with two extra weeks of swimming instruction. Thank God, I was doing too well in all of my preflight ground school subjects to get booted out of the program.

I was fulfilling my extra training when I received a letter from the U.S. government. I opened it and read, "Greetings and congratulations, Stuart Charles Apte, you have been selected to serve your country in the United States Army," etc. I was being notified that I had been drafted!. I didn't respond to the letter; I just crunched it up and placed it in the circular file under "No Way!" [Years later, I would wish I had saved the notice.]

After graduating preflight training, I departed Pensacola and report to NAAS [Naval Auxiliary Air Station] at South Whiting Field in Milton, Florida, to start primary flight training. Wow. This was what I've been working so hard for – to learn to fly. It dawns on me, just then, that I haven't the slightest idea if I'll like flying. After all, I had never been at the controls of an airplane before.

The really cool thing about leaning to fly in the Navy was that I was not starting my flying career in a Piper Cub, like most private pilots. The first airplane I flew was the Navy's SNJ, with an R-1340 air-cooled radial engine that puts out 600 horsepower. [This is the same airplane I will eventually crash-land in the Alabama cornfield.]

To my relief, I just fall in love with flying. My instructor, a Lieutenant Benniger, had been called back to active duty from WW-11, and I was his first student. Benniger, in my mind, was a cut above any of the instructors I observed. He was such a fine instructor that after I completed the 18-hour syllabus for primary flight training, my solo flight was a piece of cake.

Benniger and I were out practicing landings on a large grass field at Baghdad Field near Brewton, Alabama, with the Lieutenant, as always, in the back seat. After three or four touch-and-go landings and a couple of full-stop, taxi-back-and takeoff-circuits, Benniger instructed me to make another full-stop landing and taxi back for another takeoff. This time was different though. He said, "Set your brakes." As I was doing that I had no idea he was already climbing out of the backseat until he patted me on the head and said, "Enjoy it. This will be your first solo flight."

I just couldn't believe it. I took a deep breath and exclaimed, "YAHOO!" I quickly completed my takeoff checklist, holding my brakes briefly as I added power to take off. I climbed out to 500 feet before starting a left climbing turn to enter the landing pattern around the field. Coming back around as instructed, I shoot two touch-and-go landings before making a full-stop landing to pick him up and fly us back to South Whiting Field. Piece of cake.

As I stepped out of the airplane at South Whiting Field, reality hit me and I couldn't contain myself; I let out a loud, "YEEHAA," attracting attention from some nearby cadets and instructors. I received a bunch of thumbs up. Later, back in the barracks, there was quite the celebration as my three roommates performed the cutting of the tie – an age-old naval custom for a first solo flight. Within a week and a half, I had the joy of reciprocating the tradition as each of them completed their first solo flight.

On my cross-country flight the day after my solo, the euphoria over new flying achievement vanished in the Alabama skies and cornfield when my plane went down. Once the Naval accident board concluded their findings in a formal report, I actually got a commendation from Vice Admiral John Dale Price for the way I had handled the emergency. Not bad for a first all-solo cross-country. I was back on flying status in a few days, and my next solo cross-country went like clockwork.

I was ready for the next phase of my training.

*   *   *

I was not a Navy fighter pilot yet. There were still plenty enough training challenges ahead to either wash out or bust my ass.

My next phase takes me to NAAS [Naval Auxiliary Air Station] Corry Field, only 40 miles away from Pensacola, for training in instrument flying procedures—to learn how to "fly blind," as non-aviators say, or "on the gauges" in aviator parlance. It was also my first experience in night flying. It didn't take very long to receive another in-your-face reminder that we were in a business that did not allow mistakes.

Returning to base after a night cross-country flight, a French Navy enlisted pilot tried to land on the Pensacola Bridge, mistaking its lights for the runway at Corry Field. He not only killed himself but also two people in a car with the misfortune to be on the bridge at that moment.

I started my instrument training in a Link-Trainer, a simulator that by today's standards is quite a dinosaur, a museum piece even.

Instrument flying—flying without visual reference to the ground—requires mastering special flying skills. One must learn to quickly interpret what the gauges are saying and to believe in them and fly by them. "Seat of the pants" sensations lead to vertigo, a spin most likely, and death.

I had to learn the use of a gyro horizon, an instrument that shows both the position of your wings and the rate you are turning or descending. In the early portion of training I could only use basic instruments without the help of the gyro horizon. This involved learning how to make standard rate turns while climbing or descending, having only the airspeed indicator, altimeter, rate of climb or descent needle and the turn-needle-ball instrument.

I also learn how to fly a basic radio range in order to make an instrument approach and land the airplane during inclement weather conditions. Eventually, I actually practiced the same syllabus in the airplane, except I was "under the hood" and unable to see outside of the cockpit.

I preformed my first 200-mile, round-robin, cross-country night flight without incident.

I had learned to scan and believe my instruments. No vertigo for me!

NAAS Saufley Field was my next training base in the crowded sky around the Pensacola area. We trained in formation flying, aerobatics, tactics and air-to-air gunnery, shooting at targets towed by another airplane, with a 30-caliber machine gun mounted on the cowling between the propeller and my windscreen. We called some of the airplanes "whistlers," because they had a hole in the propeller that was created by firing while the machine gun was out of sync with the engine, sometimes caused when the engine is in an over-speed condition.

My instructor was a Marine first lieutenant who dearly loved aerobatics. This was the first formation flying I encountered, but certainly not the last during my 18 months of training. It could get pretty hairy up there. One of my classmates locked wings with another airplane and had to bail out. The only damage to him other than his ego was a humongous black eye when the parachute riser – a portion of the chute with a large buckle – smacked him dead center in his left eye.

Lieutenant McIntyre, most certainly a frustrated fighter pilot, had been flying the AD-Skyraider, a high-performance, single-engine dive-bomber, instead of fighter planes. He taught me basic aerobatics such as wingovers, chandelles, aileron rolls, loops and Immelmens, a maneuver named after the World War I German ace, Baron Von Immelmen. With acrobatics, I found my niche in flying.

Lieutenant McIntyre's thing, his calling, was inverted acrobatics. So, after he thought I was proficient enough with standard aerobatics, we started practicing maneuvers upside down, and I learned the difference between pulling positive G's and pushing negative G's. If I pull back on the control stick creating positive G's, the blood drains from my brain and I black out [I already know what that is]. If instead I rapidly push the control stick forward, I create negative G's, forcing blood into my brain and causing a 'red out.' [I soon learn what that is.]

The first time I attempted to perform an inverted loop, I dove down to pick up the necessary speed, rolled upside down, and pushed the stick forward to begin climbing upside down. As I reached the top of the loop, the plane ran out of airspeed and stalled. What happened next was good training, but scary as hell.

My plane went into an inverted spin. To visualize that, imagine a plane on its back, spinning and falling like a rock toward the earth. And I'm in it. I need to think clearly. I need to think recovery. And, I need to think it now.

I kicked the opposite rudder from the direction of the spin to stop the aircraft's rotation, pulled back on the throttle, reducing power, and pulled back on the control stick to make the nose of the airplane drop. This is just the opposite recovery procedure for a standard spin and somewhat difficult to do after practicing standard spin recoveries.

By the time I had the aircraft fully under control, climbing back to initial altitude, I felt like I have tears or sweat in my eyes. I rubbed my gloved hand across my eyes to dry them. What I saw on my glove pushed me to near panic: my glove was red with blood! Thinking that I somehow severely damaged my eyes – a malady that would put an immediate end to my Navy flying career – I made a beeline for Saufley Field, probably flying that SNJ trainer faster than it had ever been pushed before.

Immediately after landing and securing the aircraft, I got a ride over to sick bay. Though I described the horrific discovery of bloody eyeballs with as much heartfelt detail as possible, the flight surgeon simply put his arm around my shoulders and, with a chuckle, told me that I merely had a severe "red out," caused by the rupturing of the small capillaries within my eyes. Talk about relief.

Recall now, if you will, that at this time I have been through 16 weeks of preflight, primary flight training at South Whiting Field where I soloed, have completed basic formation flying, air-to-air gunnery and combat maneuvers, and I am training in basic instrument flying, when I receive a letter from the U.S. Air Force, calling me up to flight training as an Aviation Cadet. Uh, a little late, wouldn't you say? The world turns in funny ways, and Lady

Luck is a wonderful woman still by my side, just as she has been for most of my life.

* * *

In the Navy, in addition to the stages that Air Force trainees went through, the neophyte always had waiting for him, out in the ocean, a certain grim gray slab, namely, the deck of an aircraft carrier, and with it perhaps the most difficult routine in military flying.

–Tom Wolfe, *The Right Stuff*

After Corry Field, I moved on to NAAS Barin Field in Foley Alabama, where I could become a real Naval Aviator if I could learn to land on an aircraft carrier.

The first thing that caught my eye when I drove onto the field were the bright white outlines painted on the runways to simulate the deck by forming the dimensions of an aircraft carrier. And, they damn sure don't look very big to me. "Holy shit," I mumble out loud. "Am I going to have to land in a space that small?"

To begin, I had to learn and understand what every movement of the LSO's [Landing Signal Officer's] paddles meant and how to make my aircraft immediately comply with the LSO's commands. I can only do that by trusting those commands explicitly. Each movement can actually mean the difference between life and death, not only for me, but also possibly for other pilots in the air and crewmen on the ship. Not complying with the LSO's signals might result in crashing onto the deck, creating a fouled deck, making it impossible for the other aircraft in the air to land right away, even though they may be low on fuel.

Our LSO is Lieutenant "Shaky" Spell, a highly decorated WW-11 officer. I have to believe that his nickname Shaky comes from the way he handles his paddles. His paddle movements are so descriptive, that they without a doubt communicate what he wants you to do. At times he is almost shaking them.

I learned to fly a pork-chop-shaped landing pattern, flying at no more than five knots above stall speed around the field with landing gear down and full flaps. This seemed like a simple task the first morning I fly the circuit, just to get the feel of the area. Take my word for it: by afternoon, the thermals created by the rising temperature makes my airplane feel like it is a bucking bronco that is trying to drop out of the sky, and keeps me very busy. At this moment, I shuttered to imagine what it feels like trying to land on a carrier the size of the small box painted on the runway, under the conditions of a deck pitching up and down, back and forth while my plane fights thermal effect. I knew I would soon find out.

There's talk of an advanced cadet who, flying an F6F Grumman Hellcat of World War II fame, had finished his advanced training at Kingsville, Texas, and was back in the Pensacola area to do his final carrier qualifications. Like me, he first had to qualify doing FCLP's [Field Carrier Landing Practice] before going out to a carrier, the U.S.S. Monterey, to do his final qualification landings.

As the story goes, he was feeling like a real hot fighter pilot after completing his first catapult shot and the seven take offs and landings aboard the carrier, which was steaming along 50 miles out in the Gulf of Mexico. Before landing at Barin Field, he was observed diving down to pick up speed and screaming along close to 380 miles an hour, just a few feet above a nearby cotton field. Probably wondering what the loud noise was, one of the cotton pickers stood up at just the wrong moment and was decapitated by the propeller as the plane flew by. From that time on, the field has been known as Bloody Barin Field. Even early on in my primary flight training, I had heard of Bloody Barin Field. But, I had envisioned that the field got its name because of all of the cadets that had been killed there practicing field carrier landings.

No doubt about it, I have become a good stick and rudder man by this time. I learned faster than most because I was blessed with what my instructor reported as "superb hand/eye coordination," and I was ready to qualify ahead of schedule.

Finally, the big day came. Time for my qualification carrier landing.

A flight instructor led our formation of eight cadets, consisting of two divisions of four planes, out into the Gulf of Mexico, to do our carrier qualifying on the U.S.S. Monterey, a light cruiser hull that was converted into a small Jeep aircraft carrier during WW-11.

One division of planes was sent up to 3,000 feet to circle, which is called dogging, while the other four-plane section was put into a right echelon formation at 800 feet. The Monterey was moving rapidly at close to 25 knots. To perform a carrier break, an instructor pilot was leading our echelon formation of four planes just off to the right side of the carrier until abeam the ship's superstructure. He peeled off in a relatively steep turn to the left, extending his landing flaps and putting his landing gear and tail hook down. Three seconds later, I pressed in my left rudder petal, adding a little power with the throttle, while moving my control stick to the left and slightly back at the same time, which puts the plane into a turning left bank.

Full flaps. Gear down. Tail hook down. Canopy open. Mixture full rich. Propeller low pitch, high rpm. Final landing check. At the same time, descending, watching my airspeed, altitude, wingtip position to the carrier, and keeping the airplane ahead of me in sight. I am almost working by reflexes because I am too busy to think about what I have to do. My training thus far is so complete that I am as cool as a cucumber, and everything is going by the numbers.

At that moment, the ship actually looks bigger than I thought it would, after hearing all the stories about landing on a postage stamp. The Navy's training is so good that on my first approach and landing I am so in the groove that the only signal I receive from the LSO is a slight "come-on" and a "cut" right at the end of my approach, to which I add power, then smartly cut my power off, releasing the slight right rudder pressure I was holding, making sure I keep my wings level.

My touchdown and rapid deceleration after my tail hook grabbed a cable, which the Navy calls a cross-deck pennant, was almost as I have envisioned during the many hours I spent thinking about the landing. Then the arresting gear petty officer gave me a signal to set my brakes as the crew removed the cable from my tail hook. I quickly read my before-takeoff checklist and got the signal from the fly-one officer to lock my brakes and advance my throttle to takeoff power, all of which I do immediately. All this is happening so fast that it is hard to believe it is happening to me. When he gives me the go signal, I quickly released my brakes doing the short takeoff run to get airborne.

With 38 knots of relative wind, the ship's speed, plus the actual wind coming down the deck, I am able to reach the 65 knots necessary to get airborne quickly. "Wow, I did it," I shout for no one to hear but me. "Almost as easy as falling off of a log," I smile to myself.

I pulled my throttle and prop lever back to climb power, and cranked my canopy closed, unzipped the pocket in my flight suit's left shoulder, get out a cigarette and Zippo lighter, and lite up. Even though I was now feeling quite confident of the tasks ahead of me, I have to pay attention and continue my left climbing turn to remain in the landing pattern. I only have a few minutes of relaxation to inhale a few puffs before putting the cigarette out and cranking my canopy open again.

Now on my downwind leg, I extended full flaps and pulled the handle releasing the tail hook. I made sure that the fuel mixture was full rich, pushed my propeller control lever forward to low pitch, giving the engine full RPM, and quickly did my checklist. I'm not even breathing hard as I turned final on my approach, seeing the LSO give me a harder left turn signal to properly align me up in the groove. My glide path must be right on schedule because this time the only other signal that I get, other than the in-the-groove signal, is a low dip, meaning I am slightly high at the end of my approach, and a cut.

This touchdown and landing was a photocopy of the previous one. As was my takeoff, climb out, cigarette break, and the beginning of my flight around the landing pattern. That is, until I am on my downwind leg. I am not paying that much attention to the aircraft two slots ahead of me, the one that is on final approach at this time. By now, I don't even know for sure who is in that airplane. I found out a few minutes later that it was Joe Schmitt. Joe evidently did not respond to a high dip signal quick enough and was landing long, which evidently prompts him to dive for the deck. To my horror, he hit long and bounced off the port [left] side of the ship, crashing into the water.

Whoever is commanding the ship at that moment, either the skipper or the duty officer, made a critical error by turning the ship hard to the starboard [right], which brought the back of the ship directly over the now sinking airplane. The port screw [propeller] hit part of the airplane.

The aircraft ahead of me was just turning base and I can see the LSO frantically giving him a wave off, which is an automatic go around. At the same time, someone on the radio instructed all of us in the air to "clean up" our aircraft, climb to 3,000 feet and commence dogging in an elongated, stretched-out, circular holding pattern until given a Charlie signal to come back down and re-enter the landing pattern.

"Holy shit!" I whispered to myself. "Poor Joe is a nice guy. Maybe he's not the greatest stick and rudder pilot, but a very smart book guy who can recite verbatim from the training manuals." I cleared my head – better keep my mind on the tasks at hand, bringing my landing gear up, flaps up, throttle and RPM back to a climb setting, and pulled my mixture control back a bit to start conserving fuel. Who knows how long we may have to circle?

As I was climbing up to our 3,000-foot holding pattern, I could see exactly what was happening and the scene quickly brings me back to reality. This is not a game, but a very dangerous job that I am pursuing...

Finally, the USS Monterey turned back into the wind, and they gave us a Charlie signal to come down and re-enter the landing pattern. With only six aircraft trying to qualify, the pattern was not stretched out quite as far as it has been. Another change in the scenario was the speed of the carrier. With a damaged screw [prop], the Monterey is not able to do more than 18 knots. The greater the difference there is between the carrier's speed and my aircraft's speed, the greater the difficulty to slow and stop. Nevertheless, my next four passes are in the slot and I qualify with ease, going six for six without ever getting a single wave off. Only one other cadet in our group manages to do the same.

After leaving the flight deck and going to the pilots ready room, I heard an announcement over the loudspeakers from the ship's captain saying, "I know everyone will be very happy to hear that NAVCAD Joe Schmitt was picked up by our plane guard destroyer escort, and thankfully he only has minor cuts and bruises to show for it." One of the officers in the ready room jokingly says, "Joe's probably enjoying the medicinal brandy carried for just such emergencies."

I spent the next 48 hours living aboard the USS Monterey before it steamed back to port in Pensacola Harbor, watching and photographing the other cadets as they try to qualify. I can't tell you the relief and pride associated with having completed this very important phase of my training. I was now qualified to continue on to advanced training in Texas.

I am also now qualified for something else: non-flying naval officers are required to wear black shoes with all of their uniforms. Having carrier qualified, I am a part of the flying Navy where officers wear brown shoes with all of their uniforms except dress blues and dress whites. This means I'm able to buy and wear a pair of brown shoes with my khaki or aviation green uniform. Naval Aviators are known as the brown-shoe Navy instead of the black-shoe Navy. Naval Aviator's feel like we are a cut above the average Naval officer, and we like the idea of having something more in our dress code to show it.

No one can blame Joe Schmitt when he decides to DOR [drop on request], which means quit flying. The quit chit turned in the very next day removed him from the duties of a Naval Aviation Cadet, and now required him to spend the balance of his four-year enlistment obligation as an enlisted sailor. After 16 weeks of preflight and more than 55 weeks of very intense flight training, to drop out or even wash out at this stage would be heartbreaking and even devastating to me. The fact is, I made a commitment to myself to become a Naval Aviator, and failing to do so was simply not an option.

* * *

Those who remained, those who qualified for carrier duty—and even more those who later on qualified for night *carrier duty—began to feel a bit like Gideon's warriors.* So many have been left behind!

–Tom Wolfe, *The Right Stuff*

"I see that you want to be a fighter pilot, and by your records it appears to me that you would be a very good one."

I was standing at ease, in smart Parade-Rest posture, before a Marine colonel when I heard those welcome words. I had now transferred to NAAS Kingsville, Texas, my new training base. The colonel's next words almost knocked the smile off my face.

"I suggest that you take your commission in the Marine Corps. You see, only ten or fifteen percent of those that stay in the Navy will become fighter pilots. The Navy's primary job is flying anti-submarine patrol."

To tell the truth, I was quite impressed by the Colonel's stature and demeanor, and the rows of ribbons below his Navy wings. But I had already made up my mind before entering his office. I thanked him very much, but insisted that my greatest desire was to become a carrier,-based tail-hook pilot, and just to make sure of that, I planned to volunteer for all-weather night fighters, a strictly voluntary flight assignment that never seems to have enough volunteers.

When I had arrived at Kingsville, I found the two advanced fighter training classes ahead of my class training in a split syllabus, flying both the F6F-5 Grumman Hellcat and the F8F-1 Grumman Bearcat. The Hellcat, sporting an R-2800, 2000-horsepower engine with a large four-blade prop, is the plane that won the war in the Pacific, having shot down more Japanese airplanes than all the rest of America's fighter planes combined. The Hellcat is armed with six .50-caliber machine guns, three on each wing that are bore-sighted to have converging fire at 150 yards. The Grumman F8F Bearcat, which never actually got into combat before WW-11 was over, was designed especially to intercept and shoot down the

Japanese Kamikaze suicide bombers. The Bearcat has the same big 18-cylinder Pratt & Whitney R-2800 Radial engine that is in the Hellcat but it is 30 percent lighter and 50 mph faster, which gives it extremely high performance. But with only four .50-caliber machine guns, two on each wing, it's not quite the amount of armament and strength of the Hellcat.

The Grumman Hellcat fits me like my mama's lap.

I feel like we are made for each other; everything about her feels just right to me. The way it responds to my touch during takeoff, during landings, during formation flying, and especially during gunnery exercises makes me once again wish I had been born earlier so I could have flown this magnificent airplane in air-to-air combat during World War II in the Pacific. Then again, who knows what could have happened? I may not have survived the war and would have missed out on one whole helluva lot of great fishing.

It becomes obvious to me now that air-to-air combat is my forte. I am easily the top gunner in my advanced training class, where we shoot at a sleeve towed behind another aircraft at various altitudes from a variety of starting positions.

I completed the entire advanced fighter-training syllabus in faster-than-average time, and found myself on my way back to the Pensacola area to Bloody Barin Field to prepare for my final visit aboard the U.S.S. Monterey. Next on the Navy's training list is to be catapulted off the deck of the carrier instead of doing a running takeoff, as I had previously. And now I would be flying the high-performance Hellcat, instead of the SNJ Trainer.

Thankfully, I felt so comfortable in the Hellcat that the next phase of training, field carrier landing practice, felt just right and I whizzed through it in record-breaking time. Then I had to wait a few days for some of my fellow cadets to catch up and make a large enough group to fly out to the carrier.

Finally the big day arrives.

Reveille comes at 5:30 a.m. on this particular day, and I jump out of bed, quickly dress in my highly-starched, washed khaki uniform and, of course, my brown half Wellington boots. I don't know why, but I am particularly hungry this morning and it looks like some of my fellow cadets are the same.

Navy breakfasts are always outstanding: scrambled eggs, soft-boiled eggs, bacon, sausage, and the always-present SOS, which stands for "shit on a shingle." It's actually chipped beef on toast, still one of my favorite breakfast dishes. This morning, I limit myself to only one cup of good Navy coffee, thinking that I would rather not have to use the relief tube, which is situated under my seat in the airplane. Someone in our little group makes a joke, saying something about this being the condemned man's last meal, and someone else quickly and sternly says, "Knock it off!"

At our lockers, near the flight line. I slip into my flight coveralls, stop by the parachute loft, and check out a parachute, once again hoping that it will not be needed. I sign a yellow sheet to check out the airplane, and head to the flight line where the plane captain, an enlisted aviation mechanics mate, is standing by to relieve me of the parachute and place it in the airplane's bucket seat. I do a quick walk-around as part of my preflight check and climb into the airplane. As I sit on the parachute, he helps me get the chute strapped on around my shoulders, chest and thighs, then hands me the shoulder harness over each shoulder to secure into my seat belt buckle. While doing this, he informs me that he has already pulled the propeller through the correct amount of blades to make sure there will not be a hydraulic lock when I start this big 2000-horsepower engine. He climbs down, securing the steps back into the fuselage and gives me an "all-clear" thumbs up.

My watch tells me that I am operating right smack on schedule. Smoke comes from some of the other eight airplanes, signaling the start of their engines. I turn on the battery switch, and the crackling sounds of static from the radios along with the whirring sound of instruments warming up are music to my ears. Am I ever ready for this day? You can bet your bottom dollar I am. As I've said numerous times before when asked, "I was born ready!"

Following procedure, I first complete my cockpit checklist and then my pre-start checklist. Next, I get another "all-clear" thumbs-up from the plane captain and hit the start switch. The engine coughs once, sputters once, and catches as I advance my fuel lever to full rich, briefly admitting the exhaust smell into my open cockpit. I perform a quick check of all my instruments: oil pressure rising, oil temperature coming up, and idle RPM in the green. I quickly read my pre-taxi checklist out loud to myself, call the tower for a taxi clearance to the duty runway, and I am instructed to follow two other airplanes that are already taxiing ahead of me.

"Roger Wilco, Kingsville tower, Navy Six Five Niner Four," I respond. Making sure that my parking brake is firmly set, I give the plane captain the thumbs out sign with both hands, which instructs him to remove the chocks from under my wheels. After he moves off to my left wing and gives me thumbs up, I release the brakes and add power to start taxiing to the duty runway. With the large radial engine in front of me blocking my view, the only way I can see in front of the airplane is to make S turns while I taxi, clearing my vision first on one side of the plane and then on the other. The F6F Grumman Hellcat is a tail dragger, meaning that the airplane has two main landing gears under the fuselage and a rather small wheel under the tail.

This is a beautiful early spring day, with a clear blue sky that reminds me of the Gulfstream. The early morning temperatures signal the absence of fair weather Cumulus clouds in the sky. Later in the day, the sun will warm the earth's surface and columns of air will rise, creating a layer of cumulus clouds that you will only see under this kind of stable weather condition.

Looking up as I taxi, making S turns, thinking about the possibility of this being my last flight in the Grumman Hellcat that I enjoy flying so much, I briefly wonder, *What's next in my life? Will I screw this up? Wash out?* The radio static in my headset is abruptly quieted with, "Navy Six Niner Five Four, Navy Baron tower, over."

"Navy Baron Tower, Navy Six Niner Five Four go ahead," I reply.

"Navy Niner Five Four, continue to the run-up area at the approach end of runway zero niner and standby for your flight clearance."

"Navy Niner Five Four, Roger that. Out," I quickly reply.

S turns make for very slow progress, so I scan all of my engine instruments while taxing. I'm also trying to keep from visualizing what my first carrier landing in this high-performance aircraft will be like and what I might expect from my first catapult shot.

I carefully slide into position alongside the other two Hellcats that are doing their engine run ups. I set the parking brake, advance the throttle just enough to get the prescribed RPM necessary to perform all of the engine pre-takeoff checks.

The fourth Hellcat in our division easily slips into the space designated for him, and initiates his engine run up.

Now the radio crackles with our clearance: "Navy Six Niner Five Four is cleared to the U.S.S. Monterey's radio beacon. After takeoff, maintain runway heading until the remaining three aircraft have joined up. Then proceed to the Papa November Sierra radio beacon and climb to 7,500 feet maintaining Visual Flight Rules. After the PNS radio beacon, proceed directly to the U.S.S. Monterey's radio beacon maintaining VFR."

I repeat back my clearance. The tower clears me into position to hold, then clears each of the other three aircraft into position to hold for 10-second staggered takeoffs. This is a procedure we trained for while in Kingsville, Texas.

I don't know how or why I've been selected to lead the formation out to the carrier, but it immediately gives me a feeling of responsibility. It's a feeling that I will have many times during my career in the Navy and later as a pilot with Pan American World Airways.

I quickly call the other three classmates and tell them we will be called the Able Flight. It's just a little play on words, since apt and able have the same meaning.

"Navy carrier qual flight, you are cleared for a staggered takeoff."

"Navy Six Niner Five Four, Roger Wilco, rolling."

Holding my brakes briefly while advancing the throttle to take-off power, then with my brakes released, holding right rudder to compensate for the torque and with a quick glance at all the engine instruments, I am on my way. My airspeed indicator moves slowly at first. Then, like a living thing feeling freedom, my Hellcat accelerates faster and faster until, with a very slight backward movement of the control stick, I am airborne. I quickly roll the aircraft to the right to help eliminate some of my prop wash, and then back left to the runway heading, gear up, canopy closed, throttle and prop back to climb power.

My fellow classmates join up smartly as I follow my clearance, climbing up to 7,500 feet and turn to overhead the PNS radio beacon. "Okay Stu," I say out loud to myself as if a tutorial, "remember, as the lead airplane, you have to make all of your maneuvers very smoothly, so that flying in your formation is easy for the other three aircraft."

We are simultaneously listening on two different radio communication channels, our standard training communication channel, talking to each other, and, of course, the emergency guard channel that all aircraft in the air and two-way radioed stations on the ground listen to in case someone has a MAYDAY emergency.

I have pre-selected and identified the carrier's low-frequency radio beacon on my second ADF radio range receiver, so just as I overhead the PNS radio range, I flip a toggle switch and my bird dog ADF needle points 30 degrees to the right of my present heading. First giving the pilot in the airplane flying my right wing a rapid head movement to the right, I roll toward him into a very smooth right turn, rolling my wings level with the ADF needle pointing dead ahead. Looking out into the Gulf of Mexico, there's water as far as I can see, but no aircraft carrier. I flip the receiving toggle switch up once more to double check, and once again confirm that I am correctly heading for the carrier's beacon. With a sigh of relief, I hear the proper Morse code identifier. About 30 minutes later, I'm in radio communications with the Monterey, and soon I have her in sight on the horizon.

My flight of four aircraft will be the first to qualify this magnificent morning. The sea is smooth with what looks to be just a light chop, and the Monterey's wake is visible for more than a mile.

We are cleared to descend to 1,000 feet, and overhead the carrier from astern flying a right echelon formation. We quickly change from flying in a two-plane section, two-section division formation into flying in a four-plane right-echelon formation to perform the standard carrier break for landing separation.

I have already started a gradual descent from 7,500 feet, and continue my descent to level off at 1,000 feet. Passing the Monterey's superstructure, I pat the top of my head twice and point to my wingman, a signal passing over the formation lead, and roll into a sharp left bank, putting my landing gear handle in the down position, select full flaps, push the propeller control lever forward to full RPM, mixture control lever forward to full rich, and add some power to compensate for the turn, and drag from the landing gear and flaps.

Rolling the wings level at the correct wing tip distance from the carrier while continuing my slow downwind descent at 80 knots airspeed, I quickly read over my carrier landing checklist. Landing gear, down in the green; mixture, full rich; flaps, down; propeller, full RPM; tail-hook, down. "Oh shit!" I exclaim, reaching out to pull the t-handle that releases my tail-hook.

I memorized and performed everything on a standard landing checklist, but this landing was not on a runway, and I had overlooked one very important item—the tail-hook. And that's the value of checking and rechecking in your head each critical step. A petty officer is looking through binoculars on landing gear and tail-hook watch, and providing I do not have my tail-hook down in time, I will be given a wave off. A mandatory go-around in order to execute another landing approach, would give me a bad grade for that approach, much more important than any grade I've ever achieved in college. This grade has to do with life and death.

Abeam the ship's stern at 400 feet, I roll into a left turn while continuing my descent. I'm looking at the LSO, who is giving me a steeper left turn signal with his paddles. My response is immediate, even though I believe my turn is already steep enough. It is both a written and an unwritten law that the LSO's signal is a command that has to be followed, although only one is mandatory; the wave off signal necessitating an immediate application of power and a go-around.

His paddles signal me to roll my wings level and slightly reduce my power setting. At the same time, he continues to give the in-the-groove signal, meaning my descent is right on glide path. Just before reaching the carrier, the LSO signals a cut, and I immediately chop my power while still continuing to fly the Hellcat down to the carrier's deck.

My heart skips a beat when it seems as though the airplane makes a slight bounce, but my tail-hook grabs the number three cross deck pennant – the arresting gear cable – bringing me to a rapid stop. Whew, a landing rather than a go-around ... what a relief!

Holding my brakes while the arresting gear petty officer disconnects my tail hook from the cable, I quickly review my after-landing checklist and before-takeoff checklist. I'm thinking that I'm going to make a deck launch, a running takeoff like I did on the six qualifying landings and takeoffs with the SNJ during primary flight training.

I knew that I was going to experience a catapult takeoff sometime during these seven qualifying landings and take-offs, but I thought it would probably be on my last takeoff, before returning to Barin Field. The arresting gear petty officer hands me off to a taxi-control petty officer who signals me to continue my taxiing forward toward the starboard catapult officer. All taxi movements on the deck of an aircraft carrier are very, very precise and dangerous as hell. But taxiing into position to be hooked up to the catapult is not only precise, it is damn scary. There is no S turning to see where I am going, just following hand signals from a taxi man slightly in front and off the left wing of my airplane. When he gives me the signals to hold my left brake to make a slight left turn and add a little power, all I can see in front of the airplane is water.

With the signal to hold both brakes, I promise you that I have them both locked. Next, he gives me the signal to extend my flaps, do a control check, and complete the take-off checklist. I quickly nod my head and give him thumbs up, signifying that I have complied with his signals. He now turns me over to the fly-one officer who gives me a signal to hold both brakes and advance the throttle to 100 percent takeoff power by holding his left hand above is head with his fist closed, and making a rapid circular motion with the first finger of his right hand. I do so while taking a quick scan that all my engine instruments are in the green. Remembering to put my head back firmly against the headrest so the rapid acceleration doesn't knock me unconscious or even make me see stars, I quickly put my right elbow flush into my stomach with my right hand around the control stick to keep the aircraft from going into too steep of a climb, stalling and crashing into the ocean.

The fly-one officer gives me the *am-I-ready?* Double-thumbs-up signal and I answer it with a left-handed salute, immediately locking my left thumb around the throttle to make sure that I continue to have full takeoff power.

There's no way that you can imagine the feeling of acceleration, going from a dead standstill to 85 knots in about 85 feet. Hell, I can cast a fly farther than that.

I am airborne and climbing out almost before I know what has happened. It's an amazing experience, even better than I have anticipated. I quickly make a right clearing turn to get my prop wash out of the way of the next airplane, and then continue straight ahead, climbing to 500 feet before starting my left climbing turn to re-enter the landing pattern for my second approach and landing.

"This time," I say to myself, "I'll not forget to pull the release handle for my tail-hook."

The next five approaches, landings and deck launches were textbook style and I ended up with an overall 3.9 grade out of a possible 4.0, finishing off this phase of my advanced fighter training. Now all I have to do is circle the carrier at 3,000 feet, waiting for the other three cadets in my division to complete their six qualifying landings and join up with me to fly back to Barin Field.

The only remaining requirement before getting commissioned as an Officer [Ensign] in the U.S. Navy and designated a Naval Aviator is about one month of all-weather flight training in Corpus Christi, Texas. I love it when a plan comes together.

Now it's back to Texas again, probably for the last time. After I checked into the all-weather training unit at NAS Corpus Christi, It did not take very long to get a taste of what being a naval officer will be like. I was issued a card that permitted me to eat at the officer's dining room, to which I have to contribute a certain amount of money out of each paycheck. But I am now getting paid all of $129 a month instead of the $96 a month I was receiving as a basic Naval Aviation Cadet. And I am billeted in the junior BOQ [Bachelor Officers Quarters] instead of a barracks.

Corpus Christi is the only place I have ever been where the airport would go on instrument landing conditions because of a dust storm and a rainstorm at the same time.

Flying a Navy SNB-5, twin-engine Beech craft, I spent half of my training time in the command pilot's left-hand seat and half in the co-pilot right-hand seat. After completing this very intense five weeks of all-weather flight training, learning how to fly ADF [automatic direction finder] approaches, MDF [manual direction finder] approaches and most important of all, GCA [ground controlled approach] which will allow me to land with the lowest ceiling and visibility. This last phase of training before finishing my 23 months of extensive ground school and flight training was soon to be finished.

The Navy issued me a white instrument card, which stated, "S.C. Apte, Ensign USNR-R has met the requirements for a STANDARD instrument clearance rating." Wow. I was still about a week away from getting my commission, but this certainly was a morale booster, signifying that I was qualified to execute takeoffs, landings and filing IFR [Instrument Flight Rule] flight plans.

My passion for fishing was not forgotten during this time. Instead of going into Corpus Christi with the guys on Friday nights and Saturday nights, I would often take both a spinning rod and a fly rod and spend numerous hours under the floodlights at the end of the pier behind the officers club, catching more saltwater trout than I care to admit. The officer's wardroom quickly became accustomed to having fried, boneless trout fillets included in their Sunday morning buffet breakfast. Judd Hill, a fellow Cadet from

Florida, joined me on a number of the night fishing escapades. Some nights the fishing was so good that we stayed up until dawn was breaking over Laguna Madre, putting our daytime activities on the back burner. On the plus side we never had to clean any of the fish. After the first time, they gave us a great big washtub that we tried our best to fill over its rim. Judd stayed in the Navy and became the commanding officer of an elite F8U Crusader fighter squadron in Viet Nam, before retiring as a full commander in 1972.

With the prospect at hand of becoming a Naval Officer and a somewhat hot fighter pilot, I did go into Corpus Christi the following Saturday afternoon with my mind set on buying something befitting this stature, like a powder blue Pontiac convertible. My mind was quickly changed by how much it cost and the Pontiac-Oldsmobile dealer said that he had a fantastic deal on a new 1953 Oldsmobile Rocket 88. The spin involved the General Motors Hydromatic plant burning down and this particular run of Olds 88's did not have automatic shifting, but it had a manual stick shift on the steering wheel, making it a drag racing dream. Manual shifting did not bother me whatsoever, as my first car was a hand-me-down 1935 Ford V-8. It had a tooth missing from first gear and it sounded worse than a broken coffee grinder until shifting into second gear.

I called home to ask my dad to wire me $200 for a down payment on this super deal. Feeling like I was sitting on top of the world, I couldn't wait to drive to NAS Corpus and show off my new toy.

The very next day five cadets and I climbed in my chariot, went into town to a drive-in restaurant that is known as The Body Exchange. This is a place where a car loaded with college girls would drive up next to a car full of cadets, first with our windows rolled down getting to know each other, then more often than not with doors open. It became a game of musical chairs, changing from one vehicle to the other and sometimes joining together where both cars would head for a secluded beach at Padre Island to swim and at times engage in a little romance. It proved to be a great way to break-in my Rocket 88 for things to come in the future.

After passing my final instrument check-ride with flying colors, the day finally arrived. I wore the highly-starched dress white uniform, still sporting the soon-to-be-changed NAVCAD epaulets. A total of 15 newly designated Naval Aviators were lined up to receive their Wings of Gold. Some flew AD Skyraider dive bombers, others TBF Turkey torpedo bombers, and a couple of us that went through fighter tactics flying the F6F Hellcat.

We stood at parade rest for what seemed like hours while the Chief of Naval Air Training congratulated all of us and asked if there was anyone in the crowd who wanted to pin their son, husband or boyfriend, to please step forward. The Naval Air Station band played marches until finally they softly played Anchors Away, and Admiral John Dale Price slowly walked down our line and carefully pinned the wings on those of us who did not have a love-one there to do the honor.

The hard work, the intense training, the anguish and hardships had finally paid off. And I don't mind a bit saying that I was damned proud of myself.

* * *

I'm an Ensign, by gum, and off I scurry to downtown Corpus Christi to the Army-Navy Uniform Store. It's time to get measured so that all my uniforms are properly tailored and I can look the part of an officer.

I'm excited. I try on Aviation Greens, Tan Gabardines, Dress Blues and of course high-collar Dress Whites. What a great wardrobe of uniforms, but there's a new rub: They're no longer furnished courtesy of the Navy. As a commissioned officer I get the dubious privilege of paying for them myself.

Uncle Sam takes full advantage of the problems encountered by each new young naval officer. Shortly after receiving my commission, I sign up for a Navy loan in order to purchase this new wardrobe. I get paid every two weeks and a percentage of my pay gets withheld as payment back to Uncle Sam. For some reason, this loan is known as "A Dead Horse." It's funny, I thought. I'm about to ride into the jet age on a dead horse.

Okay, now it's back to NAAS Kingsville Texas, only this time I think I'm the real deal, a full-fledged Naval Officer sporting my glistening wings of gold.

As I returned the Marine MP's salute going through the main gate, I have the feeling I could conquer the world.

This would be a whiz-bang 10 days of jet training, starting first with a two-seater TV 2, the Navy's version of the Air Force T-33 Shooting Star, which in turn is a lengthened fuselage version of the F-80.

But first, it's back into a pressure chamber, something I experienced before flying the Grumman Hellcat in advance training. I'm again wearing an oxygen mask, being brought up to 32,000 feet, instructed to perform certain duties while wearing the oxygen mask. I'm handed a deck of playing cards and asked me to name each card as I take it out of the deck, showing it to the Navy flight surgeon in the chamber with me. Next I'm instructed to take my oxygen mask off, continue the show-and-tell with the playing cards. At this point they teach me to perform "grunt breathe," which involves taking a deep breath, bending over, tightening my stomach muscles, bearing down and grunting. This intends to help force any oxygen in my blood into my brain.

I do pretty well for at least a minute before anoxia takes effect and I pass out. As soon as the flight surgeon puts the oxygen mask back on me and selects a 100-percent oxygen feed, I snap out of it, just a bit groggy for a moment. But this serves as an experience of what I might encounter flying jet fighter planes at high altitudes.

No matter what type of high-performance aircraft you fly, it's vitally important to know where every switch is located and to be able to touch every switch, control and instrument in the cockpit. I sit in the cockpit of the TV-2 until I can perform a blindfold cockpit check by touching all of the gauges, switches and controls that the instructor calls out. Even though I will only be flying this airplane for today, I had to know all of the emergency procedures, especially how to eject – the only way out with a parachute. Today's TV-2 flying time is to get my mind working faster than it ever had to work in piston fighter planes. Jets fly more than twice as fast as prop planes, and this one is only a short interlude to flying the high-performance carrier-based Panther Jet.

After going through an abbreviated 2 ½-hour syllabus of approach to stalls, extending and retracting the speed breaks to slowdown from high speeds, making two touch-and-go landings and a full-stop landing, Lieutenant JG Pete Johnson, my instructor, had me taxi back to the gas pits. He exited the back seat, telling me to make sure all my fuel gauges show full, and before takeoff, gang-bar the fuel switches in order to have all the small auxiliary fuel tanks flow into the main fuel tank.

Flying the T-Bird, as it is affectionately known, was certainly easier, quieter, smoother and actually more fun than anything else I had previously flown. Easier because the controls were lighter to manipulate and there is less to do, especially during takeoff. Just push the throttle forward to 100-percent RPM, and when sufficiently airborne put the landing gear lever in the up position. Unlike the Grumman Hellcat, once airborne there was no pulling back the throttle to decrease manifold pressure, pulling back the RPM lever to match the manifold pressure, closing the canopy and cowl-flaps, easing the mixture control back in order to reduce the fuel flow–and to do all of these things before exceeding any of their structural limits. It most certainly left me with a feeling of forgetting to do something, which isn't a good thing when you're flying high-performance airplanes that can kill you within the blink of an eye.

Pete was waiting at the approach end of the runway to talk with me on the two-way UHF radios that the enlisted airmen at the end of the runway have in case someone is on final approach without his landing gear down. The only words I heard from Pete on each of my five approach and landings: "Looking good" and "Nice one." On my final full-stop landing, he said, "Okay, see you at the line shack."

This had been a full day of hard flying, and I felt completely rung out, ready for a hot shower and a cold beer. It was 4:30 in the afternoon and we had been at it since 7 this morning. "I have very little debriefing for you, Stu," Pete said with a wan smile, his face looking as tired as I felt. "You have well-deserved thumbs up for this phase of jet indoctrination, I'm happy to say. Let's meet at the 0 club in one hour and you can buy me a drink."

Later, in the Officers Club, Pete told the bartender, "I'll have the coldest Papst Blue Ribbon you have in the cooler, please."

Without pausing and not yet looking directly at me, Pete said, "Stu, you are a fine pilot." He turned to face me now, as though a dramatic announcement was forthcoming. "I'd be pleased to have you fly my wing."

Despite the theatrics, I could tell he meant it. It's about the highest compliment any budding fighter pilot can hear from an instructor. I was so proud that my heart nearly burst through my chest. I told Pete how much I appreciated his words, and that I was now especially eager to conquer my next exciting training phase: learning to fly the F9F-2 Grumman Panther Jet.

While the next day was considered a day off from flying, it was a grueling 10-hours of studying about the Panther Jet's operating procedures. I needed to memorize takeoff speeds, approach and landing speeds, climb speeds and probable stall speeds, abnormal procedures, emergency ejection procedures, and study diagrams of where all of the switches and controls are located. I even found a Panther that was in for a maintenance check and logged some time sitting in the cockpit, getting the feel of where everything is located. I faced a four-page written exam, a blindfold cockpit check and, according to my instructor Marine Captain Bob McNally, I would be safe for solo, which is the only way the single-seat Panther jet can be flown.

Right from the get-go, just sitting in the seat, I felt flying the Grumman Panther was going to be a dream come true. I guess, just like thousands of other Naval Aviators before me, I was fast becoming a Grumman fan.

Day one's syllabus is almost a clone of my one day flying the TV-2 Shooting Star. With one major exception being there's no backseat with an instructor pilot ready to help in case something goes wrong.

As things turned out, nothing did go wrong. After going up to 10,000 feet I did a series of maneuvers to get a feel for the controls that would be critical in a landing configuration—extending the speed brakes, putting the gear and flaps down, maintaining 300- to 500-feet-per-minute descent rates.

Later, in a series of landings and takeoffs, with Captain McNally in a jeep at the approach runway, I flew the pattern and landings with a smoothness that seemed to please the Captain and certainly had me smiling under the oxygen mask.

Ringing wet with sweat from excitement and fatigue, I feel like a million dollars as I navigated my way back to NAAS Kingsville. I was almost squirming in my seat with anticipation of flying the Panther Jet in a fleet fighter squadron.

With the field in sight, I called, "Kingsville Tower, Alfa Tango Uncle 201 three miles south for landing."

The reply came from a female voice that sounded rather sultry, momentarily distracting me. "Roger Alfa Tango Uncle 201, you are cleared to overhead runway three one for a carrier break-and-landing. Wind is two niner zero degrees ten knots, altimeter is two niner niner five. Call turning base."

Her voice lingered in my head. Sure would be nice, I thought, to have some female companionship to help me celebrate my first day flying the F9-F Panther. But I knew I still had six or seven extremely rigorous days of flying ahead of me before completing the program, and finding out what fighter squadron I would be assigned in the fleet.

Quickly refocusing, I extended the speed brakes to help slow me to 200 knots, maintaining 1,000 feet as I over-headed runway 31. Approaching the far end of the runway, I did a fast roll to the left, trying to look sharp in case my instructor or anyone else was watching.

I went through the standard routine of gear down, full flaps, speed-brake-retracted, starting a 300- to 500-fpm descent while rolling out downwind at a wingtip distance from the runway. Abeam the approach end of the runway, I start a left turn planning to roll out lined up with the runway, without a long straightaway. At the same time I call, "Kingsville Tower Alfa Tango Uncle 201, turning base, gear down 3 green."

Immediately the same sweet-sounding voice replied, "Roger 201 cleared to land." Damn, I thought, sure would like to see what she looks like.

It seems like I'm in total command, flying this bird as though I have 500 hours in it. I roll my wings level just before reaching the runway approach lights, just giving me three seconds of straightaway before touching down, about 800 feet down the runway.

Cocky now, I'm hoping a lot of people were watching what a carrier speed break and landing should look like.

"Two zero one, you're cleared to the Alpha Tango Uncle ramp."

"Roger that, Kingsville."

You'll never guess who was waiting for me at the ramp. No, not my imagined babe in the tower, but instead the beaming face of Captain McNally. He walked to my plane after I shut the engine off.

"Hey, Stu, I just did a bit of boasting to those two instructors standing over there." He motioned toward the line shack behind him. "You made a great carrier break, approach and landing – good enough for one of the instructors to ask if that was a new instructor flying."

You can just imagine how those words made me feel.

The next day was another of familiarization with the airplane, shooting touch-and-go landings on the first hop, and some formation flying with my instructor on the second hop. Fortunately, it went just as smoothly. Not only did I finish the training with flying colors, I'd earned the respect of my instructor.

While one might figure at this stage that I was so full of myself that I could barely get my head in and out of a cockpit, that wasn't the case at all. If anything, I'd come to respect even more the mortality of man and how a life can end in a fraction of a second merely by one bad decision or moment of indecision. Flying jets leave little room for error, because things happen so fast that without banking on solid training and experience, you might as well sign your death certificate.

Now don't call me conceited. Put yourself in my place, recognize the great thrill of flying through the air and controlling such magnificent machines, and you'll better appreciate the satisfaction of successfully completing all the rigorous training sessions required. That my instructors were complimentary served as icing on the cake.

As we have seen in Chapter One, in the months ahead an F9-F Panther would almost kill me in the skies over the Florida coast. The reason I survived was my training. I knew exactly what to do the instant a warning light came on. And I did it fast!

* * *

After my Panther ejection, while recuperating in the Portsmouth (Va.) Naval Hospital, I continually broke out in a severe case of hives. Sometimes the palms of my hands would break out and on other occasions the bottoms of my feet. At times my eyes would swell shut almost like that night at NAAS Sanford when I ran out of fuel while trying to taxi in. The doctors started running numerous allergy tests and decided I was allergic to some inhalant in the Virginia tidewater area. They recommended my being transferred to the training command in the Pensacola, Florida, area as a flight instructor.

After getting out of the hospital and being put on non-flying status for more than a month, I was able to pass a flight physical. When checking back into VF 81, I was told all of my squadron mates had already checked out flying the F7U-3 Cutlass and thought it was a great hot rod under certain conditions.

Commander Harders, my commanding officer, informed me that he had been notified of my impending transfer as an instructor in the flight training command because of allergies. Of course, I felt crushed.

"Sir, if I have to leave this squadron, is there anything you can possibly due to get me into another fighter squadron in NAS Jacksonville?" I pleaded while standing at a rigid attention.

"I'm flying to Washington day after tomorrow for some meetings at the Pentagon," he replied. "I'll see if there is short-handed squadron in Jacksonville and at the same time find out how much clout I have."

"Thank you, sir," I said emphatically. Taking one step back, giving a smart salute and doing an about-face, I left his office.

That afternoon I was issued the classified secret manuals on the Cutlass and told to study hard. I was to be scheduled tomorrow afternoon for the first of three simulator periods, after which I'd have a written exam and a blindfold cockpit check.

The next three days seemed to whiz by at the speed of sound, and I was now ready for the first of three FAM [familiarization flights] in an airplane that was completely different from other airplanes. The controls were different, the power settings were different with strange names, like TOT [Tail Osalatory Temperature] instead of TPT [Tail Pipe Temperature]. The power settings in this jet fighter were made by the TOT, not by the percentage of the N1 turbine, requiring a whole new thought process of using temperatures instead of RPM.

This hot rod was an innovative but flawed jet fighter plane. It had a delta wing, twin rudders and no tail, sporting two Westinghouse J46 WE-8B engines with afterburners. Sitting on the ground it looked like a praying mantis because of its extended nose gear, making it necessary to climb in and out of the cockpit via a long ladder that was hooked on the side of the cockpit. It was also one of the first to have an all-hydraulic control system. No cables went to the ELEVONS, which did the job of elevators and ailerons that were on all other jet fighter planes.

Lieutenant Mike Service, our squadron maintenance officer, who was to be my chase plane, with a sly grin, told me I would be holding on during my first afterburner FAM take-off flight. The Cutlass with afterburners had a higher rate of climb from takeoff to 20,000 feet than any other airplane in the Navy or Air Force.

This first flight was to merely get the feel of this altogether different aircraft. Making an afterburner takeoff was not quite the same shocking acceleration that you receive when getting a catapult shot, but it certainly was a kick in the ass different than a normal takeoff.

Climbing out to 15,000 feet, I practiced slow flight, putting the landing gear, flaps and slats out. This dirty condition would be the way I would have to configure when coming in for landing and it was best to get used to the feel at 15,000 feet instead of 1,000 feet.

Next I cleaned up the bird, accelerating to 350 knots, making some steep turns in each direction while maintaining my altitude. I told Mike that I wanted to do a full roll in each direction, and he replied, "Have at it, Stu, and while you're at it why not do a loop."

Eee – Yoww! The Cutlass was extremely light on the controls and highly maneuverable, its performance far better than I had imagined. Pulling up from the loop I heard Mike's voice on the radio.

"Okay Stu, join up. Let's take her down and head for the barn. My fuel state shows close to bingo time." His transmission quickly brought me back to reality.

"Roger that, sir," I replied while looking over my shoulder, finally spotting him.

After joining his wing we continued our descent on a direct heading for Oceana, where Mike called for a carrier break and landing permission. I anticipated having a different sight picture after adjusting into the landing eye seat position because of the high nose attitude on its approach to touching down. I was pleasantly surprised how soft a landing it made. Now it was a matter of taxiing to the designated parking area, setting the parking brakes, moving the throttle and fuel to off and waiting in the cockpit until ground personnel hooked-up a starting unit. Sometimes as much as 10 minutes after shutting down, the J 46 would light off again, necessitating the starting unit's availability for blowing the fire out.

Mike suggested that I wait until tomorrow morning for my next flight before the cumulus clouds start building up and creating turbulence. My second FAM was to be my first supersonic flight ever, and I was damn sure excited about joining the small, elite group of sonic boomers known as the "Mach Busters."

Falling asleep was not easy I was still riding on the high of my first Cutlass flight and had a multitude of thoughts racing through my head. When I did finally drop off it was in a very deep sleep and my alarm signifying morning seemed to happen quickly.

In no time at all I showered, shaved, dressed and was at the officer's dining room while it was still dark. While having a good cup of Navy coffee I was in luck this morning and able to enjoy one of my favorite breakfasts, SOS, chipped beef on toast. Emergency and flight procedures were flashing through my mind as I finished eating.

At the squadron Quonset hut, I quickly got out of my uniform and wiggled into my G-suit [anti-gravity suit] before walking into the pilot's ready room to see what aircraft and what time I was scheduled. Almost like reading my mind, the flight schedules officer assigned me the same airplane I had yesterday. Some airplanes have idiosyncrasies and I was pleased that this one, as far as I could tell, did not have any.

Once again Lieutenant Mike Service was going to fly chase for me on my last familiarization flight; he already signed out his airplane and was walking out towards it. Taking off – joining up – and climbing out to 30,000 feet went as expected. This time we headed 30 miles out over the Atlantic Ocean. VF-81 and sister squadron VF-83 have the only supersonic airplanes on the east coast of the U.S. and were already guilty of broken windows and the likes created by sonic booms. We were going to break the sound barrier twice, once individually and then in formation.

Acceleration was rapid as I eased over into a slight descent. Coming around-the-horn with the throttles lighting the afterburners, I approached and went right through Mach 1, only noticing a slight shutter at the moment I exceeded the speed of sound. Truthfully, if I hadn't been watching my Mach Meter, I probably would not have known that I had joined the Mach Busters. Next we joined up in a slightly spread combat formation, climbed back to 30,000 feet, pushed over, lighting our afterburners in unison, and accelerated through Mach1 together. With another notch in my gun belt, Mike suggested he join up as my wing-man and I lead us back to Oceana.

Just like yesterday, all went well and I was scheduled to go back up without a chase plane at 1:00 right after lunch. My feelings were remorseful, thinking about having to leave this great group of fighter pilots and an airplane I was starting to enjoy, and once again going into the unknown.

The F7U-3 Cutlass has the first Martin-Baker ejection seat, where all you have to do is put your feet in the stirrups, reach up and pull the face curtain to be on your way out of the airplane. It is equipped with the first Chain-Link parachute that did everything for you, opening automatically at or below 10,000 feet. I'm pleased to say I never had the necessity of trying either of these new and improved innovations. [Two of our future astronauts, Wally Schirra and John Glenn, also had the pleasure of flying the Cutlass in 1954.]

Then the day came when I was asked to report to the skipper's office. The bad news: I was being transferred out of VF-81. The good news: Instead of being transferred to the training command, I was going to another top fighter squadron, VF-173 at NAS Jacksonville, Florida, one of the first squadrons to receive the high flying, supersonic North American FJ-3 Fury. The Fury is beefed up for carrier landings, a hopped up Navy version of the Air Force F-86E Sabre Jet, sporting a larger J65 Sapphire engine.

Shortly after checking in with the squadron commanding officer and executive officer, I was assigned my collateral duty as first lieutenant of the squadron. This is a job title, not a rank. I was to be in charge of squadron security, deployment and all squadron equipment that was deployable. They quickly brought me up to speed, issuing the classified Secret FJ-3 manual to study, showing me an aircraft undergoing maintenance in the hangar. I could spend all the time necessary learning where the switches and gauges were in the cockpit prior to getting a blindfold cockpit check. The next day I had a six-page, open-book written exam on the airplane, abnormal procedures and Naval Air Station area rules – as much a learning session as an exam.

Send me in, coach, I said to myself a couple days later while being briefed for my first Fury FAM flight. I'm a bona fide Cutlass pilot and anyone who can fly that bird can fly anything; or so I thought.

There were numerous bugs to contend with, like occasional

engine seizures due to some severe lubrication problems, which could cause the engine to seize up. That makes it necessary to either eject or, if you're high enough and near enough to the field, make a dead stick landing. I remembered that with an engine seizure, the hydraulic pumps are no longer operating and allowing only a certain amount of control movements before they freeze, making it a bad day to fly. Like any new fighter plane being delivered to the first fleet squadrons, it's their job to do a shakedown. Fleet pilots are generally aware of the extent of flight testing performed on the planes prior to their being assigned to the fleet or training squadrons. Fleet pilots know how to fly the plane they are in, how fast and how high it will go, its G limits, stall speeds and general flying characteristics. The FJ-3 was also prone to engine flameouts, but probably not much more so than many other jet fighters of its day. During this briefing I was told the J65 engine also suffered from occasional catastrophic turbine blades failures, which would cause the engine to shed its turbine blades and sending them flying out the side of the fuselage.

One very different quirk this airplane had was nicknamed the JC maneuver; easy to get into but difficult to get out of. I'll explain: While Bob Hoover, the test pilot, was on his first high-speed flight with the FJ-3, he made a slight over-correction for altitude and moving his elevator a bit too quickly. It caused the plane to pitch sharply. He inadvertently moved the control stick to compensate, causing the plane to pitch in the other direction; each correction put his plane into a more violent maneuver. His every movement in the cockpit was remotely filmed and everything said was tape-recorded. This maneuver was so violent that "Jesus Christ!" was the only words recorded. The FJ-3 Fury was the first airplane to have a flying tail active all the time. This means the whole hydraulically boosted horizontal stabilizer, not just the elevator, moved grossly and accentuated the pitch effect induced by the stick movement in the cockpit. Hence this maneuver was known as the "JC Maneuver."

Even after being made aware of this maneuver and knowing the only way out of it was to neutralize the controls, my first couple of flights easily had me approaching the JC Maneuver. It was easier to get into above 35,000 feet where the air was less dense and the

Fury's service ceiling was 49,000 feet. One time I did a zoom climb to 55,000 feet, high enough to see the full curvature of the earth, before pushing over into a high-speed Mach 1+ descent. Approaching the speed of sound, my airplane went into an almost uncontrollable roll to the right which I countered with left aileron to no avail until I was almost upside down. I reached a dense enough altitude for my opposite aileron application to take effect. At altitudes below 40,000 feet, the Fury – while in a slight descent – would punch right through Mach 1, making only a slight roll to the right and easily corrected with left aileron.

I only had a total flight time of 44 hours in the Fury when VF-173 did a full squadron deployment to Leeward Point, Guantanamo Bay, Cuba, for gunnery exercises. I spent 16 days practicing various types of air-to-air gunnery, firing our 20 mm cannons at a cloth sleeve being towed by one of our squadron mates. Each airplane's bullets were painted a different color, leaving a residue on the sleeve and making it easy to see who was getting the hits. Once again this was my forte.

Being the new boy on the block, one of the newest members of the squadron, I was the designated tow guard for our first day's shoot. Thereafter each morning, a senior pilot would deal a playing card to each member of the squadron under the rank of Lieutenant Commander. The person with the lowest card would fly the tow plane, dragging the target banner on a cable at which the rest of the squadron would fire its 20 mm cannons. The pilot with the next lowest card would fly a position on the way to the gunnery range and back as tow guard. This was to keep other aircraft from inadvertently flying into the cable if the pilot did not see the banner. We practiced mostly high–sided and low–sided firing runs with an occasional flat firing run. It was important to remember not to fire from a "sucked" position, coming in from too far astern angle, meaning you might end up hitting the tow plane, which has happened in the past.

On our 15th day, I received the low card, making me the tow plane for the second firing period of the day. Lieutenant Jameson was my tow guard. All went well during the shoot and he joined up flying next to the banner on our way back to Leeward Point, where I made a low pass pulling the release handle and dropping the banner alongside the runway. Lieutenant Jameson joined up on my right wing as we climbed out to 1,000 feet, circling to the right side of the field in order to come in for a carrier break over the runway. The rest of the squadron had already landed, and I was rolling out after touchdown when I glanced back over my left shoulder to see how close my wingman was behind me. All I could see was a big ball of fire and black smoke coming up 150 yards before the runway.

Lieutenant Jameson was an Annapolis graduate, married with a new baby, but he had the least amount of total flight hours and FJ-3 hours in the squadron. The accident investigation board suggested he turned too tight on final approach at too slow an airspeed, stalling the Fury without enough room to recover and crashing to the ground. Once again the sign posted in almost all of the operations and ready-rooms hit home: "Flying itself is inherently safe…But very unforgiving of mistakes." Two days later we left Gitmo and flew back to NAS Jacksonville, where we were scheduled to practice FCLP's [Field Carrier Landing Practice] at Navy Mayport in preparation for going aboard the USS Bennington [CVA-20] as the first FJ-3 squadron to land on an aircraft carrier.

Now the strangulated hernia that I received ejecting out of the Panther Jet reared its ugly head, sending me to the Jacksonville Naval Hospital for more surgery. It necessitated my being off flight status flying operational jet aircraft long enough to keep me from being Field Carrier Landing qualified, which would not allow me to stay and deploy with VF-173. Despite some of the Fury's early pitfalls, it was by far the best airplane I had the opportunity and pleasure to fly in the Navy.

When released from the hospital and back on flight status, I received orders to report to Fleet All Weather Training Unit Atlantic as an instrument instructor, renewing instrument tickets for fleet pilots. Because I was not yet medically cleared for flying jet aircraft, I was checked out as an instrument instructor flying the twin-engine SNB-5, instructing multi-engine patrol plane pilots. This continued for the next 3 ½ months until medical gave me the go-ahead to flying jets again.

Now I was checked out and became an instrument instructor flying the TV-2 two-seater jet, instructing fighter pilots needing to renew their instrument ticket. Some months I instructed in both aircraft, teaching two different syllabuses. This was my job until I was released from active-duty in December 1955.

* * *

The image of a hell raising, drunken, hard flying fighter pilot perceived by the general public due to stories, movies and possibly some personal observations since World War I, may not be a totally unjust one.

Not long ago a preflight classmate of mine who retired from the military after 25 years of active-duty wrote to me explaining that the title Fighter Pilot applies to all aviators who fly tactical aircraft used in hazardous air-to-air and air-to-ground combat operations. Many pilots, regardless of the aircraft they fly, are fighter pilots in mind and spirit as evidenced in their brazen lack of fear and determined win-win warrior aggression.

Fighter pilots are a close-knit band of patriots and warriors, in love with their unique death-defying profession. They relish the proud camaraderie inherent among inspired daredevils who daily live close to violent death in the skies and who particularly enjoy frequent celebration of their good fortune in surviving another exhilarating flight.

To this day, as I write these words, I am proud to have been one of them, flying for my country, in the United States Navy.

* * *

"I now know why men who have been to war yearn to reunite. Not to tell stories or look at old pictures. Not to laugh or weep. Comrades gather because they long to be with the men who once acted at their best; men who suffered and sacrificed. I did not pick these men. They were delivered by fate and the military. But I know them in a way I know no other men. I have never given any one such trust. They were willing to

guard something more precious than my life. They would have carried my reputation, the memory of me. It was part of the bargain we all made, the reason we were so willing to die for one another. As long as I have my memory, I will think of them all, every day. I am sure that when I leave this world, my last thought will be of my family and my comrades....Such good men."

– Author unknown

CHAPTER

FOUR

TARPON COME FIRST!

Pan-Am Can Wait

It's December, 1955. I'm out of the Navy, and need a job. But not just any job! I need one that won't get in the way of fishing.

I received job offer letters from several major airlines including Eastern, Pan American, United and American. But it seemed to me that Eastern Airlines, being Miami-based, would be ideal for me to combine flying, earning a living, and my very ambitious fishing pursuits.

I headed down to N.W. 36 Street in Miami, near the airport, and filled out Eastern Airlines' lengthy application, took their physical exam, and spent almost seven hours complying with the rest of their application process.

Eventually, at my final interview with Eastern Airlines, I was sitting across the table from the Chief Pilot, a fellow by the name of Captain Kearns – a name that I will never forget. He was gruff throughout the interview, and at the end he actually said, "You should be thankful that Eastern Airlines is going to hire you."

I looked him dead in the eye, picked up my completed applications from his desk, ripped them into three pieces, flung them across the table, got up, and walked out of the building. I was thinking. *Who does this SOB think he is? I'm an ex-Navy fighter pilot and I should be thankful for Eastern Airline's interest in me? The way I see it, any airlines should be thankful for my interest in them.*

"Adios, Eastern," I said as I walked out their door.

Walking a bit farther up the street, I ran into a couple of guys who had been AD-6 dive-bomber pilots in my last Navy Air Group. Bill Taylor and Jack Miller had just been hired by Pan Am and were really excited about their offers. First, Pan Am guaranteed they'd be based in Miami for at least a year. On top of that, they were given the option to fly long hauls carrying freight on four-engine, non-pressurized DC-4s, or short hauls to the Caribbean Islands with passengers on twin-engine Convairs. I knew which one I'd choose – long hauls carrying freight, because that meant a lot of time off between flights.

I couldn't help telling them what just happened to me at Eastern Airlines. They could tell I was pissed off. And when I get pissed off, I go fishing. That's just what I did then. I packed up my fishing gear and headed down to the Florida Keys with another friend–Jerry Kirk, a firefighter from Coral Gables. Jerry was to become one of the esteemed "Four Sportsmen," a group destined, including myself, to become gear testers for Pflueger Fishing Tackle and Ted Williams Fishing Tackle Company. We headed down to a place called Popeye's on Conch Key, about 60 miles north of Key West.

It cost us near nothing to stay there. I had Mom's Worry, the boat I purchased as soon as I got out of the Navy. We spent a wonderful, soul-satisfying better part of a month fishing in the Keys. It was soul-satisfying for sure, especially the day that I hooked a monster tarpon.

Conch Key was little more than a fast 15-minute run to a little group of islands named Arsnicker Keys. The grapevine had it that quite a few tarpon hung out in that area, and tarpon was what we wanted in our crosshairs.

With a gentle southeasterly breeze blowing, we set ourselves up to drift from the westernmost Arsnicker Key toward the first point of Nine Mile Bank, a shallow area that runs from Man-of-War Key to the easternmost Arsnicker Key.

After drifting only 50 yards, we went over the top of a small group of very large tarpon. So large that when I saw them on the bottom, my first thought was, "How in the world did all of these big logs end up on the bottom way out here?"

Using a medium-weight spinning rod and eight-pound-test line, I used a three-inch top-water plug made in Miami that had a catchy sounding name, Leaping Lena. If worked properly, it could certainly live up to its name. While retrieving it with an action known as "walking the dog," making it splash back and forth on the surface like a scared, wounded fish, a monster-size tarpon inhaled it. The strike sounded like a large concrete block being dropped into the water–a sound probably heard all the way to the first point of Nine Mile.

Immediately upon feeling the two sets of treble hooks, she leaped five feet into the air, shaking her head with such vicious velocity it's a wonder that the plug stayed hooked and my light line did not break. All big tarpon are females—I've seldom caught a male that exceeded 100 pounds– and it seemed obvious to me that this big beauty was in the 150-pound class.

Jerry agreed, emphatically. "Holy crap!" He shouted, also loud enough to be heard all the way to the first point of Nine Mile Bank. "Stu, this tarpon has to weigh more than 150 pounds. Are you going to break it off?"

"Are you kidding me?" I replied, my voice indignant. "I don't care if it's Moby Dick, I'll fight it to the end."

After that first wild jump, this magnificent fish settled down to a swimming contest, at first taking us into Nine Mile Bank, then a little ways out to the Gulf of Mexico, all the while heading in a northerly direction.

Two and a half hours into the fight, I managed to get a yield out of her by pulling down and back toward the tail with my rod. "Okay Jerry," I said, "she might just be ready to bring in. Make sure that the big gaff with the five-foot handle is handy."

"Are you sure you want me to put this gaff into the mouth of this monster?"

"If I'm able to lay her alongside the boat, that's exactly what I want you to do."

And that is exactly the way it went. I finessed her alongside the boat and Jerry, even with some second thoughts of what he was about to do, reached out and put the gaff-hook into her lower jaw exactly the way I told him to. All hell broke loose as she came half out of the water once again, furiously shaking her head and snatching the gaff-handle right out of Jerry's hands, smacking him alongside his head with it. The blow damn near knocked him to his knees.

We were still attached, even though it was with spider-web-like, eight-pound line. So once again the chase was on, with Jerry at the controls of the boat and my now cramping fingers wrapped around the spinning rod and reel.

The hook-up took place about 2:30, and now the sun was setting on the horizon, and soon it would be dark. With both of the 25-horsepower engines in idle forward gear and us following the now-tired fish, I asked Jerry to get out the emergency kit and make sure my spotlight worked.

We followed her into the mouth of one of the main channels on Nine Mile Bank and back out along the Gulf of Mexico side, all the way past the first stake marking the entrance to Man-Of-War Channel. We sparingly used the searchlight only when we thought absolutely necessary.

This fight turned into a battle using Braille methods. How we managed to follow her through that winding channel is beyond me. Now smelling or feeling something in the incoming tide out of the Gulf of Mexico, she seemed to increase her tail beat and we had to increase our speed with the boat. She made a beeline to Little Conchie Channel and soon thereafter right into the much bigger and deeper Conchie Channel.

I could hear and feel that she came up on a half-hearted, head-shaking jump and taking a deep breath, I said, "Jerry it's now or never. That jump should have made her even more tired, and I'm going to try and bring her alongside the boat again, so be ready with the three-foot gaff-hook and the spotlight."

Once again taking a big chance at this stage of the fight, I carefully eased my first finger of my right hand onto the spool in order to apply just a slight bit more drag, knowing that after such a fight my 8-pound-test line probably shrank to only 5-pound test.

Lady Luck was still with me. The line didn't break as I eased her alongside the boat. Once again it became the moment of truth for Jerry. I mentioned to him not to shine the spotlight directly on the tarpon but off to the side, yet close enough to allow him to see the fish and put the gaff-hook into her lower jaw.

Jerry did an excellent job under extremely adverse conditions. With a shake of her head, the tarpon's lunge for freedom snatched the short-handled gaff out of Jerry's hand, and once again this big Madame was off the gaff and swimming. This time, though, my flimsy spinning line gave up the ghost and I had to admit being tired and also glad she was free.

Now, for the first time, I became truly aware of the buzzing mosquitoes. I've never seen so many mosquitoes in my whole life, and I've seen my share. They were so thick you couldn't even see through them with the spotlight. Since about an hour after dark, Jerry had been applying liberal amounts of citronella bug dope on both of us.

We could hear a large generator and saw lights on the mainland at Flamingo. Very carefully we slowly eased our way toward the marked channel leading to the new marina that was under construction. Now we were killing handfuls of mosquitoes with each swat.

The lights were into our faces and so bright it was difficult to see the landing. After tying up the boat, we climbed ashore and a night watchman quickly met us. "What the hell are you doing here, and where the hell did you come from and why?" he growled.

After giving him an abbreviated version of what happened, he told us to come inside the watchman's shack away from the mosquitoes to spend the night. We gladly accepted the invitation, because the shack cooled us with air conditioning and the thought of spending the night outside amid those swarms of miniature Draculas didn't exactly appeal to us.

The next morning – full of itchy welts – we managed to borrow, so to speak, 10 gallons of gas just to make sure we had enough fuel to cross Florida Bay and make it back to Popeye's at Conch Key.

During that fishing trip, on several days Jerry left to go to

Coral Gables for his duty as a fireman. Like a dream, a fantastically lovely 18-year-old, true redhead from the hills of Tennessee snuck into my little room, undressed and slid under the covers with me. Thrilled with this unexpected gift from the gods, I embraced her with abandon. Trouble is, on about the third interlude on a day that I didn't go fishing, I learned that she was married to one of the men working at Popeye's.

When I told Jerry about it, he went bonkers. "You must be the luckiest son of a bitch in the world," he said, a look of total envy consuming his face. I just looked at him without saying a word, but you couldn't have wiped the silly grin off my face with an electric sander.

February rolled around, and it was time to find a job. Back in Miami now, I headed over to Pan American World Airways. With all my credentials and necessary papers safely tucked under my arm, I entered the building while still a little leery from my experience at Eastern. Unlike Captain Kerns, Pan American's Chief Pilot welcomed me aboard with a hearty handshake and a pat on the back, saying, "We're delighted to have a naval aviator like you on board."

By the end of February 1956, I have become a DC-4 Third Officer. The third officer's role is as the extra copilot, a non-rated pilot, who has been checked out in piloting the airplane but does not have the same qualifications as the Captain and the First Officer. The Captain and the First Officer both have an ATP [Airline Transport Rating], and the First Officer is the first copilot. It's necessary to have at least one rated pilot in the cockpit at all times during the flight. So, either the Captain or first copilot has to be in the seat next to me when I, the Third Officer and relief copilot, am operating the aircraft. On the long hauls across the Atlantic or Pacific Ocean, we carry a Second Officer, who is the navigator.

Later, when I fly the DC-6 and DC-7 four-engine pressurized aircraft, we carry one or two Flight Engineers, a First and a Second, on the very long hauls. As an example, on the around-the-world flights it will be necessary to carry a large complement in the cockpit consisting of the Captain, the First Officer, a Second Officer as a navigator, the Third Officer as a relief copilot, a First Engineer, and a Second Engineer. These airplanes will have sleeping berths somewhat like a Pullman berth on a train in that they pull down from the ceiling right over some of the first-class seats. I will always remember the strange feeling that I have stepping on the back of a first-class passenger's seat when climbing out of my berth. It is a chore dressing while in a half sitting and half reclining position in one of those berths.

The non-pressurized DC-4s generally flew below 10,000 feet, so pilots weren't required to wear an oxygen mask. The DC-4s also did not have any radar, so we could not detect the large cumulonimbus clouds that hold the kind of heavy rain and hail that can tear planes apart. [As they had almost torn my Panther apart in the skies over Florida, as related in Chapter One.] Radar can also be very helpful when flying around the mountains of Central America and South America, which was where most of our flights took place.

One of the routes we had was called a 10-Day Western Sector, carrying freight up and down Central America and the north coast of South America. I staged my flying out of Guatemala, making the ports of call at Honduras; San Salvador; Managua, Nicaragua; San Jose, Costa Rica; and finally overnight in Panama. The next day, we would head east, leaving Panama and fly to the Columbian and Venezuelan cities of Cartagena, Barranquilla, Maracaibo and Caracas.

Sometimes, we stayed overnight in Caracas at the Intercontinental Hotel. Other times, we stayed right near the airport at the Macuto Sheraton Hotel, depending on our schedule. This had us flying up and down Central America and the north coast of South America, which wasn't too bad of a deal, providing you didn't eat or drink the wrong thing and contract "Montezuma's Revenge," an amoebic dysentery that's less than fun to deal with.

The 10-day Western Sector is perfect for my fishing lifestyle. My favorite assignment was hauling freight from Miami to Buenos Aires, Argentina, making all of the ports of call. I could get in my whole month's flying while only being away from Miami 74 hours. Where could I find another job that allowed me so much free time? With a long-range crew consisting of a Captain, First Officer and two Third Officers, we could fly continually around the clock without taking crew rest in a hotel anywhere.

The cargo version of the DC-4 had two bunk beds rigged up in the extreme back part of the cockpit, so we could take some down time there sleeping or just relaxing. We would fly from Miami to San Juan, about a four-hour flight, spend a few hours on the ground for transferring cargo, and head out to Caracas. The flight time from San Juan to Caracas was a little over 3½ hours. Our next leg was around 3½ hours to Dutch Guyana, then a couple of short hops to British Guyana and French Guiana. The next four legs of the trip were probably the most dangerous, flying inland over the Brazilian jungles to places like Manaus, Belem, Brasilia and Bello Horizonte, depending on the cargo.

For some reason, it seemed to me that I was always flying over the dark jungle at night, when I can't see the towering cumulus thunderstorm buildups, with some around the Amazon River area as high as 50,000 feet with the strength to rip our airplane apart. Our radar consisted of two sets of bloodshot eyeballs up against the windscreen, watching for the lightning flashes in order to pick holes around the worst portions of the storms. Our only means of navigation beside dead reckoning was our ADF [Automatic Direction Finder] needles, which more often than not point at the nearest lightning flash.

When we got close enough to some of the destination cities, we picked up the VOR signal, which was basically only a line-of-sight signal like a VHF radio, only good for around 30 miles at the low altitudes we are flying.

Radio communication was almost entirely on High Frequency long-range radio that seems to have more static than audible voices. Nevertheless, we had specific places where we were required to give our position report, and our ETA to the next position point. The ETAs have to be accurate within five minutes; if we miss calling in a position, alarms go off.

Flying into Rio de Janeiro often presented a challenge. We generally tried to have all four pilots in the cockpit, recruiting the maximum number of eyes looking for other airplanes. More than once while on final approach, another airplane cut in front of us, requiring us to execute a missed approach and come around for another landing.

From Rio our next stop was Montevideo, Uruguay, a six-hour flight, where on final approach we would only be a few hundred feet above the mast of the World War II scuttled German monster battleship Graf Spey.

The first morning when I flew over the site, the scene gave me a feeling that is still hard to describe, when ghostlike shadows of the childhood scenes I had witnessed off Miami's beaches came flooding into my mind.

* * *

Suddenly, it seemed, after a little more than a year and a half of flying freight throughout North and South America and the Caribbean, I found myself on my first passenger flight ever. That particular first flight provides a story I have repeated many times, and always with a chuckle.

It is August 11, 1957, and I am called out from a standby pool at the Condado Beach Hotel to operate as the third officer, relief co-pilot, on a flight from San Juan to New York. These flights take approximately nine hours of in route-flight time over water. Because the DC-4 is a non-pressurized airplane, we fly at an altitude between 7,000 and 9,000 feet; we don't want the passengers, or especially the pilots, to pass out during the flight. At these altitudes, the passengers are able to breathe and the pilots don't have to wear oxygen masks.

Being an over-water flight, we have Loran navigation. With this older type of navigation system, a pilot lined up the electronic squiggles on the screen, and then switched modes and re-aligned the squiggles a few more times to get into the last and most important mode. The pilot then very carefully counted the micro seconds before plotting the plane's position on the Loran navigation chart. As I mentioned earlier, we did not have radar on the DC-4 and therefore could not see the cumulus clouds that often build up as thunderstorms over the Gulf Stream in this part of the Atlantic Ocean. You can probably imagine what happens every time we fly into the thunderstorms, at one of the worst turbulence penetration altitudes. The plane dances a jig all over the sky, and we have 60 to 70 very airsick passengers. Hence, these DC-4 passenger flights were nicknamed, "The Vomit Comet."

We were scheduled to depart San Juan at 4 p.m. local time and arrive at Idlewild Airport [now JFK Airport] at 1 a.m. My logbook shows that we actually got airborne at 4:47 p.m., and that I make the take-off, flying the first portion of the flight. This is probably the first flight the Puerto Rican passengers aboard have ever made. The captain or the first officer makes a duty watch list so the crew knows when it is their time to rest.

About four hours into the flight, the first officer, Bob, taps me on the shoulder and says, "Okay Stu, it's my time in the barrel. The air mattress is blown up under the navigation board, so go take a nap."

I am all for that idea; I have been enjoying my most recent two-day layover in San Juan perhaps a little too much. But, after all, I am 27 years old and believe in experiencing life to the fullest. "I'm about ready for a little shut-eye. Thanks, Bob," I reply. I am extremely ready to get a few hours of rest before arriving in New York.

I reach down on the right side of my seat and pull up on the lever that allows me to push my seat back far enough from the control wheel to get out of the cockpit. With a chuckle, I say, "I'll see you when we get to New York, Bob." I move down the two short steps into the navigation area and extend my arms while stretching my back after sitting in the same position for four hours. I take off my shoes and hang up my shirt, then settle down on a double-size air mattress. Sleep seems to come almost immediately as I stretch out under the covers.

I really don't know how long I have been asleep but it seems like no time at all when a warm body slips under the covers and presses against me. It is immediately obvious that this form is a very well-endowed female.

Never even whispering a word, we start hugging and kissing, and playing touchy feely. When she reaches down and unzips my pants, I almost have a climax right then and there.

Before long, we are entwined like two love-crazy snakes. We're in the heights of passion when the blackout curtain separating the cockpit from the navigation area pulls aside without warning, admitting a fatal glow of light. Next, I hear a click and a slightly brighter green hue of light flows into the navigation area.

Either the captain or the first officer is at the Loran navigation panel shooting a navigation fix. Whoever it is briefly steps on the side of my ankle. "Oh, excuse me," he whispers, and from under the covers, I let out a soft, slightly annoyed moan. Through all this, my phantom lover and I are still together as one, gripping each other with an endearing hug.

The Loran set goes black as it is turned off, and the blackout curtain enfolds us once again to ensure our privacy – we hope. The curtain admits an eerie glow of light, as he officer goes back into the cockpit area. The moment the curtain is closed we continue our lovemaking without skipping a beat. The thunderstorms that occasionally bounce us around seem to only add to the rhythm of our movements.

When we are finally done, my mystery companion, with a parting hug and kiss, whispers in my ear, "I'll see you when we get to New York, Bob."

"I'm Stu," I reply.

I feel her entire body stiffen and the temperature seems to drop 10 degrees. She slips out of my arms in a nanosecond and scoots off the air mattress without so much as a word.

True story—so help me God!

These were the years when flying was dangerous and sex was safe…

CHAPTER

FIVE

FROM HIGH FLIER TO FLATS GUIDE

Resetting the Crosshairs of My Future

One evening in early1957 I received a telegram from Pan-Am giving me a two-week notice that I was being furloughed—airline lingo for being laid off. I knew the score: these things happen in aviation. Things get tough, companies lay off pilots. Things get better, they call them back. It's all based on seniority, not performance in the cockpit. {Sub-standard performance in the cockpit gets you grounded at any time.]

OK, I was out of a job—at least temporarily. But the more I thought about my situation, the more I realized there was an opportunity here, an opportunity to totally reshape my life.

"What are you going to do, son?" asked my father tenderly. "You going to check with United, American or Delta?"

Dad mentioned these three because they were at the top of the airline group that had aggressively wooed me when I was getting off active duty from the Navy. What I said next took him totally by surprise.

"I've decided to do something that I've always wanted to do," I announced. "I'm going down to the Coast Guard office."

I told my father that I intended to fill out the necessary paperwork, study for a couple of weeks in preparation for the written exam, and obtain a captain's license to operate a motor vessel for hire. I was going to be a fishing guide—more exactly, a Florida Keys flats-fishing guide.

At first, dad thought I was kidding. "That's one of the funniest ideas I've ever heard," he roared.

To go from flying the skies to plying the waters for fish indeed seemed an unlikely venture to stake my entire future on, more like a frivolous escapade than a solid career. But I was dead serious: I was willing to take the gamble against failure. This momentous decision inevitably created the new pathways that shaped my life into the incredible journey I have experienced. At that time, my fondest dreams could never have foretold the world of fishing that would be mine, the company I would enjoy, the places I would go. But right then, I only knew one thing for certain: A whole new ball game had just begun!

I moved into a one-room shack sporting a double bed with squeaky springs, a washbasin and a toilet in Little Torch Key Trailer Park, about 25 miles north of Key West. Showering involved using the trailer park's common shower stalls. Talk about a Spartan existence. But on the plus side, I only had to pay $20 a week rent.

Even though I was a fledgling guide, I was no amateur when it came to fishing experience. My tenure with Pan Am would later provide an education in fishing that few people could have afforded. I would have the opportunity's to fish every continent except Antarctica, including Africa, Iceland, Europe, Canada, Australia and New Zealand, South America and Central America, numerous islands in the Caribbean, and, of course, every coastline of the United States. My magic carpet was provided by Pan-Am's cockpit authorization, which I would write out myself, and get to the airport early enough to be in operations when the captain of the flight showed up to do the paperwork. If by chance he didn't know me, which would have truly been the exception, I would introduce myself and ask him to sign the jump seat authorization.

With this type of authorization, I was able to board the flight along with the crew. My baggage would be on the flight just the same as any passenger or crewmember. Not only was this a fantastic perk, after the airplane was taxiing out, I would also generally move back to first class if there was a seat available. The ability to fly like this allowed me to fish in many places around the world that I never would have had the opportunity to go. This perspective served me well in my future career as a fishing guide – and world-record holder.

There on Little Torch Key, I'm a 26-year-old, ex-Navy fighter jock, a bachelor who'd been laid off from Pan Am as a pilot and turned loose on a great adventure in the Florida Keys. I took to my new role as a fishing guide with relish, eager to learn all I needed to help my anglers catch fish and enjoy their experience.

I already knew all about fishing gear, casting and the best techniques to make a fish strike practically anywhere on Earth. But I didn't know the area around Little Torch Key well. It took more than a month of running around, scouting fish and learning about where the fish were and weren't before I had my very first customer, a half-day charter. The fees for half days were $35 and $55 for a full day, but remember that this was in 1957, when that kind of money didn't look so bad.

In early 1958, Pan Am decided they had laid off too many pilots and called me back. I immediately went back and had to have a new flight physical, after which I promptly arranged to have a 90-day leave of absence, without loosing seniority, during the height of the tourist guiding season. This would be without pay but would allow me to return to the Lower Florida Keys flats as a bonefish guide—which is exactly what I did, with immense pleasure.

My flying/guiding life was fine throughout 1959, then in December Pan-Am did it again: they jettisoned 450 of their more-junior pilots. Now I was back to full-time guiding. By then my guiding business had begun to blossom. I had built up a bit of a steadily growing following of clients, and I'd just built a house on Little Torch Key the year before. The house was built of concrete block and stucco. The interior, roof inside, and all the beams consisted of knotty cypress. All of the cabinets in the kitchen were custom built out of knotty cypress. It was beautiful to me, and cost around $11,000 to build. I did some of the grunt work myself. My brother, who was an electrician and his friends, did the electrical work

I lived down there full-time and during this period I gave out

13 keys to my house to New York-based flight attendants. Only years later did I discover that local people considered me the Hugh Heffner of Little Torch Key.

And with good reason: These flight attendants would catch a flight to Miami, take a Greyhound bus and get off on Little Torch Key, then parade and jiggle their way a mile down the dirt road to my house at the very end of the road. My nearest neighbor lived half a mile away. Talk about total privacy!

Only a few house rules existed. No. 1: Drink all the booze you want, but just bring some with you on your next trip. After all, we used to bring plenty of duty-free booze in from our flights. Speaking of bearing gifts, a number of stewardesses flew to Africa on a lot of their flights, on the DC -6s and long-range DC-7C planes. They brought back beautiful, intricate wood carvings, having them made into magnificent lamps and other things. My house took on the persona of a true world adventurer, with all the interesting artifacts from the ladies and my own coterie of curios. Another benefit of having these lovely visitors is that I'd be off on a flight and some of the gals who came down made sumptuous dishes and froze a lot of them for when I'd be home alone.

Rule No. 2: If you want to go swimming, there are no bathing suits or clothes. You could take five steps from my front door and dive off the seawall or tiptoe down the steps into 15 feet of gin-clear water. Sometimes as many as five gorgeous babes would be splashing around with little ol' me, all of us naked. Most of the gals from the Scandinavian countries showed no inhibition at all, and after a while even the shyest flight attendants would finally peel off their suits and join the fun. The word soon spread among a number of the more adventurous stewardesses that Stu's Keys retreat offered relaxation, privacy and letting their hair down – without any Pan Am snoops around or hassles with the typical lounge lizards who stalked them at the Miami hotels where they usually stayed between flights.

Now, I'm sure you're thinking that here's Stu, a young, healthy bachelor who happens to be an airline pilot, cavorting with all these sweet young things in the buff, and he's scoring like Shaquille

O'Neal at a basketball dunking contest. And you'd be right. Hey, a gentleman I certainly am, but I'm also a red-blooded, American male who's quite fond of the female form. Could you blame me?

I spiced up the libations with two specialty drinks. I made a stinger with two parts brandy mixed with half a pint of White Cream de Menthe. I'd shake it with ice and pour into an already-chilled Old Fashion glass filled with crushed ice. The other I called a rum dumb punch, made with Myers rum, laced with Ronrico Purple Label 151-proof rum, topped off in a tall glass of ice with Hawaiian Punch – the latter disguising the potent alcohol content.

One day I placed a big pitcher of stingers on the seawall with full glasses all lined up. Four of us frolicked in the water, skinny-dipping as usual. Also at that time I owned a young German shepherd named "Worry" that I adopted even before her eyes opened. I was the first figure she could see so I was imprinted in her memory. I fed her with white bread dipped in milk, a baby bottle, and little pieces of white meat chicken.

One of the girls walked up the steps to go to the bathroom and hollered, "Stu, something's wrong with Worry."

I climbed out of the water to see that Worry, now five months old, looked like she was having a fit. Worry yelped, cried and flopped all over the ground. I picked her up, cradled her, and felt terrified that she may be experiencing some form of a seizure. And that's when I glanced over at the glasses of stingers – they were all empty. Evidently the young pup decided to follow my example a little too closely, in which case I'm sure she woke up the next morning with quite a hangover because she acted quite contrite.

Even after being laid off and not flying, I found myself still surrounded with never-ending groups of lovely ladies, coming down to visit whenever they so desired. If you think getting paid to fish and enjoying all the beautiful women a man can desire is a dream, you're right.

Even in 1962 after I got married, phone calls kept coming. My bride, Bernice, would answer the phone and the gals would ask for me. She'd hand me the phone with a playful frown and they always ask the same thing: "So tell me, Stu, are you married now or what?"

Of course the word gradually got around to all the lovely ladies that Stu was now a happily married man, and that "Stu's Keys retreat" was under new management.

By this time, my reputation in the world of sport fishing was expanding even beyond the Florida Keys, actually worldwide. I did a full hour with ABC's "Wide World of Sports;" where I was one of two guides. Jimmy Albright, my idol when growing up, served as the other guide. This was a fly-rod tarpon tournament using 12-pound-test tippet between two of the greatest anglers of that time: Joe Brooks, ABC's fishing expert, and my mentor, and Al "A.J." McClane. Joe was angling editor for *Outdoor Life* Magazine, and Al, angling editor for *Field & Stream* Magazine. The production required a huge amount of footage with a crew of six cameramen and six guides with boats to handle them and their equipment.

To decide which angler fished with which guide, Roone Arledge, then President of ABC Sports, flipped a coin. "Heads, Joe fishes with Jimmy; tails, he fishes with Stu."

To me, Jimmie Albright was "The Man." Whenever I drove to the Keys, beginning in the late 1940s, I'd crane my neck when passing through Islamorada in the hopes of catching a glimpse of Jimmie. He did things in the fishing world I'd only dreamed of. Just to be in Jimmie's league in a tournament meant a lot. To do it for national television, on ABC's "Wide World of Sports," surpassed my wildest dreams.

Roone Arledge stayed at my small house on Little Torch Key to oversee this gigantic production. Arledge and I hosted about 15 people each morning, but they never replenished the supplies, as did the lovely flight attendants. Now picture in your mind my 1,100-square-foot house. It included a garage and workshop, 196 feet of concrete seawall leading to the water, a master bedroom and living room/dining room combination, and a bar going around the dining room where we ate. With all the production people, guides, Joe and Al hanging around, my place looked like an overstuffed mushroom.

Joe Brooks and I "won" the tournament, with four tarpon to Jimmie and Al's one. Our biggest was a solid 120 pounds and the only one they caught was estimated at 90 pounds …The crew shot so much exciting footage that they wanted to return two years later to shoot a new opening, a little bit in the middle, and a new closing to became the pilot film for all of ABC's "American Sportsman" series. Joe Brooks and I were in that together. Curt Gowdy also came down to do the on-camera introduction for the series.

The ABC "Wide World" we originally shot in 1962 was scheduled to air on a weekend in November 1963. It was pre-empted by the funeral of President John F. Kennedy. It did finally appear on TV, and Dante Fascell, the U.S. Congressman at the time for the Miami District, including the Keys, cited it in the 88th Congressional Record, with an invitation for all his constituents to watch it.

I loved those early years guiding out of Little Torch Key. Television exposure certainly didn't hurt my business any. And as my reputation grew, my circle of friends and acquaintances widened considerably – including a number of celebrities and VIPs.

During my last two years of full-time guiding, before going back to flying with Pan American in late1964, I was on the water for hire more than 330 days each year. Like a farmer when it's harvest season, you work every day and when not guiding, I would go fishing myself. In each of those two years I made more than $40,000, but lacked retirement or medical benefits and the future of having more time to fish myself.

Bernice was less than thrilled with my return to the cockpit, to say the least. Going back to flying not only meant a big cut in income back then, but she still harbored the insecurity of knowing about all the stewardesses who came down the road to visit during my early bachelor years.

My first year back at Pan Am as a first officer on the DC 6 I only earned $7,800 – quite a comedown indeed in finances. But building an aviation career seemed the right move for me at the time. I had enjoyed my "fling on the flats," guiding. But it seemed time to move on, professionally. As things were to turn out, this was another fortuitous decision that helped bring me to where I am today.

Once I started flying again, I grabbed every opportunity I could to return to international fishing, destinations far from my usual haunts in the Florida Keys.

When asked which countries I fished most in the 1960s and 70s, I would have to say Panama and Costa Rica. In Panama was a place called Club de Pesca Panama, which translated to the Fishing Club of Panama. On the phone was Ray Smith, a Texas oilman. As he described the club, I'm thinking that this should indeed be an interesting spot–a camp carved out of the jungle that over 100 miles from the nearest electric light bulb.

I felt ready, willing and able to check out this far-flung fishing Mecca. However, little do I know that Ray had an ulterior motive: He wanted me to manage his camp.

We could only arrive at the camp by plane, either landing on the water with a seaplane or on a deserted WW ll military emergency airstrip, then proceeding to the camp by boat. Ray arranged for a charter plane to fly Bernice and me from Panama City to the little ex-U.S. military emergency landing strip at Hockey. There, a 31-foot Bertram picked us up near the mouth of the river and deposited us at the lodge.

The next 10 days were nothing but fishing and relaxing. I was in the middle of doing them both real well when Ray popped the question. He made me a very interesting offer, "Would you consider leaving Pan Am to become the General Manager of Club de Pesca Panama."

Manager? Me? After being in this gorgeous setting for 10 days, after sampling the lifestyle and the fishing, I was quite tempted. But, I had to admit to him that I'd already heard through the grapevine that managers don't last long around there.

I tactfully explained to Ray that the only way I would quit Pan Am to take such a position was with a 10-year guaranteed salary. At this time, because the fishing was so seasonal and wouldn't require my presence at the camp for the entire year, we negotiated $25,000 a year. But Ray inevitably balked at meeting my 10-year guarantee, so the deal to be his manager fizzled.

We did negotiate a deal, however, that was more to my liking.

I agreed to take a 90-day leave of absence from Pan Am the next year, 1965, and come down to the club to teach his captains and mates about light-tackle and fly fishing; take some of his guests out on charters; and possibly do a film. He was thrilled by my offer and showed it by more than doubling my Pan-Am salary.

I spent a great deal of time and energy teaching the captains about conservation – the *why's* and *how's* of releasing fish. Naturally, someone has to be the angler while the captains and the mates are learning about light-tackle and fly fishing, and I filled the role with relish. I caught a number of world-record fish, all in the name of teaching. One of them was a 58-pound dolphin, also called *mahi mahi,* or a dorado as more commonly known in Central and South America. I bagged the big dolphin on a 12-pound-test tippet with a fly rod. That's still the record to this day and is the longest standing saltwater fly-rod record.

I also caught a record 136-pound Pacific sailfish using a 10-weight, two-piece, rather willowy fly rod made by the Spin Master Company in Miami. My fly reel was a Fin Nor #3 [the famous Wedding Cake model] they gave me in 1958. This fish became and still is the second-longest-held saltwater fly-rod record and to this day has the place of honor on our living room wall.

My other favorite destination in the 60's was Costa Rica.

In 1965, Carlos Barrantes, who owned the only fishing tackle shop in San Jose, Costa Rica, called and asked if I'd be willing to fly down.. After spending the night there, I would join him on a flight through a mountain pass to the Caribbean side of the country to "research fish" for tarpon, snook and weird-named freshwater species up the rivers.

That was like dangling an ice cream cone in front of a five-year-old kid. There wasn't much money in it, as I recall, but I would have done it for nothing. Just the thought of research fishing in exotic areas truly lit my fire. When he said that he would also take care of all my expenses, I was sold on the deal, lock, stock and barrel.

I flew to San Jose and spent the night, and the next day Carlos and I climbed aboard a small, single-engine airplane. We flew over and around the mountains, landing on the beach at the mouth of the

Parismina River. Carlos brought along a 9.9-horsepower outboard on the airplane that we put on a Cayuga, an 18-foot dugout canoe.

We fished up the lagoons and at the mouth of the rivers, and I truly thought I had died and gone to heaven. The snook and tarpon action was just awesome. Big tarpon rolled everywhere, and they'd never seen or heard an outboard motor before. Silver kings would come out of the creeks from the lagoons into the main lagoon early in the morning, single file and right on top. You could cast a fly to them, make a few strips and get hits left and right. It was simply some of the most fantastic fishing I ever experienced.

Carlos wanted me on this trip to see if I thought the fishing was good enough to open the first fishing camp on the Caribbean side Costa Rica. I, of course, told him that American fishermen would go absolutely crazy with this kind of fishing, providing he had a decent place for them to stay and reasonable food.

He bought the area at the mouth of the Parismina River where there stood an old schoolhouse that had been hurricane damaged. Carlos renovated it, built a number of small cabins, and hired an elderly American lady to do the cooking. It did quite well, and I went back there several times a year thereafter and enjoyed the great fishing.

I also encouraged Carlos to check out the fishing in September and October because I heard big snook lurked along the beaches, which he quickly did and changed the lodge's schedule to include the fall months. He had been opening in January and closing in May because of the rainy season. Carlos ran it for a couple of years before he sold it to a gentleman named Jerry Tricome from Chicago who had a fishing camp in Canada. In no time, we became fast friends.

With fantastic pictures of big tarpon, snook and freshwater species that we found way up the rivers, I wrote a couple of magazine feature stories about fishing at Parismina Tarpon Rancho – the name Carlos originally gave it and remains so today.

One story I really like is "Black Night for the Silver King," which you'll read in a later chapter, so named because I used to walk to the mouth of the river along the beach after supper. Using a bait-casting outfit, level-wind reel, big plugs or jigs, I'd wing 'em way out toward the other side of the river, casting at an angle up-river. While working the lures back I would hook some tremendous tarpon, often one after the other. The water had a lot of phosphorous in it, and I took a lot of super night pictures.

But fishing in the wilds presents hazards. Late one day before a typical evening fishing adventure, we were up the river fishing in one of the lagoons when a big bushmaster snake swam right in front of the boat. Being bitten by a bushmaster with little chance of immediate medical help makes you wonder how important it is to go fishing.

That same jolt of fear flashed back into my mind a few hours later. With a new moon – which actually is no moon – making it so dark that the phosphorus in the water became my main lighting source, I waded along the edge of the surf. Taking care not to walk out too far where it abruptly drops off, I waded out to where the waves rhythmically hit me around the waist and receded below my knees. All went well enough as tarpon showed up as expected until one of the rollers reached my thigh, and I felt something brush against me in the current.

My heart lurched at the thought that a big bushmaster sinking its fangs into me and filling my body with a deathly dose of venom. When it turned out to be a water plant instead, I breathed a sigh of relief so loud that any bushmaster in the vicinity probably got the hell out of there. Things that go bump in the night in the Costa Rican jungle are the kind of things you never forget.

CHAPTER

SIX

SOME OF THE MOST EXCITING FISHING ON EARTH!

The Palolo Worm Hatch

Creates Tarpon Frenzy

As a fledgling guide in 1958, my experiences in going fishing on my "off days"—without a client in the boat—proved to be as valuable and rewarding as I had expected. The advantages of scouting the vast reaches of the Florida Keys flats, with their complex tidal currents and intricate fish movements, were obvious. When clients booked an outing, I was ready for them. But a huge bonus to my off-days fishing was provided by Mother Nature, who, in her subtlety and wisdom, revealed some of her most ingenious secrets to careful observation and my persistence in being on the water.

That's how one of the most bizarre events in all the outdoors first came my way. I was alone when it happened, but this time, retelling my story, I'm hoping to take you along:

The air has an eerie quality to it, and I realize with a rush that the flats are quiet. No fish are moving. It's late May in the Florida Keys – the prime time for fishing. The giant tarpon should be migrating; bonefish and permit should be raiding the flats looking for crabs and shrimp; fish of all kinds should be on the prowl, fattening themselves on every other kind of thing that swims. Instead, not a creature is stirring.

I turn my skiff around and head for home on Little Torch Key, hoping tomorrow will be better, that I will get a client, and that the fish will return. I cut through the Bahia Honda Bridge, leaving the backcountry, and heading southwest down the Atlantic side. The wind is calm and I hug the rocky shore in six feet of water over the coral heads. Suddenly, my eyes bug out at the sight of literally thousands of tarpon.

Tarpon are "nymphing" like big trout, coming to the surface and gulping down some kind of food, then rolling under again. Schools of them, along with bonefish, permit, big mangrove snapper, all in a massive feeding frenzy. I shut down my engine and anchor to watch, totally mystified because I haven't the faintest idea of what's going on. Mind you, I'm no stranger to fishing, having been born and raised in Miami and seldom without a fishing rod in my hand since. And I know this area of the Florida Keys better than most. But this is the wildest, weirdest phenomenon I have ever witnessed.

I sit hypnotized for a few moments before it occurs to me to pull out a fishing rod and find out what is making these giants act like this. I know it has to be something unusual. I tie on two or three different streamer patterns, and have an occasional take. Then I notice literally millions of small, fish-like things about the size of my little finger swimming in the water. The tarpon are inhaling gobs of them with each gulp. In an area half a mile long by a few hundred yards wide, the fish are jammed in so thick feeding on these tiny little critters that I feel as though I can walk across the water on their backs.

Finally, I take out an old standby tarpon pattern, yellow feathers with a red hackle neck, and start having some success. I hook fish after fish until my arms ache from pulling them in. They are still slamming at the flies when the day succumbs to pitch-black darkness, and I finally have to leave to make the long run back home. It is my first experience with the strange little creature with the habits of a recluse that have since given me some fantastic days of fishing – the Palolo Worm.

"What the heck is a Palolo Worm," you ask. "And what is their purpose, other than causing fish to go bonkers?"

Frankly, I'm still not entirely sure. But I have learned that they live among the reefs of the Atlantic and Pacific oceans. Normally, they hate daylight, even moonlight, and only come out of their holes in the reefs on the blackest of nights to feed on vegetation on the coral. Then, as its spawning time approaches, changes take place in its body. The worm, about an inch long, can be either male or female, and the last third of its body takes on a new color – pink in males and greenish gray in females, with the latter full of eggs and the former with sperm. Rachel Carson wrote about this worm in her book *The Sea Around Us*.

In late spring on an outgoing tide in the late afternoon, generally on a quarter moon, the worm comes up to spawn. Each worm swims to the surface, their swollen rear ends twisting and writhing almost independently of the front half. Nature has different jobs for each half: the front portion will stay behind on the reef, perhaps back in the single rut, while the back half separates and explodes like a volcano, spewing its eggs or sperm into the outgoing tide. The area, covering acres, allows the eggs to immediately combine with the sperm, and swift changes take place, the division of cells, the differentiation of structure. By evening of the same day they have become tiny larvae spiraling through the sea.

While this is all happening – in fact, even before it begins – fish know about it. They recognize the very day, perhaps the exact hour, when the hatching will begin. Somehow, nature's radar puts the word out early.

Throughout the Florida Keys, the tarpon's normal migration pattern is to the east and north, up the coast. Thousands of tarpon begin as early as April to make the trip. But just before the Palolo Worm hatch, the tarpon migration ceases, and the fish turn westerly to the coral reefs to await an orgy of feeding.

For fishermen, three conditions herald this hatch. First, the hatch must occur on the outgoing tide in late afternoon and on into the early evening. This is probably so the new worms are able to spend their first hours in the darkness before dawn. Second, the Palolo worm hatch usually commences on the first quarter or the last quarter of the moon. It seldom occurs on the full moon because of the light, and yet it never takes place on the new moon when absent of all light. Third, the hatch must have fairly calm or stable weather conditions. If the weather is very rough during the expected hatch time, there will be a small hatch, with some worms and some fish, but nothing like a full-scale event.

A normal hatch lasts over a period of three days. In a tumbling crescendo of worms and fish, the first evening provides a banquet of bounty, and the fish come in swarms. The second evening is by far the peak of the frenzy, with the largest amounts of worms and fish together at once. The third evening is still a pretty wild happening, but the amount of worms begins to taper off, along with the predators gobbling them up.

I've seen as many as an estimated 3,000 tarpon jammed into an area half a mile long and a quarter-mile wide, plus a grab bag of every kind of predatory fish you can imagine working their way between the glistening Silver Kings. Apparently there are enough Palolo Worms for everybody. If you cast an orange and yellow fly, or cockroach pattern with bucktail and grizzly for the streamer, those fish will smack it like you've never seen before.

The earliest I've encountered a worm hatch is during April off the Marquesas Keys, 35 miles west off Key West. I believe it probably happens earlier than that around the Dry Tortugas, 40 miles farther west. That's usually the start of the hatch, and the occurrence continues up the coast as the spring wears on. I've discovered hatches at Bahia Honda Key, Pigeon Key and Sunshine Key in the lower Keys. Many flats on the ocean side, and some on the Florida Bay side where there is live coral, also have hatches. I know of hatches at Indian Key, Long Key, Tavernier Key, Key Largo, Cape Florida and undoubtedly others farther north that I don't even know about. I even heard about one hatch that took place in a condominium canal.

The fact is, even after all the years I've been fishing, I haven't spoken to many people who know about the Palolo Worm hatch

– not even professional guides. Most of them work all day and quit at 4:30 p.m., just as the hatch is beginning. They have taken their clients back to the dock by the time the Palolo Worm is opening its fateful little ceremony right on their own stomping grounds.

One of the greatest hatches I've ever witnessed was at Bahia Honda Key on a calm afternoon with tremendous storms building up out at sea. The biggest waterspout I've seen, big enough to be a giant tornado if it had been over land, is steaming down the coast, sucking up water. But it never comes inland, and our weather stays completely calm. Seemingly turned on by the storm's electric elements, the worms boil up by billions, and for a dedicated angler, it is like being in heaven.

Besides the number of big tarpon I hook and release, I toss my fly into schools of fish and come up with five-pound mangrove snappers, eight-pound bonefish, and assorted other denizens that had crowded in for the feasting.

Since it coincides with the tarpon's migration patterns, I suspect that the hatch of this tiny worm has something to do with the tarpon's reproductive cycle. That's only a guess, mind you, but I theorize that perhaps the worm, full of reproductive hormones, might trigger those same reproductive hormones in tarpon. If any fishery biologists have data on that, I sure hope they come forward with it.

I think the major tarpon migration is tied in with the weather patterns, with cold and warm water conditions governing the route and timetable, just as they govern many other fish migrations such as with marlin and sailfish. Of course, where big tarpon go, other fish are sure to follow – like sharks. A shark's favorite meal is tarpon. They follow the schools of Silver Kings, waiting for a mishap or careless behavior. Then they strike quickly and fatally. One year, I witnessed a hammerhead shark longer than my 18-foot skiff grab a 100-pound-plus tarpon that I was fighting on a fly rod. The shark snatched it up midway, snapping its huge jaws around the tarpon's belly, and shook it like a terrier, with its head out of the water. The shark probably weighed close to 2,000 pounds. It was at once a frightening and fascinating spectacle.

For many years, the Palolo Worm's annual show was called the "red worm hatch" in the Keys, but the worm is not red. While the males have a pink body, the females are usually distinguished by an orange or rust body and a green head. Some of the flies I tie resemble this combination, the hot head of orange right where the feathers are tied to the neck. On many tarpon flies I use an orange thread to tie the fly. I've found that orange seems to excite big fish more than any other color, perhaps because it resembles the Palolo Worm's coloring.

When I use a spinning outfit or casting rod, I try an orange bucktail jig or a Bill Smith lure, orange and yellow. They seem to work as well as anything because during a hatch feeding frenzy, most fish will eat almost anything that comes along.

I make it a point to shut down my outboard at least a quarter of a mile away when approaching a tarpon area. Tarpon don't like the sound of an engine, and they spook. It can take them 45 minutes or more to settle down after some unthinking boater has plowed through with his outboard roaring, or even idling.

After I've shut down my engine, I either pole the boat to the spot I intend to fish or use my electric trolling motors to approach. The fish apparently don't mind that sort of disturbance to their habitat. In the hatch area, most people anchor rather than tying up to their push pole, which is a common method on the flats. On the ocean side of the Keys, the bottom is usually too hard to plant a pole, but the anchor will hold nicely. I always use a small float at the top of my anchor line, with a quick-release snap attached to my bow eye. If a big fish can't be turned and it's necessary to pull up and go after it, I simply drop the quick release snap and take off. The float will show me where the anchor is when I return.

The tarpon that feed during the Palolo Worm hatch come in all sizes, from 50-pound youngsters right up to 250-pound behemoths, so I generally gear up with 15-pound-test line if casting, or 16-pound-test tippet for my fly rod. This is not selective fishing, as in choosing the fish you cast to, the kind I most prefer when on the flats. This is complete bedlam, when you cast your lure and know something out there is going to try and eat it. It might be a tasty five-pound mangrove snapper or a world-record, tackle-busting giant tarpon. Of course, the fun is in the challenge of getting the fish to eat your lure and the knock-down, drag-out fight. I release all of the tarpon I catch.

The Palolo Worm Hatch happens every year. If you missed the chance last year, head on back when there is a quarter moon and a late afternoon outgoing tide in the spring. Try to book your guide to fish at this unorthodox time. (With the Palolo Worm hatch your objective, your cocktail hour and dinner can wait!) Look around the shallow flats, and if you notice that the fish are gone, make haste for the nearest ocean-side reefs – and brace yourself for a truly amazing spectacle.

The Palolo Worm is here.

CHAPTER

SEVEN

TED WILLIAMS;
A FISHING FRIENDSHIP

Rubbing Shoulder's with an American hero

You cut a freshman college class to go fishing. What happens? Does fate punish you? No! You end up meeting Ted Williams.

A chance meeting brought me together with Ted Williams in the late fall of 1948. At the time I was attending the University of Miami as a freshman and had cut a three-hour Botany lab, my only class that day, to spend a couple days fishing for snook in the canals alongside U.S. 41 leading to Naples.

It was an over-cast, blustery fall day in South Florida, just cool enough to keep the mosquito population from being too active. I left my house in Miami around 3 o'clock in the morning and drove down U.S. 41–also known as the Tamiami Trail–to the Marco Canal area in order to arrive by daybreak. I'd heard that jumbo-size snook had been cruising the incoming tide, looking for a meal.

After what I considered a very successful morning, having caught four nice snook over 10 pounds and two of them easily over 15, I headed back toward the Tamiami Trail to see if any of the schools of smaller snook were busting the minnows along the runoffs from the Everglades.

I drove a 1941 De Soto that had seen better years. My fly rod poked out the left rear window, waving in the wind as I cruised along at 45 miles an hour, looking for feeding fish.

After driving 10 to 15 miles, I didn't see any indication of snook chasing minnows on the far bank. Then, a flurry of feeding fish busted loose in one of my favorite places. Pulling over to the side of the road, I jumped out almost before Betsy came to a full stop. You have to be quick in order to get a fly to these fish while they're still feeding, before they move on. Well, I was quick but not quick enough, and by the time I got a fly line stripped off the reel, they were gone. I stood for a while looking, but to no avail. I wound in my fly line, hooked my popping bug on a snake guide and wrapped the loose line around my reel so I could dash into action if I found more fish down the road.

Five miles farther down the road I saw a guy casting a fly, so I pulled over to watch. In no time at all it became obvious to me that he knew what to do with his fly rod. I got out of Betsy, carefully walking behind him and over to his left side, making sure I wouldn't hinder his casting.

After watching him make beautiful presentations to the far bank of the canal, I asked, "Having any luck?"

He neither responded nor acknowledged my presence, not even glancing toward me. I stood there watching while he made three or four more casts and thinking that maybe he's so engrossed in casting that he didn't hear me.

"Have you caught any snook yet today?" I queried, this time a little louder, he might be hearing impaired.

It seemed obvious that with the mention of the word snook, he figured I'm not just some tourist driving toward Miami and trying to pass the time of day while stretching their legs. Without so much as interrupting the cadence of his cast or turning toward me even a little, he replied, "And just what do you know about snook?"

Being a little feisty myself, I self-assuredly responded, "I know enough about snook that I caught four this morning over 10 pounds each, and two over 15."

That stopped him cold in his tracks. He half-turned toward me, his eyes examining me for the first time. Now I definitely had his complete attention. "And just where on this earth did you do that?"

For the first time he notices the fly rod sticking out of Betsy's back window and my Dade County, Florida, license tag. "In the Marco Canal," I said.

"Yeah, then what the hell are you doing over here?" He answered sharply, as if disbelieving my assertion.

"The big cruisers that we spot swimming along before we cast our fly to them only move a few hours after daybreak," I replied. "And it's after daybreak."

The man now realized I wasn't just making up tall tales about catching snook, and that indeed he must be in the know about snook fishing in these parts. As he wound in his fly line, he coyly asked, "Where is this fantastic place in the Marco Canal?"

"I've never checked the mileage on my odometer, and it would be difficult to describe the spot with so many curves and areas that look alike," I replied. "But I plan on going back there tomorrow morning for a few hours after daybreak, before returning to Miami. You're welcome to meet me in the parking area at Royal Palm Hammock on the cut-off to Marco from U.S. 41 at, say 6 a.m. and we'll catch daybreak where we're going to fish."

I don't know this guy from Adam, but I'm thinking it would be nice having company, especially someone who casts a fly like this big dude does.

"Where you staying tonight?" he asked.

"I'll be sleeping in old Betsy," I said, as I waved my arm toward the old De Soto, "in the Royal Palm Hammock parking area."

"Are the mosquitoes pretty bad during the night?"

"Yep," I replied. "But I have plenty of mosquito dope, and it's cool enough to only leave one window cracked an inch."

He answered immediately. "I'm staying at Weavers Camp just a few miles up the road, and only 20 minutes drive that time of the morning," he said while slowly walking to his station wagon. "See you at 6 a.m., sharp." He emphasized "sharp" loudly, as if a drill sergeant.

"Boy, wish I could afford to stay at Weavers Camp," I mumbled to myself.

Five forty-five the next morning seemed to come around all

too fast. Curled up on the back seat and wrapped in a blanket, I awoke with someone rudely knocking on my window and a bright flashlight shining in my face. It scared the shit out of me for a moment. I reached for my .22 pistol on the floor but stopped when I realized the time and who was probably rousting me out of a deep sleep.

Uncovering from my blanket, sitting up yawning and stretching, I unlocked the door and stepped out into the dark morning. My wristwatch says 10 minutes to six and I quickly think this fucking big dude sure is anxious as all get out. But the words that instead came out of my mouth showed no anger.

"Good morning," I said, "you're right on time to do battle with some big linesides." Snook, with the long, dark lateral line across the length of its body, are sometimes called such.

The new dawn was already showing in the eastern sky. "Let's go," he said. "I'll follow you with my car." He walked over and got into his station wagon, engine still running.

I love to fish as much as anybody, but couldn't help but muse that this fellow sure seems damn anxious to tangle with a big one this morning. The least he could have done is bring me a donut or cup of coffee. I climbed into the front seat, started Betsy's engine and headed out of the parking area to the Marco Road.

Twenty minutes later, it was light enough for me to recognize where I wanted to pull off the road and wait for the cruisers to show.

Not wanting to waste any time, I quickly started assembling my two-piece fly rod. Having left it rigged, all I needed to do now is line up the guides, push the ferrules together, pull some fly line off the reel and make sure my hook on the fly is still sharp. I'm ready.

Looking back at the big guy's station wagon, I could see that he was doing about the same.

Fishing that morning was almost as good as the previous day. I only caught two, and my new-found friend managed to out fish me, catching three nice snook, all over 10 pounds. His biggest looked to be a good solid 15 pounds while both of my fish weighted at least 15 pounds.

The flow of cruisers coming in with the current stopped just as quickly as it started. It seemed like in no time at all my watch said 10:30. The action was over. Time to get ready for the 70-mile drive home.

While I was disassembling my rod and putting the tackle away, the tall one walked up with a piece of paper in his left hand and his right hand extended, casually saying, "My name is Ted Williams. What's yours?"

After telling him, he says, "I sure enjoyed fishing with you, Bush. My phone number in Coral Gables is on this piece of paper. Give me a call next time you're going fishing."

With that, we went our own ways.

Not being a baseball fan to the point that I hardly even knew the Boston Red Sox existed, I had no idea Ted Williams was anything but just another guy who knows what do with a fly rod. And so began a friendship that lasted more than 40 years.

One afternoon a month later when I got home from classes at the University of Miami, my mother greeted me. "Some man by the name of Ted Williams called three times today, leaving his phone number each time. And his last call he sounded a little agitated that you had not return his calls."

"Mom, I don't know a Ted Williams," I said.

"He claims to have fished with you on the Marco Canal and had some good snook fishing," mother replied.

"Oh, that big dude," I remarked, the memory coming back. First I put the books in my bedroom, changed out of my college clothes into something more comfortable, and still not knowing that Ted Williams was anything special other than a big guy who casts a good fly line, I called him.

The phone rang so many times that I nearly hung up. A lady's voice finally answered, "Williams's residence."

"Is Ted Williams in?" I ask.

"Um, I'll have to look and see," she answers wearily. "Who's calling please?"

"Please tell him it's Stu Apte, returning his call."

"Stu who?" She asked, the first of many, many times those words

119

were to be uttered on the phone. For some reason that's the response I usually got when calling, and just for grins decided to put that on future license plates: Stu Who?.

"Just tell him the Stu he fished with in the Marco Canal."

Waiting at least five minutes, I was again getting impatient and close to hanging up before I hear a man's voice. "Stu, I was in the middle of tying a bonefish fly, sorry you had to wait." Without hardly taking a breath, he asked, "There is a great wading tide for bonefish tomorrow ... you want to go?"

Short and sweet – no small talk – right to the point. I soon came to recognize that this is "Ted Talk," with just the important things said. Luckily, with only three classes each week, the next day was free.

"Sure," I answered. "Where do you plan on going?"

"I store my skiff in a warehouse on the water in Coconut Grove. It'll be a short run from there across Biscayne Bay to Soldier Key."

Following his lead of no idle chitchat, I asked what time he wanted me there. Again, I still do not have the slightest inkling who Ted Williams is.

Ted said, "How about eight o'clock. There's an outgoing tide until just after 10 so we'll be able to catch the last hour of the outgoing tide and the important first couple of hours of the incoming tide. That will give us the best fishing for tailing bonefish."

"Sounds good to me, what can I bring?" I asked. "Lunch?"

"No, Bush, I'll have everything we need. See you at eight o'clock and be on time"

"Don't worry about that, and thanks." By this time I'm wondering why in the hell he keeps calling me Bush.

That evening Bill Lewis, a fishing friend and classmate, called asking if I wanted to go snook fishing tomorrow. I casually informed him that I was going bonefishing at Soldier Key with some big dude I had met last month while snook fishing on the Marco Canal. "I gotta tell you, Bill, he's one helluva fine fly fisherman."

"Yeah? What's his name, maybe I know him?"

"Ted Williams," I replied. Almost before I got the words out of my mouth, Bill almost sucked all the air out of my ear through the phone, "Holy shit, do you mean Ted Williams, the Ted Williams, the great Boston Red Sox baseball player?"

"Damned if I know if that's the same guy," I replied. "But now that you mention it, I did notice that he has a Massachusetts license tag on his station wagon. I'll probably find out tomorrow and will let you know."

And that was the first inkling of just who this big dude actually was.

I am not ashamed to say that Ted out-fished me that day, catching three bonefish for each of mine. We managed to stay out of each other's way, helping each other when needed and started the bonding of a lifelong friendship.

Our friendship had to be put on hold during the time I was going to Mexico City College from 1950-1951, and when Ted was called back into the Marine Corps as a fighter pilot in 1952.

During his Marine Corps stint, a Navy flight surgeon who was Ted's Marine Air Wing's flight surgeon in Korea became the flight surgeon for my Air Group at NAAS Oceana, Virginia in 1953. The first time I met him in sick bay, he said, "Hmm, Ensign Stuart Apte ... can you be the same person Ted Williams talked about while I was his air wing flight surgeon in Korea?"

Before I could answer, he asked, "Did you and Ted do a lot of fishing together?"

I told him that I'm indeed that man. "Small damn world we live in," he said with a headshake. "Ted mentioned he heard a younger fishing buddy of his was a naval aviator, a fellow fighter pilot, and to keep an eye out for him. Can't believe I actually ran into you."

Yes, a small world indeed. As a matter of fact, not many people know this, but while in Korea Ted served as the wingman on numerous missions with future astronaut and U.S. Senator John Glenn.

We were both out of the military in 1956, and that's the next time I heard from Ted. He was back playing major league baseball for his beloved Boston Red Sox, and I was now flying as a Third Officer for Pan-American World Airways, Latin American Division out of Miami.

By 1957, during the first of three layoffs by Pan American, I'm living in my little rented one-room shack at Little Torch Key Trailer Park, trying to develop a name as a back-country fishing guide. Ted would drive down early in the morning for a long day of fishing with me and then drive back to his Islamorada home about 60 miles up the highway. This became his ritual until I built my house at the end of the road on Little Torch Key in 1958.

Sometimes when fishing became slow in the Islamorada area, Ted would call to go fishing or to learn about the action in my area. One day, he drove down with a friend from Boston, with his own backcountry skiff on a trailer. It so happened that I was booked for the next four days. It was February 24, 1960, and my client list grew longer and longer now that guiding entailed my full-time pursuit. So, I suggested that Ted follow me, watching for my hand signals for when and where he should stop to fish.

We had a perfect early-morning tide situation, with the last of the outgoing through the beginning of the incoming tide. We were after tailing permit near Upper Harbor Key. It was a perfect weather day for being on the water.

We stopped within 150 yards of each other to wait for the tide to change. We hoped to see permit on the shallow flats facing the Gulf of Mexico, but nothing happened for the first couple of hours. I could see that Ted was getting antsy. He shouted across the calm water, his voice booming. "Hey, Bush, you sure there's permit around here?"

Cupping my hands around my mouth I yelled back. "Just hold your water and be patient a little while longer. For some reason the tide isn't coming in as strong as it did yesterday, which sometimes happens on the Gulf side of the Keys. They'll start showing up when we get a little more water."

And show up they did, ones and twos at first. Then, as though someone opened the gate, schools of eight to 10 permit started streaming onto the flat in the incoming tide. By now I was busier than a cat trying to cover up poop on a cement floor because my clients, a husband and wife, had a doubleheader hookup and each fish took off in opposite directions. We got a lucky break when the fish suddenly headed in the same direction. I'm polling like a demon following both permit to keep them from stripping all the line from their reels. They managed to get all the line back and landed both permit, and went on to catch a Florida Keys Grand Slam: catching a permit, bonefish and tarpon in the same day.

When I last looked toward Ted's boat, he was on the bow with a spinning rod while his friend struggled to keep the boat going in the direction of fish Ted kept pointing at. Teddy, as I'd started calling him, landed his 18-pound, 8-ounce permit. The feat was accomplished on 8-pound-test line and an artificial lure, which won him the Spin Casting Division of the Metropolitan Miami Fishing Tournament that year.

Later in 1960, while Ted stayed at my house on Little Torch Key, the executive vice president of Sears, Roebuck and Company flew their chartered airplane into Key West and hired a limo for the whole entourage. The reason for this meeting was to have Ted Williams sign a $100,000 annual contract, lending his name and talent toward marketing, developing and endorsing a line of in-house sports equipment, specifically for fishing, hunting and baseball equipment. His official title was Chairman of the Ted Williams Sears Sports Advisory Staff.

Ted later told me that they wanted to fly him to Chicago for this meeting and signing, but he was not about to give up three days of our fishing together to do it. And so, as the saying goes, if Mohammed won't come to the mountain, bring the mountain to Mohammed.

Ted's signing of the contract therefore took place in my little house, and thereafter we celebrated a mile up the dirt road at Little Torch Key Tavern. We enjoyed a fantastic dinner of deep-fried Florida lobster tails prepared by owner May Gillespie, along with her special French-fried potatoes and onions combination. We topped it off with May's wonderful chocolate layer cake ala-mode. Other than myself, this was everyone's introduction to deep-fried lobster tail, and they couldn't stop raving about the great flavor and taste.

Speaking of Sears, their test base for sporting equipment

was located in Fort Myers, Florida. And it was in Fort Myers the following year that Ted nearly drowned in front of a gathering of media members. While operating a powerboat meant to be cut in half to demonstrate its unsinkability, the boat unceremoniously sunk. Ted ended up in the drink and had to be rescued. I can only imagine what the media folks wrote about that.

In 1959, Ted asked me to do him a favor and take golfer Sam Snead fishing for bonefish. He wanted me to teach him how to use a spinning outfit and to cast accurately. Sam was Ted's partner in his fishing tackle company, and being one of the company's tackle testers, I obliged.

Sounds like fun I thought, taking one of the all-time great golfers bonefishing. Fun? I'd rather have spent the day pulling out nose hair. After we finally got on the water – Sam canceled two prior dates – by day's end I silently wished this outing had been canceled too. Sam, who often bragged about being a self-taught golfer and never had a lesson, did not want to be instructed or told anything. Worse yet, he was very abusive in the boat and the same off the water too, cussing and cursing like a wild man. After that day I promised myself that Sam would never fish with me again – ever.

Two years later, Ted once again asked if I would do him a favor by taking Sam fishing again. Memories of the ill-fated trip I endured with Sam flamed to the surface. I

"Ted," I said calmly but firmly, "this is the first time I ever refused doing something for you, but I made myself a promise two years ago that I'd never let him set foot in my boat again."

Ted at first looked at me sternly, and with a knowing smile finally nodded. I think he knew full well why I cared not for the company again of Slammin' Sammy Snead.

In 1961, my soon-to-be wife Bernice adamantly suggested I start a guest book, especially since all of my guiding trips were now operated from my house. Teddy Ballgame was one of the first to sign my guestbook. His comment: "One of my best students."

While some may have felt slighted by this – remember, I was a full-time guide and spent many hours on the water – to me this represented a very sincere compliment. Although not a fishing guide,

Ted became a master at the sport, probably for the same reason many considered him the best hitter in the history of baseball: he was a perfectionist. Indeed, although I was a guide and he the angler, I learned a lot fishing with Ted, such as how to use a push-pole to motorlessly propel a skiff.

Often when fishing together, Ted ended up doing the poling while I enjoyed the fishing. He didn't seem to mind too much, as poling a skiff is certainly strenuous exercise. Besides, as he put it, "Bush, whenever I put you anywhere near the proper position for a cast, you make it a good one."

He was a true friend and mentor but he was also an angler susceptible to the emotions all go through when fishing. Often he'd become frustrated when I tried polling him into position for a fish he really wanted to cast to. As a perfectionist, Ted was a student of everything he did. He was long on instructing techniques but short on patience with anyone who could not quickly understand and perform. I have been told that a lot of people put me in the same category. Maybe this comes with being a fighter pilot, where if you don't do it right, you're dead. I prefer thinking that it comes with wanting to be the best that you can be, by proving something to yourself. Believe it or not, Ted and I both at times admitted in vulnerable moments that we have an inferiority complex – yes, the great Ted Williams admitted that to me. But we both agreed that that's probably the basis for the driving force needed to make us excel.

I'm certainly not a physician, but I'm certain that Ted had a tendency toward hypoglycemia. This tendency reared its ugly head whenever Ted's blood sugar was low. For example, in 1959, when we would go fishing for a full day in the lower Keys, I noted that Ted struggled with a slight overweight problem. He would eat a normal breakfast and only take two grapefruits in the boat for his lunch. I could watch his demeanor transform from enthusiastic smiles in the morning into words by late afternoon that would make a vulgarian wince when something was not to his liking.

Before we had dinner at Little Torch Key Tavern, the only game in town, he became very difficult to have a conversation with. By the time he was half finished with dinner, his demeanor once again would slip back into the Ted Williams that so charmed and delighted my mother. After basically dieting for half of the day, he would now eat at least one whole pint of vanilla ice cream for dessert. The sugar seemed to transform him into a gregarious, smiling, outgoing person.

I ended up with 13 $1 bills from numerous bets that Ted lost to me. He'd write on the dollar bill what the bet was for, and then sign and date them. These are all on the now-rare silver certificates from the 1950s and early 1960s. Of course, the same thing applied to me if I lost the bet ... difference is, I saved all of his dollar bills and he no doubt spent mine.

In 1988 we did make one serious bet about what the core consisted of inside a fairly new monofilament fly line. We were helping out with kids for an Under-15 event being held in the Upper Keys. Ted thought the fly line was an almost transparent extrusion without actually having a solid core in the middle. I patiently explained to him that I have been using this Shakespeare/Pflueger fly line since its inception a few years back, and I guaranteed him that it had a solid monofilament core in the middle.

Being a show-me guy, Ted said he was told just the opposite of what I am telling him, and furthermore he said confidently, "I'll bet you $100 that it doesn't have a core inside."

I knew I was right and wanted my friend to save face. "Teddy," I replied, "put away your hundred and let's bet a dollar bill like we used to do. You can write something on it like 'I lost this bet to Stu because I was a disbeliever.'"

Characteristically, Ted wouldn't relent. "Bullshit, Stu," he bellowed. "Either put up or shut up."

"Okay, my friend," said I with hint of joking contempt, "it's your money that you're going to lose." About that time, Jimmie Albright happened to walk up and, Ted still holding onto my hand, said, "Jimmie, you're a witness to this bet I just made with Stu. I bet him $100 that these mono core fly lines are extruded like this, without a core in the middle."

Jimmie agreed, and I soon returned with the fly line in a new box. I let Ted look it over, and then I tied a double overhand knot around the end of the fly line with 20-pound Dacron and promptly pulled the finish off the monofilament core. The proof of what I'd said could not be denied.

"Okay, Stu, that made a believer out of me," he growled. "I owe you $100 ... I'll catch up with you in the next day or two."

The following week, Bernice went into Ace Hardware in Islamorada just as Ted came out. He gave her a $100 bill and asked that she give it to me. I called him that evening and tongue-in-cheek said, "What's the matter, TW, don't you have balls enough to look me in the eye when handing over the hundred?" He groused a bit, looking for the right words to say but not coming up with any.

One of my favorite reflections of Ted occurred in 1968. I was no longer a backcountry guide taking clients out for tarpon, permit and bonefish. I had been back flying airplanes for Pan Am since late 1964. Ted and I were again doing quite a bit of fishing together, and he had just returned to Islamorada from a great Atlantic salmon fishing trip at his lodge on the Miramichi River, in New Brunswick, Canada.

Ted was raving about the fantastic fishing he had just experienced in his own private pools on the river. I guess I was feeling my oats that day, or something, because I do remember pooh-poohing Atlantic salmon fishing, something that I had yet to try, when he invited me to come fish his camp with him. I could tell by the expression on his face and his body English that I had somehow offended him. We were so used to gigging each other, just for fun, that I didn't give it another thought.

He kept bugging me about it and in the summer of 1971, I finally took him up on it. I found out that Atlantic salmon are indeed a great fly-fishing game fish. I also heard through the grapevine that his camp provided access to an outstanding fall salmon run, when fish average a bigger size fish than during summer. But Ted never invited me to go, seemingly pleased that I finally recognized what he'd been saying all along about the tenacity of Atlantic salmon.

Talk about a long memory, one day in 1975 Ted yacked on and on about preparing for his next Atlantic salmon trip in a couple of months at his camp in New Brunswick. I unwittingly took the bait.

"Hey, Teddy," I asked, "when the hell are you going to invite me to go salmon fishing with you on the Miramichi again?"

Ted replied with unmistakable vengeance in his voice. "You had your fucking chance, Bush."

Studying the triumphant sneer on his face, I knew exactly what he was referring to. I also knew better than broach that subject again.

CHAPTER

EIGHT

A PAIR OF ACES

Big Fish, Unforgettable Anglers

Countless anglers of all description and temperament climbed aboard my boat Mom's Worry throughout the years. So many different people, so many days on the water—the images blur together, fade beyond immediate memory. But some of the anglers who have fished with me remain sharply etched in my thoughts, fixed their by their deeds and words. Two who strongly fit into that category are Ray Donnersberger and Scottie Yeager.

Similar to Jimmy Stewart in appearance, Ray Donnersberger stands very tall, lean and sinewy. Ray can fight a tarpon like nobody else I've ever fished with. He lives and works in Chicago, but his love for fishing compelled him to also own a house on Lake Michigan.

When I first met Ray, he was fishing in Islamorada in the Florida Keys with Cecil Keith, Jr. Cecil and Jimmy Albright were the best guides in Islamorada in the 1960s, along with George Hommell, who was also superb on the flats. As a matter of fact, when clients asked me back then which guide I'd recommend in the Islamorada area, I'd say that if I had to hire a guide for myself, George would probably be the one I would choose. He was extremely knowledgeable, a very hard worker, and I'd been told he was easy to be with in the boat. While George is still with us, Jimmy Albright and Cecil Keith Jr. have passed away and are probably looking down on their beloved tarpon fishing grounds.

When I first guided him in 1960. Ray was the only angler

I've ever known who was not only truly right-handed, but also somewhat ambidextrous. He could wind successfully with his left hand. You should always wind with your dominant hand; if you are right-handed, wind with your right hand. And yet I see most right-handed anglers using their left hand to retrieve line – it's no wonder many of them lose fish. Ray was an exception: he could wind with his left hand even though he clearly was right-hand dominate.

Unlike most anglers who need a lot of coaching and still can't cast properly or see fish on the flats, Ray was fantastic at both, casting and spotting fish. I learned from him and he learned from me; it's the perfect combination to have in the boat. It would be a great understatement to say we make a good team. Every year I guided Ray, he won the prestigious Fly-Casting division for tarpon in the Metropolitan Miami Fishing Tournament [MET]. When Ray fights a tarpon, it's as if he's fighting for his life. Battling a 100-pound-plus poon on fly is strenuous work, requiring extreme concentration. Ray's deep, heavy breathing keeps him from being starved of oxygen. Ray continues to fight the fish tooth and nail right to the very end.

Ray D, as I'd gotten used to calling him, was the only angler that I would book for more than one week at a time, and I booked him the last two weeks of the MET to fly fish for tarpon. The only year that Ray D did not win the fly-fishing tarpon division occurred when he brought in a tarpon that would have been a tournament record of 126 pounds. As I was gaffing that fish, the rod blew up at the exact moment that Ray applied just a little needed extra lifting pressure on the rod. We voluntarily disqualified the catch, even though it was a moot point whether I had gaffed the fish before the rod broke or not. If we knew for sure that I had, it would have been a legal catch. But the rules state that a broken rod disqualifies your catch. Ray D didn't walk away empty handed though; he is awarded the Philip Wylie Tough Luck trophy, which brings to mind the noted author for whom the trophy is named.

Philip Wylie and I fished together once, back in the late 1970s. But when I was in my early teens, I practically devoured all of Philip Wylie's books on fishing. He had two characters: the captain's name is Crunch and the mate Des. They run a 40-foot charter boat from

Pier 5 off Biscayne Boulevard in Miami, but would also come to the Keys with their skiff and fish in the backcountry. I read Wylie's books over and over, all the while dreaming that one day I, too, would get out on a charter boat and fish the backcountry of the Keys.

My parents knew unequivocally that from a very young age I was totally addicted to fishing, and my dream was of big-water, big-boat, big-fish adventures. On my 13th birthday, my dad booked an offshore charter boat out of Bakers Haulover in North Miami Beach to take us out for a half day. Well, it was rough and we hadn't even arrived at the fishing grounds when my mother became deathly seasick, which in turn blew back on me and made me sick—the only time in my life I have been sea sick, or air sick, or anything like that. I caught my only fish that day on the way back in. It was just a bonito, but it was still my first-time-ever, deep-sea fish and the beginning of my fulfilling a dream.

I still have some of these books that Philip Wylie wrote fiction about Crunch and Des: *Fish and Tin Fish*, *The Big Ones Get Away*, and *Treasure Cruise*, to name a few. His Crunch and Des stories usually appeared in the *Saturday Evening Post* magazine before they went into hardcover books. His book of true fishing experiences, *Denizens of the Deep*, is one of the best you'll ever get your hands on. He also was a superb essayist on social issues. He was my boyhood hero whose image was never tarnished or forgotten.

Ray D is a man's man, the kind of client that every guide prays for. He was just a very, very gentle person. When it comes to fishing with a fly rod in the Keys, tarpon is the one species, next to bonefish, that most people come looking for. Ray was such an addict that he couldn't wait for the tarpon to arrive during their regular season. He used to call me from his office in Chicago and say, "Look, if the fish show up in January, February or March, give me call and I'll fly down and we'll give 'em a lickin'."

And I did just that. One year, tarpon showed up early and I learned a lesson. The long-range forecast was for the weather to be fantastic, so Ray jumped on an airplane that night, flew into Miami, rented a car, and drove to Little Torch Key where I lived, which is

28 miles from Key West. We got out on the water the first thing in the morning, but around midday a fast-moving cold front pushed in and the fish all disappeared. Ray didn't seem to mind. He was pleased we had tried it – but I never chanced that again during the winter and early spring because it can easily turn into a waste of time and hard work for nothing.

Even after I returned to flying in 1965 with Pan Am, Ray and I remain very close friends. We fished together at every chance. We also headed out to Montana to trout fish in the West. On one occasion, Ray took me to the Anglers' Club of Chicago in the early 1970s, and after that one visit, some 30 years later I am made an honorary life member of this renowned club. I am only the fifth person in their more than 50-year history that they have honored in this way.

In 1971, Ray D and his wife, Doro, rented half a duplex on Big Pine Key in the lower Florida Keys, and I rented the other half of the duplex with my wife, Bernice. Our plan was to fish for two weeks. Ray had never caught a permit on fly, and when the weather was cooperative, I would have the honor of poling him around for permit. Ray D, in turn, would pole me over the flats when the conditions are right for tarpon, all fly fishing, of course.

Well, cold front after cold front after cold front came through, making conditions lousy for tarpon fishing. But, as luck would have it for Ray D, the conditions were fine for permit, as they are the last game fish to leave the flats with bad weather and the first to return. So we did an awful lot of permit fishing. Ray D got numerous shots, but never hooked one of those wily Florida Keys permit during those two weeks.

We were down below Key West permit fishing one day. While I was polling Ray, he finally said, "Listen Stu, I'm not going to fish any more until after you fish. You have not had a fishing rod in your hand this whole trip."

"No, no, no, Ray – a deal is a deal," I said. Well, just as he sat down with his line all stripped out, and I said, "Ray, here come two nice permit, get up now, hurry!"

But Ray just sat there stubbornly, insisting that I cast to them. I knew these fish were going to just swim on by, so rather than debate and lose an opportunity, I jumped up and grabbed his fly rod. I made one cast and put the fly in front of the lead permit. He ate it! I caught that permit and it won the fly-fishing division of the MET that year. As I've always said, it's more important to be lucky than good.

We filleted that permit because we had to kill it for the tournament weigh-in that was required at that time. It provided some mighty fine eating. Our wives wound up making a bouillabaisse, as I had brought in a bunch of nice-size mangrove snappers—as well as blue crab, stone crab claws and lobster—from the canal right behind our duplex. Just to broaden the feast, our wives drove to Key West and bought fresh oysters and clams from a seafood market. Man, we enjoyed a fantastic number of meals out of that scrumptious bouillabaisse.

The next day the weather was a little better but still not good. We permit fished out in front of Big Pine Key in the morning, where we find numerous tailing permit. Ray had a couple of shots without any success, so we pulled the boat out of the water and went in for lunch. As we sat there, I thought of one of my go-to, ace-in-the-hole spots where I'd had great tarpon fishing. I told Ray, "You know, my friend, there is a very big shallow bank that I have found tarpon close to under similar conditions down near Key West." I knew that the tide should be coming in across this bank, warming up the water as the sun beats down on it. This would create warmer water on the down-current side, and if there are any tarpon around at all they should be drawn right into the warmer water.

We drove to Key West and launched the boat at Garrison Bight Marina. We ran to an area that I had nicknamed "The Jewelry Store," a code name just like others for hotspots we want to remain secret. This area on the National Geodetic Charts is actually called Pearl Basin.

We had not quite reached the flat when we knew we were in business. We see a tarpon roll quite a ways out in the deep water, where our 18-foot push-pole won't reach bottom. We did not have a trolling motor, but that didn't stop us. Ray was almost paddling with the push pole to get us close, when, just under the surface in the slightly warmer water, I saw some shapes. I made a very long presentation into this hue of color. A tarpon immediately ate the fly, and I set the hook by pulling the fly line with my left hand while striking the fish at the same time with the rod in my right hand. The silver king jumped toward the sky with a typical vicious head-shake, tossing the fly back at me.

It looked to be about a 65-pound fish, not a big one for sure, but by golly it had been the first opportunity to cast to a tarpon that I had in almost two weeks. I picked up and cast back to the hue of color, and the slight northeast breeze blew my fly a little off to the right of my target. "Doggone, Ray," I said, "I missed the shot." I started to strip the fly line to re-cast, and I'll be a tarpon's uncle if a fish doesn't eat it. I don't see her until she chomped the fly, and I set the hook. Oh … how world records are caught!

When this fish takes off into Northwest Channel, we fire up the engine and take off after her. After a 40-minute, tough fight in the deeper water, I have it near the boat. Just when I think "I've got her" – a jinx in fishing if there ever was one – the big tarpon takes off again in deep water. But then it makes a mistake. The tarpon runs up on a fairly shallow bar out in the middle of the channel. All that fish needs to do is stay in the 35- to 40-foot depths of Northwest Channel and fight like hell, making it is almost impossible to lift it to the surface using 12-pound-test leader tippet.

As I work the fish on the shallow bar, I handle it a lot better and can apply the amount of "down and dirty" pressures to roll the fish under and break its spirit. Ray D has never gaffed a fish in his life, but is ready to give this brute a try. It's truly a badge of courage when you agree to gaff one of these big critters. I tell him to reach under the belly of the fish and hit her with the two-handed gaff, rolling it over in one swift, powerful motion – and he does so, just like that.

We brought the fish in and weighed it. The official scale at the Key West Yacht Club put our tarpon at 154 pounds, a new world record by three pounds. What jubilation we enjoyed! Ray was immensely happy that he'd done his part to put a record in the books.

Interestingly, I was told some weeks later by a prominent member of the yacht club that the official scale could easily be 10 percent off unless some sort of adjustment was made to balance it. Ray and I both thought this fish was considerably bigger than the scale showed it to be, and 10 percent of 154 pounds would make it another 15-plus pounds. Considering all the tarpon Ray and I had seen over the years, we estimated that fish to be 169 pounds or so, and its length and girth measurements confirmed our thoughts. But, it went into the book as 154 and that's the way the cookie sometimes crumbles.

* * *

And Scottie Yeager? Definitely a filly of a different color, and she's the level of grit and competitive spirit you'll seldom witness. Here's how she persevered to nab a magnificent billfish—on freshwater bass-fishing tackle!

We are fishing the sailfish rich waters off Panama's Club de Pesca at Pinas Bay (now called Tropic Star Lodge). Scotty has brought in a huge sail, but we have not been able to revive the fish so that it can be successfully released.

It was now apparent that the fish is dead. Through 45 minutes of pitching and heaving, the rain-drenched anglerette and crew have taken turns at giving the fish artificial respiration. We hold the sailfish's bill and the front part of its dorsal fin with the boat idling forward, thus forcing water into its mouth and out its gills. Unfortunately this is a vain attempt to bring the sailfish back to life.

Hanging over the side of this rolling boat to support a nine-foot sailfish, as we and the mate have been doing, is a Herculean task. I have no doubt that some of us will have bruises that will last a week. The weary mate finally let go of the dead Pacific sail. We look up sadly at Scottie Yeager. The West Palm Beach Shores anglerette is sobbing. A mixture of tears and rain run down her cheeks as she watches the dead sailfish sink out of sight into the Panamanian depths.

A member of the fairer sex who grew up loving fish and fishing, Scottie is an outstanding conservationist. She has fished hard and expertly. On what has been an exceptionally rough and stormy day, she hooked, played, landed and released seven of Pinas Bay's famed sailfish. As we slowly head back to the Club de Pesca de Panama, I sit back and admire this woman. She has whipped fish after fish on 20-pound-class line, and then cried when one of them could not be released alive.

The next day, a light wind ripples the surface, but otherwise the sea is calm. The moody tropical weather is on our side this very important July day. Soon after we leave the dock, the mate puts a ballyhoo over the side and we troll it slowly over the sun-warmed water. There is no hook in the bait, as it has been rigged as a teaser. Using a teaser is one of the best ways to bring a sailfish to the surface so it's lured within reach of the caster.

The governing rules of most fishing clubs like the International Women's Fishing Association are tough. The angler must cast the lure and retrieve it from a dead boat, which means a boat not under power. If the angler casts to a fish from a moving boat, it qualifies only as a trolling catch.

Scottie is armed with a 6½-foot fiberglass plug rod and an Ambassador 6000 plug-casting reel that I myself have modified to conform to the I.W.F.A. regulations. I have removed the anti-reverse mechanism and preset the drag so that it cannot be adjusted while a fish is being played.

The reel is loaded with 200 yards of 15-pound test fluorescent monofilament. There is a six-foot shock leader of 20-pound-test monofilament, to which is connected a short piece of wire. An oversized, ungainly looking chugger-type of wooden plug is attached to the wire leader.

Scottie is going to try to catch a Pacific sailfish on light freshwater casting tackle – a feat that only a handful of expert male anglers have ever accomplished.

Trolling baits with or without hooks can be a tiring and sometimes unrewarding method of fishing. It's possible to spend many long hours with nothing more to do than watch the baits skip across the sun-glistening surface of the water. During the first hour or two it seems easy to stay alert, but after that, most fishermen start relaxing and are lulled into a sleepy state by the warm sun and the gentle rolling of the boat. But the top anglers stay aware of such moments and maintain a readiness, because many fish have been hooked only to get off the line because the anglers were too slow in responding.

Fortunately for Scottie, this doesn't happen today; a long dark shape suddenly materializes just under the surface and gains rapidly on the skipping ballyhoo teaser.

"Sail!" I yell, but Scottie has seen the fish too and is poised to cast. The skipper reduces speed and slides into neutral gear as the mate reels in the ballyhoo decoy. The hungry sailfish rushes aggressively at the teaser bait, but the mate deftly plays his part by keeping the decoy just tantalizingly out of its reach, drawing the fish ever closer to the stern of the boat.

"It's a beauty," I say as Scottie places the big plug within three feet of the now very frustrated sailfish. *Ka-pop, crash, splash.* Scottie works the plug almost violently and the sail sees it and attacks in a fury of foam not 30 feet from the boat. Scottie slams the hooks home and the stung fish takes to the air.

As the cobalt-blue torpedo greyhounds at the surface, a veil of sunlit spray seems to hang in the salt air. The handsome head shakes in a desperate effort to throw the plug, its strength transmitted through the line to the straining anglerette.

The engine is in gear again and the skipper tries to keep up with the sailfish, but we are too slow and are losing distance. Still, the line holds. As the little rod that has really been designed for largemouth bass bends double, the fish leaps mightily and throws the plug.

A massive sigh in unison consumes the boat. Scottie retrieves the lure and I inspect the hooks for damage, but only a small piece of flesh has been torn from the sailfishes' mouth.

Nonetheless, Scottie has hooked her first sailfish on plug-casting tackle. The mate rapidly puts another ballyhoo teaser over the side. Scottie remains alert, searching the water behind the bouncing, diving teaser through her green polarized glasses.

Another sailfish, a large one, comes right in on the bait. Everything goes like clockwork. When the teaser "escapes" the sail, it turns its fury on the big wooden plug, hitting it with its bill, trying to stun or kill it. Scottie's reflexes are spring-loaded and she strikes hard. The plug goes flying through the air and lands 20 feet away from the fish. The startled sailfish seems to look right at Scottie in disgust as it turns tail and runs.

Even so, Scottie is exhilarated. "Wow," she exclaims, "what a way to fish for sailfish."

We lose that teaser bait to a yellowfin tuna that comes up without warning. I watch as another ballyhoo teaser is quickly put over the side. The interruption caused by the uninvited tuna is brief, as a pair of sailfish comes up from behind our wake.

"Yahoo," I yell, "we must be at a sailfish convention."

Both fish want that bait badly, and the mate has a job keeping it away from them. It seems as if nothing will spook the two sails, and Scottie's plug lands in front and between them. Both fish scramble for it and the smaller fish wins the race, as is often the case.

When the fish grabs the plug, Scottie braces herself and strikes several times. Using every bit of timing and coordination necessary, she embeds the hooks into the hard mouth of the sailfish. The violence of the first few minutes of runs and jumps makes it seem as if the sailfish is trying to gain its freedom by making us cower with a show of force. But Scottie is still the master, and it isn't until the battle is halfway won that the hooks tear loose and this fish, too, is free.

Some say 13 is an unlucky number, but Lady Luck is like the weather–fickle and unpredictable. Scottie's 13th sailfish of the past two days is giving the mate fits. It darts from side to side, taking vicious, accurate swipes at the teaser. As the boat slows, I wonder how Scottie has strength enough left to cast, much less to play another fish. As these thoughts race through my mind, I watch in wonder as the big plug sails through the air and lands just alongside the sail's left eye. As if attracted by a magnet, the plug immediately becomes the all-consuming interest of the sailfish. It forgets the ballyhoo, and in anger and frustration, lunges at the plug.

Scottie sets the hook again and again. The sharp sting of hooks going through flesh and bone puts the sailfish into a frenzied leap only 40 feet from the boat. Scottie has her hands full holding onto the little rod. Just keeping the rod tip high and giving enough slack by bowing to the fish when it jumps is a full-time job.

The skipper has the boat in gear again and does the best he can to keep Scottie from losing too much line. Leap after leap, jump after amazing jump, the sailfish puts on an aerial display that is ample reward for any fisherman. It tail-walks across the surface, throwing its dorsal from side to side. Scottie is determined to land this one, if only the line doesn't break and the hooks hold.

As if it received a second wind, the fish comes the last few feet to the surface with regained speed, and jumps twice. But the vigor it had before is lacking in these last jumps. Now the fish swims away from the boat, putting its shoulder into it, like a horse pulling a plow. Again it is taking line, but this time, only a little bit.

Scottie grits her teeth and begins pumping again. Now the tables are turned, and Scottie begins to steadily gain line. The fish looks beautiful as the sunlight reflects off its spread dorsal fin. Precious monofilament now fattens the spool, and the sailfish is only 20 feet from the boat. With two short, fast pumps, Scottie slides the sail within reach of the mate's waiting gaff. He strikes expertly and the fish thrashes and throws water all over us. The gaff holds, and the captain jumps down from the bridge to grab the sail by the bill.

We get underway as rapidly as we could, for we have some two hours of running before reaching the dock at Club de Pesca. Back at the dock, it is an extremely happy Scottie Yeager who watches the scale go up, up, and up to 90 pounds – a fantastic feat for anyone using that kind of tackle suited for fish less than one-tenth the size of that sailfish.

This time, Scottie is too happy and excited to cry. Her new I.W.F.A. record took her only 40 minutes. But what an exciting span of time it has been. Scottie is all smiles as we shake her hand, and congratulations go all around.

CHAPTER

NINE

WINGS OVER VIETNAM

Supporting Our Troops—Pan-Am Style

My experiences in flying the skies over Vietnam in 1966, while the war there raged on, came about because of a tragic loss in the Pan-Am family. Harold Gray, President of Pan American Airways, lost a son in the fighting. Lieutenant Commander Harold Gray was a naval aviator flying a F4H Phantom when he was shot down while on a mission.

Harold Gray turned the loss of his son into a living tribute to the downed pilot's memory. He donated the services of Pan Am's then-aging DC-6 fleet to fly military personnel into and out of Vietnam when they were slated for a little R & R.

Pan Am proffered just enough openings to fill a temporary assignment over a four-month period to operate a daily flight from Hong Kong to Vietnam. Wanting to see what was actually happening over there, I took a cut in pay when volunteering my service as a first officer to become one of three crews performing the inaugural flights to some of the garden spots of Vietnam–like Da Nang, NHA Trang, Cam Ranh Bay and Tan San Nhut, the airport in Saigon.

When Bernice, my wife of nearly five years, and I packed our bags and took off, we thought we were headed for another great adventure. We envisioned living the high life in the Hong Kong

Hilton Hotel, but it turned out that Pan Am had other ideas. The Empress Hotel sits across the bay in Calhoun, China, a moderately priced, reasonably clean hotel. It was to be Home, Sweet Home for the next four months.

This was going to be a bare-bones operation. Gray was charging the U.S. government a whopping $1 per flight for the DC-6s – that's per flight, not per person – as a contribution in his dead son's memory. An added twist to participating in the inaugural flights would be the presence of Bill de Lima, an old-time captain from the school of gruff-talking, demanding SOBs who expect their utterances to be worshipped and never questioned. Because of his prima donna demeanor, very few first officers want to fly with him. Before leaving the U.S., I made one of my many tongue-in-cheek statements to crew scheduling, boasting that I could fly with any captain and keep him out of trouble. So guess who gets stuck as Captain Bill's first officer on the inaugural flight?

We met briefly at the Empress Hotel while Bernice and I were checking in at the front desk. Captain Bill is tall, well built and looks younger than his mid 50s, the single life after a divorce evidently agreeing with him. Although robust in appearance and used to being in total command, I got the impression that de Lima is somewhat lonely.

Bernice and I dragged ourselves to the room, unpacked and showered, washing off the grime from our long flight. Finally we decided that no matter what time our watches were saying, we were hungry and more than ready to find a place to eat. When we stepped out of the elevator into the lobby, Captain Bill was folding an English newspaper he'd been reading, and waved us over.

"Have you given any thought about dinner?" he asked. We replied in unison, "We're starved."

Captain Bill had arrived in Calhoun three days before we did, giving him the opportunity to check out a few local restaurants. Leaving the hotel, following Bill's quick pace, we walked a couple of blocks, then turned down a narrow street. After another half a block we began to sniff strange and almost sweet scents as we neared the eatery Bill had in mind.

The restaurant was a large, open room with at least 60 tables. Once inside, the aroma was almost pungent. Two-thirds of the tables were already packed with Chinese men, women and children. Their ivory and ceramic chopsticks could be heard clicking away, only occasionally overridden by conversation.

Captain Bill was familiar with the required procedure of seating yourself, so we followed his lead. Looking around, I noticed we were the only Caucasians in the whole place. Naturally, the menus displayed only Chinese script—like hieroglyphics to us. Luckily, this is also a dim sum restaurant. Teenagers parade from table to table with large trays strapped over their shoulders to support the weight of many wicker baskets of steamed delicacies.

As the waiters sauntered past the table while singing out the type of food being carried, I got their attention and pointed a finger to my eye and then at their wicker baskets. They nodded with toothy grins and lifted the lids for me to see what they held. I figured that if it wasn't moving and looked edible, I'd give it a try. I ordered by pointing at the baskets, then at our plates. Almost everything I sample was delicious. I have always been especially fond of pork and shrimp, which are some of the main dishes, though there was an occasional surprise that does not spend much time in my mouth. I realized I would probably never know exactly what some of these dishes are, but if the taste is good and we don't get sick, who cares?

We're so impressed with the wonderful amalgam of tastes and flavors that Bernice and I return to this restaurant two or three times every week for the four months we lived in Calhoun. We also discovered that the Sunday brunch at the Hong Kong Hilton was not to be missed.

Betty McDonald and Sue Johnson, two of our attractive flight attendants, have a suite of rooms at the Hong Kong Hilton, which make us wonder how they can afford such luxury on their meager salaries. But we should have guessed: It turns out that an assistant manager is having an affair with one of them. Their fun lasts two and half months before someone gets wise, and the manager gets canned, and the two girls have to vacate the premises.

Delayed, our inaugural flight departed Hong Kong at 10 a.m.

in order to arrive in Da Nang around 2 p.m. After four grueling hours of flying a new route into a hostile environment, we parked the aircraft, knowing we were sitting in an area where the Viet Cong periodically lobbed rockets and mortar rounds. We unloaded our cargo of returning military personnel and several big tubs of ice cream, which we would carry on every trip into Vietnam. Meanwhile, the gas truck rolled out and started the refueling process, while a couple of enlisted Marine airmen climbed up on our wing to replenish the oil in each of the four engines. Three other enlisted personnel went through the airplane, picking up and cleaning up. They were trying to hurry the reloading of around 90 other Airmen and Marines, all eager for R & R. In the cockpit, we were just as eager as our passengers to get the hell out of there.

We had a kind of unwritten captain and co-pilot agreement in Pan Am, that we would take turns making take-offs and landings, in order for both captain and co-pilot to stay proficient. Captain Bill made the take-off out of Hong Kong and the landing at Da Nang, so now it was my turn to fly the return leg to Hong Kong.

Our flight back to Hong Kong was a little faster than the outbound leg, with a tail wind, and uneventful until we were an hour out from the airport. Pan American operations called to tell us there was a heavy fog bank rolling into to the airport. We were all pretty tired from the stress of flying to Vietnam for the first time, and the message added to the tension that was building in the cockpit as we got ready for an approach and landing in a very heavy fog.

Hong Kong airport had a very good ILS [Instrument Landing System], and the British also had a renowned radar-guided GCA [Ground Control Approach]. I considered myself to be of peak proficiency in both types of operations. Unless the fog was so bad that visibility was below the absolute minimums permitted for landing, I expected to bring us safely home.

I started getting out our ILS approach charts. "Let's do a descent check," I said to the captain and Paul Reinders, the flight engineer. In the DC 6, the flight engineer's station during take-off, climb-out, approach and descents is a removable jump seat between and just behind the captain and the co-pilot.

Twenty minutes out, Hong Kong Center turned us over to approach control. The first words to us: "Good evening and welcome back, Clipper six one zero five. Sorry that I have to inform you the fog has occasionally gone below our ILS minimums but not quite below the GCA minimums. The wind is from two nine zero degrees, twenty gusting to thirty knots. You are number one for the approach. Would you like to fly an ILS approach being monitored by GCA or a GCA approach while watching your ILS?"

I replied, "Stand-by one." Captain Bill was being very adamant about my shooting an ILS approach; but it was my landing and I added, "Hong Kong approach Clipper six one zero five, we will make a GCA approach while monitoring the ILS." I had been forewarned about this approach during an airport qualification slide presentation about the islands, which were actually mountain peaks jutting out of the water as high as 1,000 feet. We'd be flying between them. They are always a concern, even in a no-wind condition, but with this much wind blowing from my left beam, my approach had to be precisely on track.

I could just imagine Captain Bill getting red in the face and I heard him mutter under his breath, "I'm the damn captain of this ship." But by now, pressing on, I ask the flight engineer to perform an approach-to-landing checklist. "Flaps fifteen degrees," I said as I put the flap handle into the proper detent myself, not waiting for the captain's assistance. Continuing the descent while slowing down to my approach speed, I called, "Flaps twenty-five, gear down," just as approach control cleared us to continue the descent to 1,000 feet. Paul reached forward and selected the landing gear handle into the down position, as I called for a landing checklist.

Approach control now turned me over to the final GCA controller, who immediately says, "Clipper six one zero five, start a shallow turn to the left – now stop your turn. Clipper zero five, you do not have to make any further verbal response to anything I say until after landing. If you do not hear me for five seconds, execute an immediate missed approach go around." Captain Bill responds, "Roger, final controller."

"Clipper zero five, start your descent at 500 feet per minute

– you're going slightly above glide path, increase your descent – you are now on glide path and on track, you're on glide path and on track".

At this point of the approach, Captain Bill, while watching the islands on the radar screen, started giving me a "cockpit GCA," making it impossible to concentrate on what the final controller is telling me to do. I just tuned both of them out of my head and flew the ILS approach. Captain Bill hollered something a couple of times that I ignored, focusing all of my concentration on needles on the panel glowing in my face, flying a very precise ILS because of the islands' proximity and the crosswind.

Breaking out of the fog right over the runway approach lights was somewhat disorienting. I was holding a 45-degree crab into the strong crosswind from my left, and it being night time with wisps of fog partially obscuring the runway lights, I had to force myself to hold the airplane in the crab until just before touching down.

The final approach controller said, "Clipper six one zero five, that was an excellent approach under some adverse conditions."

Yeah, right! He didn't know about the adverse conditions I had in the cockpit. "Do you have any comments for me?" he asked.

"Many thanks for taking me by the little finger and leading me home," I replied. Captain Bill now took control of his airplane, as he had the only tiller wheel for steering the nose-gear while taxiing.

Taking a deep breath with a sigh of relief, I asked Paul to perform the after-landing checklist. After we were in our assigned parking area, wiping the sweat from my forehead, I asked him to perform a block's checklist.

Captain Bill de Lima had not said a word to me since I ignored his comments while flying the approach. Pan American operations had our limo waiting for us just after we exited the airplane. The ride to the Empress Hotel, walking through the lobby and the ride up the elevator, felt like icicles in the winter. Not a word was spoken by any of the three of us. Betty and Sue, sitting all the way in the back of the limo, were chatting about something in hush tones.

I barely got to my room, kissed my wife, took my shoes off, my mindset on having a good hot shower, when the telephone rang. It was Paul Reinders calling to tell me what a great job I did despite the antics of Captain Bill.

This was the first of many flights I would make with the infamous Captain Bill de Lima, Flight Engineer Paul Reinders, senior stewardess Betty McDonald and her cohort Sue Johnson. The next afternoon, crew scheduling called to ask if I would mind flying the next trip with Captain Bill. I told them to let me think about it for an hour and call me back, which they did. During the interim period I talked it over with my wife, telling her some of the details of the flight, and we both agreed that it would probably be the worst scenario and it was behind me. So when crew scheduling called back telling me they were having a problem getting a first officer to fly with him, I replied with, "Okay, but you'll owe me one."

I hadn't been off the phone five minutes when it rang again; this time it was Captain Bill calling to ask if we had any dinner plans. Shaking my head and winking at my wife, I said, "No sir, why?" He said, "Would you mind meeting me in the lobby for a libation at five o'clock?"

"I would be glad to if Bernice is also invited," I said, to which he replied, "I'm sorry that it came out that way, but of course I meant for her to go also." We agreed to meet him.

During our second cocktail, I had the impression that Bill had come as close to an apology as he ever has in his adult life. He patted me on the shoulder and said that I made a very fine approach and landing under tough conditions ... and that he just found out we were scheduled to fly again tomorrow. "I'm pleased that it's you," he snorted, evidently figuring I felt the same. I took a deep breath, swallowed and thanked him for the kind words, and glancing at my wife told him, "I, too, am looking forward to flying with you again."

Hey, my momma told me that you can catch more flies with honey then with vinegar.

We are back on schedule with a 6 a.m. departure that should get us in and out of Vietnam by 1 p.m. and back to Hong Kong before 6 p.m. each evening. Our schedule had us flying to Vietnam and back the same day and having the next day and night off, which actually was a day and a half off between flights because all of our departures were scheduled to be in the early a.m.

Our next flight was to NHA Trang, a helicopter/air cavalry jumping-off hotspot of fighting, about 100 miles down the coast from Da Nang. This time, for a change of pace, the now-mild-mannered Captain Bill let me make the takeoff out of Hong Kong and the landing in NHA Trang. Everything seemed to go very smooth on the flight and within the cockpit, to the point of it almost being relaxed and enjoyable. That is, as relaxed and enjoyable as it can be when flying over Vietnam, where you know you are probably being shot at with small arms fire by the Viet Cong, especially going in and out of Cam Ranh Bay and Da Nang. These were two of the places where the VC was heavily embedded in the jungle not far from the airports' perimeters.

Two days later we made our first landing at Cam Ranh Bay, an airstrip made out of metal mats. It reminded me of a couple of World War II movies with John Wayne I especially liked, "The Flying Leathernecks" and "The Fighting Seabees." Our approach route was to take us near a couple of small islands just offshore that reportedly had VC hiding in the jungle. We had no intention of flying over them. The airstrip itself was only about 200 yards beyond the beach, which was patrolled by our own troops.

Our approach and landing was uneventful, but before we could even offload all of our military passengers, we noticed the fire trucks and crash crew screaming out toward the approach end of the runway. An Air Force twin-engine C-124 Caribou had declared an emergency and was on final approach, its port engine feathered with smoke and flames still streaming out of it. The pilot did an excellent job landing with his left engine out.

Our passenger list this time consisted of Air Force and Army personnel. It is not too surprising to see the difference in the demeanor of those going on R & R from those returning to their duty station. The ones leaving on R & R are all perky, slapping one another on the back and telling jokes. The troops disembarking from Hong Kong are quiet and look like they can use a vacation or even a good night's sleep.

The Air Force operations officer informed us that we should hold our brakes, rev the engines up to full power before releasing our brakes, in order to get as much speed quickly as possible. Upon liftoff, we were to start executing a chandelle [a climbing 180-degree reversal of direction] to the left, staying within the perimeter of the field. Reports had the VC in the nearby jungle shooting with small arms fire at almost every departing aircraft.

Bill made a standard PA announcement, which also included briefing the passengers and our flight service about the type of takeoff and climb out we are going to execute. To be honest, I was glad that it was my leg to fly, as I know what kind of aerobatic pilot I was in the Navy and I do not know about Bill's aerobatic skills.

The take-off was almost like being a hot fighter pilot again—maximum takeoff power, pulling back on the yoke as the DC 6 reached flying speed.

"Gear up," I barked, while rolling the airplane into a hard left bank, making a steep climbing left turn at only five knots above stick-shaker, stall speed. "I feel like I'm flying an airplane again," I exclaimed over the loud drone of the engines during takeoff power.

We were maintaining maximum power until the flight engineer informed me that number one engine cylinder head temperature was rapidly approaching red line temperature. I replied, "Bring them all back to rated power until we pass 1,000 feet climbing and then go to climb power." At this point I was concentrating on not flying directly over any of those little islands just offshore.

Our flight back to Hong Kong was a piece of cake, not seeming to take as long going back this time as it had the past. Here it had been a little more than a full week and I was feeling like a veteran. The weather in Hong Kong was clear, with visibility unlimited but with what seemed to be a constant strong crosswind from the left. No sweat at all, compared to my first approach and landing in the fog there at night.

Our limo ride back to the hotel was kind of quiet because we were all tired, but there was a comment or two about our takeoff out of Cam Ranh Bay. Betty McDonald, our senior stewardesses, said, "Hey Stu, a couple of the Army guys sitting in the back got sick before you even got the wings level right after we took off." With a chuckle she added, "I told them I thought it was a blast and to hold on to their ass because you're on your way for a hell of an R & R good time."

Not every round trip was a piece of cake. Unfortunately some of our navigation is by guess and by gosh: two Automatic Direction Finders that often swing and point to every lightning flash from every thunderstorm. As you come within range, one of the radios is tuned to the frequency of the next station to which you want to navigate. Whoever is handling the radios on that leg of the flight then listens to the identification code, which is broadcast in Morse code, to make sure that we are navigating to the correct beacon. Each radio beacon has its own identifier code.

On one trip, unknown to us, North Vietnam had set up a false radio beacon that was broadcasting the identification code of the next beacon along our route of navigation. We bit on the ploy, the same time I am putting the bite on breakfast. At the controls, Bill takes a jog to the west toward the bogus beacon and follows it for close to an hour. I finish breakfast and pick up our navigation chart, because something doesn't feel right to me. Within a few moments, I was trying to convince Bill that we should not be heading toward the north, and that we were not on the proper outbound tract from the last radio beacon we flew over.

Bill grudgingly gave in, turning back toward the south to intercept the proper tract toward Da Nang. We are flying over a cloud cover and could not tell that we were over the Gulf of Tonkin. Twenty minutes later we had a couple of U.S. Air Force F-4D fighter planes pull up to us, one on each side. They were close enough for me to see a thumbs up from the one on my side, while at the same time the other one called us on 121.5, the international guard channel, saying, "Hey Pan Am, aren't you a bit off the beaten path?"

Without skipping a beat, Bill replied, "We were lured toward a bogus radio beacon."

"Where's your destination, asked the F-4D pilot.

"Da Nang" was all Bill replied.

The pilot continued, "If you turn right 15 degrees, you should be dead on. Have a good day. We have to watch our fuel state. With that, they both went into afterburner and accelerated; climbing to a much higher fuel saving altitude than the 17,000 feet we were flying."

We had been told to stay at least 3,000 feet on a high steep final approach into Da Nang, and on the descent to kick our rudders back and forth, making the airplane slip and skid. This creates an illusion of the direction of flight, making it much harder to be hit by the VCs small arms fire. I couldn't resist saying, "Are we having fun now, boys? And I took a cut in pay to come out here and play."

I certainly would not have been so glib at that time had I known that we were about to go from the probability of small-arms fire by jungle-lurking VC, to a very real attack—big time!

Just a short time after we had shut off our engines and deplaned our military passengers at Da Nang, the Viet Cong started lobbing rockets and mortar rounds onto the field, most of them hitting around the aircraft parking area. I had bought my first Nikon camera with a motor drive and a telephoto zoom lens in Tokyo on my way to Hong Kong. Everyone on my airplane left and headed for sandbag-lined shelters. Everyone except me, that is – I had my Nikon out shooting pictures. I got a good sequence of one of our Air Force B-57 Canberra's that was parked between protective sandbags being hit. The two-man crew was just lighting off the engines to go out on a bombing mission. They both got out okay, and I snapped pictures of them making a rapid departure from their airplane, which is what I did as well a very short time later.

As one might expect in a war-torn atmosphere, weird things can happen. While in a shelter and hunkered down with a bunch of the military, Betty proved to be more adventurous than any of us had imagined. She accepted an invitation to go on a fast-fire mission in "Puff the Magic Dragon," a C-130 equipped with 20mm Gattling Guns protruding out of several window mounts of the aircraft. They were just going to take off, do a quick circle around and lay down a high velocity of suppressing fire in the area that the rockets and mortar rounds were coming from. Shouldn't be gone more than 30 or 40 minutes total, she was told. And it looked like we will be on the ground for at least two hours, with this disruption in our plans.

I would venture to say she is probably the only flight attendant in history to serve an Air Force crew while on a firefighting mission.

On our way back to Hong Kong, flying at 19,000 feet in basically a cloudless sky, I noticed a lot of smoke on the ground. We were actually flying almost directly over an area being dive-bombed. It looked like they had hit an ammunition supply, because suddenly there was a big flash with a lot of smoke. Then, all too quickly, whatever was happening was beyond our vision.

Now that we had become aware of these happenings, in days to come we would see numerous bombing attacks on the North Vietnamese from our airborne vantage point.

* * *

Our flights to Vietnam were almost becoming routine; about as routine as flying into an area that is often under siege can be. My four-month temporary assignment was rapidly coming to an end when the Pan Am chief pilot called and asked if I would consider extending for another month or so with Captain Bill de Lima.

"We would like you and Bill to set up flying military R & R, staging out of Taipei Formosa to Vietnam," he explained.

Neither Bernice nor I had ever been to Taipei, and she did not have to think about it very long before saying, "Sure, why not. It will be like putting another notch in our belt of places we have been."

So there we were once again, off and running on a whole new adventure.

Captain Bill de Lima, Paul Reiners, the flight engineer and I ferried one of Pan Am's DC-6s, with Gretchen, Paul's wife, Bernice, our two stewardesses and a small crew of Pan Am mechanics to Taipei. It was immediately obvious that flying from here was going to be a different type of operation. This airport was by far more military than it was civilian. There are guarding groups with heavy machine guns and anti-aircraft guns along many of the taxiways and runways. It looks like they are expecting an attack from mainland China any moment.

Our hotel was much smaller than the Empress Hotel in Calhoun, and right on what seemed to be the noisiest main street in town. After a bit of haggling with the assistant manager at the front desk, we manage to get our room changed to the top floor, which made for less noise and better sleeping conditions. Once again, home sweet home. For another month.

The limo Pan Am had arranged for the crew pick-up at the hotel to take us to the airfield was stopped at the front gates by guards armed with machine guns and a very serious looks on their faces. They searched the limo every time we went through the gate, coming in or going out. Wow, talk about tight security.

The first night's takeoff was mine, and I had studied my approach plates and departure procedures that afternoon before taking a nap. Our departure procedure for this airport had us making a hard right turn shortly after takeoff, flying to a radio beacon while climbing to 2,000 feet before turning back on course, still climbing. Seemed to be taking us quite bit out of our way for no apparent reason, other than it was the published departure in our Jeppsen manual, and that was what I was going to fly. Because it was such a long flight, Bill tried talking me into not flying the published departure but to climb out right on course, which would probably save 10 to 15 minutes. I had no intention of not following the published procedure, and in once again opposing The Great Man's wishes created a new sore point between us that would eventually grow into a serious wound.

This was to be our longest flight since we had been out there. We are going all the way to Saigon's Tan San Nut airport; a grueling six and a half-hour flight. Our departure time was scheduled for 4 a.m., in order to get us to Saigon by 11 o'clock in the morning. With a probable two hours on the ground, we expected to arrive back in Taipei around 7 p.m. in the evening.

The air traffic going in and out of Tan San Nut was by far the heaviest I have encountered. It seemed as if there was a plane taking off or landing every two minutes. Saigon Center had us on radar

50 miles out and vectored us into a slot behind a number of other landing civilian and military aircraft.

After we finally landed and taxied in, the plane was serviced by a dozen or so tiny Vietnamese men wearing little more than loincloths. They worried me immensely. I had the feeling that any of them could be Viet Cong, but officials assured me that they were all checked out security-wise. Still, I never stopped worrying about them and how easy it would be to sabotage the plane, killing 90 American servicemen and our whole Pan Am crew.

The good news was that our return trip flight was planned to be 40 minutes shorter because of tailwinds, and we thought we might even throw another log on the fire and get back to Taipei an additional 10 to 15 minutes faster than that. Our flight back was a little bit difficult for our two stewardesses, as the first three hours of the flight had us bouncing around on the edge of a jet stream that was the creator of the tail wind. Other than that, as the saying goes, all's well that ends well. And we actually got back in time for a nice dinner.

On our next run we were headed back to Da Nang, departing Taipei at an ungodly four a.m. Soon Bill and I would be at it again.

Our forecast flight time was five hours and five minutes, which meant five cups of coffee and around five cigarettes each. This trip was my time to do the takeoff and landing in Da Nang, something I really like doing. Jinking our way around those islands was something that brought out the old fighter pilot feelings in me.

Paul completed his walk-around pre-flight, the stewardesses checked the cabin area and got most of the military personnel on board. Bill and I did a rather quick cockpit preflight, at which time I reviewed our published departure procedure, a Pan Am procedure, with both Bill and Paul. Bill said that the published departure procedure was a bunch of hooey, a figment of some desk jockey's imagination. Once again, because it was a long flight, he wanted me to climb out on course. I emphatically said, "No way, Jose. I just finished briefing on the departure route I am definitely going to fly."

Bill was having another of his "I am the captain and supreme commander" moments that I thought went out the window with my first approach in the fog at Hong Kong's airport.

"Captain, if that is the departure routing you want to take, you go ahead and I will watch out of my side window for any trees or terrain," I respond calmly but firmly. "I damn sure don't know what's out there and neither do you."

Here we go again, I figure, picturing Bill's face turning red. But I'm thinking that if we're all going to die, it's not going to be because I made a dumb shit mistake.

"Okay, hotshot, you'll soon see that I am right," said Bill. Paul turned sideways and gave me a wide-eyed look with his brow all wrinkled up.

"Pre-start checklist," Bill said in a commanding voice. Paul cleared his throat and started reading the checklist. He glanced at me in between items, to see if I was in fact going to let Bill do it his way. I truly was not a happy camper but decided that discretion was the better part of valor, not wanting to have a Cane Mutiny in the cockpit of the Pan Am airplane.

Bill told me to call the tower for startup clearance, which came back with an immediate okay to start. With all four engines running, Bill called for a pre-taxi checklist and asked me to call for taxi clearance. I did so, believing for the first time that he was actually going to fly his own departure route.

We completed the pre-takeoff checklist, the takeoff checklist, and before you could say "Wild Bill" we were cleared for takeoff and rolling down the runway. Bill was most certainly a good enough aviator, even if from the old school. His takeoff procedure was precise and smooth, and yet sometimes I thought that his head was not on the same planet as mine. As we were climbing out of 1,200 feet, I was starting to see what looked like treetops just below us. But in this quarter-moon starlight I wasn't quite sure until all of a sudden I was positive that we were flying damn close to the treetops.

I grabbed the yoke sharply, pulling back for an immediate climb as I screamed out, "Maximum power, now."

"What the fuck are you doing?" Captain Bill screamed at me loud enough for the people in the back of the airplane to hear.

"Shit!" I exclaimed. "I could see trees just underneath us and I fucking-A did not want to die."

Paul interrupted Bill's words. "I'm pretty sure that I could see trees from where I was sitting also."

"Bullshit, Stu! You tell them in the back what happened, and you better pray that nobody is hurt."

Our intercom bell rang just as Bill's words were out of his mouth, and Betty, our senior stewardess asked, "What the fuck was that all about? I have probably been scared out of 10 years of my life."

"For some reason our departure route had us flying over an uncharted small mountain and we had to take that evasive maneuver to keep from flying into a tree," I explain. "Is everyone in back okay?"

"Yes, I think so, except for having the shit scared out of us," she said. "It's a damn good thing we were still in our seats and strapped in and that all of the military are so regimented they do not unbuckle their seatbelts until told to. We are all good."

Here we are off on a five-hour flight to one of the hotspots in Vietnam and I anticipated either getting the silent treatment or a red-faced reaction. I thought to myself, "Stu, just do all that you can to make it a safe flight."

Thank God for my Navy and Pan Am training, and for having made up my mind some time ago, that no matter what, I was not going to let another pilot kill me.

The rest of our flight was uneventful until we were in the process of offloading our military passengers. The Viet Cong once again decided to lob mortar shells and fire rockets into our vicinity. This time I scrambled down the steps like everyone else and ran for a bunker that is sheltered with sandbags.

Sue, our other flight attendant; possibly being a little jealous of what Betty told her, asked if she could go with a helicopter crew that was getting ready to depart on a quick hop to lay down suppressing fire in the area they thought the ordinance was coming from. Our flight attendants were not young girls – in their mid to late 30s – and old enough to know better, having been with Pan Am around 15 years. Can you imagine one of them in years to come, telling their grandchildren what they did while in Vietnam?

After the "all clear" was sounded, we crawled out of our bunkers, brushed off the dust and dirt, and continued getting ready for our flight back to Taipei. Luck was still with us; our flight plan had us picking up part of the jet stream less than an hour after our takeoff, and that cut around 40 minutes off our time enroute. We got back to the hotel in time to get cleaned up, change into civvies and go to dinner, with time to spare. What a day at the office!

Our flights became smoother after that, routine in fact. I now had the good Captain Bill de Lima's attention, seeing things my way on flying the published departure routes and other procedures. All went well both going and coming. Then again, the thought ran through me that I'd still rather be on the ground in Da Nang with rockets and mortar shells exploding around my vicinity, than to be at Saigon's Tan San Nhut airport, having my aircraft serviced by some Vietnamese that I thought could be Viet Cong.

I started feeling like maybe I was pressing my luck, and that I should take a little bit off the table before the next role of dice. So, the next morning I was on the phone talking to the Chief Pilot in Hong Kong. This time I was very adamant about my not ever flying back to Tan San Nhut, and I was about to volunteer myself back to my home base in Miami, where with my seniority I should have already entered into 727 training and a considerable raise in pay.

"Stu," he pleaded, "if you would do one more flight back to Da Nang with Bill, I will personally arrange first-class transportation back to Miami for you and your wife, and then 10 days off to re-acclimate yourself before going back on the schedule. We are about to wrap up the Hong Kong to Vietnam piston flying, so I will have a number of crews available."

I did not have to hesitate a second before answering. "You've got it, sir!"

I kept my promise—made a final uneventful run with Captain Bill. And my Chief Pilot kept his: / Bernice and I had reservations on a Cathay Pacific Airways flight to Hong Kong, where we overnighted, this time at the Hong Kong Hilton Hotel. Then we flew on Cathay Pacific the following evening to Tokyo. From there we transferred to the Pan Am Tokyo to Los Angeles nonstop, getting there in time to clear U.S. Customs, and catch the American Airlines nonstop flight to good old Miami, Florida.

Our Vietnam experience was behind us now. Ahead lay the new challenges of mastering the 727 tri-jet so many pilots loved. But I would never forget the experience: the teeming cities, the vast ever-changing skies, the jungles where the Viet Cong lurked and fired at us, the heart-stopping rocket and mortar attacks, the scowling Captain Bill, and the happy faces of the troops we carried to a little rest and relaxation from the pain and sweat of duties in a war they were not allowed to win.

CHAPTER

TEN

A JUNGLE RIVER'S
RECORD-FISH TREASURE

Where Fishing Becomes Adventure

"Faraway places with strange-sounding names..."

The feeling Rodgers and Hammerstein described so evocatively in one of their songs calls to the bold and curious among anglers. I certainly am no exception, always at the ready to head for the places where big fish are said to be lurking. In the 1970s, a visit to Guyana became one of my priority destinations. A small country (about the size of Idaho) on the northern coast of South America, Guyana is sandwiched between Venezuela on the North West, Brazil on the South, and Suriname and the Atlantic Ocean on the East. It is a land that includes dense jungles and dark rivers of strange big fish. Come along, as we head there on a very special adventure: To try to find and land the biggest freshwater fish ever taken on a fly.

Off to my left a jaguar screams, to the right a monkey chatters and a Jabiru stork sails slowly across the river directly over the pool ahead of my boat. I am standing on the slim crossbar seat of a 12-foot aluminum skiff that is being handled by my host Peter Gorinsky, while we watch the surge that tells us fish are actively feeding.

Ten yards away in Guyana's murky Rupununi River, a huge

body rolls lazily, the coil of its back flashing silver-dollar size scales on a girth bigger than a man's thigh. Long wavy dorsal fins start almost two thirds of the way back on top, and bottom, converging at its' tail to form an arrow-like point. The whole tail assembly is a blushing red. Blended into the olive drab of its body, it forms a cornucopia of color as bizarre as the fish itself. At least six feet long, cigar-shaped, flat-headed and sharp under-slung jawed, the giant arapaima – the largest freshwater game fish in the world – looks as near a throwback to prehistoric times as anything now alive. I have come to these dank jungles in January of 1972 to take one with a fly rod.

This prehistoric-looking fish is believed by some to be a first cousin to the tarpon because of the shape of its head, particularly the upturned mouth, large scales and a rudimentary lung that's filled with oxygen each time the beast rolls to the surface and gulps air.

No one has ever taken an arapaima while fly fishing, and in fact few outside Guyana have caught one on any type of tackle. I'd read that the last expedition took place in 1947, more than 25 years before my trip; a small group from the Explorers club, Dan Danforth, Phil Skeldon and Robert Avery, guided by Tiny McTurk were the only other American fishermen to have caught these prehistoric looking game fish, but the anglers used heavy tackle and fought the 100-pound-plus goliaths for more than an hour. I feel my fly rod and 12-pound-test leader might make the fight an interesting, if not impossible, challenge. As the fish rolls to the surface, I gauge the distance, lead it about 15 feet and drop the fly just ahead of the direction that it's traveling. I count to four as the fly sinks and start a slow retrieve, stripping in two feet of line with my left hand. After half a dozen strips, a couple of armloads of line decorate the bottom of the boat. The line just stops moving. There is no strike, not even the slightest tug, but I know the big fish has come up from behind my fly and closed its cavernous jaws on it. I jerk the rod tip up and to the side sharply and double haul on the line with my left hand, once, twice, three times in rapid succession, setting the hook.

The fish blasts off in a long run that sizzles the stripped line through my fingers. Almost immediately, it jumps. I see it is not the biggest fish in the Rupununi, but nothing to be ashamed of either. With three fourths of its bulk clearing the surface, I judge it to be about 5-feet long and over 60 pounds. It crashes back down and bores deep into the water, then zooms up, breaks the surface, and tail walks halfway around the boat. My rod bends like a tuning fork.

"It's going to break!" yells Peter, my guide and partner for the day.

I let up, but not much. During a lifetime of fighting giant tarpon, I've never broken a rod. But I don't want to break my leader and lose the first arapaima ever hooked on a fly.

"Get that lip gaff," I call to Peter.

Peter picks up the gaff but holds it like its hot. Only then does it occur to me that he's never used one.

"When I get the fish to the side of the boat," I tell him, "slip the hook into its mouth coming out of the it's lower jaw and hang on!"

I gain more line, and just when I have the arapaima lying on its side next to the boat, Peter reaches over the gunwale and, to my horror, grabs the 12-pound leader in his hand.

"Don't grab the leader!" I shout.

Peter drops it, and we go through the gaffing lesson again.

"You can grab the heavy mono just above the fly," I say, trying my best to control my excitement. "I've got 11 inches of heavy monofilament from the fly to the line, so you can grab onto that. But don't touch the light stuff ... it'll break."

Then, what does he do? He grabs the light leader again. I shout again. Now it dawns on me that he simply doesn't understand what I'm talking about.

This third time, I bring the fish close in. Peter makes a stab at it with the gaff and misses. The arapaima shudders wildly and runs off a quick 50 feet of line before I can stop it. I know now that I am going to have to bring this one in alone. A tricky proposition to be sure, but I've lip-gaffed a lot of tarpon over 100 pounds with the rod in one hand and the gaff in the other.

Once more I maneuver the arapaima alongside the boat, both

of our mouths gaping. I switch hands on the rod, bend over the gunwale and drive the sharp gaff hook through the fish's lower jaw, pinning it to the side of the boat. In seconds, it's mine – the first arapaima ever landed with a fly rod.

I lean back in the boat, laughing, and let the thought wash over me that this is only the first half day of my three-day safari, and there are plenty of bigger fish out there, some over 200 pounds, waiting to be taken.

This mission to attempt to bag the world's biggest freshwater fish on a fly meant traveling a couple of thousand miles by jet, half the night in a beat-up Land Rover, and most of a day by canoe and outboard up a wild jungle river. I've caught more giant tarpon than I can count, including two world-record specimens of 151 and 154 pounds, on a fly rod with 12-pound leader, and racked up many more records on saltwater game fish. This arapaima, however, rests upon a special pedestal in my mind because it's as big as many ocean fish, and you can't just walk out your back door and hang one on.

Our Guyana safari started with a call from my good friend Kay Brodney. An unusual woman, Kay is perhaps the planet's top female fly-fishing angler. I was her guide in the Florida Keys in 1962 when she took the women's' world record 137-pound tarpon on a fly rod with 12-pound tippet. Now, Kay is anxious to try something different, and I have to agree the arapaima will fill that bill nicely, in spades. Big ones over 200 pounds are not uncommon, and some estimates say arapaima run as long as 10 feet and weigh upwards of 400 pounds – they're monsters.

While the Amazon Indians have been harpooning arapaima for centuries, very few have been caught by sportsmen. The only place in the world they inhabit is the Amazon basin and a few of its tributaries such as the Rupununi River. The location is Guyana – formerly known as British Guyana. It's a frontier featuring vast coastal plains, broad savannahs, deep rainforests and liana-hung jungles. The place teems with gaudy macaws, tiny hummingbirds and giant blue butterflies. Jaguars stalk the country with few enemies other than 15-foot, alligator-like caimans and giant anacondas. The rivers burst with multi-toothed fish, like the brutish black piranha, which grows to five pounds or more.

Georgetown, the capital city, represents an amalgam of Portuguese, European, African, Chinese, East Indian and Amerindian living and loving side by side. Peter Gorinsky fits well into this picture, his blood mixture of Scottish, Wapashoni Indian and Polish all somehow producing quite handsome features. Peter arranged our visas and the governmental permission to enter the backcountry, first to Lethem, then to Karanambo, and on to the Rupununi River.

Just outside Georgetown is a primeval wilderness, largely unexplored, home of the three-toed sloth, peccary or wild pig, vampire bats, inch-long leaf-cutting ants, and a startling variety of birds like the brilliant-plumaged cock of the rock, whose colorful mating dance is like a Vegas lounge show featuring several dozen males at the same time. There are dense forests of purpleheart and greenheart trees with logs so heavy they won't float, and they'll only be transported downstream on rafts. The Amerindians use purpleheart for unique wood-skin canoes by felling the tree and carefully skinning it out with wedges, probably just as their ancestors have been doing for umpteen generations.

Our safari penetrates an area that by Cayuga – dugout canoe – is 11 days from the nearest settlement. We make it in a few hours, however, in an ancient DC-3 and a bouncing Land Rover, arriving early the first morning at the Manari Ranch Guest House.

In the Rupununi district, the day breaks noisily. The sun appears suddenly, peeling back the sky with layers of purple, flashing red and incandescent yellow. Trumpeter birds and guinea fowl screech and parrots chatter. It's fresh, like a summer morning on vacation, even in January. On the Manari Ranch's windowsill sits a tame parrot that greets us with "Happy Birthday" over and over.

We spend some time getting rigged up and learning about the arapaima's habits. Its favorite food is, naturally enough, another fish, the arawana. Small arawana have a greenish back with silver sides, so I tie some flies with leftover tinsel from the ranch's Christmas tree decorations, and some added Mylar to give it flash in the dark water. The inside of the fly is white bucktail, and saddle hackle producing a large fly, 5½ inches long, tied on a super-sharp Equal Claw number 254, 5/0 hook.

Peter tells us a little of what to expect. "It's a half-day trip to the Rupununi from here. We'll be in two boats with electric trolling motors. In this area you have to sleep in hammocks around a campfire to keep jaguars and caimans away." Peter says we'll fish from an island in the middle of the river, away from deadly bushmaster and fer-de-lance snakes, and ticks.

"Caiman will still be around, and maybe we can do a night caiman hunt," says Peter. "You can get right next to them, you know." I twitch, the thought not at all comforting. "We'll live off the land because it reduces the weight of carrying lots of supplies," he adds. "We'll catch anything we need to eat."

On the way to our campsite on the Rupununi, we stop off at Tiny McTurk's ranch, a uniquely Polynesian-style place with thatched roofs, broad porches and no window screens. McTurk was one of the first settlers in the area. Stories are told about how he entertained visiting VIPs with exotic meals served on fine China, with mellow silver and expensive Irish linen tablecloths, though the floors in the big house were the same as they are today – plain dirt – and chairs consisted of apple crates. We never complained and he never apologized for them.

McTurk led the arapaima expedition of the famed Explorers Club in 1947, when a 148-pounder was taken on rod and reel. For his own fishing, McTurk brings in the huge arapaima on "jugs," much the way Mississippi river fishermen take big catfish. He baits a finger-sized hook with a 2½-inch-square chunk of arawana, ties it with a clothesline to an inverted gallon jug, and casts it afloat. When an arapaima takes the bait, the jug's flotation soon tires the fish, and McTurk paddles out to collect his prize. He claims to have taken arapaima in excess of 200 pounds that way.

At Karanambo, the Rupununi gives itself back to nature. It is the dry season, and the river is low and narrow. In some places the jungle all but leaps across the water, closing its trees overhead. Our two boats, a 12-foot skiff and a smaller Cayuga loaded with three-day's supplies of equipment and staple foods, continually drags bottom. Numerous deadfalls, logs and snags left over from last season's high water, created by torrential rains, snap our outboard's shear pins at an alarming rate. Finally, as insurance for our return trip, we fabricate some shear pins from the handle of an old cooking pot. Our campsite, called Simoni Lake, was last used in 1947; the hot, stifling jungle has since completely reclaimed its ground.

We set to work immediately, chopping out jungle growth to open a place for our hammocks. A crude table is fashioned from small trees we have cut, and onto it we pile canned goods, rice, celene flour, a grated root similar to the Spanish yucca, and citrus fruit grown at Manari Ranch. We have no perishables. As our only insurance to returning to civilization, the supplies look surprisingly meager.

The Rupununi River is, in its own way, as inaccessible as the tangled jungle. We boil all our drinking water and wash at the edge of the sandy beach. There is no walking into the water. Everything has teeth. Everything bites. Everything is dangerous. In one area, I notice long, thin, stick-like fish rising slowly to the top in a vertical position. "Electric eels," Peter instructs. "They come up and take air, then go back down again. They stay in the exact same place, so you can watch them rise again and again. But you wouldn't want to cast and hook one; it's guaranteed to be a shocking experience."

From our camp I can see the big arapaima rolling not more than 150 yards away. Peter explains the area to me. "Five lakes come down from the Kanuku Mountains like a string of sausages, and then the Rupununi starts. Each of the lakes has a different depth and supports different fish. In the shallowest you get the lukunanis, the natives name for peacock bass, and arawanas, and in the deeper lakes are the saber-toothed biaras, gruesome looking fish with two large fangs that come out of its lower jaw and penetrate two holes in its upper jaw. When hooked, they jump like a tarpon and run like a bonefish. Some weigh up to 30 pounds."

Still speaking of the area's lakes, Peter continues, "After the first two lakes, the others are deeper and have rocks on their bottoms. Fish are everywhere, but the arapaima prefers the shallower lakes. One lake in particular is about a mile long, not very wide, and about

10 feet deep. The arapaima comes right to the surface to breathe. In one lake, there are only about 10 arapaima because the lake doesn't support very many fish that big. Preparing them as air-dried fish, natives have killed enough arapaima to cause the government to place these large wonders on the endangered list."

At one time, the arapaima migrated out of the Amazon basin only into the Rupununi. They've since spread downstream to the larger Esequibo River, and are now in the mouths of many rivers.

"Arapaima have a lung mechanism like tarpon," Peter goes on. "Arapaima doesn't leap like a tarpon, but I have seen some jump. The largest arapaima I've seen was eight feet, maybe 200 pounds."

Within a couple of hours of setting up the camp, the first arapaima ever caught on a fly rod was part of my angling history, as I described earlier. I'd say that fish weighs 60 pounds – small as arapaimas go. I have my heart set on a much bigger fish, but the exhilaration stays with me while I hold it up for pictures and long after I have released it. I don't want to kill such a small fish when I know I have a chance at taking a much bigger one. It is now about 2:30 in the afternoon and I am anxious to get back out, but there is a lot to do at the camp before dinner, and I am assigned the job of putting something on the table that night.

I take my fly rod and walk up the beach to take some of the big lukanani, the peacock bass marked with flaming red gills and alternating bands of pale yellow, dark grey and forest green. They fight at least as well as any large-mouth bass I've tried, and they are better on the table. But my attention keeps wandering out to the big deep pool in the center of the lake, where the huge arapaimas sit in wait for me.

Kay and Peter are fishing at the other end of the island, and not having too much luck. They have each hooked one, but lost them after just moments. The afternoon is wearing on, and after I have caught enough fish for dinner, the arapaima become really active again. Big ones are making those long slow rolls, moving easily, just like so many of the tarpon I've stalked. This kind of roll produces strikes. The fish are active, but not fearful or annoyed. Actually, the arapaimas have little to fear, and apparently no enemies other than man and an occasional jaguar, which might catch them in the shallows. Their highly sensitive lateral line warns them of any approach in the cloudy water. They easily out swim the caiman, and their mouths are big enough to swallow piranha. Predators pretty much leave them alone.

I call to Maurice Barlow, "Let's get our butts back out there and see if we can catch another fish." He quickly agrees and we shove off in the direction of the rolling arapaima. There is no anchor aboard, so we improvise with heavy round stones tied to long lines, setting the boat fore and aft in the current, preventing it from swaying in the wind.

I quickly hook into another fish, but the hook pulls loose and I lose it. It is almost dusk and the campsite is fading into the gloom off our stern. The fire needs stoking, and we think about going in. But then a big arapaima rolls in a looping, lazy curve, headed straight for us. I false cast the 9-foot fly rod twice and the large, glittering green fly sails 80 feet and plops softly into the murky water, just ahead of the fish. I count to four, and then begin my special tarpon retrieve.

When I'm working a fly, I hold the rod tip toward the water, the butt right in my belly. I don't pump the rod at all; it stays steady, pointed right at the fish. I feel everything that happens on the end of the line. After a couple of strips away from that big fish, my line stops. No pull, no jerk, just stops. That is it; I haul back on it, two, three, four jerks backward. The fish suddenly blasts off on a powerful surging run. I get busy, clearing the line I have dropped onto the deck, letting it zip through my fingers. Maurice pulls in and stows our two rock anchors and gets ready to paddle or motor after the fish, if necessary.

"Boy," I shout, somewhat breathlessly, "this one feels a lot bigger than the last one, but I don't know how much."

It tows us from one side of the river to the other, then downriver, away from the camp. Then it makes a long run back to where I hooked it, under a big overhanging tree in the deepest part of the river. We use the trolling motor to stay with it against the current so as not to put too much strain on the leader.

The fish jumps then, majestically, in an almost slow-motion

sequence, and we can see it is big, over 6-feet long, well over 100 pounds. It shakes its head like a big wolfhound, spraying water for a dozen feet in every direction, and takes off on a long, straight run. The raw power is awesome. Just then, the light, which began to fail when I hooked the fish, fades altogether.

In the tropics, the day ends like someone pulling down the blinds. It's dusk for a few moments, then it's black dark. You can't see your hands in front of your face. And out there the biggest freshwater game fish ever hooked on a fly rod is plummeting up and down the river while the only thing connecting it to me is a flimsy 12-pound tippet monofilament leader.

From the first sight I know it is over 100 pounds, and visions of the legendary 200-pounders I've sought all my life flash in and out of my imagination. The darker it becomes, the more active the idea seems. I begin to feel like Captain Ahab attached to his white whale. Your senses are sharper in the dark, and I can swear this fish is out to get me. It rushes up to the side of the boat, jumps, shakes viciously, and dives for the bottom. Maurice, the boat and I are soaked to the bone. There have indeed been stories about native boats being overturned and crushed by big arapaima, and more than once during these rushes we fear that same thing happening to us. I darn sure didn't want to be an arapaima disaster story. The fish charges us five or six times before I can feel its strength ebbing.

In about 25 minutes, I think the arapaima is pretty well whipped. I am ready to gaff it, when I realize that Maurice, like Peter earlier, has never before lip-gaffed a fish, and I will have to tell him how.

"Pick up that lip gaff," I tell him, "and shine the light on the fish so you can see what you're doing." I hand him a small penlight that I've slipped into my pants pocket. Maurice drops to his knees at the side of the boat, while I stand on the crossbar seat to control the fish better.

As soon as the light beam hits the arapaima's face, all hell breaks loose. The fish lunges up at the light, thrashing wildly. It crashes against the gunwale right next to my seat and wrenches the boat sideways. In the pitch dark, I feel the thin platform slip out from under me, and suddenly I am pitching down toward the water.

There is no way I want to be in that black water with this enraged arapaima and those gangs of piranha. Nighttime is meal time in the jungle, and given half a chance, a dozen different things would gladly turn me into a table d' hotel.

I jerk sideways, turn my body in midair, feel my ankle crack against the gunwale, and finally crash land in the bottom of the skiff. It takes me a moment to realize I'm in the boat, and with a sigh of relief I'm back in the game – glad not to be some critter's dinner and to find the rod and line still intact. The arapaima never touches the boat, and although it has run off about 50 feet, it is still firmly attached. By this time it's totally fatigued and lying on its side. Once I collect myself and find no broken bones, I realize it is a mistake to try and gaff the arapaima in the dark so we decided to beach the giant.

We half lead, half drag the exhausted fish to the shallows at the campsite, yelling for help. In a foot of water, Peter gaffs the arapaima and drags it onto the sand. Even then, it has not finished fighting. The fish shakes off the gaff three times, but is too tired to escape. The only thing I can think of to say is, "Holy shit! I actually got him."

I know it's the biggest freshwater game fish ever landed on a fly. Looking at the huge prize, our exciting weight estimates run from 180 pounds up to 220. The arapaima measures 82-1/2 inches long and 39 inches in girth. I knew that a tarpon of that dimension would weigh about 160 pounds but I have been told arapaima weigh heavier. It is another dozen or so hours before we will know for sure, since the only official scale is back at McTurk's ranch. We can't make the trip at night, and that makes for more anxiety.

It is past eight at night, and we begin to worry about caiman, or even a jaguar, coming to eat the fish and maybe us. I veto the idea of stowing the fish under my hammock. The last thing I want is to contest my catch with a jaguar, regardless of the record possibilities. We build the fire up high, and I pace the camp most of the night, hearing every sound twice. Out in the lake, other arapaimas continually rise to the surface, slapping their huge tails as they dive for the bottom again. Whether they are doing this to ward off predators or to frighten small fish, the sound is an eerie addition to my worries. The fight keeps flashing through my mind and I relive it a dozen times before dawn spears the eastern sky with its red and yellow streamers. Resting in the hammock, I inadvertently drop off into a deep sleep of exhaustion...

With the smell of the now-decaying arapaima drifting into the dank jungle air, a jaguar screams nearby, quickly bringing me out of my much-needed sleep. The first rays of sunlight descend onto the Rupununi River and fill my blinking eyes.

I know the only thing I will have to take back home is pictures. Even the arapaima's skin will not survive a full day in the sun. That won't make Bernice, my wife, too unhappy; with two world-record tarpon already gracing the family room wall, there isn't much room for a giant arapaima.

We load the fish into the skiff and cover it with banana leaves against the burning sun. It loses a lot of moisture anyway. At McTurk's, the arapaima tips the scales at 161 pounds, and considering it has lost water equivalent to 10 percent of its weight, the fish most likely weighed about 180 pounds when caught. Even so, at 161 this arapaima is the largest freshwater game fish ever caught with a fly rod.

The next day we have to leave the Rupununi, and my fishing is over. Kay is never able to land one, but Peter has taken a fine 40-pounder on fly to become the second man to do it. Right then, I'm thinking I'll be back for another try. There's a 200-pound arapaima down there, somewhere, that's got my name on it.

CHAPTER

ELEVEN

THE MAGNIFICENT 747

Getting My Wings on the Big Bird

First flown in 1969, the Boeing 747 is one of the most remarkable moving objects ever created. Today's version, the 747-400, can fly 416 passengers about 8,380 miles. The tail height is 63 feet, 8 inches, the equivalent of a six-story building. The plane has six million parts, 171 miles of wiring and 5 miles of tubing. Wing-tip to wing-tip measures 211 feet, 5 inches. The plane cruises at about 565 miles per hour and can carry 57,000 gallons of fuel. Since its inception, the 747 has flown 2.2 billion people—the equivalent of nearly 40 percent of the world's population—some 20 billion statute miles. That's 42,000 trips to the moon and back.

Part of my good fortune in aviation was to fly one of the first 747s ever built, late in 1969, not long after the plane had first been rolled out of Boeing's big hanger. The original versions of this magnificent monster were without the digital advantages of today's models and other technological advances that have gone into the evolving aircraft. Still, they were 747s, clearly something special.

The first 747 I ever saw was at night. It was an awesome sight, sitting on the tarmac, surrounded by the bright glow of floodlights. A few nights later I would fly this new, gigantic monster of a plane pilots were calling "The Aluminum Cloud." This initial 747 experience and others to come would become major highlights of my aviation career.

When I was a young Navy fighter pilot, I learned that date of rank is very important each time you come up for promotion. By that, I mean the exact date and time a person receives his or her present rank as an officer. During the 34 years I was on Pan Am's seniority list, I learned the same is true when applying for a pilot's position with an airline.

Each time there is an opening on a bigger and faster airplane or at a different base-station domicile posted on the bulletin board, it's awarded by seniority number figured by date of hire. As you might suspect, the bigger and faster the airplane you fly, the more money appears in your paycheck.

In November 1969, I was awarded a First Officer slot on the Boeing 747. Pan Am was the first airline in the industry to order and receive this new, oversized, state-of-the-art airplane. The move included a considerable raise in pay from my position as a 727 First Officer.

The 747 was so new to the airline industry that no one had a training simulator. Pan Am made a mockup of the cockpit, consisting of drawings and photographs of the pilot's instruments and engineer's instruments. This was our procedural trainer after completing three weeks of extensive ground school, learning about the many systems that operate the airplane.

This so-called cockpit mockup was located in a small room in Pan Am's new training facility on 36th Street in Miami. We would sit in a chair either on the Captain's side of the cockpit or on the right side where the Co-Pilot sits. One person would read the checklist and the other would touch the item and give the proper response. The instructor would say, "Touch each instrument, each control, and make them come alive."

This procedural trainer became known as "The Paper Tiger." You would understand why if you spent eight hours a day, six days a week, reciting normal checklists, abnormal checklists, emergency procedures and normal call-outs while making believe you're in an airplane going down the runway and climbing out to the assigned altitude. It took quite an imagination to dream this up, and even more of an imagination making believe you were flying.

The Paper Tiger certainly was not as good as a simulator, but I soon found out it did help as a procedural trainer. Twelve of us – six Captains and six Co-Pilots – flew to Roswell, New Mexico, in early December 1969, where Pan Am took delivery of the first two 747s from Boeing. Both of these airplanes were so new they still had Boeing markings on the tail instead of Pan Am colors.

My flying mate was Captain Henry Frantz, a DC 8 Check Captain. I had never met Captain Frantz and quickly learned that he was a true gentleman. Pan Am had all of us in a motel about 25 minutes driving time to the airport, where we spent most of our waking hours studying. We had been informed in writing that both of Pan Am's chief pilots went through their training at Boeing in Seattle, Washington, with an average flying time of 24.5 hours including their type rating ride with the FAA. Their dispatch said they most certainly expected the same from us. Flying time in this airplane is very costly, and they wanted us to be ready to start flying the inaugural 747 flights to Europe in early February.

It was 8 at night when Henry and I had our first look at this magnificent monster. We were scheduled to spend the next four hours sitting in the cockpit; two hours each in the Captain's seat with the other in the Co-Pilot seat, doing all of the same simulations we did in the procedural trainer. Only this time, it would be the real thing.

The next morning would be more of the same, but also with a systems ground school instructor asking questions and answering ours. I was actually starting to feel comfortably at home in either the left or the right seat, and could hardly wait to get this fantastic ship into the air. Henry, on the other hand, kept talking about how big it was and how he hoped he could handle such a big plane.

Seeing that Henry was rattled about the plane's size, I gave him a tip from my Navy experience. My primary flight instructor in the Navy had told me not to worry about anything outside the cockpit, but to just fly my seat and the rest of the airplane will follow. That philosophy has certainly worked for me every time I checkout on a different type of airplane. But all Henry would do is shake his head side to side, mumbling something to himself about how big this bird was.

After lunch we spent an hour doing a preflight aircraft walk-around with the instructor, then four more hours sitting in the cockpit making sure to memorize exactly where each instrument and control is, and touching them without looking. Tomorrow morning we were going to get a blindfold cockpit check.

Neither one of us had a problem with the blindfold cockpit check. Almost all the instruments and controls in Pan Am's airplanes are in the same basic area.

Now we headed back to the motel to study, making sure I have memorized all the power settings, airspeeds, flap settings, call outs and procedures before my first flight at 8 tonight. Henry and I are scheduled for three hours in the airplane; one hour was familiarizing us with the way the airplane feels in the air and how it responds to control inputs. Then we would each spend an hour staying in the landing circuit, shooting touch-and-goes.

At least those were the best-laid plans of mice and men, as the saying goes. Henry said that he was still intimidated by the 747's size, and suggested that I make the first takeoff, letting him get better acclimated to the size of the airplane while I'm flying. And that was just hunky-dory for me, because I always hated waiting my turn. Even when I was boxing in the Navy. I'd be cold with my insides jumping until I stepped into the ring. Then I would feel an adrenaline rush that seemed to start with a warm glow, slowly rising from my feet up to my neck, and I would feel very calm. From then on, things seem to almost happen in slow motion.

Henry was in the Co-Pilot seat and I was in the left-hand, Captain's seat. The flight instructor was sitting in the jump seat behind me. The Flight Engineer will be experiencing his second time operating at the Engineer's panel. A Check Engineer was strapped into the second jump seat behind the flight instructor.

All four engines were running after completing our pre-start and start checklists. Henry called for taxi clearance to the duty runway. Taxiing this big bird was going to be my biggest challenge. I remembered to overshoot each turn on the taxiway in order to have all 18 wheels remain on the taxiway.

We completed all of our checklists and I was lined up perfectly on the runway centerline. Holding the brakes, I advanced all four throttles to near take-off power. The Flight Engineer was in position, waiting for my command as I released the brakes and called for takeoff power.

As we rumbled slowly at first down the runway, all the instruments looked good and at 80 knots on the airspeed indicator, Henry made the first call-out of "eighty knots." This is the speed when I have enough rudder control to let go of the tiller steering handle I used for taxiing. Henry's next callout was "V1," a speed that's predicated on the actual runway length, field elevation, temperature, barometric pressure, relative wind and takeoff gross weight. This very important call-out signifies a position the airplane is on the runway. If a problem occurs before V1, it's mandatory for the pilot to stop the airplane, knowing there is enough room left to remain on the runway. After V1, it's mandatory to continue the take-off, rotating the airplane at VR – the proper speed for the airplane to get airborne.

The next call-out I was waiting to hear was "V2, positive rate of climb," a safe speed to initially maintain climbing the airplane and call out, "gear up," bringing all 18 landing gear into their wheel wells, eliminating lots of drag.

Henry Frantz must have had a premonition when he suggested I make the first takeoff while he handled co-pilot duties and watched.

Just after VR, with the 747 barely airborne, we flew into a flock of large Sandhill cranes, ingesting one of them into my number one engine, destroying both first stage and second stage turbine blades, and immediately creating one hell of an engine fire.

I was at the controls of a 747 for the first time, just off the ground, with the outside engine on the left wing on fire. Not a simulator! The real deal—a brand new Boeing 747.

The panel was alive with warning lights and the engine-fire audio alarm, a loud rapidly clanging bell that seemed to be almost in your head. This was the kind of emergency we had trained hours to handle, without fumbles or heart-stopping panic.

While making the proper emergency engine fire callout's, my

primary job is to still fly the airplane and decide on whether we need to dump fuel before returning to land on three engines, or leave our landing gear down, while returning to immediately land.

We were light enough to make a right turn, remaining in the landing pattern, but everyone agreed with my suggestion to climb out straight ahead, bring the landing gear up and do our emergency and abnormal checklists before returning to the field. At this light gross weight, the 747 can climb out if necessary at 800 fpm [feet per minute] rate of climb, operating almost like nothing was wrong.

Thirty minutes later, I was making my first of what would eventually be many three-engine ILS approaches and landings in the 747, most of them being simulated in training. Landing this great big, magnificent airplane with an engine out seemed easier than I could have imagined. The 747 is so massive it creates a tremendous ground effect lift, cushioning each landing.

After shutting down the remaining three engines and completing all of our checklists at the airport facility, I was ringing wet with sweat and damn sure ready to get out of the seat. It was nice receiving accolades all the way around from my fellow airmen. Henry, with more jest than truth, said, "Hey Stu, now you know why I thought you should go first."

To which I replied with more truth than jest, "Uh huh, thanks one whole helluva lot."

If I had been worried or wasn't sure of my abilities to check out in the 747, this first takeoff with an engine-out approach and landing most certainly would have eliminated any of those thoughts. Talk about a confidence builder!

The next week and a half gave me a couple more periods at the controls, and more studying in order to pass the seven-hour FAA oral exam on the many systems of the airplane. Not being good at reading schematics or engineering, I memorized the FAA portion of the aircraft and operating manuals. I believed it was all a waste of time and effort to memorize stupid things like the designation of the oil used in the engines or how each of the systems work. Who cares? I don't want to know how to build the airplane, just how to make each of the systems work properly so that when something goes wrong and a warning light comes on, I know how to take care that problem.

For those reasons, I am much more concerned about passing my oral exam, then passing my rating ride in the airplane. Sitting in a room that housed the Paper Tiger mockup, I was having that old, cold feeling with my guts in turmoil when the FAA inspector came into the room and introduced himself.

For the next six and half hours I regurgitated everything I had ingested into my brain about the systems of the 747. I guess I did okay, as the inspector said, "Mr. Apte, I think that's enough. You have an 'up' on your oral exam."

Actually, I believe the only reason he knew my answers were correct is that he kept referring to his 747 manuals and seeing I was repeating the instructions verbatim. Like high school algebra, I forgot most of it almost immediately, because I didn't need to know much of it in the first place.

The big day arrived a little sooner than I had anticipated. Henry and I were scheduled for our ATP – Airline Transport Rating – ride in the world's biggest airplane, the 747. This time the FAA Inspector wanted Henry to go first, which was okay by me, thinking I'll be able to watch what was happening. But this was not to be the case. Instead, they told me to go downstairs and relax in the first class seats for the next couple of hours while Henry went through the ringer. They would call me to come back up when my turn came.

With the seat tilted back, my eyes closed, I tried visualizing all the maneuvers Henry was putting the plane through. By the time we were on final approach, it seemed like much longer than two hours had gone by, despite my watch telling me otherwise.

When we landed, I thought, "Wow, that was a damn firm landing, especially for the 747." Henry then brought the airplane to a complete stop, turned off the runway, and taxied halfway back to the approach and take-off end of the runway before stopping. We sat there for 10 minutes before the FAA inspectors voice came on the public address speaker, saying, "Okay Mr. Apte, you can come up now."

As I topped the spiral staircase to the upper deck, the cockpit door opened and Henry, looking utterly defeated, said, "Stu, I got a 'down' on my rating ride."

Oh shit, I thought, now it's my turn in the barrel. Immediately entering the cockpit, I noticed it was the Check Engineer at the Engineer's panel. There should be no screwing up on emergency, abnormal or regular checklists.

My two hours in the barrel seemed to go by quickly. I performed all the normal, abnormal and emergency procedures necessary for a rating ride, both on the ground and in the air.

After taxiing back to the terminal, shutting all four engines down and completing all of the necessary checklists, I motorized my seat back and waited for the bad news. The Inspector, who was sitting in the Co-Pilot seat, was busy filling out a form attached to his clipboard. When he finished, he slowly turned toward me, giving a *thumb up* indication with his right hand and saying I did a good job. He handed me a temporary certificate stating that as of that date, I had a Captain's type rating on the B747.

I had to take a deep breath to keep my emotions and tears from showing. The moment was almost as emotional as receiving my wings in the Navy. I would begin as a Co-Pilot. Then, when the opening came, I would be Pilot in Command of the biggest, fastest, and longest range passenger jet in the world. To this day, I cannot fully describe the pride I felt at that moment—nor the "Thank you, God Almighty" I said in my thoughts.

CHAPTER

· TWELVE

SHADOWS IN THE SEA

Sharks, Tarpon and Savage Encounters

Day is just breaking on the Florida Keys. It's quiet, the breeze light. A typical spring morning, with the first flush of sun on the horizon promising a bright day. The tide is due in shortly. Conditions are almost perfect for tarpon fishing. February is a little early in the year, perhaps, since the giant tarpon, in excess of 100 pounds, seldom crowd into the passes before April or May. But I have caught them as early as January, and some big ones have been spotted in the channels around Key West.

I stop off at Big Pine Key to pick up Bob Beech, a young biologist who teaches at Sea Camp, and we drive the 28 miles to Key West in high anticipation, never realizing we are about to witness the assassination of a king.

We launch Bob's bonefisher skiff at the public ramp on Garrison Bight and head for a narrow flat near Northwest Channel, about five miles away. Tarpon are very sensitive to motor noise, so once there we shut down the outboard and switch on a little electric trolling motor, helping it along with a push-pole. We want to get close to the fish without spooking them. These tarpon, however, are not lollygagging around. Big ones roll onto the surface, slap their tails and dive for the bottom.

"The natives are restless," I say lightly to Bob. "Something has them stirred up. Usually, in this channel on an early morning tide, they are relaxed, feeding and you can see them slow roll as they break water, burble, and grab a lung-full of air."

"Yeah," he answers in awe, "but look at them. There must be five or six hundred in there." He stabs the push-pole into the soft mud flat and ties the bow to it. We begin casting, both using plug tackle, 15-pound-test line, white-and-red, Upperman-style, 5/8-ounce bucktail jigs. After 45 minutes, we haven't had a single hit.

"What do you think?" I ask finally, "Feel like cranking up and trying another spot?"

"Might as well," Bob says. "How about trying that permit spot you've been telling me about? It's for sure these fish aren't interested."

Just then, working my lure back, I feel a slight tap. Not a hard hit or a strike, but a light touch. Sometimes a tarpon does that. It will come up from behind, swimming just fast enough to engulf your lure, and close its mouth. All you feel is a tap or a stop until you come tight. I horse back on the rod and sock it to him, with three good slams–bam, bam, bam–to sink the hook into the tarpon's bony mouth. I feel the solid tug that says a big one is on the other end of the line. The warmth of adrenalin pumps through my veins in an instant, and I shout, "Yahoo, Bob! I finally got one of these critters to eat."

Line peels off my reel as the big fish hauls out into the channel. It jumps immediately, doing so again, its gills rattling, and I can see it is well over 100 pounds.

"Get your camera ready and maybe we can get some good jump shots," I say. But the fish won't come back in, instead insisting on staying as far from the boat as possible. I can't turn it.

"Never mind the camera," I instruct, "Pull that push-pole out and fire the engine up. We'll have to follow this fish before it takes all of my line."

Normally I can handle a fish this size in 30 or so minutes on plug tackle and 15-pound-test line, but there is no way I can stop this one. It is super tough. After about 40 minutes, the tarpon is closer to us, and when it comes up to grab a gulp of air in its rudimentary lung mechanism, I can see why this fish is extra-tough. The jig is snagged just behind its neck, a little forward of halfway between its head and dorsal fin. Somehow it has gotten hooked there instead of its mouth. With this kind of foul hookup it is impossible to guide the fish, turn it or exert any kind of control. When I pull toward the boat, the fish feels it in the middle of its back. No matter how much pressure I put on it, I can't do much to lead it to the boat. It moves toward deeper water.

Northwest Channel is 25 to 30 feet deep in this area and the big tarpon will sound, rush around on the bottom, then surge up to roll as it pleases. Finally, it turns toward the boat, and thinking the fish is yielding to my pressure, I yell for Bob to get his camera ready again.

"It looks like it's going to come up right next to us," I shout. Then I see the massive dark shadow. A monster shark is charging at the tarpon.

Both fish flash under the boat and suddenly there is a loud crash and a sickening lurch to the small skiff. The huge shark has careened off the bottom. I fall sideways, grabbing for the gunwale as the shark passes a yard away from my eyes, its powerful tail and dorsal fin swishing up out of the water – a massive hammerhead. Its grotesque, flattened, airplane-wing head swings into a sharp bank and it twists around, following the tarpon back under the boat.

Even with the hook in its back, the tarpon does a matador's job of avoiding the shark. As the big hammer closes in, the tarpon nimbly sidesteps, slipping away from the powerful rushes, turning, twisting, making the attacker miss by a quarter of an inch.

"Run at it!" I yell to Bob. "Charge the shark. Maybe we can scare it off."

A tarpon is agile, and a hammerhead, even though it's the most maneuverable of sharks, cannot simply run up and catch a healthy tarpon. I've watched tarpon out-turn, out-swerve, out-jump, and out-maneuver hammerheads and bull sharks, even after they've been hooked, released and nearly exhausted. This one, however, seems to be playing a losing hand. I reach down for my pliers to snip the line. If the tarpon needed help, a free rein would aid its escape.

The hammerhead, well over 14 feet long and crowding half a ton, has a single-minded goal: a tarpon dinner. It sweeps in incessantly.

Before I can cut the line, it suddenly went slack. The shark, missing a wild lunge at the tarpon, has simply brushed the 15-pound monofilament and its sandpaper hide has done the rest. We drive at the shark with the skiff, but that too fails to deter its freight-train charges. The monster is not to be frightened away by a mere boat not much bigger than itself.

"Keep shooting pictures, Bob. We might as well get some good pictures."

"I'm out of film," he answers glumly.

"Stay close to them," I encourage. "I'll get my camera."

Over my shoulder I see the shark rush at the tarpon, and this time the hammer connects, slamming the wide head into its side and throwing it six feet out of the water. As it comes down, the massive fish blasts the tarpon again, showering silver-dollar size scales into the air and littering the surface for yards around.

The punishment is taking a heavy toll. The shark now changes tactics. Almost leisurely it stalks the tarpon, sensing a kill. It edges ever closer until, only a few feet away, it dashes in, head swinging, to butt the courageous tarpon into unconsciousness. In seeming slow motion, it smashes the tarpon near the tail, in the belly, but it didn't yet take the tarpon head on. Finally, jaws distended, it moves in for the kill.

I at once feel the terrible helplessness of watching my favorite fish assassinated by a shark combined with the curious fascination of being involved in raw, natural spectacle of violence. We see the jaws snap once, and it is all over. It seems like half the tarpon has disappeared. The hammerhead sweeps past, turns in the blood-smeared water, and finishes the job with one gulp.

Nature's most effective and feared killers, sharks are a constant menace to anything in the sea, but certain species seem to favor tarpon as prey. Whether this is because the tarpon grows to a size that gives sharks their money's worth for the effort or some other reason, great hammerheads and bull sharks hover near schools of tarpon wherever they are found around the world, particularly along migration routes and spawning grounds. When a tarpon feeding frenzy occurs, sharks become a danger not only to the fish but to man as well if he gets in the way.

Fishing with Lee Wulff while filming a CBS "Sports Spectacular" TV show several years back, I suddenly see a shark rush in at a tarpon Lee had on. It is a greater black tip, an eight-footer, lean and fast, the same shark that is popularly known as a spinner shark. Lee quickly breaks his fly leader to give the tarpon a chance to escape. The fish is not exhausted and appears to have enough energy left to elude the predator's fearsome serrated teeth. The black tip rockets in so fast nothing can change the inevitable outcome. It slashes a big chunk out of the tarpon with one bite.

Writer A. W. Dimock, who recorded his catches of tarpon from a canoe in the early 1900s, recalls times when big sharks eyed his frail craft as though making a decision to attack either his hooked tarpon or himself. Though it never happened, Dimock said he felt, more than once, that the shark had measured him for a meal.

Another famous Keys guide, Captain George Hommell was guiding a young woman customer along tarpon alley behind Big Torch Key. The woman had hooked into a giant tarpon estimated at 200 pounds, certain to be a new women's world record on 20-pound-class line. After a long fight, the tarpon was close and George was poised to sink the gaff home. Just then, a tremendous hammerhead 18 feet in length came rushing up the channel between the flats. Without any hesitation, it nailed the tarpon right at the boat with one bite, shearing off one-third of the big fish. The giant hammerhead spun around and swam back to the bottom to swallow that portion.

George, as shocked and disappointed as his client, asked if she would like to have the rest of the fish – the head and remainder of its gigantic body – to mount as a memento. She said yes, so he heaved it into the boat before the hammerhead could get it.

As the balance of the tarpon was pulled from the water into his 16-foot skiff, the shark came roaring back and slammed into the boat's bottom with its back, then raised up alongside looking wildly, its eyes apparently searching for the rest of its fish.

George, fully aware of the danger from a shark that exceeded his boat in size, hit the starter button to fire up his 40-horsepower engine and get out the hell out of there. The hammerhead, not to be put off, grabbed the whirring propeller in its teeth and stalled the engine. Throwing the outboard in gear, Hommell hit the starter button again, and once more the shark clamped down on the prop. The third time, George turned the engine to high speed, hit the starter, and leaped away, getting the boat on plane immediately to escape the snapping jaws. He raced directly across the channel to a shallow mud flat and ran up high and dry. The hammerhead hung around for 45 minutes, cruising back and forth, trying to figure a way to get the rest of the fish. Blood streamed from its mouth from the propeller cuts, but this was little deterrent. The shark was ready to do battle with whatever had taken its tarpon.

Science has yet to come up with a reason for the head design of one of nature's monstrosities, the hammerhead shark. There are several different species including the common, great and bonnet head, and they are found in warm oceans all over the world. The great hammerhead stretches to 18 feet or more, according to fishing guides who have measured the size against their skiffs. In the 1940s, when commercial fishing for the vitamin A found in shark livers was big business, the hammerhead was highly prized. Its enormous liver was worth as much as $500.

Whenever I see a hammerhead shark, beginning in January and going on into July in Keys channels, I know there will be tarpon around too. It is a 100 percent certain clue. Hammerheads follow the schools of tarpon as they apparently detect a scent, and sharks have the most highly developed olfactory organ of any fish.

A hammerhead or bull shark, ready for a meal, will harass a school of tarpon by swimming around and around it until they're forced into a milling ball. The shark will smash into this concentration of fish, trying to injure one with its head or body or rake its teeth across one. In so doing, it will pick up the scent immediately. Swinging its head back and forth to locate the source, the shark will dog the injured tarpon as long as necessary – even 24 hours or more – until it wears down its prey and rushes in for the kill.

A 1,000-pound shark takes a lot of fuel to keep going, so a 100-

pound-plus tarpon makes a fine meal, a touch more satisfying; it would appear, than several 20-pound fish of some other species.

Bull sharks, greater black tips and duskies all are hell on tarpon. The dusky shark is primarily a pelagic, deepwater fish, which ranges from Africa to the Gulf of Mexico and New England, but it frequently swims right into the shallow flats after the schools of tarpon. A bluish gray on the back and white on the underside, the dusky reaches as long as nine feet and weighs up to 500 pounds. A dusky will attack swimmers, and is not scared off by a dozen humans.

Jim Kline, at that time a diver at the Miami Seaquarium, once had his diving helmet knocked off by an aggressive dusky, right in the shark tank, but wasn't injured. Phil Case, also at the Seaquarium in those years, didn't fare so well while transferring a nine-footer with a shark net. The shark crashed through the net and bit Case, then swung around and sliced Captain Bill Gray's leg open below the knee. The wound took 52 stitches to close.

In Costa Rica, the three main rivers where tarpon migrate far inland to spawn are the San Juan, the Colorado and the Parismina. January to May, and again in October, great schools of bull sharks harass and feed on the spawning tarpon.

Apparently adjusting readily to fresh water, bull sharks have been caught in the Atchafalaya River in Louisiana, 160 miles from the Gulf, and also in Mira Flores locks in the Panama Canal. Although the bull shark is also a true pelagic shark, it very closely resembles the world's only freshwater species, the Lake Nicaragua shark, a proven man-eater. Some scientists believe a monstrous overflow of the lake, eons ago, carried the sharks down to the ocean where they adapted to salt water. I prefer to believe it happened just the opposite, that bull sharks followed tarpon runs up the river, and adapted to fresh water before the lake became landlocked. They certainly don't mind shallow water or freshwater if it means a tarpon dinner.

Sports fishermen in Central America as well as in the Keys lose tarpon by the dozens to aggressive bull sharks. While not as agile as hammerheads, they are more aggressive.

At one time I was guiding Ray Donnersberger, trying for a fly-rod tarpon in the Metropolitan Miami Tournament. He hooked a very large one, around 150 pounds, in the Bahia Honda area of Florida Bay, when a big bull shark slashed in. I cranked up the engine and ran toward the shark, hoping to scare it off. It moved away, but turned and came back immediately to harass the tarpon. I brought out my .38 revolver and put several slugs near it, but the big bull kept coming back until finally it brushed the leader Ray was using, and broke off the fish. The tarpon zoomed away then, but we never knew if it ultimately escaped.

I haven't lost many tarpon to sharks because I've found that you can run the boat at them and, many times, scare them off. I have used the .38 a number of times, too, but usually nothing works once a shark has the scent of a tarpon on its mind. Tom Paugh, former Editor of *Sports Afield*, and I were tarpon hunting in the backcountry behind Big Pine Key and Little Torch Key, running from one point to another in four or five feet of water. I saw a large dorsal fin and wake up ahead, and ran the boat right up behind it. It was a big hammerhead, probably 12 feet long. The boat disturbed the shark and it started swimming faster to stay ahead of us. I eased the power off so we stayed just about on its back, keeping its tail just under the bow.

The shark was finning like mad to keep in front and I could see it occasionally turn halfway to look over its shoulder at us and swing its airplane-wing head back and forth. Then suddenly, after a few minutes of being followed, the shark whipped around, turning on a dime even at that speed, and in an eye blink crunched its teeth into the bottom of the boat. It knocked a sizeable hunk of gel coat off the bottom as it struck, as if to say, "Okay buster, get off my back or I'm ready to fight."

I veered off and let the shark go on its way, only too happy that it was also willing to forgive and forget. No doubt we could have outrun the shark if it had pursued us, but if we stayed to harass it further, there was no telling how the encounter might turn out. The hammerhead is one of the fastest-turning fish in the ocean. Its grotesque hammerhead undoubtedly lets it make a shorter turning radius, as well as giving it wonderful peripheral vision. Like an airfoil or a planing surface, the brute uses its head to bank steeply as a fighter plane, maneuvering after smaller and quicker-turning prey.

That shark is big enough, should it become enraged, to easily break the boat apart by crashing against the side, or swamp us with a few sweeps of its tail and cause the boat to sink. I decide that kind of play might not be too healthy. There are numerous records of sharks attacking boats, and winning.

A man named R. P. Straughan followed a big tiger shark in his little skiff off Miami a few years back, staying over it as the shark cruised along a shoal. The day was flat calm, so both adversaries could see each other clearly. Finally, the shark apparently became irritated at the chasing game and swam off about 30 feet, turned, and charged. It smacked into the boat dead center and lifted the stern clear out of the water. Straughan hung on, not knowing what else to do, and was terrified as the shark made pass after pass, and violently careened into the boat. Because Straughan ducked into the bottom, he thinks the shark could no longer see him, and finally left.

Charlton Anderson and a friend were fishing off the south coast of Florida when, without apparent provocation, a big shark rushed at their boat. It bit a hole in the bottom "as big as your head," according to Anderson. He stuffed a sweater into the hole and baled furiously until they could reach shore.

Sharks have the strongest biting power of any fish in the sea, as strong as 18 tons per square inch, yet most of them feed not by crunching but by grabbing hold and wrenching their bodies sideways, chewing, using the powerful muscles of their tails to twist and turn their heads. The whole fish is designed to bite, hold and rip chunks out of its victim.

Giant tarpon, even the biggest ones in the 200-pound range, are not a very good match for a bull shark or a hammerhead that weighs five times as much. Many tarpon are almost bit in half the first time a shark gets close enough to snap its fearsome jaws.

Roy Lowe, a well-known and gregarious fishing guide who was one of the very early tarpon guides in the Bahia Honda area, says he turned into a shark hater when he became a tarpon guide.

Roy often fished from a small skiff that he towed behind a larger inboard cruiser, and he carried a big shark rig on the boat. If a hammerhead or bull shark began to harass his tarpon, he'd slap a huge bait on a finger-sized hook, use a chain for a leader with half inch line, and fish for the shark. When it was hooked, Roy would bring it up close to the boat and dispatch it with a .30-06 rifle. Some sharks, he says, took a dozen shots before expiring.

Writers, from time to time, have been fond of endowing the shark with human attitudes and thought processes, but the fact is that sharks are even dumber than most fish. To put it straight, a shark is a real dimwit. The cerebrum, that portion of the brain we call the thought center, is highly developed in man and the great apes, and seems to be smaller as the need for reasoning diminishes. Fish in general have a comparatively small cerebrum, and sharks have the smallest of any. They are, however, magnificently designed to fit their element, the sea, and to eat. Like other predators, they sense weakness in their prey, and never hesitate to move in when ready for the kill. They have been around, by some estimates, as long as 40 million years, without little physiological evolution.

In the *Book of Tarpon*, published in 1911, A. W. Dimock tells of an encounter at Boca Grande, Florida, one of the great tarpon fishing areas of the world. "Untrammeled and fresh, the tarpon could play all around its foes, and by watching for danger signs I helped it escape when the fish grew weaker. I pulled the canoe quickly beside it to remove the hook and free the creature from danger. I was too late, for when within reach of my hand the tarpon rose half out of the water, its body already circled by those rows of cruel teeth that never give up their prey. The jaws closed with a crunch as the great fish swirled, dashing water and blood into my face. Then I saw that a second shark had swallowed the head of our quarry. I turned to the captain and said, "Cut that line, quick as you can. I've had all the shark I want for today."

Of all the tarpon I've caught, I've had shark harassment on about five percent of them. That doesn't mean, of course, that sharks were not around all the time. They are not always ultra-aggressive. The hammerhead that Bob Beech and I photographed was not overly aggressive as sharks go. It may not have been hungry at the time, but simply could not pass up a free meal in the way of a tarpon in distress.

Most fishermen are not really aware that a shark is after their tarpon until it's too late. All of a sudden the fish is hit, and just as suddenly it's over. Occasionally, though, even the most rapacious sharks are cheated, and a tarpon will survive to fight another day.

Not long ago I was fishing with Flip Pallot—one of the country's top anglers, TV personalities, and one of my best fishing partners—in the Sugarloaf Key area. Flip was polling at the time, and I was casting a fly to a very large tarpon. The fish took the fly and I set the hook to begin a marvelous aerial battle. It jumped half a dozen times, ran all over the bay, and was in and out of the water like the big, husky, hard-fighting fish that it is.

After about 35 minutes, I brought it to the side of the boat. Flip lip-gaffed it, a precaution that holds the fish but does not kill it. Then we saw that this very large fish had a wide crescent of scales missing on its side. It had previously been shark-bit but not during this fight because the wound had begun to grow new tissue and a large glazed area had formed over it. We guessed it had occurred two or three weeks before. The tarpon easily weighed more than 180 pounds, and the teeth marks formed a huge crescent on both sides, the bite area as large as a garbage can lid. I don't know if it could have been a huge dusky or bull shark, but it had to be much larger than any hammerhead I have caught, considering the size of those jaws. Perhaps it was a great white, but of course I'll never know.

Flip and I don't kill the tarpon because of the controversy that might have developed over its fighting ability after the shark bite, even though it was potentially a world record. Instead, we slipped the lip gaff out of its mouth and gave it artificial respiration until it was breathing strongly. With a helping shove, it swam off; a lucky tarpon that has not only escaped the worst predator in the sea but also survives an encounter with man.

Each new spring since then when I see the first signs of the tarpon run, with big ones stacking up in the channels around Key

West, I think of that big courageous silver king we let go. I sure hope it's still out there, somewhere.

CHAPTER

THIRTEEN

ENGINE OUT!

A Nasty Encounter at 31,000 Feet

Pan Am's Chief Pilot wanted to see me in New York. I had been doing training flights in the big new 747 and felt pretty confident about my performance. Not to worry.

I was surprised, however, when I learned the Chief Pilot had called me in to congratulate me: I had set a record for completing a type rating with the least amount of 747 expensive flight time of anyone: eight hours and forty-seven minutes. I later found out that I ranked eighteen in the world to receive such a rating, including the Boeing test pilots and the Pan Am chief pilots. It's good to be in on the ground floor.

The first eight months of operating the 747 proved to be quite difficult. The airplane was magnificent, with redundant backup systems. But the Pratt & Whitney engines had two major problems. One had to do with the stator veins malfunctioning and dumping the engine oil overboard, making it necessary to shut the engine down before running without oil – the result of which would cause the engine to seize or catch fire. Each of these engines cost more than $1 million dollars and the company obviously wouldn't take kindly to a crew that unnecessarily destroys one of them. The other had to do with the engine burner cans malfunctioning during takeoff power's high-temperature, probably because they were made from the wrong kind of metal. The immediate quick fix for this was to add water injection during takeoff, and whenever possible make a reduced power setting takeoff.

I can remember more than one takeoff from London's Heathrow airport on hot summer days, a full load of passengers aboard going to New York's Kennedy airport. I wasn't sure we'd clear the hotel outside the airport perimeter on our climb, and our butts probably chewed the material out of our seat cushion on those occasions.

On some Atlantic Ocean crossings, an airplane would end up with one engine shut down due to losing all of its oil, and sometimes another engine would be operating only with reduced thrust. Despite these glitches, there were no catastrophic happenings, thanks to the training and skill of almost all of the Pan Am pilots.

Starting my second year as a 747-rated First Officer, I did have a happening that I felt certain was going to cost me my job. The incident was unavoidable, and my actions necessary. But I stuck to the earlier vow that I had held steadfast though my aviation career: I was never going to let another pilot kill me when I was sitting in the cockpit, right seat or left seat!

Pan Am requires the Captain and First Officer to meet in the operations office to check the weather, routes and double check the fuel for the trip. Since getting a type rating on the 747, I made it my personal job to arrive in operations at least 30 to 40 minutes earlier than the Captain so I could do all of the necessary checking and paperwork before he got there. One of the reasons for doing this was that I knew my next step up the ladder probably would be as a 727 Captain, and I wanted to immediately feel comfortable in that position.

This is the first time I met the infamous Captain Smiling Jack, as he was called behind his back. His reputation as a grumpy, difficult captain preceded him. I heard that many First Officers called in sick when contacted from the reserve pool, if they learned the trip would be with him. I also found out through the grapevine that he had an extremely difficult time checking out on the 747. Just as in Vietnam with all the wicked rumors about Captain Wild Bill deLima, I can fly with anyone and make it a safe flight. In fact, Wild Bill and I flew together for almost four months before we parted under very friendly conditions. I felt I had earned a healthy measure of respect on his part.

Our trip this one particular evening to Paris Orly airport was scheduled for seven hours and 40 minutes en route flying time. In addition, throw in 35 hours layover time in Paris and probably an eight-hour flight back to Kennedy. But I figured it would be a piece of cake, as my chances of ever having to fly with Smiling Jack again are very slim.

Jack was very pleasant in operations and asked if I had been on the airplane very long. "Been on it for more than a year," I replied. "I was in the first-class back in December '69."

He raised an eyebrow when he noticed I had already made out our take-off performance data bug sheet. This 3-by-5-inch sheet showed our V1/Vr/V2 speeds along with the gross takeoff weight and total fuel on board. Maybe he was impressed, because while we were riding out to the airplane, he asked if I would like to fly the first leg to Paris.

"Absolutely, Captain," I replied, adding, "Thank you. I seldom get to make the takeoff and departure at Kennedy." I immediately dispelled all the bad vibes about this fellow, chalking them up to rumors one shouldn't believe until you find out for yourself.

My first job entering the cockpit was to program our present position, latitude and longitude in each of our three INS's – Inertial Navigation Systems. Once that is properly done, this fantastic system – the same one astronauts used descending to the moon – will navigate to each of the nine waypoints I'll insert along our route. Now the procedure is for the other pilot to check all the latitudes and longitudes of present position and all the waypoints.

It was a typical early November night with a mist-like rain blowing in the wind. The flight was sold out, and we were off the blocks and taxiing right on schedule, which is a little unusual with a full passenger load. Luckily this flight is scheduled to depart around an hour before the airport gets really busy with departures.

Jack was performing like an excellent co-pilot and we were airborne, doing a noise abatement climb, before climbing out to our assigned altitude. Jack was making a long announcement to the passengers over the P.A. and I engaged the automatic pilot, hooking it into the INS while I was handling the radios and making position reports. We encountered an occasional brief chop while passing through portions of the jet stream.

Prior to reaching a position overhead Gander, Newfoundland, we received our oceanic clearance and started our climb from 29,000 feet to our assigned altitude for the ocean crossing of 31,000 feet. And then the engineer informed us we are rapidly losing oil in number three engine. Almost in unison, Jack and I asked the engineer to swap gauges, to make sure it wasn't a gauge malfunction.

"Did that before I said anything," he replied.

"Keep a close eye on number three oil pressure gauge, and if the pressure starts to drop we'll shut her down," I said. "Jack, call Gander radio and inform them of our possible engine shut down, find out what their weather is and also check on Goose Bay's weather."

"We will continue across the Atlantic, even if we shut the engine down," Jack responded with a surly degree of authority.

About that time the flight engineer said, "The oil pressure is fluctuating and starting to drop. We'd better shut her down."

"Okay, let's do it by the book," I said in full command of the situation. "Abnormal checklist, engine shutdown."

With the engine shut down and secured. I asked Captain Jack once again to call Gander radio and get both their weather and Goose Bay, Labrador's, weather, and to tell them we are descending to 30,000 feet and returning toward Gander. With these words I eased some power off, starting a turning descent, and at the same time reached and turned the landing lights on to make us more visible to other aircraft.

Captain Jack grabbed the yoke with both hands, trying to stop me from turning the airplane back toward the nearest land.

"Damn it, Jack, let go the fucking yolk!" I screamed at him.

Still fighting me for the controls, he said we could at least go across the Atlantic to somewhere in Europe.

This was starting to become a dangerous situation, and I reached behind the right side of my seat to unlatch a water fire bottle. With a threatening motion I said, "Let go of the fucking yolk or I'll mash your head in with this fire bottle."

He could tell that I was dead serious and immediately released his grip on the yolk. I put the fire bottle along side my seat, just in case I had to actually make good my threat. Stopping our descent at 30,000 feet, I re-engaged the automatic pilot's altitude hold position, inserted present position direct Gander in the INS, and once again in a softer but still authoritative voice said, "Captain, please get on the radio and inform Gander Center that we have descended to 30,000 feet and we're returning to overhead and land at Gander airport. And while you're at it, find out their weather and Goose Bay's weather."

While leaving Kennedy airport, Jack informed me that this was definitely my leg and I was to fly the airplane, and he would handle the co-pilot and radio work. Now I reminded him of those words, saying, "Jack, you told me this was my leg and I was to fly the airplane and you would handle all the radio work. Now damn it, get on the radio to Gander Center."

While he was talking to Gander Center, my brain was telling me I had just committed mutiny on a United States flag-carrying international airline. At the very least I figured I'd be fired, and might also have to serve time in a federal penitentiary. But the thought quickly flashed in my head that at least I will be alive to be fired, not to mention more than 300 passengers on board who wanted to continue breathing as well.

The Gander and Goose Bay weather reports involved a heavy fog, and the nearest airport still open on the east coast of the U.S. was New York's JFK.

Now feeling in total charge of the situation, I said, "Jack, ask Gander Center for a clearance from our present position INS direct to New York, and at the same time find out where our next nearest operational airport is located."

That present position INS direct to New York came through almost immediately with a clearance to descend to and maintain 28,000 feet. The INS was indicating it would take us two hours and 40 minutes at our slower three-engine speed.

Each time we were handed off to another control center, their first words were, "Clipper one fourteen, I understand you have one engine shutdown, is that correct? And would you like to declare an emergency at this time?"

The first time we were asked if we wanted to declare an emergency, Jack looked over at me and I said, "Negative, tell them if we have to shut another engine down, we will then declare an emergency."

The weather at JFK had deteriorated since our departure some hours before; it was still above my minimums, but below Captain Jack's minimums for having less than 100 hours operating the 747.

After receiving our first descent clearance from New York Center, Jack asked if I would like to make the ILS approach and landing, to which I replied, "Yes sir, I fully intend to bring this big bird back to JFK in one piece."

Now I leaned toward my left and suggested that he make a quick announcement to the passengers, who would think we are descending to land in Paris, and to briefly tell them why we are landing back in New York.

Right after receiving the information on what runway was in use at Kennedy; I briefed Jack and the flight engineer on the ILS and possible missed-approach procedure, and completed a descent checklist.

Breaking out of the clouds about half a mile from the runway on final approach, we were cleared to land. Because our shutdown engine was inboard, the approach and landing was considerably easier than it would have been if we had an outboard engine inoperative. A shutdown outboard engine would have created a great deal of yaw.

Pan American Operations had all of the available ground personnel waiting at the gate to greet the passengers as they disembarked. I never did find out what they did with more than 300 passengers. My job was finished for the night – and maybe forever. As tired as I am, I doubted that I would have a good night's sleep worrying about my future. My only consoling thought: I'm alive to fish another day, even though I may not be allowed to fly again.

As the days passed, I waited for the other shoe to drop, for that phone call from the Chief Pilot's office telling me to make myself available posthaste.

The week went by slowly, without a word from the Chief Pilot or the Director of Flight Administration's office, so I showed up at operations in uniform for my next scheduled flight. While walking to operations from where the crew bus dropped me, I ran into the one and only Captain Smiling Jack. He actually crossed the street to greet me, asking how I was doing.

He started off by saying, "Stu, I didn't get a chance to tell you, but you did a very good job making a three-engine instrument approach and landing."

Beaming and relieved, I said, "Thank you very much, Captain, it was a difficult night."

He then went on to say that in a conversation with the Chief Pilot earlier that day he had confirmed that we indeed should have continued across.

I guess I got a little red in the face. "Let's take a quick trip to the Chief Pilot's office now, and if that is what he thinks, I have been working for the wrong airline these past 15 years," I said with no small measure of defiance.

"I don't have time, Stu," he said quickly. "So let's just forget the episode."

I nodded, but felt positive that in fact Jack didn't say anything to anyone about what happened. If he had, I'm sure it would have at least drawn an inquiry from somebody.

That was the last time I saw Captain Smiling Jack. A couple of months later I heard he took early retirement, and that bit of news didn't disturb me – and I'm sure many others at Pan Am – a bit.

Photo Section

A setup postcard picture 1931 on Miami Beach. I was 8 months old and my brother Marvin was six years old. (Preface)

1944 my brother Marvin is home on his first leave after more then a year in the Pacific. At 14 years old I still had an angelic look. (Preface)

1947 Senior year picture at Gordon Military College in Barnesville Georgia. (Preface)

April 1955 Stu at home on a 10 day leave. (Preface)

My fantastic parents. The best anyone could ever hope for.
(Preface)

My parents on a fairly late in life cruise. (Preface)

Stu's Preflight graduation picture. (Chapter 1)

Young Stu Apte,Navel Aviator. (Chapter 1)

A division of F9F Panther Jets in right-hand echelon for a carrier break. (Chapter 1)

Stu with three acquaintances from Portsmouth naval hospital (Chapter 1)

Certificate designating completion of the SAC survival school.
(Chapter 1)

We had 30 in our original preflight class and less than half of
them ended up getting their wings. (Chapter 3)

Stu as Cadet Officer of the Day (COOD) in Preflight
(Chapter 3)

SNJ's in left echelon formation during primary flight training at
NAAS Saufley (Chapter 3)

Lieutenant "Shaky" Spiel, the best LSO that brought me aboard the carrier. (Chapter 3)

SNJ landing on USS Monterey. (Chapter 3)

Stu on the left with two other cadets during F6F Advanced training. (Chapter 3)

F6F Grumman Hellcats on the U S S Monterey , waiting their turn for a deck launch. (Chapter 3)

F6F Grumman Hellcat on the catapult. The most difficult thing was to release the brakes while seeing nothing but water in front. (Chapter 3)

Cat-shot F6F Grumman Hellcat from USS Monterey. Notice the short distance to get airborne. (Chapter 3)

YAHOO! Finally made it... (Chapter 3)

We sure looked young. That's an F9F-2 Panther Jet in the
background. (Chapter 3)

Stu checks out some of the Navy's new radar equipment during his last assignment on active duty as an instrument instructor. (Chapter 3)

The Four Sportsmen 1957, tackle testers for Pflueger and Ted Williams tackle. Bill Curtis, Coral Gables fireman Jerry Kirk, Ed Luise and Stu Apte (Chapter 4)

One reason tarpon come first. (Chapter 4)

Bringing in a brace of snook to prove it is good fall fishing.
(Chapter 4)

Young Stu with a wooden push pole. (Chapter 5)

1960, Stu's Navy guide picture. (Chapter 5)

Joe Brooks's world record tarpon that pulled me out of the boat twice. (Chapter 5)

May 1961, Stu in the water with Joe Brooks's world record tarpon. (Chapter 5)

Joe's 120 pound tarpon succumbed to too many retakes.
Standing, Al McClane and Joe Brooks. Squatting, Jimmy
Albright and Stu Apte (Chapter 5)

1962 Stu sitting under Joe Brooks's world record tarpon.
(Chapter 5)

April 1962, Ray D. helps Stu bring the Metropolitan Miami
Fishing Tournament winner into the boat. (Chapter 5)

Polalo worm and one of my worm flies from 30 years ago.
(Chapter 6)

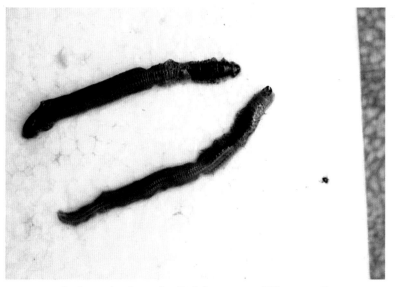

A closer look at the Polalo worm. (Chapter 6)

Rare picture of a water spout during the Bahia Honda worm hatch. (Chapter 6)

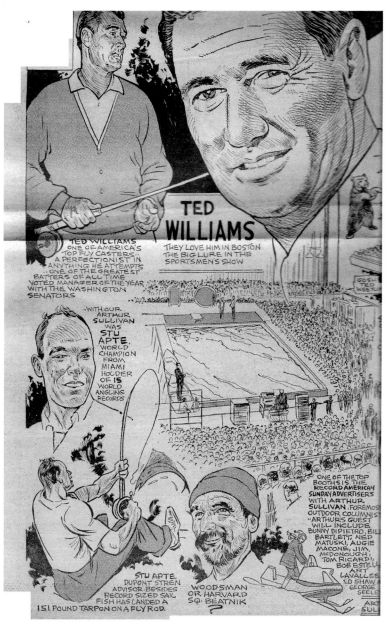

Boston newspaper 1970 Ted Williams and Stu Apte (Chapter 7)

TW and SA at New England Sportsmen Show (Chapter 7)

Ted and Stu managed to catch this bonefish on a windy winter day. (Chapter 7)

Louise Kaufman, Ted's lady friend that stood by him through a couple of wives. (Chapter 7)

TW and SA with bonefish photographed by Louise Kaufman. (Chapter 7)

They caught a double grand slam, two permit, two bonefish, and two tarpon in the same day. They kept these to be mounted as a memory of this fantastic days fishing. (Chapter 7)

Ted's 18 pound permit that won the Metropolitan fishing tournament spinning division. (Chapter 7)

Stu and Ray D. with 154 pound record tarpon. (Chapter 8)

Scotty Yeager happy with mixed emotions (Chapter 8)

Stu and Ray D. hauling aboard the Metropolitan Fishing
Tournament flyrod winning tarpon. (Chapter 8)

We carry plane loads of pilots and ground personnel. What a
feather in a VCs cap to sabotage this bird. (Chapter 9)

A sleep of exhaustion while returning to Vietnam after 10 days
of a well deserved R&R in Hong Kong. (Chapter 9)

A Marine F8U Crusader landing at Da Nang. (Chapter 9)

A B-57 Canberra fueled, armed and ready to go on a mission at Cam Rahn Bay. (Chapter 9)

My flight engineer engineer Paul Reinders eyeballs the whole
fueling procedure. (Chapter 9)

Bernice and Gretchen Reinders pose with the Taipei aborigine
ladies. (Chapter 9)

Best to travel the busy streets of Taipei in a bicycle driven
rickshaw. (Chapter 9)

9 April-66

Dear Stu,

By now you can believe that I am damned weary of adhering to an opinion contrary to yours and then being forced to admit that you were right, to wit: I insisted that the airplane with the stack fire at TAIPEI airport was a C-46; you said it was a C-47; it was a C-47. You said you saw terrain go by the plane when I said it was impossible because of our position (2 MILES South of TPE airport) and our altitude (1270') at the time. You saw it; there is an uncharted hill 1230' high exactly on track of our pull-up procedure. WE HAVE MADE 4 DEPARTURES DIRECTLY OVER THAT HILL BECAUSE OUR JEPPESEN CHART DOES NOT CORRECTLY REFLECT ITS PRESENCE. TWO PLANES HAVE ALREADY HIT IT (USAF & CAT). But no one has told us of it. Yesterday I made the first day

T.C. of my life from ~~TPE~~ and got the scare of
my life when I saw where we had been. Any
kind of wind component would have arranged
a mass funeral. Notams are now out and
I am writing a crank letter to Jeppesen.
Apparently a cruel fate is saving us for

Capt. Stuart Apts
% Pan Am – Piston Crew
Miami International Airport
Miami – Florida
U.S.A.

Sender's name and address
Bill de Lima
THE EMPRESS HOTEL
KOWLOON / HONGKONG

AN AIR LETTER SHOULD NOT CONTAIN ANY
ENCLOSURE; IF IT DOES IT WILL BE SURCHARGED
OR SENT BY ORDINARY MAIL

The Flying Geese Aerogramme Form
Printed by HING SHING PRINTING FACTORY
Form approved by Postmaster General Hong Kong No. 2068

BY AIR MAIL
PAR AVION
AIR LETTER
AEROGRAMME

an ignoble death in our dotage during a
fight in a whorehouse. Sorry I missed
saying goodbye.
But I will now. Goodby
Bill.

Captain Bill de Lima's letter from 1966 Pages 1 and 2
(Chapter 9)

The first evening at the Manari Ranch, Stu artfully ties a fly using Christmas tree tinsel that catches the big one, while Kay Brodney and some kids watch. (Chapter 10)

Our little outboard struggles while towing the supply boat. (Chapter 10)

Maurice Barlow stirs the pot while Bernice preparers a delicacy
in our home away from home. (Chapter 10)

Peter lifts my 65 pound arapaima that I had to lip gaff myself.
(Chapter 10)

Kay does a great job lip gaffing Peter's first and only arapaima.
(Chapter 10)

Kay Brodney and Peter Gorinsky inspecting my arapaima.
(Chapter 10)

Stu and his crew hoist the ariapima up for a picture.
(Chapter 10)

At 161 pounds it was almost too big to weigh.
(Chapter 10)

Pan Am's 747, sometimes called the aluminum cloud.
(Chapter 11)

A partial view of the 747 gauges. (Chapter 11)

Suddenly there is a loud crash and a sickening lurch in the small skiff. (Chapter 12)

This time the hammerhead blasts the tarpon again, showering silver dollar size scales littering the surface for yards around. (Chapter 12)

This time the hammerhead connects, slamming its wide head into the tarpon's side. (Chapter 12)

Finally, Jaws distended, it moves in for the kill. (Chapter 12)

Another nice black marlin. (Chapter 14)

Aye mate it's a grander. (Chapter 14)

A monster black marlin. (Chapter 14)

You know you have a grander when the blood runs out of your glove. (Chapter 14)

It jumped out of the water but can still be dangerous.
(Chapter 15)

Jerry and Guide Fernando pleased with the results of a nice
catch. (Chapter 15)

Hey Stu we've got another nice one. (Chapter 15)

Release him gently, Jerry instructs Fernando. (Chapter 15)

Alfonzo's right-hand man happily displays my catch to the camera. (Chapter 16)

Alfonzo Alvarez caught the sibling of my roosterfish. The only two rooster fish caught in three weeks of fishing. (Chapter 16)

JoJo Del Gurcio doing his thing on Australia's black marlin.
(Chapter 17)

JoJo fighting a black marlin. (Chapter 17)

Jo Jo's marlin makes another jump. (Chapter 17)

And another jump. (Chapter 17)

The first of many salmon on the trip. (Chapter 18)

Stu tails an average Laxa salmon. (Chapter 18)

Jim Chapralis looks at his Laxa salmon as he wades to the bank.
(Chapter 18)

Both Stu and his gilly are pleased with landing this nice salmon
in the waterfall pool. (Chapter 18)

The dark clouds and rays of sun on Stu's salmon and face give it a dramatic look. (Chapter 18)

Stu admires a nice sea run brown trout caught in one of the holding pools. (Chapter 18)

Hey Jim, how much do you think this one weighs (Chapter 19)

Stu gently releases a nice brown trout while his guide Jim
Loudin watches. (Chapter 19)

Some of South Island's rivers were lined beautifully with wild flowers. (Chapter 19)

Stu admires a nice brown that was duped by a number 18 dry fly in one of the South Island Lakes. (Chapter 19)

Left to right, The General's pilot, Stu, General Torrijos and Bob Griffin. (Chapter 20)

General Omar Torrijos and the leading female officer in the Panamanian Army. (Chapter 20)

John Havlicek with his wife Beth on the left and my wife Bernice on the right. Photo taken by the ABC film crew after I was whisked off the airplane. (Chapter 20)

John Havlicek takes advantage of a rainy day for his first wahoo (Chapter 20)

Getting ready to run to the fishing grounds. (Chapter 20)

Finally, we are off on our first and only day of filming.
(Chapter 20)

Jimmy Lynch wires Flip while Dick waits his turn. Pat Smith and Bruce Buckley seem preoccupied in the other boat. (Chapter 22)

Dick Butkus relaxing. (Chapter 22)

Stu and Dick watch the teasers as Flip scans the waters for fish. The original name of the boat was Wet Dream, which ABC would not allow. (Chapter 22)

Stu and Flip making wahoo ceviche. (Chapter 22)

Dick teases while Stu stands ready to cast a fly. (Chapter 22)

Dick looks down at the teaser while Stu works his fly and Flip
watches. (Chapter 22)

Flip bills Stu's sailfish as Dick Butkis looks on, putting icing on the cake during an ABC's American Sportsman filming. (Chapter 22)

Stu and Dick are happy after a successful day filming, putting icing on the cake. (Chapter 22)

Left to right Bernice, Joe Brooks, Mary Brooks and my German Shepherd Worry, early 1960s. (Chapter 23)

The first Fall in our log house. (Chapter 23)

A herd of elk walking single file in my front yard. (Chapter 23)

My wolf dog Lobo felt right at home in Montana.
(Chapter 23)

Curt's grousing with the camera crew has everyone laughing. From the left Jason Miller, Curt Gowdy, camp owner Henry Norton and Stu Apte. (Chapter 24)

Sometimes like throwing 5 gallons of water. (Chapter 25)

A gill rattling jump right next to the boat. Up-up
(Chapter 25)

And away! (Chapter 25)

Every jump a different one. (Chapter 25)

Is this one the 200 pounder! (Chapter 25)

Part of the happy crew of stewardesses just boarding clipper flight 801 for Tokyo as one of my two flight engineers watch. (Chapter 26)

A map of Russia's Kola Peninsula. The eye of the upper fly is
pointed to Murmansk and the eye of the lower fly is pointed to
Umba. (Chapter 27)

The Umba eight in Murmansk Russia. Starting on the left is
Randy Moret, Sandy Moret, Stu Apte, Bud and Ted Berger,
Dave Robinson, Dave Beshara and Steve Zuckerman.
(Chapter 27)

Our first look at this World War II vintage airplane that was to take us to the Umba, had Randy Moret asking if it was safe. (Chapter 27)

Shaking our Aeroflot captains hand, I also wished him good luck. As Dave and Randy said cheese for the camera. (Chapter 27)

The only outboard powered boat in the area causes us both frustration and anxiety at different times. (Chapter 27)

We caught lots of Atlantic salmon this size. (Chapter 27)

Dave Beshara didn't mind fishing late. (Chapter 27)

Our group getting ready for what became an almost nightly
dinner of either Atlantic salmon soup or potato soup, followed
by boiled salmon, for a fine dinner. (Chapter 27)

Dave Robinson with one of his first Atlantic salmon ever.
(Chapter 27)

I enjoyed teaching these Russian children how to cast a fly.
(Chapter 27)

General Schwarzkopf and Stu Apte--A good team. (Chapter 28)

General Schwarzkopf and Captain Sean O'Keefe. (Chapter 28)

Stu congratulating General Schwarzkopf on a job well done--
kicking butt on a triple digit fly rod tarpon. (Chapter 28)

Wade Boggs and Stu Apte with Wade's 38in. snook.
(Chapter 28)

Stu and Carl Yastrzemski YAZ, at the New England Sportsmen
Show (Chapter 28)

Stu and Ken, The HAWK, Harrelson New England sportsmen
show (Chapter 28)

Stu and Miss Massachusetts Cathy Munroe 1968 first runner-up Miss America (Chapter 28)

Stu and Carl Yastrzemski, YAZ at the New England Sportsmen Show (Chapter 28)

Tarpon Alley West growing to meet Bernice's needs. (Chapter 29)

Mary Hamilton in front of my Bozeman Montana townhouse.
(Chapter 30)

Mary Hamilton happy with her first bonefish caught fishing
with me and my dear friend Captain Steve Thomas
(Chapter 30)

A happy camper on our first trip to Tropic Star Lodge in Panama. (Chapter 31)

Jeannine still thought this dinner party was to celebrate our first anniversary of living together. (Chapter 31)

I finally got everyone's attention. (Chapter 31)

Jeannine was speechless and dumbfounded when I said, "Will you marry me?" (Chapter 31)

Paul and Helen Wingrove congratulate Stu on making a wise choice. (Chapter 31)

Some of the instigators of this wonderful night Ginny and Dick Campiola with young Richard in front, my pseudo-son José Wejebe, Bette and Dave Beshara. (Chapter 31)

Left to right... Kay Ford, José Wejebe, Stu and Jeannine, and the man who married Stu Apte, Pat Ford. (Chapter 31)

She's on her own....almost! (Chapter 31)

Jeannine being attended to by her daughters, Cindy and Lynda
(Chapter 31)

Part of my newfound family, Lynda on the left and Cindy on
the right. I have truly been blessed (Chapter 31)

Our son-in-law Terry Adams gave Jeannine to me. (Chapter 31)

Apte clan; Sitting left to right Elsa, Marvin, Steven, Debra.
Standing left MG, Linda, Stanley, Laura, Stu, Jeannine and
Tasha (Chapter 31)

A German chocolate wedding cake shaped like a tarpon
(Chapter 31)

Yes my darling I will love you forever.. standing behind, our
oldest daughter Lynda, my good friend Pat Ford who performed
the ceremony and my older brother Marvin. (Chapter 31)

The bride cuts the cake. (Chapter 31)

Just two kids in love... (Chapter 31)

CHAPTER

FOURTEEN

THE ONES THAT GOT AWAY

They're Gone…But Not Forgotten!

About 100 years ago, a poet named Eugene Field wrote this about fishing:

> *I'd never lost a little fish,*
> *I'm free to say;*
> *It always was the biggest fish*
> *I caught, that got away.*

I know how he felt. Although I'm fortunate to have fished all over the world and caught many incredible fish, the mental images of countless equally incredible fish that got away never leave my memory. This includes a potential world-record, giant tarpon suddenly disappearing into a swirl of foam, a monster brown trout sliding slowly back into a trout stream, a neon-flashing blue marlin throwing the fly and refusing to take it again, and monster sailfish, bonefish and bass I have lost.

The disappointment, frustration, and even rage of those moments come back to me now, along with a kind of satisfaction knowing that I did my best under the circumstances. It's a strange, warm feeling that emanates from fishing itself that's all about the challenge. If I knew that every big fish I hooked would be landed, the whole pursuit would take on all the excitement of a visit to the corner drugstore.

Considering all the ones that got away from me, my clients

and fishing companions, I ask myself if perhaps destiny influenced which fish was landed, and which was lost. Was fate in control? Or perhaps we influence fate itself by learning from our failures and having our more-experienced hands ready for future challenges.

The answer may be yes and no. Some fish are lost due to overconfidence, inexperience, or simply the angler's failure to take the situation in hand with confidence, authority and without a moment's hesitation. Some fish become lost due to equipment failure such as broken swivels, hooks or rods. Other fish get off the hook or break off due to freak accidents. And sometimes the only answer is, as the then Editor-in-Chief of Outdoor Life, Lamar Underwood, told me, "Some things are just not meant to be." This, perhaps, is one of the more important aspects of fishing to take to heart – you are going to lose fish and they're going to be big ones. The lost fish, quite commonly the biggest ever hooked, continues to grow in the memory of the hapless fisherman, and gradually becomes one of the most important fish of his life.

You can argue that the bigger the fish, the bigger the disappointment in losing it. Take the giant black marlin off Australia, for instance. Peter Bristow is a fishing captain widely known for the granders he catches hereabouts – marlin weighing over 1,000 pounds. In Cairns at the beginning of the 1977 spring season, Bristow weighed in his 100th marlin over 1,000 pounds.

While granders are certainly quite a feat, fishermen have a grander dream – becoming the first person to catch the one-ton marlin, a 2,000-pounder. The 1977 season was the best in the memories of those who fish the Down Under black marlin fishery. Point in case, Bristow's client Jo Del Guercio landed 77 marlin in 21 days of fishing, including four fish that weighed 1,000 pounds or better, and six others estimated at 950 to 1,050 pounds, all tagged and released. Jo Jo's granders weighed 1,176, 1,196, 1,245 and 1,323 pounds. But the largest one, of course, got away.

"It was the only fish that ever frightened me," confides Bristow. "We hook the fish at four in the afternoon and its strike is simply terrifying. We're trolling away from the sun, and it appears as if a king mackerel is jumping over the bait. But no, it's the bill of this giant fish appearing. About six feet later its dorsal comes over, and what seems like ages the tail goes past. It is horrifying."

The mammoth fish crashes the bait and slowly swims away, taking line, traveling due east. After 10 minutes, the fish stops and comes to the surface and just lies there, raising and lowering its dorsal fin. Black marlin are so large they have few enemies in the sea, and even the giant tiger sharks gives them a wide berth unless they're sure the marlin is almost dead and cannot use its awesome spear. Bristow, by this time, has backed the boat close to the fish, and Del Guercio winds double line on his reel. It is time for the wireman to grab the heavy wire leader and pull the fish close enough to gaff. Bristow stands on his flying bridge, shouting instructions.

"Then the fish decides to jump," he relates. "It jumps three times at the stern not more than 10 feet away in three positive moves. First it strikes its bill out and stops, it strikes its head up and stops, and two-thirds of the fish come out of the water. As I said, it's 10 feet from the stern to us, at a right angle."

"I'm standing on the bridge and looking straight at the fish's eyeball, and there's still a third of the fish in the water," he continues, the excitement consuming him as he envisions the moment. "The girth is at least 10 feet because I imagined putting my arms across a side of the fish and wrapping them around it. It is monstrous."

The huge black marlin sinks slowly back into the water, then rises up again, three times. The wire man, stunned, just stands there looking at it. Del Guercio, who has caught numerous marlin over 1,000 pounds, is speechless. Bristow, who personally has taken five marlin over 1,200 pounds, is awestruck.

"Del Guercio asks me what I thought, and I say let's take a shot," says Bristow. "If the damn thing's going to lie on top, let's take our chances. You may never see that thing again. It's like a whale."

Bristow begins to back the boat closer to the giant fish, leaving a relatively inexperienced man on one of the gaffs. They slam the first flying gaff into the fish just across its hump. A perfect shot, but the second gaff man, the inexperienced one, hesitates a second too long. The fish takes advantage of the lag and surges, turning the coil of leader wire lying on the deck into a kink. The wire breaks, and suddenly the fish, which has been so docile, becomes a raging monster. It dashes itself against the pull of the gaff, hauling the boat backwards.

"The second gaff man just stands on the cockpit with the second gaff in his hands while the other deckie is yelling that the wire's broke," Bristow recalls. "Everyone is stupefied. I want to go back, shorten the gaff rope, cleat it off, and get the second gaff into the monster fish. But the fish decides to go down."

Within seconds, Bristow weighs the question of putting the boat in gear and ramming ahead to drag the fish up again, but fears it will rip the gaff out. He hesitates, momentarily, and the fish begins to move. The seas are heavy with a 15-knot wind. The boat is being dragged backwards at about eight knots into the swirling, heavy seas. Water begins to surge over the stern, and in the blink of an eye, two feet of water floods the cockpit.

"I'm ready to get off the bridge and cut it loose," Bristow says. "It's like being towed by a whale; the most frightening thing I have ever been through. Then, in a half a minute that actually seems like half an hour, the fish rips itself away from the gaff."

Conservative estimates put that fish between 1,500 and 2,000 pounds, and Bristow laments the seconds of indecision that perhaps cost them the prize. But Bristow puts it philosophically: "It's a sport, and you can't accuse anybody of failing to doing something. But, if we'd been more aggressive, we'd have gotten that fish. There was a chance at first of getting a second gaff into the fish, but the crewmen hesitated for just one second. He missed his chance. He didn't have another one. Neither did I. It was the worst experience I have ever been through and never want to experience it again."

Bristow could not talk on the VHF radio for two hours afterward. "I still wake up in the middle of the night just thinking about that fish."

Missed fish can cost you more than records. When your catch's poundage determines the outcome of a tournament, it can mean lots of money going down the drain. Such occurred at a Bass Master Classic, the Super Bowl of freshwater fishing where the country's top professionals compete three days for a $100,000 prize.

To put the kind of skill required for this type of competitive fishing event into perspective, the fisherman has to move into strange territory, practice for eight or nine hours, and be able to find the proper depths, cover and schooling patterns of native largemouth bass. It also takes a measure of luck, even for top pros like Bill Dance, Roland Martin, Tom Mann and Paul Chambley, to fish three days and win. The Master Classic is an invitational event whose participants must be the top scorers in six other tournaments. But the prospect of a $100,000 winner-take-all purse puts big-time pressure on them, too.

Bill Dance recalls how he once fished the classic at Clark Hill Reservoir on the Georgia-South Carolina border. "I go over a place to establish a pattern, but it's difficult when I know four or five baits might work but I like to fish just one. I try the Timber King Spoon and start taking fish. Everything starts coming together on the plus side. I have a lot of confidence in my lure, the pattern and my ability. When a fisherman is fortunate enough to get all that together, he's lucky. It's a rare feeling."

Fishing every type of cover, Dance mixes it up from shallow to deep water, the points, the ridges, the underwater humps, and finally, "stumbling into an area that is loaded with fish."

He begins to catch bass as quickly as he can cast. Not big bass, but large enough to amass tournament points. By the first day's end, the weight of his limit of 10 bass puts him among the top finishers. The next day at the same spot, Dance begins scoring again. In spite of some motor trouble costing several hours, in 10 casts he catches six nice bass that at the day's closing puts him in third place.

It's the last day of the classic, late in the afternoon, and Dance decides to hit the same area. He continuously catches so many bass he sets a yet unbeaten record, a 10-bass limit every day of the classic. As he is fishing feverishly, Lee Wulff happens by with a film crew for one of the tournament sponsors, and begins shooting footage of Dance taking fish after fish. With his 10-fish limit in the live well, he begins culling while fishing in water 37 to 42 feet deep. This resulted in a sort of musical chairs as Dance catches a fish and searches his live well for a smaller one to release.

It takes time, but suddenly a big fish of about five pounds strikes. "But I'm playing to the camera, not concentrating hard enough to catch the fish or paying attention to what I am doing," says Dance. "I pressure it too hard, and the fish jumps, shakes and throws the hook not six feet from the boat."

All that dramatic fight is filmed. The camera crew moves off, and Dance still has a half hour to better his score. On an impulse, he asks his partner to try the engine – it's dead. Just then, another boat passes, and with a variety of frantic signals, Bill Dance's team manages to flag it down, transfer Dance's fish, and make it back in time to beat the clock.

The final weigh-in shows Dance with 48 pounds, 14 ounces of bass, good enough for second place. Ray Breckenridge with 52 pounds, 8 ounces takes top honors and the hefty check of $100,000. Do the math and you'll see that Dance's five-pounder would have clinched the championship – making it a $100,000 bass that got away.

"I still see that fish in my mind a lot," Dance laments. "I've lived that last half hour over and over again. But what I learned that day was far more important. Fish the deeper areas close to where I find a school. Always. If I had fished all three days in the deeper water, my total would have been larger. And plenty of times since then that's paid off for me. It was a hard lesson, but worth it."

And yet, missing a fish you wanted very badly can actually make you feel a lot better if it greatly benefits someone else. That's happened to me more than once. At the tiny Caribbean island of San Salvador, I was on the charter boat Flying Fisherman trying to find new territory to fly fish for blue marlin. What we found may amount to a hitherto unknown blue marlin fishery at the Eastern Bahamas edge of the Atlantic.

As close as a quarter-mile from shore, Captain Rick DeFeo begins raising marlin. The barrier reef there drops off about 60 feet before plunging over the edge to 2,000 feet of crystal-clear blue water. Late in the morning, we raise a small, wild blue marlin that's really lit up and eager. My fly rod is rigged with a floating shooting head that has 12 feet of high-density sinking tip attached to an 8-

foot leader with 18 inches of 15-pound-test tippet and 11 ½ inches of 100-pound-test bite tippet tied to a popping bug. At this time, no one has ever caught a blue marlin fly fishing and I hope to be the first.

We stop the boat and tease the marlin in close. I begin to false cast as the marlin lunges wildly after the mullet teaser, lit up like midnight blue neon. My fly lands a foot away, and I chug it one time. The marlin crashes it as though starving to death. I set the hook three times, and the marlin, 45 feet from the stern of the boat, comes up shaking his head. On the fifth shake, the small hook pulls loose. But the fish does not leave. It continues to charge around the boat, looking for its mullet.

I try over and over to interest it in the popping bug, which the fish damaged badly, but it will not take again. Finally, I tell Pete Rayner, known as the Flying Fishermen because of his aerial traffic broadcasts on the radio in Miami, to try the fish on spinning tackle because that's never been done either. Since I could not turn the trick with a fly, perhaps he can with spinning tackle.

The hook-up is almost immediate as Pete drops in a small mullet on his 12-pound-class spinning outfit with 14 feet of 200-pound-test leader. He sets the hook, and the blue takes off on a sizzling run but stays within 100 yards of the boat. It sounds to about 200 feet but does not go farther. It surfaces 50 yards from the boat and tail walks back and forth across the stern. Bill Noll, the mate, is ready with the eight-foot gaff, and in seconds that fish is landed. A relatively small blue at 102 ½ pounds, it is nevertheless the first blue marlin entered for the International Spin Fishing Association record. So, what's lost by one fisherman can be gained by another.

In thinking about that fish, I am happy and proud that even though I didn't catch it, someone else did. If I had another chance at it, I would not do anything differently than I did that day. Perhaps, as some down-home philosophers might say the lesson of fishing is that all human beings, particularly anglers, need to learn that what they want most is simply sometimes not meant to be. As Herbert Hoover so aptly put it, "All men are equal … before fish."

BLACK NIGHT FOR THE SILVER KING

Things That Go Ker-Splash in the Dark!

It is black. Ebony. Total darkness, only the night, and you.

And the fish: the giant tarpon.

Of all the places I've fished in my lifetime, few have more of the "Old Man and The Sea" flavor of fateful necessity than Parismina, Costa Rica. At times I feel like I can walk across the water on the backs of rolling tarpon. But this time, it is even more compelling. Night fishing for silver kings on a wild jungle river brings with it elements of danger, apprehension and anxiety – even outright fear. It's a blood-pumping adventure that rivals any roller coaster ride.

The big river rushes past me in the pitch black. I brace my feet solidly to fight the stiff current as the black volcanic sand disappears upriver into the crouching jungle trees. Low-lying clouds hang overhead and blot out the riotous display of Venus and the Milky Way. I hold my hand two feet from my eyes and see nothing. I'm not afraid of the dark, but in all my travels, I have not experienced this kind of dark before.

The Parismina River sluices out of the jungle to a 150-yard-wide mouth pouring into the sea. It is fresh water; its small delta has built a natural breakwater between its steady outflow and the wide Caribbean Sea. That breakwater, a few hundred yards away, halts the incoming seas only momentarily. Big waves crash over the shallow sand bottom and surge into the deeper river mouth, forcing a constant battle between freshwater and saltwater as tides and currents vie for fleeting supremacy and bring food to its denizens.

The mouth of this river is a long way from civilization, with not even a distant glow of city lights to instill a sense of security. The realization of not being anywhere near help in the event of an emergency is at once exhilarating and consuming. Jungle crickets chirp fitfully, and it's the only sound I hear except the gurgle of water around my legs and the distant crash of surf against the sandbar. The water's turmoil occasionally rolls a dim phosphorescent light across the horizon, the only visual reference that up is not down.

I squint in this infrequent phosphorescence to glimpse my fishing partners and guide in silhouette, who I'm supposing still stand less than 50 feet away. At that moment a sudden bump against my calf terrorizes me. Is it that bushmaster I saw in this area earlier in the day or a deadly fer-de-lance caught up in the swift current? I slap at whatever it is, feeling the solidness of a mahogany branch that elicits a gasp of relief so guttural I can only suppose that any self-respecting jaguar in the area immediately hauled ass in the general direction of Nicaragua.

But my relief is short lived. I sense that the shallow water where I'm standing extends only a few feet before dropping abruptly to 10 feet, which only serves to revive my growing paranoia of the ghostly surroundings. But a tentative, hesitant tap on my line distracts me. A giant tarpon has come up from behind and inhaled my Wiggle Diver lure. I haul back on it to set the hook once, twice, three times, and feel a solid stop. I smack it again, and suddenly the water explodes with a fury that sends droplets showering over me. Dark as it is, the giant body looms up in glistening flight above the black water, and the bizarre jangling of its rattling gills resonates in the jungle.

"Bueno," my guide shouts, "sabalo grande." Here he's been standing behind me all this time and I didn't realize it.

After a bewildering battle, during which I blindly ran up and down the surf where at the time I teeter-tottered at the edge of the drop-off, the big fish finally succumbs. It's every bit of 110 pounds, and I hope beyond hope when releasing it that I won't hear the commotion of exploding water around it, signaling that a big hammerhead just finished it off. Luckily, there's only the cricket chirping as the great animal revives after a brief rest and pulls out of my grip to swim away, with no damage done on either side of the line.

These big tarpon, none smaller than 40 pounds and few larger than 140, herd themselves into the river mouth in numbers so great that at times it's hard for the average human to imagine. The tarpon are followed into the river mouth by sharks: schools of big bulls and hammerheads ranging to 800 pounds or more. It's certainly not a dive zone unless one has a death wish.

All day I have been fishing with host owner Jerry Tricomi in what's called the California Lagoon where we've scored heavily on big silver kings. As we dock our boat at the ramp, I overhear Miguel, one of the young guides, talking about the night before. I whimsically ask him about the fun at the local cantina. No, he says seriously, he's doesn't have senoritas on his mind at the moment, only fishing at the Parismina River mouth at night for sabalo.

But Miguel shyly admits there's a problem: The tarpon have taken all his favorite lures, and to be able to fish, he'll have to borrow some. I quickly fill the ensuing silence with a promise that I'll share anything in my tackle box for a chance at those nighttime monsters.

That night, we gather on the beach. Jerry, Miguel, Fernando, another guide and I parcel out the lures: Nickelure white bucktails, Magnum Rapalas, and big gang-hooked Creek Chub Wiggle Divers. Armed with a plug rod and 17-pound-test line, I see that the guides are using heavier 25- to 30-pound test on big spinning and heavy-duty plug-casting tackle. We spread out along the black sand beach, ready to be surprised.

On my first cast, gradually getting used to working totally by feel, I have three hits before I can react and hook a single fish. The big tarpon need not strike hard for their food; they simply swim up behind something and close their bowling-ball-size mouths over a tidbit. So, unless the fisherman is completely alert, the silver king recognizes something is amiss and opens its huge maw again, dropping the lure before the fisherman's reflexes have a chance to act.

Next cast, another fish grabs my lure. It's a big one. How big I'll never know, as not wanting to stick around and fight, the massive poon simply turns and swims away, its tail insultingly waving bye-bye.

Before I can reel in my third cast, I feel the light tap that the silver king initially makes. I strike it hard, zapping the hooks to it with three backward jerking motions, and the fish swirls in a circular pattern to burst out of the water in a fearsome leap, gills rattling wildly, drenching me with water. The phosphorescence in the water bathes it in a greenish, eerie light, and it appears like a sheet-covered skeleton dancing in the black nothingness. I feel the chills racing up and down my spine. I have to remind myself that I am fishing, not witnessing some strange voodoo nightmare.

The fish crashes down and submerges, putting massive shoulders into the line pull as it starts to follow its brothers out to sea. With 17- pound test, I have little chance of turning it unless I resort to some trickery. I give it the old down-and-dirty treatment. Instead of holding the rod high and letting the fish lean down against the pull, I shove the casting rod tip down into the water and fight against the pull with a downward and sideways motion, in effect tripping the fish.

It rolls under and comes back jumping, spraying the ocean with the cold light of a million fireflies, then crashes back and heads seaward again. I use the same trick, stomping down hard before it can get up a good head of steam and waltz away with the line. Soon, it is beaten and lying exhausted in the surf. Fernando wades in with a release gaff, snags the lower jaw, and extracts the plug.

Taking the plug from a tarpon in the 80-pound range can be a ticklish operation. If the fish lunges at the wrong time it can do a turn-about and spear you with those treble hooks. From a painful experience I had in Key West a few years ago, when a tarpon and

I were tethered together this way and the fish continued to thrash wildly, I can tell you that it's no fun being gored in such a manner.

Fernando releases the tarpon but it continues to lie there in need of a long rest or a helping hand. He walks it along the beach to aid in respiration, and finally the fish recovers enough energy to swim away. Whether or not it later became a sharks' dinner is anyone's guess, but likely once it survives the first few minutes of release, it's probably home free.

Next, it's Jerry's turn to hook into a big one. However, this brute isn't desirous of any beach blanket bingo games. After two feisty jumps, its shoulders set and away it saunters, pausing only momentarily over the breakers 200 yards out before plunging off into the inky depths. We surmise that the normally effective Albright knot has failed due to a bad tie, no doubt caused by Jerry's disorientation in the super-black night while tying it.

The dangers from a popped line are negligible, but a thrown plug blasting back at you through the air can be extremely dangerous. The big, saltwater Wiggle-Divers weigh about 1½ ounces and armed with two sets of over-size, super-sharp treble hooks. A big fish writhing out of the water with its head shaking violently makes the plug a lethal weapon when it's shaken loose. The plugs often shoot out of a fish's mouth with slingshot force and have been known to rip out eyes, sever throats and lodge in unmentionable places.

One fish does almost that to Fernando. I make a long cast along the river and the current bows my line so far I cannot feel where the lure is. As I quickly retrieve, a tarpon grabs it. I zap it, all hell breaks loose, and the fish erupts in a six-foot jump. Instead of surfacing where I think it will, however, it explodes out 50 feet away from me but only a dozen feet from Fernando. I feel the line go slack, hear the gills rattling, and Fernando's surprised shouts. I figure the fish impaled him with my plug, but then he laughs and starts yelling about being nearly drowned – this big'un inundated him with about 40 gallons of water, and Fernando stood there as if a winning football coach just doused with a bucket by his players.

Eight minutes later, another tarpon chews right through the 100-pound-test mono leader on my casting tackle, and gains its freedom without having to go through the entire fight. We would have released it anyway, as we do all tarpon not entered for record. Poons aren't that good to eat – fortunately for them – and the biggest thrill is winning the fight and releasing them unharmed.

We catch so many fish that evening in a two-hour period that when the other rancho guests hear our stories, they insist on joining us the next night.

Even 25-pound-test line won't stop some 100-pound fish when they decide it's time to vamoose. And it can be a devil of a job to budge one that turns its side to you and "dogs" in the strong current, refusing to get off dead center. The usual way is to pump high, reel down quickly, and try to gain a few feet of line. This can wear your arms to limp noodles in no time. So, when Jerry hooks into a particularly stubborn specimen, he doesn't try to pump it in against the tide and current. He simply walks backward up the beach away from the water, slowly enough to not pull any line off the reel. This pulls the fish in closer, at which point Jerry runs forward to the water's edge and reels furiously to gain line on the reel. He wins the battle and ultimately lets the tarpon resume whatever the hell it was doing before making the mistake of chomping Jerry's offering.

The following night, we build a big bonfire high up on the beach so we can see, but not close enough to scare tarpon. Four guests join us on the volcanic black sand, and just as with us, these new adventurers quickly recognize a big difference between daytime tarpon hunting at Parismina. Indeed, by day anglers fish wide lagoons where there is no current; it is sight fishing to rolling fish where they pick out the fish they want and cast to it. They stay in a boat where the guide can paddle if the fish strays to the end of the line, or he can crank up the engine and follow the fish until it tires. At night, on the other hand, you may be on the beach but you're much closer to playing by the tarpon's rules, not yours. You can't follow the fish, and it can use its strength, speed and the currents against you. You're fighting much bigger odds, and the only way to come out on top is to strike fast, fight hard, and give it all you've got.

A little knowledge about tarpon fishing doesn't hurt, either. Muscling those giants to you with the down-and-dirty technique makes the big fish roll under and come up sputtering. I imagine it disorients and confuses them in much the same way the night does us anglers.

By day, the scenery is exotic, some of the most beautiful tropics I've ever witnessed. All around is raw jungle: exotic, hypnotic, eerie sights and sounds and scents. Birds of all colors flash and screech; spider and howler monkeys appear everywhere; the occasional grunt or scream of a jaguar brings your mortality to the fore. And at night, all your senses are on fire. But most of all, there is tarpon, sabalo, silver king ... that's the greatest essence of Parismina to me.

CHAPTER

SIXTEEN

A PARADISE LOST

Fishing Exploration—Plus a Rendezvous With Nicaraguan Kingpin Anastasio Somoza

In the early 1970s I was living in Miami again while flying full time for Pan Am. When I answered the phone one day, the voice on the other end gave a Latin hint, even though his English was flawless.

The caller was unknown to me. Alfonzo Alvarez, on a trip to Miami from his home in San Salvador, had looked up my phone number in the Miami directory. Our conversation started with the formalities of an introduction and he got right to the subject: Was I interested in coming to San Salvador to do some exploratory fishing in a beautiful area on the Pacific Ocean north of El Salvador called Bahia De Jiquilisco?

To me there are not many things more exciting and rewarding than exploring new fishing grounds, so of course I expressed great interest in hearing the details. I invited Alfonzo to stop by my house.

"Mr. Apte, those are the words I had hoped to hear from you." He confirmed my address and said he'd be over within the hour.

"May I call you Alfonso?" I answered. "Your coming over is fine, but first I must tell you that Mr. Apte is my dad's name, so call me Stu."

Forty minutes later, a taxi pulled into the cul-de-sac in front of my house and a well-built, well-dressed gentleman stepped out. As he approached, I walked out the front door, extending my right hand. His handshake and greeting was warm and he said, "I don't want to take too much of your time…ah…Stu." So I asked the taxicab driver to return and pick me up in one hour, if that's all right."

"Of course, that will be just fine," I replied, holding back a grin at his pronunciation of my name – it had sounded like a sneeze. With a motion of my arm, I said to come in and meet my wife Bernice. Sitting in the living room, we immediately got down to the business at hand. Alfonzo owned a large property with numerous cottages in an area just 45 minutes flying time from the international airport in the capital city, San Salvador. He was very flattering when he said that my reputation preceded me and he'd like to hire me to come to Jiquilisco Bay for one week at a time during the four different seasons of the year. He agreed to provide a boat and supplies to fish the whole area so I could hopefully assess whether the fishing was good enough for him to start the first fishing lodge for American tourists in the country of El Salvador. And before I could give him an answer, he said he would fly my wife and me to San Salvador and then have his pilot fly us to Jiquilisco for a look at the facilities.

Wanting to know how generous Alfonzo was going to be with payment for my time and effort, looking straight into his eyes, I said, "I will need $1,500 per week, a total of $6,000 for the four weeks, plus all expenses."

"Not a problem…ah…Stu. If we have an agreement, I will give you a check for half of it now."

"We do have an agreement, Alfonzo, and I would like to take you up on your offer to have Bernice and me fly to San Salvador to have a look at the facilities. I'm a pilot with Pan American World Airways, which gives me great traveling privileges – often for free if I ride the cockpit jump seat. That will certainly help on the expenses"

"Yes…ah…Stu, I did know of your position with Pan American. I have checked and found out many things about you, probably more then you can imagine. I will be back in Miami two weeks from today, and at that time we should set a date for your first visit with your wife."

"That sounds good to me," I said, adding, "I will make a list of questions about the types of fish, other fishing people in the area, rivers and inlets, to name a few right off the top of my head. Hopefully we can spend a couple of hours together, making plans."

"I can tell by the way you think, you are a professional and do not fool around," Alfonzo said seriously, looking right into my eyes.

Just then, the taxi driver rang the doorbell.

"Ah…Stu, I am very pleased with our first meeting," he said, as he reached into his pocket, taking out a blank check.

"Let's take care of the money when you come back in two weeks," I replied.

"That's fine, Señor. I was told that you are a man of integrity, and I see that it is so. I will see you two weeks from today. Here is my card, with phone numbers where you can reach me. I'll give you a call sometime before then."

Six weeks later Bernice and I were met by a uniformed chauffeur as we left the Pan American 727. He asked for our passports and baggage claim stubs, motioning us to follow him through immigration and customs. We waltzed through immigration, having our passports stamped, without slowing our pace. This is the way to travel, I thought. When we got to the baggage claim area, both of our bags were brought to our uniformed mentor. I didn't even recall seeing him give our claim stubs to anyone; talk about efficiency.

I had been to San Salvador many times since I started flying to Central America in early 1956 with Pan American, but I rarely had the privilege of spending the night. This made our 40-minute drive through the city into a suburban area all the more interesting. As we approached what appeared to be a large area fenced in with razor wire, a high metal gate was pushed open by one of two armed guards.

As we drove through I was slightly taken aback with the idea of having to have armed guards for protection. I could tell by her concerned look that Bernice's was wondering the same thing.

Leaning a little closer to her, I whispered, "It's probably a typical case of the haves and the have-nots. Don't worry about it – I'm sure we are in good hands."

About a quarter of a mile down a road inlaid with bricks and lined on both sides with beautiful flowers and interesting trees, we rounded a curve to see an extremely large, castle-like house. Alfonzo was standing with his beautiful wife Sonia just outside the eight-foot, carved, inlaid double doors. He motioned us to come on in.

I've been privileged to be invited into many mansions in the United States and abroad, but I have never seen a house like this one. It sported a temperature-controlled, three-foot-deep stream running through the foyer, living room and under both of the curved marble stairways that went from each side of the room to the second floor. Fish were swimming in the stream – not mere goldfish, but various sizes of very healthy rainbow trout.

After being shown to our luxurious bedroom and bath, we were invited back down for cocktails and an appetizer of jumbo shrimp cocktails. That preceded a dinner of broiled stuffed lobster and filet mignon surrounded by roasted asparagus and sweet, fried plantains.

Wow! I thought, if this is how the other half lives, send me in coach, I'm ready to play this game for sure.

Our trip to Jiquilisco was wonderfully uneventful and relaxing. Alfonzo's facilities there would certainly be sufficient to initially handle 14 anglers quite comfortably if the fishing was good. I recalled that in 1964 I described to Carlos Barrantes in Costa Rica what I considered the three important ingredients necessary to having a successful fishing lodge to attract American anglers: great fishing, great food and comfortable accommodations.

I was sure Alfonzo could provide great food and comfortable accommodations. Now, the big question became whether the most important item in this stew – the fishing – would be up to snuff. And, of course, that's what I was there to find out.

My first full week of fishing was not very productive, even though Alfonzo provided me with his favorite fishing guide. Knowing there are times of the year everywhere in the world that fishing can be poor; it had me thinking that this might be an off time for fishing in this area. Or maybe it was the new moon phase or some other factors.

Three months later I planned my second trip over the full-moon period, and Alfonso informed me he would like to accompany me to try his hand at fishing. Things were looking up; on our first morning I caught the biggest roosterfish I had ever caught. We then fished hard the rest of the day, catching only a few jack crevalle, some very small snook not even a foot long and some unwanted gaff-top catfish. This was certainly not the type of "great fishing" I had hoped for, to merit hard Yankee dollars.

The next day was more of the same, but without the excitement of catching a large roosterfish. Back at the dock I informed Alfonzo that the next morning would be the beginning of some true exploratory fishing, and we would need to carry extra fuel. Before leaving Miami for this trip, I located and purchased a United States Navy Geodetic Survey chart of the area.

A couple of hours before sundown we were sitting on the veranda enjoying delicious little deep-water conch, raw and submerged in some sort of black liquid. As bad as this looked, it took some coaxing and teasing to have me try the first one. After that, I probably ate a dozen of those half-dollar-size critters, washed down with ice-cold beer. Suddenly a large helicopter swooped right over the top of us, so close I almost dropped my bottle.

"What the hell!" I exclaimed. "Who's that?"

Alfonzo stood up, clapping his hands, saying, "Anastasio said he might stop by to spend the night and meet you. I'll tell our chef Jose that we have an additional special guest for dinner."

"Special guest, huh," I said with disbelief in my voice. "And who might that be?"

"Why, it's Anastasio Somoza, of course, the President of Nicaragua."

The helicopter must have made a fairly quick reconnaissance of the estate before coming back to land on an area specially cleared for such occasions. Three heavily armed men dressed in combat uniforms jumped out. Quickly separating, each seemed to know exactly where they should go. Then a medium-size, nicely dressed man stepped out, followed by whom I assumed was the pilot.

I was so fascinated by the happenings at the helicopter that Alfonzo had covered 50 of the 75 yards to the landing pad before I even knew he was gone. It was obvious they were old acquaintances by their handshake and pat-on-the-back salutation. After exchanging greetings, Alfonzo and Anastasio strolled back, followed by the pilot and two of the guards.

Placing my almost empty bottle of beer on the table, I stood up as they approached, facing directly toward them. Alfonzo made the introduction and, standing at attention, I bowed slightly from the waist saying, "Con mucho gusto, Señor Presidente."

Somoza offered his right hand with a firm handshake, extending some sort of greeting in Spanish that I didn't understand. Feeling a little embarrassed, I asked Alfonzo to please apologize for my inability to understand very much Spanish. But Somoza answered in almost perfect English before Alfonzo had a chance to relay my thoughts, and thereafter the rest of our conversation thoughtfully occurred in my native language.

The sun was just starting to set when someone suggested a before-dinner cocktail. That's right up my alley, I thought. Turning to President Somoza, Alfonzo said, "What is your pleasure, Anastasio?"

Without any hesitation he snapped his fingers, pointing to one of the guards and sending him to the helicopter for a special bottle of rum. I did understand the Spanish words for special rum, but little else. The guard would have been a pretty good running back, the way he hightailed it to and back from the helicopter with a bottle enclosed in an attractive cloth container.

Must be something pretty special, I thought. I had started drinking rum during my Navy flying days at Guantanamo Bay, Cuba, and almost considered myself a connoisseur. Looking at me with a smile, Somoza asked, "Stu Apte, do you ever drink rum?"

"Yes sir," I replied. "Rum is my favorite liquor."

"I'm glad to hear that, because I believe I have a special treat for you. Alfonzo, three glasses please, with some ice water on the side."

Carlos, one of Alfonzo's servants, had the glasses and the ice water on the table even before he made the request.

The easy way Somoza twisted the sealed cap from the bottle was an indication of his hand strength. He then handed the bottle to Carlos who was standing behind my chair, and with his thumb and forefinger spread about three inches, without saying a word suggested that Carlos should pour rum in everyone's glass.

"Before you taste this rum, Stu, please do me a favor and just inhale its bouquet."

Alfonzo stood up, holding his glass high and making a toast in Spanish, to which I stood up as well. We clinked glasses all the way around. Somoza correctly knew the fragrance of his rum would win my approval. The smooth, full-bodied flavor was even better than the aroma.

"Mr. President, that is undoubtedly the very best rum I have ever tasted. Now I understand why you asked for ice water on the side in case anyone gets thirsty. This is truly what I call sipping whiskey. May I see the name on the bottle, sir?"

"But most certainly, it's Flor de Cana; the English translation is Flower of the Canyon. But what you are drinking is Directors Stock, aged for 25 years."

"Is it possible to purchase this rum anywhere?" I asked the sound of hope in my voice.

"It's only available in Nicaragua. We are not producing enough for export yet, and the 25-year-old Director Stock is not for sale anywhere at this time. But I will get your address from Alfonzo and see what I can do for a fellow rum aficionado," he said with a chuckle.

Alfonzo's chef did an outstanding job preparing a dinner of super-sized shrimp and broiled lobster tails. Talk about roughing it – I'll drink to that, and I did after dinner. We polished off the bottle of Director Stock, sipping it like an after-dinner drink with our coffee.

By 9 o'clock we said our good nights and went to our individual cottages. Still sporting a slight buzz from the rum, I felt just a little bit rocky in the shower. Not wanting to get too wide awake, I did a very fast shower, laid out my clothing for the morning, slid between the sheets and was quickly deep in slumber land.

The sound of a helicopter getting airborne was the first thing I heard after closing my eyes. Thoughts jumped into my head … did something happen? Is it morning already? Quickly rolling out of bed, I could see that it was first light. My cottage was facing west so the morning sun wouldn't disturb me.

Glad that I laid out what I was wearing today, I quickly brushed my teeth and washed my face and hands. In five minutes I was out the door, still wondering where the President's helicopter went and why Carlos didn't wake me this morning like he had in the past. At breakfast, Alfonzo said President Somoza asked him to please relay his regrets for not joining me this morning. He received a call on the single sideband radio from his palace in Managua, necessitating his early departure.

I thought for a moment about what I had learned about Somoza. How he had been educated at St. Leo College in Florida and LaSalle Military Academy in Long Island before graduating from West Point in 1946. He was unofficially the 44th and 45th President of Nicaragua from 1967 to 1979. However, as head of the National Guard, he effectively ruled as a dictator.

[I was to never again meet up with Somoza, and in 1980 I felt a twinge when I heard that he was assassinated while exiled in Asunción, Paraguay, dying from gunshots fired into his Mercedes Benz limo by a group of leftist guerrillas from Argentina.]

But that morning my mind flickered back to the business at hand. "Alfonzo," I asked, "is it possible to have Jose make some sandwiches or whatever for us to eat on the boat instead of coming back here for lunch? I'm not sure how far we will run today looking for areas not heavily fished."

"No problem, what would you like?"

"A peanut butter and jelly sandwich, some of your delicious melons cut up, a quart of water and some plantain chips would be just fine."

We were in our boat and running 30 minutes later. I always feel a little adrenaline flow whenever I'm going to fish somewhere new, and that day was no exception. I guess being optimistic is part of being a fisherman, otherwise we would never leave the dock.

My optimism dwindled as the day grew older. Every tributary and every little bay had stakes pounded into the soft bottom. When the tide was high, the local natives would paddle out in their Cayugas to attach a long net extending from one shoreline around to the next. When the average 15-foot tide recedes, all fish regardless of size, between the stakes and the shoreline would be trapped. Now I was starting to understand the lack of good sport fishing in the area.

Back at Alfonzo's compound, I casually asked how many shrimp boats were in his fleet. Twenty-two, he replied; half of them drag their nets in the daytime while the other half drag during the night. "Tomorrow, I'll take you down to my quick freeze, packaging and shipping operation."

Unbelievable is the only way I can describe his operation. He must have had 40 people working in the areas where the shrimp first come in on electric conveyor belts, passing through an area being hosed off to eliminate seaweed and the likes, through an automatic sizing process where they get separated from the ones that were to be beheaded, shelled and de-veined. They all ended up in an area where they were quick-frozen at -30 degrees.

Everyone working in this large building wore white pants and white long-sleeved shirts, and what appeared to be a rubber apron and white, calf-high rubber boots. At the entrance to the building you must walk through a six-inch trough of bleach water to make sure your boots are clean.

Alfonzo's operation was approved and periodically inspected by the USDA because most of the shrimp were shipped to the United States under the label of Camarones EL Presidente [The President's Shrimp].

As far as I was concerned, the sport-fishing operation for American tourists Alfonzo hoped to provide at Jiquilisco Bay was not looking very good. At first I could not imagine not having an abundance of game fish in such a remote area, but with his vast shrimping operation, dragging the areas just offshore day and night, their nets taking thousands of fish along with the shrimp each day, it became obvious to me what had happened to the inshore fishery. The few fish surviving the shrimpers' nets would only end up caught in the local native's stake nets. And the lack of shrimp as forage reduced the presence of predatory fish.

Alfonzo had to go back to San Salvador and said he would send his plane to pick me up at the end of the week. But going out each morning was no longer giving me the rush of adrenaline. For the rest of the week I did catch some roosterfish, one unfortunate 12-pound snook that somehow escaped the nets, a few very small snook and numerous jack crevalle.

Back spending the night at Alfonzo's palace in San Salvador before catching a morning flight to Miami, I seriously broached the subject that with his fleet of shrimp boats operating day and night, there will never be the type of inshore game fishing to attract American anglers. I gave him the option of my not returning for the scheduled next two periods of exploratory fishing, but if he wanted me back for one more shot at it, I would like to bring another great fisherman friend. We could cover more areas quickly during each good fishing tide and use walkie-talkies to keep in touch. He was in full agreement to my last-ditch stand of coming back with Captain Ralph Delph as my assistant.

Three months later when Ralph and I arrived, we were met and whisked through immigration and customs via limo to Alfonzo's house, where we would spend the night.

Alfonzo did have a surprise for us. It was near harvest time on a big rice farm to the northeast side of Jiquilisco Bay. Evidently their crops have been getting decimated by thousands of white-wing dove every morning, and Ralph and I have been invited, along with the Italian Ambassador to El Salvador, to participate in a dove shoot that was a double-edged sword: One edge was helping slow down the crop's decimation, and the other providing hundreds of dove for the big Harvest Fiesta in the nearby village. [The shoot was scheduled to take place later during our visit]

When we were asked what type of shotguns we prefer, I replied that I shoot two 20-gauge, Beretta BL-4's with an improved and modified choke at home, so anything similar would be fine. Ralph quickly added, "How about a 12-gauge Remington 1100 with a modified choke and no plug, so I can get the maximum amount of shells in the magazine?"

The next day at noon found Ralph and I together, running in one of the boats at Alfonzo's compound in Jiquilisco. Ralph probably has the best nose for finding fish I have ever seen. My plan was to give him a brief look around the area that day, then each head out on our own, meeting back at the compound for lunch. I figured that between us, if there is any reasonable fishing in the area, we damn sure should be able to locate it.

This was our routine for the next four days, without having any more luck than I had previously. Now, more than ever, I was convinced that Alfonzo should give up his idea of promoting the area for American fishing tourists. It was a very serious conversation at the dinner table, when I told him he'd have to give up his fleet of shrimp boats if he ever expected to rejuvenate the inshore fishing.

"Impossible!" Was his sharp reply.

"I can understand where you're coming from, but you are paying me to tell it like it is," I said softly but firmly.

"Yes, yes…ah, Stu, it's just that I was hoping … All right, you tried and I am most appreciative of your honesty."

"Please, enjoy your dinner and after I will show both of you your shotguns for tomorrow morning's dove shoot."

You can believe Ralph Delph enjoyed his dinner. I have never seen anyone eat as many jumbo shrimp as he did, washing them down with cold beer. After dinner we walked to Alfonzo's cabin for our first look at the shotguns we would be using. This was going to be one serious dove shoot, as we would each have two shotguns and a case of shells. When I unzipped the gun case I was extremely pleased to see I'd be shooting a matched pair of 20-gauge Browning shotguns with improved/modified barrels.

Ralph had two of his requested 12-gauge Remington 1100s and an unopened case of shells. We would each have two young teenage boys to help, with one picking up the birds and the other reloading the empty shotgun.

We were awakened extra early the next morning and had a quick cup of coffee and a piece of toast before getting airborne in Alfonzo's twin-engine airplane while it was still black dark outside. We made a quick 15-minute hop across the bay to a dimly lit gravel landing strip where the Italian ambassador to El Salvador had just landed with his charter flight.

Alfonzo made the introductions and then quite descriptively told us to be prepared because the sky was going to get black with dove. He described it like an eclipse of the sun.

We had to hustle along for about a quarter of a mile, going through a gate and then being stationed at fence posts 100 feet apart as it was beginning to dawn. Everything had been done perfectly, the case of shotgun shells was open, both of my shotguns were leaning against the fence post, and my two helpers appeared to be so eager they were almost bouncing up and down.

I did a quick instruction for my loader/helper on how I wanted him to put shells in the chambers and hand me the over/under shotgun with the barrels still broken. This was an important and very safe way of handling a loaded shotgun.

Ralph remarked, "Here they come." The Eastern sky was now glowing with light orange and yellow streams of light as Ralph slid five rounds into his autoloader's magazine. I watched numerous dove fly over my head ghostlike, heading to the rice fields for their morning feed, before I brought the shotgun to my shoulder and fired twice, bringing down two of the fast fliers.

Quicker than I would have imagined, I was finished with my second box of 25 shotgun shells when it seemed to be over. Leaning the shotgun on the fence post, I stepped back to look around and noticed both Ralph and the Italian Ambassador were doing the same. That was a fantastic shoot, but not quite as good as the sky getting black with dove. I figured these people just have a tendency to exaggerate.

Then it happened. Like a gate being opened, thousands of dove came out of the mangroves, heading for the rice fields in such thick flocks that they actually obscured the sky. This had both my loader and retriever jumping up and down pointing at the sky, hollering in

Spanish before I got back to work with my Browning.

One hour later, sporting an empty case of shotgun shells and a very sore shoulder, this amazing dove shoot was over almost as quickly as it had begun. We had provided enough dove to be one of the main courses at tomorrow's village fiesta, and most certainly helped save some of the rice crop.

While the idea of having a fish camp died, I suddenly realized that this area would be incredible for wing shooters. But being a fishing dude, that thought slid from my mind as I gazed out the window of Alfonzo's plane on the way back to his mansion. It had been a good try. I'd experienced a most interesting adventure in El Salvador and in meeting Somoza, and actually didn't feel that unhappy about it all. After all, I'd kept my end of the bargain to the fullest.

Two months later when I returned home from a Pan Am flight, Bernice said that the day before a limo pulled up to our house and dropped off a case of Special Director stock rum as a present from Anastasio Somoza. I hoarded those 12 bottles of 25-year-old Flor de Cana for more than 10 years before the last bottle was gone.

And each bottle brought back many memories.

THEY'RE BIGGER DOWN UNDER

Cheers, Mate, for Giant Black Marlin

Half a world away, the land Down Under is a menagerie of great differences, of weird and wonderful animals, of a barrier reef that stands 50 miles offshore and runs 1,200 miles, and unusual species of fish with strange sounding names.

To the average American angler, lunkers mean bass that weigh 10 pounds or tarpon of 100 pounds. But at the Great Barrier Reef of Australia, the biggest of the entire world's game fish dwarf these species into insignificance. The South Pacific's giant black marlin tips the scales at more than 1,000 pounds. Fishing for them is a once-in-a-lifetime thrill and the first sighting is a never-to-be forgotten experience.

Come along, and you'll see what I'm talking about:

The spear breaks water first, waving menacingly over the bait, and the awed senses of a stateside angler are mocked by the size of the thing. It is not the slender, graceful rapier of the sailfish that every saltwater fisherman covets to decorate his mantelpiece. It is the thick, blunt, baseball-bat size cudgel of glowing ultramarine blue, driven by an underwater torpedo the size and speed of a ski boat. It is a giant black marlin. A Grander – a fish weighing at least

1,000 pounds – black marlin is incredible, a neon-flashing, dark blue game fish.

The bill rises up and a frantic two-pound baitfish is swallowed like a tadpole to a 20-pound bass. The angler counts four, five, six, up to 10 seconds during his free-spool drop back, then hears his captain shout, "Lock up!" He throws the clutch on his huge Fin Nor reel to its striking position and braces himself to absorb the crunching pull of the 45-pound drag. He winds as fast as his arm will turn as his captain bolts the diesel engines forward to set the hook. In the sudden surge, the giant is tethered, struggling at the long end of the 130-pound-class line. The ultimate trophy, the Grander, is only as far away as the angler's stamina and skill will allow it to be. From then on, it's a matter between fisherman and fish.

This year, the Australian capital of marlin fishing, Cairns, weighed in its 100th giant of over 1,000 pounds. The all-tackle record is 1,560 pounds, but even that figure is not the mark modern anglers seek. Instead it's the big one-ton black marlin – the 2,000-pounder that professionals are certain lurks somewhere off the Great Barrier Reef.

For the dedicated fisherman who lands it, the 2,000-pound black marlin will be worth the risks to life and equipment it will take, the tremendous expense, and the time it takes to gain the expertise and to fight the many battles. To the men and women who seek the legend, those are merely conditions of the quest. The prospect of taking the behemoth, which is as agile in its own element as a brook trout is in a rushing stream, is the grandest challenge of all, even if it is the most expensive.

One of those men is Mike Levitt, of Gladwyne, Pennsylvania, who is my host this November in 1976 for 14 days of marlin hunting off Cairns, Australia. Also, among the guests are Mike's brother, Skip Levitt and Ron Jones, who skippers Mike's Jersey Devil in the Atlantic. Our fishing takes place from the charter boat Yanu III, captained by Paul Whelan, with crewmen Rick Thislewait, the wireman, and Lance Knight the gaff man. At the end of each fishing day, our accommodations are aboard an 85-foot mother ship Ulysses.

Of the 11 giant marlin that Mike Levitt takes in 14 days, two are granders and one of them weighs 1,058 pounds. One blustery afternoon off Ribbon #7 Reef, Mike demonstrates not only his great dedication to the sport, but also his great sportsmanship as well.

The seas are lumpy, as they usually are; the sky is grey and threatening, as it often is during the month of October – spring in Australia. Suddenly the baitfish disappears in a swirl of spray and the cockpit becomes a madhouse as Mike free-spools the line off his reel, making sure there is no backlash, and makes ready to set the hook. Captain Whelan drives the boat forward, shouting, "Lock up ... It's a big one." Levitt straps into the fighting chair, braces himself as line pours off the big reel and smoke curls from its rapidly overheating drag.

Soon he turns the giant fish. "It's coming up," a crewman shouts, and 100 yards off the stern the monster breaks water, accompanied by a geyser that competes with Yellowstone Park's Old Faithful. The fish is a big – make that, mammoth – black marlin, bigger than any of us has ever seen. Within 30 minutes, it is within gaffing distance and Mike is yelling to the captain that it's over 1,500 pounds.

But before they can wire it, the fish dives and the fight is renewed. Then it is suddenly at the boat again. Mike clearly says, "I don't want to kill it unless it's over 1,500."

The captain hesitates. The fish is certainly much larger than any taken this week, including Skip Levitt's 1,103-pounder that was caught the day before. But is it bigger than 1,500? The captain cannot be sure.

"If we're not sure, stick a tag in it," Mike says. "Next year it will be bigger. I've already taken one over a thousand and that's enough, unless it's a new record."

The all-tackle record on 130-pound-class line is 1,560 pounds set at Cabo Blanco, Peru, in 1953, by Alfred Glasell, Jr. But, according to captains who have caught numbers of big fish, the dimensions of that record effort do not correspond with its weight. Its length and girth, they contend, suggest a fish closer to 1,300 pounds, a mark that has been bettered by several anglers, including Jo Jo Del Guercio of Ft. Lauderdale, Florida, who landed a 1,323-pound black marlin while based on the same mother ship as we are.

[An aside to the Glassell marlin is the fact that he had a professional movie photographer on the boat with him the day the catch was made. The fish was played unusually close to the boat, and the footage so good that it eventually made its way into the movie version of Ernest Hemingway's *The Old Man and the Sea*. This despite the fact that a couple of Peruvian mountains can be seen in the background in a couple of the frames. Despite months of trying, the Hollywood film crews were never able to get footage as good as the Glassell, hence a deal was made and it was used. Watch the Spencer Tracey version of The Old Man and the Sea, and you'll see Glassell's marlin.]

An entry for the 80-pound-class record was held briefly this year by Steve Zuckerman of Los Angeles, an old friend I introduced to light-tackle fishing during the three months I was at Pinas Bay, Panama in 1965. Steve's marlin weighed 1,232 ½ pounds, eclipsing D. Mead Johnson's previous mark by 14 ½ pounds, but was itself beaten only a few weeks later, on November 8, 1977, when Georgette Douwma, of London, brought in a 1,323-pounder on 80-pound-class line to claim the world record. Steve notched another record, however, which may not be beaten for some time: he became the only angler to land two 1,000-pounders in one day, and what makes this an even more outstanding catch is that they were both caught on 80-pound line.

His record fish, Steve said, fought hard for only a short time, diving deep under the boat before giving up after 20 minutes. But during that time, the fish charged the boat and ran its bill right through the bilges. The boat limped in for repairs and the weighing ceremony.

Damage to boats is an accepted hazard from the monster billfish. Del Guercio's charter boat suffered a smashed transom from one maddened marlin. Only about a 400-pound fish, the crew had decided to tag it when the fish turned the tables. It charged its attackers and rammed its blunted spear up through the transom door, into the sill, causing havoc among the crew and providing a kind of grisly humor. "Grab a hammer," one of them yelled, nearly hysterical, "and bend that damn thing over. Then we'll have the bugger."

The huge marlin spike, however, is no joking matter. People have been impaled on them and knocked senseless with one powerful swipe. The bill on a 1,000-pound marlin is more than four feet long, tapered from its 18-inch base to the thickness of a man's arm, and terminating in a blunted railroad spike. The bill is an awesome weapon the marlin uses as deftly as any Musketeer wields a sword.

Our charter boat, Yanu III, launched only a month before, already has two broken marlin bills in her hull. One marlin, a 700-pounder when boated, displayed a broken bill segment in its side. A vicious weapon, the spear commands the respect of the most swashbuckling crew. Even the average tiger shark, which inhabits the same tropic waters, gives the marlin its due.

Marlin often feed by zooming in and knocking the bait down with their bills. They then come back and swallow it head-first. Their maw is a straight pipe from mouth to stomach, and though they seem to prefer small scad of about two pounds, marlin can easily wolf down a 15-pound tuna in one gulp.

Speaking of scad, it's the favorite bait food of even the largest marlin. Similar to our mackerel, scad are caught each morning on rod and reel by the Australian boat crews and anglers in anticipation of the afternoon's fishing, when marlin bite best. Rigged so they swim naturally on the surface, dive, and then swim again, the scad will induce marlin to bite when they have not shown interest in other baits.

In late afternoon, the boats troll scad on one outrigger and a large bait, maybe a 25-pound wahoo or yellowfin tuna on the other. Another bait, a mackerel-like fish called the tanguigue, is used for baits up to 20 pounds. The large bait attracts the quarry's attention, but they invariably strike the scad first. Scad are smaller and they seem to attract other fish when trolled. Those fish, the razor gang as the crew calls them, consist of 100-pound wahoo and tanguigue that will zoom in and chop the bait right behind the hooks. Some days, we have at least 15 razor chops while stalking these giant marlin. But at 5:45 one afternoon, as I hopefully monitor my 8-

pound bonito bait, a huge fish comes grey hounding in and crashes the bait in a streaming mountain of spray, its whole body pulsing livid fluorescent blue.

The cockpit becomes bedlam as I free-spool the line on the drop-back, lock up and set the hook. It's not my favorite way of fighting fish as I'd rather stand up and hold the rod, but I slide into the big fighting chair and buckle on the harness.

The chair is greased with soap so that as I flex my legs against the footrest, the fish is pumped forward and my backside slides to and fro in the chair. I move forward rapidly and retrieve line as I slide and then I shove backward with my legs as on a weight-lifting machine. Strong legs are a big factor in fighting these monster fish, and so are strong wrists and arms when winding back 300 yards of line time after time. In marlin fishing, as well as in any other type of fishing, one key to winning is to stay as close as possible to the fish.

Some time during the fight, giant marlin, just like bonefish, tarpon or any other hard-fighting game fish, will briefly make a mistake. Bewildered, it may pause and give you a chance with the gaff. If you are close enough to the fish, you can take it. As phrased by famous Australian marlin captain Peter Bristow, "Keep as much string on the reel as you can."

If, on the other hand, the fish has gotten a distance away, it may rejuvenate before you can retrieve that line. Recovered, the fish will fight on and on. Then it can be a matter of adept boat handling to intercept the fish. The captain may turn the boat and run after a hot fish or back down on one that is close.

My marlin makes its mistake within 15 minutes, and while it lies at a standstill next to the transom, alternately pulsing its violet blue colors and fading silver, I crank the swivel to the rod's tip-top. The wireman grabs the heavy leader with his gloved hand to haul the fish in close enough to gaff.

Wiring is one of the most dangerous and thrilling aspects of marlin fishing. The wireman grips the leader between thumb and forefinger with the palm of his hand toward his face, and takes a wrap around his hand. He hauls that in, muscling the huge fish an arm's length closer, then grabs a wrap with the other hand. From 30 feet out, the leader length, the fish is towed into gaff range. Sometimes all hell breaks loose. The fish may surge anew, creating a serious threat to angler and crew. Twenty-odd feet of heavy piano wire zinging across a slippery deck, coiling and snapping at the pull of a 1,000-pound fish, can amputate an arm or leg or even decapitate an unlucky victim. Wire clippers are an essential safety feature.

My fish, docile after 15 minutes, becomes a hellion two minutes later on the wire, nearly tearing off the first deckie's gloved hand and arm. "It's not a good fish unless you feel the blood run down your arm," he mutters as he grudgingly let it go, and soon I have it close enough to wire again.

Eventually landed, the fish weighs 996, just four pounds short of the grander goal. Am I disappointed? I'll say not! The main reason for my being on the Great Barrier Reef is to shoot a film, so I only fished for marlin a total of one hour the whole trip. Even so, I am fortunate enough to tag and release one fish that weighs about 400 pounds and land a 996-pounder. Where else in this world can a fisherman go and fish for one hour and catch two marlin, one weighing nearly 1,000 pounds?

Ron Jones, Mike's state-of-the-art skipper, takes a turn at wiring an 800-pounder for Mike Levitt. No stranger to big fish, Ron is the captain of the boat off Cape Hatteras that landed a record 1,128-pound blue marlin on 80-pound-class line.

In our 14-day sting, we have 93 marlin up behind the bait, and of those, we tag and release 37. Four are boated, three weighing over 1,000 pounds. The smallest is estimated at 200, while the largest, Mike Levitt's grand release, goes over 1,300 pounds.

Jo Jo DelGuercio, one of the finest conventional-tackle fishermen in the world, fishes 21 days and takes four marlin over a grand, his largest 1,323. Jo Jo also tags six fish estimated to be between 950 and 1,050, and lands a total of 77 marlin. Other anglers report similar results to confirm Cairns as one of the planet's most fertile big-fish grounds.

The Great Barrier Reef is in the Coral Sea where the great marlin migrate, beginning at the northern tip of the Australian continent at Thursday Island, and curling down to the Tropic of Capricorn. Prime marlin fishing extends southward from Lizard Island, about halfway down along the Ribbon Reefs to Cairns. Between these two settlements is Cooktown, a major restocking port for fishing boats.

While there are some day trips that go out the 30 to 40 miles from Cairns to the reef, the ideal arrangement for giant marlin is to fish on one boat and live on another. A mother ship is used by many anglers, and ours was The Ulysses, an 85-foot, one-year old, fully air-conditioned and fully provisioned ship. It welcomed us after each day of fishing with hot showers, great food, a chance to stretch our legs as well as hobnob with the crew of another boat also anchored nearby. This arrangement allows the fishing boat to stay only 15 minutes from the best fishing grounds, and provides ultimate comfort for the guests. When necessary, the mother ship can also steam into Cooktown for provisions while the fishing boats continue stalking marlin.

Cairns itself is a city of about 100,000 people with numerous parks and beaches, some of them catering to nude bathers (sorry I missed that!) and the resort trade. The northernmost major center on the coastal highway, Cairns is also important in the sugar trade. But its springtime and life revolves around the giant marlin fishery.

Getting to Australia as well as fishing there is expensive. And, unfortunately, only those who have more than several thousand dollars to spend can hope to manage it. For example, airfare alone to Sydney is about $1,500 from most points in the United States. At Sydney, you must figure on staying overnight before going on to Cairns, and also returning. It's more than 1,000 miles, and you must stop at Brisbane to change planes.

The Australian people are among the world's finest and most accommodating, who, not unlike those in a Montana small town, cannot do enough for strangers. Even the taxi drivers are first rate, their meters registering in pennies.

The food is excellent, with restaurants of all types. Australian wines are second in my mind only to the finest California wines, and the Australian Four-X beer is an experience in itself.

Coming and going, you cross the international dateline, so that even though you lose a day on the way out, you gain it coming back. You arrive home the same day you leave Australia after at least 18 hours en route.

Other fishing inducements exist for me besides black marlin. A fish called a barramundi resembles our snook, averaging 20-plus pounds and reaching well over 50 pounds. The barramundi will take top-water plugs, flies, popping bugs and jigs. In addition, there is some of the finest, unknown rainbow trout fishing south of Sidney in the Snowy Mountains.

I've always said I'd like to fish for giant marlin on light tackle, particularly the fly rod. Unfortunately, on this trip the seas are too rough to even think about it, since in rough water there is too much separation between fish and boat in the swells, which increases the danger of break-offs.

Of course, all of us are intrigued with the idea of being the first to land the legendary 2,000-pound black marlin. It is an idea that is hard to dismiss, which is why I've repeated it as often as the pursuit of the 200-pound tarpon on fly – a feat, incidentally, that finally occurred. But back to Australia and black marlin, I saw some tremendous fish there, much larger than any we caught and surely over 1,500 pounds.

California's Kaye Mulholland reportedly hooked the largest fish her captain had ever seen in Australian waters, but finally cut it free after an eight-hour battle that lasted into darkness. Angler Neville Green landed a fish that was half eaten by sharks, and its remains weighed in at 1,463 pounds. Peter Bristow, the charter boat skipper of whom I've spoken about in this book, has lost count of the granders he has taken himself. But he has seen five or six, he says, that are "monsters, horrible monsters."

Indeed, the fabled two-grander black marlin is out there, lurking off the Great Barrier Reef. Catching it is only a matter of time, and money.

CHAPTER

EIGHTEEN

VIKING TREASURE

Atlantic Salmon in Iceland: Like No Other!

In a quiet pool the size of a football field, between the waterfall and where I stand in my hip waders stripping line from my fly reel, the air-clear water teems with masses of Atlantic salmon. It seems like a whole world of them. They jam into the pool, stacked like so many shimmering cords of wood, each waiting its turn at the rapids. The fish the Romans named, "Salar," The Leaper.

Single salmon move restlessly, milling around, joining into ever tightening schools, intermittently leaping into the air so that at times a half dozen fish are airborne. I absent mindedly reach up to adjust my polarized glasses, as though they are playing tricks on my vision. I have not expected to see so many Atlantic salmon in all of Iceland. My fishing partner, Jim Chapralis, agrees.

At one time or another, we had both fished the salmon rivers of Norway, Ireland and Labrador. On those trips, it seemed that the waters were too high or too low, too muddy or too clear, or too seldom filled with fish. Now, the Laxa i Kjos, this swift, transparent ribbon only an hour's drive from bustling Reykjavik, holds the promise of being a salmon fisherman's ultimate utopia.

"I'm going to try a dry fly," I announce.

Jim grins. "Go ahead and be stubborn about it, but you've been warned."

True, I had been told that salmon just won't take a dry fly in this river, but it's the way I prefer to fish, and I am determined. I quickly strip off a length of line, tie on the White Wulff, and shoot out a long cast. At the same time, Jim drops a Blue Hairy Mary wet fly into a group of two-dozen fish and begins working it slowly across the current. Nothing happens.

The fish ignore both of us. Twenty minutes go by as we cast to them, teasing, coaxing and courting them. Sometimes a fish leaps, playfully it seems, over our lines, leaders and flies, but there are no takers.

"I've got one," Jim says. Then just as quickly," Nope, he's off."

Finally, at the end of a drift, a salmon rises to my fly. The hook pulls out almost immediately, but contrary to what I have been advised, it takes my dry fly. I change tactics slightly, trying to provoke more action. I slip a Portland Creek Hitch on a #8 Blue Charm, which is simply a half hitch wrapped around the body about one third of the way back from the hook's eye. This method, also called "The Riffling Hitch," was developed in eastern Canada and is quite simple, and often deadly. The fly skates across the surface, leaving a V-wake. I hold my rod tip up and strip in slowly. It was more than one fish could resist.

The water dimpled under my fly and I feel the strong pull that spells salmon. My trout rod doubles over and the reel shrieks as line zips off of the spool. The fish jumps four times, thrashing toward the waterfall before its strength starts to go. It turns downstream and jumps again, my reel screams as though its gears are burning up. Just as suddenly as the mad dash begins, it ends. The salmon has reached a deeper pool, giving it a false feeling of security. Reeling furiously, I work my way downstream toward this Viking-like spirit. The wild leaps and hard fighting runs are just too much for my adversary. From my newly acquired position, I pump and reel until finally the fish scraps across the gravelly bank and I haul it out by the tail – 10 pounds of beautiful Atlantic salmon. It is the first in a number of adventurous encounters on a dream-fishing trip with some of the hardest fighting salmon in the world.

This trip to Iceland, like so many of the best fishing trips I've been on, was conceived under unusual circumstances halfway around the world in Nepal. A mutual acquaintance of Jim Chapralis and mine is Jim Edwards, managing director of Tiger Tops, an unusual lodge in Nepal's Himalayas. Edwards, a British subject who married a lovely Icelandic girl, brings his family home to Iceland for the cool summers.

The last time I spoke with him, Jim told me about the fantastic salmon fishing in Iceland's rivers, Laxas as they are called there. He insisted that Jim Chapralis and I visit them in the summer. Believe me, he didn't have to ask twice. We scheduled it for mid-summer, July 10-19, in three separate areas.

Jim and I climb aboard Icelandic Airways flight 500 out of Kennedy airport at 9:30 p.m. and settle down to sleep. The flight takes only six hours and arrives at 7 a.m. local time. I wake Jim with a not-so-soft, "Hey, the suns up, it's time to fish."

Jim cocks a half-opened eye at his watch. It is 7:05 a.m. "Go back to sleep," he says. "The sun stays up all summer in Iceland."

Approaching the coast of this strange island of dazzling ice and black lava, I look down at the pale sea. The wakes of fishing boats point their Vs away from land, moving out of a wall of ghostly fog. Cod, haddock and herring boats are following the strong tradition of Iceland's men of the sea.

Since the Vikings first settled Iceland in 874 A.D., fishing has been important, and still is today– for commercial boats, the dinner table, and more recently, sport. I checked the guidebook Jim Edwards had given me to find out more about the fishing.

Norsemen from Scandinavia and Celts from Ireland settled Iceland, and the resultant mixture was successful in many ways. The women are among the most beautiful on earth. Of all the Nordic peoples, Icelanders, alone, produced great literature in the Middle Ages. The birth rate is the highest in Europe, and the death rate one of the lowest in the world – seven per thousand. Though there are 200,000 people in an area of the size of Kentucky, most live in 14 towns and 40 villages on the coast.

Because their island depends on fish for 90 percent of its exports; in 1970 the Icelanders extended fishing jurisdiction to 50 nautical miles and pollution jurisdiction to 100 miles. This protects the important spawning grounds of the continental shelf and puts the brakes on over-fishing by numerous countries whose boats ply the North Atlantic.

Jim and I are, of course, not intent on over-fishing, but anxious to put as much pressure as possible on every salmon we can find. After a 45-minute bus ride into Reykjavik, we are met at the terminal by Paul Johnson, who with his partner Jon Johnson, leases the fishing rights to our first salmon river, the Laxa i Kjos. Paul greets us with the friendliness and warmth so typical of these Viking descendents, and we immediately feel like old friends. He explains that our fishing areas are carefully staked out.

"The government sets aside very strict fishing regulations," Paul says, "allowing only a few rods to each stretch of water." The Laxa i Kjos, which he pronounces as Loxa Keltz, is a 10-rod river where they allow a maximum of 10 rods to fish on a river each week, but it produces about 2,000 salmon in the 90-day season. He goes on to tell us about some of the great pools with names I can't pronounce, such as Fjarjusbreida, Hubdarbakshylur, and Helguholtskvorn. The names and the Icelandic language, carryover from the Vikings, and haven't changed in 1,000 years.

"You'll be fishing an easy name first, though," Paul promises. "The first day, you can try the Laxafoss, one of the most celebrated pools in the river."

Since we are not scheduled to fish until the next day, Jim and I rent a Volkswagen to drive the 50 miles to our lodge, with a stop at Jim Edwards' place. Chapralis "fakes me out" by professing his inability to handle the VW's four-on-the-floor gear shift and I get the dubious privilege of driving the whole trip. Distracted I may be, but I am still determined not to miss any of the unusual scenery.

Rolling through the barren countryside, it was easy to see why the American astronauts trained in this part of Iceland for their moon landing. It's a harsh land, where wood is so scarce a property buyer pays for all driftwood rights as we do for mineral rights here in the United States. The sprawling Vatnejukull Glacier is larger than all the glaciers in Europe combined. There are 700 thermal springs; our word "geyser" comes from Iceland's Great Geyser that spews up a 180-foot column of hot water. There are 30 active volcanoes, including Oska, which had its latest eruption in 1961, and Surtsey, which came boiling out of the flat sea belching fire and steam in 1963.

All this activity makes for interesting weather patterns, and you can experience almost any kind on any given day. Temperatures, though, average a mild 31 degrees Fahrenheit in January and a San Francisco-like, 52 degrees in summer. Warm winds from the Gulf Stream hold off the Arctic blasts.

Far off in the distance the snow still drapes the mountain tops, and moist air blowing in from the sea brings a wall of thick fog over us without a moment's notice. In two miles, it is clear again. The road meanders through the flat meadows with sheep and horses grazing, and over streams where geese paddled. Finally, we're at the lodge, rested, dressed for fishing, and out in the late afternoon sun, standing in a fabulous salmon pool of Laxa i Kjos.

After our first success, we have numerous hook ups as our luck seems to change. Jim moves to the other side of the river and strikes a fine strong salmon that has him climbing goat-like over the rocks as the fish heads downstream. He is using a very light split bamboo fly rod and a light tippet that doesn't allow for any horsing around. I watch as his fish jumps, runs, then jumps again as Jim clambers after it, giving line, cranking stubbornly, pumping. Eventually, 200 yards downstream, Jim ends the drama splendidly, tailing a fine 9½-pound Atlantic salmon.

We find that long casts are not necessary, and more than once I labor the point, only extending a few feet of fly line beyond the rod tip. With one fish, I drop the fly right at the foot of the waterfall and let the current bounce it out of the surface. A salmon takes it on the splash and the fight is wild before I tail a 13-pounder. This area at the falls is thick with salmon preparing for their amazing leaps upstream to spawn. Reportedly, Atlantic salmon refuse to eat during their spawning run, but at certain times each day they strike anyway, for whatever mysterious reason, and it is possible to hook as many as two or three fish on a single retrieve.

These Icelandic salmon are not of great size, but they fight like heavyweights. One fish rolls right out of the water at my dry fly, but misses it. He repeats this maneuver three times, and I am sure I'll get him. Broad shouldered, it looks as if it will easily go 25 to 30 pounds. On such great salmon rivers as Quebec's Moisie or Norway's Alta, this fish would hardly grab rave notices. But in Iceland, where the average salmon might run 8 to 12 pounds, fish of this size are not only considered outstanding, but rare.

Iceland has about 60 salmon rivers that rate among the best anywhere, and most of the people fish for salmon as well as trout and char. Today, when some of the Atlantic's finest stock has been virtually depleted through illicit netting off Greenland, Icelandic hopes are still bright. Atlantic salmon fishing not only holds its own here, but is also improving. Since 1970, the Laxa i Kjos has noted yearly increases of about 24 percent in salmon, bolstering its reputation as one of the world's greatest Atlantic salmon rivers. There are many reasons for this, including conservation and maintenance programs, as well as vigorous stocking methods.

Icelanders are quick to explain that their salmon do not migrate to the Greenland salmon rendezvous area where the Danes, especially, have each year been hauling out thousands of tons of migrating salmon from the British Isles and Eastern Canada. Many other countries have permitted their commercial fisheries to heavily net their own waters. Norway was a good example, as were most Canadian provinces.

Commercial netting has been all but abolished in Iceland, and they have enforced regulations that allow only a 90-day season for sport fishing that begins the last week of June, although good salmon fishing could probably be enjoyed an additional 40 days on some rivers. Fishing is not permitted between 1 p.m. and 4 p.m., relieving the rivers of heavy fishing pressure.

The next day at the Paukufoss pool, Jim and I stand with our guide, Stephan, just below another waterfall and watch dozens of salmon congregate at a sharp bend.

"Crouch low on that big rock," Stephan warns me.. "They may not scare away, but they certainly won't take, if they see you."

Lying practically on my belly, with the fly tied to a 6-lb.-test tapered leader; I am using an 8-weight fly rod, the same one that I have used many times in the Florida Keys for bonefish.

Though I can see that Stephen has chosen his favorite Nighthawk fly from my box, I have picked out the Muddler Minnow, a trout fly. I crouch low, my eyes barely peeking over the huge rock, and begin flicking the fly into a small area of the bend. Sometimes I let the fly drift au natural to the fish; other times I give it a little action. They refuse to take, though a couple of times I do move some fish.

Jim is having the same problems. "Uncatchable," I hear him mutter.

I am about to agree. Just a few more casts, I figure, maybe five minutes more. Okay, three minutes, and then back to the lodge for lunch. We'll be late once again. I can't help but see a big one show with a slow, deliberate roll. I want to hit him, hit him fast like you sometimes do brown trout fishing. But with salmon, you wait until the fish turns. I tighten up the line with my left hand while raising the rod with my right, setting the hook.

With a start, I suddenly become aware of this fish's probable escape route: first downstream, then down the chute into the canyon. You have to anticipate where a fish will go before he does it, especially in a treacherous area like this. The salmon circles the pool twice, then flashes out into the fast current. I leap up and run after him, trying to head him off. Then I have to cross the river, which oozes cold water over the tops of my hip-waders. I scramble over the rocks, thankful for the felt soles on my waders, lifting my line away from the crevices and tightening up again, pressuring the fish, coaxing him away from places that might chaff my light tippet. Then he gives out. I ease him into a backwater behind a large boulder. Suddenly, it seems, he is at my feet and I am lifting him out by the tail, a hefty 15 ½-pounder. This is one day I don't mind being late for lunch.

The fishing hours are strictly controlled. We start at 7 a.m. and fish until 1 o'clock in the afternoon, then break for lunch and a three-hour rest. We can go out again at 4 p.m. and fish until 10 at night. Since daylight lasts the full 24 hours in the summer around the Arctic Circle, we sometimes get only three hours of sleep before we are at it again. Curiously, we don't get tired, but I'm not sure whether that's from the change in time zones, the lack of nightfall or the excitement of watching those multitudes of fish.

It is here I see another phenomenon that supports one of my pet theories. Standing over the largest pool of the Laxa in late afternoon just as the tide comes in, I observe a huge concentration of salmon gathering at the river mouth. Each time the same peak conditions occur – floodtide and late afternoon on the full or new moon–it happens. There is a big push of fish invariably moving into the river from the ocean. I have observed this hundreds of times with my favorite game fish, tarpon, and am not too surprised Atlantic salmon follow the same pattern. The lower pools of Laxa i Kjos jam with a thousand fish. By morning there are only 100 or so left after the masses have made their way up river during the night.

When our three days of fishing are over, I have landed 24 salmon, Jim has taken 13, and between us, we have hooked well over 100. You might ask why so many got away. Well, the honest fact is simply that Jim and I decided not to use a net, tailer or gaff, and to handle all of our own fish. Of course our gillie thought we were out of our minds. Gille is a European name for a guide, who is also responsible for taking care of the river.

My best day was July 12 when we fished only in the afternoon. I landed five salmon of 9½, 10, 11½, 12½, and 14 pounds, and three smaller ones. Jim took a 16 ½-pounder that day, the biggest of our trip. On each of the other days we landed fish in the 10-pound range, with our average weight for the whole trip about 9½ pounds.

Icelandic fishing, like practically any good Atlantic salmon fishing, is quite expensive. In the early 1970s, a visitor could count on at least $150 a day to fish the superb rivers like Laxa i Kjos. Today, the prices have risen to astronomical levels.

When we fished Iceland, the price was inclusive of accommodations with food and guide service. Jon Johnson leased the river through the farmers' associations, and their costs have increased in proportion to the falling off of good Atlantic salmon fishing there and in other parts of the world, and with the skyrocketing market price of Atlantic salmon. In 1971, a premier river would lease for $80,000 just for the 90-day season, plus other expenditures for accommodations, management, gillies and local transportation. Today, as in the '70s, the lessor takes a high risk and barely makes a profit. Whatever the cost, without this strict management, the Atlantic salmon might be doomed.

While I prefer the lightest tackle I can use, the traditional salmon fly rod is a long, two-handed affair for roll casting with heavy lines and leaders. One British doctor is fishing slightly upstream from us with a heavy rod and 18-pound leader, enough to keep the salmon hanging on forever or to hoist a full-grown fish right out of the water. When he learns I am fishing with an 8 ½-foot trout rod, 6-pound test leader and #8 hooks, he ambles over to see how I am doing it. I catch two fish as he stands watching and I try to explain the technique, but he never really understands.

All too soon it is time for us to leave. After a short visit with our friend Jim Edwards and his lovely wife – herself a striking example of the Nordic beauty of Iceland's women – we reluctantly climb into the plane for home. I can't help thinking that Leif Ericson sailed from here in a Viking ship 500 years before Columbus, and landed on the American continent. I know life must have been harder then, but I wonder if he was as anxious to return to Iceland as I am.

COLD, CLEAR WATER AND MONSTER TROUT

We're Talking New Zealand

From very near the top of the globe, to very near the bottom, it's about 11,161 miles as the crow flies, from Iceland to New Zealand. Despite their distance apart, the two countries have in common the freshest air on earth and pure, absolutely-clear rivers and streams. The waters of both hold brown trout, but where Iceland's browns are a side-show augmenting its superb Atlantic salmon fishing, New Zealand brown trout fishing is the finest on earth. And the Mataura River on the southern end of South Island is the finest dry-fly trout stream in the world.

While the journey from Miami to South Island, New Zealand, takes one to the far side of the globe and into the opposite of whatever season we're in, what's that to a Pan-Am pilot who happens to be an avid angler? Why, nothing at all.

The Mataura River practically runs through my friend George Kennedy's backyard. George managed a slaughterhouse a few miles downriver from his property and felt as passionate about trout fishing as I did.

I made my first visit there in 1969, and after dinner George took us to a spot about three miles behind his house for my first look at these fabled waters. I peeked over a high bank and gazed into the clear, ambling river. A number of brown trout were gently cruising on the surface where an eddy in the current created a good place to feed. Some of those fish would have weighed as much as 10 pounds, and it was not easy for me to just stand there and watch them.

But the steep bank was no place from which to fish, and after all, we were just dinner guests. So I made a careful mental note as to the location, and two hours later, after having made my excuses to the Kennedy family, I was chest deep in water making 90-foot dry-fly presentations from the other side of the Mataura to those same trout.

These beauties had not been pressured much because, for the most part, New Zealanders don't bother to cast that far for their fish. With such an abundance of trout at that time, they didn't have to. But 90-foot casts were the only way to this bunch. At that distance I was still able to take two. Of course I missed four or five others because with so much line out there it created the inevitable big line bow, and setting the hook was tricky. The biggest trout I caught that evening weighed only six pounds. Only six pounds? I can't really say I was broken-hearted.

The Mataura wanders through rolling countryside in sight of snow-clad peaks, which provide a backdrop of unbelievable grandeur to match the unbelievable fishing. I found the Mataura River itself reminiscent of Henry's Fork of the Snake River in Idaho. Most of the people who live in this part of New Zealand are descendants of the Scots, and at times you get the feeling you are fishing in Scotland. Fishing Guide Peter Cullen even referred to our small dry flies as "wee lures."

But most impressive of all to me was the manner in which the Mataura is fished. While I did have to wade in deep to reach those trout behind the Kennedy home, that was the exception rather than the rule. Some mornings I never even bothered to don my waders, because I knew I would be able to fish successfully from the bank all day. These banks were about four feet above the level of the river, and I would walk upstream until I saw a trout large enough to deserve a presentation.

I would quickly crouch to keep out of sight while I kept an eye on exactly where that fish was, casting from a lower profile so as not to spook the fish. Occasionally I would have to get into the water, because debris or some other obstruction on the land would prevent a clear presentation. More often I'd simply cast from the bank. Most of these presentations were within 50 feet, and sometimes I would even get as close as 20. The main point is that all the fishing I did was selective casting of dry flies to trout I could clearly see. This was my kind of fishing, for it reminded me of stalking bonefish on the flats near my Florida Keys home.

Much of the Mataura River, like the stretch on the Kennedy land, is on private property. While in many areas of the world this could prevent the average angler from reaching the riverbank, in the area of the Mataura – which is called Southland and is the southernmost providence of the country – agreements have been reached with many landowners to keep permanent or semi-permanent routes to the river open to the public. At these points the Southland Acclimatization Society has erected Anglers Access sign boards. In most cases these signs mean that the angler and his vehicle may pass through private property by pre-arranged agreement with the owner. At times these routes may be temporarily blocked off, but usually they're open and point the way to good fishing for everybody.

In addition to the Anglers Access spots, in many unmarked places a trout fisherman has only to request permission from the landowner to pass through his property to the river, and it will be granted. New Zealanders are wonderful people and I found them to be among the friendliest and most cooperative I've met anywhere.

The Mataura is New Zealand's best-stocked brown-trout water. While there is year-round fishing, fly fishing is best from the beginning of December [their summer] on, but as I'll relate later, I experienced a hatch during my November trip that was nothing short of spectacular. In fact during my trip I caught more than 100 brown trout, and only one of those fish weighed less than two pounds. The average trout went about 3 1/2 pounds, but I also caught many five and six pounders. While November may be considered a pre-season month by New Zealand standards, I really had no complaints.

In fact, the only November problem I encountered was seagull nesting. I found them all along the banks of the Mataura, and they were bothersome when they flew near me because their shadows occasionally spooked the fish.

I can also report that these browns were the hardest fighting I have caught anywhere. The female trout, called hen-fish by the New Zealanders, were the most active and did the most jumping.

While the Mataura River browns run big, the flies they like best run small. Sizes 14, 16 and at times even 18, in any of the quill ties are productive. Early in the season the 14s are used, but after the beginning of December when the water temperature begins to rise and the days begin to lengthen, the smaller hatches are more frequent. This applies particularly to the lower Mataura.

As to patterns, I recommend buying flies locally wherever you are fishing. I was able to purchase the necessary flies in the town of Gore at the tackle shop for only 15 or 20 cents apiece. They were well tied and the Mataura trout liked them just fine. I used the following patterns successfully: Peveril, Red Tip Governor, Kahaki [the natives pronounce it with three syllables] Queen, Greenwell's Glory, Quill Cochy-Bondhu, Dad's Favorite, Twilight Beauty and Green Manuka Beetle.

As an example of the right tackle, I think it's worth mentioning that I was using a three-piece, 5-weight, eight-foot fiberglass rod with a matching reel and line. Sometimes I would use a double taper or sometimes a weight-forward line. With such an outfit you can cast as far as you have to in order to reach the fish, without too much danger of spooking them. People using heavier line, however, do spook the fish. Of course, a perfect compromise outfit is not always just exactly right for each given situation. What I should have had when I was making those early 90-foot presentations was a floating shooting head with monofilament running line. This would have enabled me to make the long casts with a minimum of line drag, and I would have lost fewer fish.

However, everything was in working order on what I must rate as one of the finest days of freshwater fishing I have ever experienced. It began about 1 p.m. when I saw the rise in the water from my car. I parked near the Otoma Flat Bridge and waded, and in rather short order I took six brown trout on a #18 Dad's Favorite dry fly, similar to a Quill Gordon. And, as usual, I had missed a number of others.

After this action subsided somewhat, I walked upstream for about a mile and was just rounding a bend when I saw a large shape swimming upstream in about four feet of water. I knew it was the biggest brown I had ever seen, and I wished that I'd had a big streamer among my files. But right then was no time to change flies so I decided to go with what I had on the line.

I cast the Dad's Favorite about eight feet in front of the moving target. I simply could not believe my own eyes as I watched that monster brown come up off the bottom. It was huge, and it simply engulfed that tasty little tidbit I had placed in its path. The fight that followed can only be described as rough and tumble and I somewhat sheepishly admit to wading right out to the fish and standing directly over it while fighting.

After 15 minutes of this, the big trout finally tired enough for me to work him back into the shallows. In fact, it was so shallow the fish was swimming on its side just to stay in the water. As I gently tried to beach it, the old fellow gave a big flop back toward deeper water and, since I was using only a two-pound tippet, I naturally let him have his head. However, he was pretty tired and I was soon able to lead him around again toward the beach. Then, just as I was certain I had him, he shook his head once and to my utter dismay I saw my prize break off and swim slowly away. I could have easily kicked it back onto the beach with my foot, but believing he had earned his freedom through a fault of mine, I resisted the urge. Had I lost a 200-pound tarpon on fly, I could not have felt more dejected.

I soon discovered that it was not the tippet that had broken, but the hook. For some reason it had snapped high on the shank above the bend. I am pretty good at guesstimating the weight of fish, and this brown trout would have topped 15 pounds for sure and, in fact, to my eye it looked closer to 20. How many anglers have had a chance to cast to, much less fight, a fish of such majesty?

But the day was not to be a total loss – far from it. In fact, what took place during the remaining hours of daylight took much of the sting out of that major setback. At about 4:30 p.m., I experienced one of the famous Mataura evening rises that I had been hearing about since my arrival. I was walking downstream toward my rented car when I observed two fish in the center of the stream head-tail nymphing. I stopped short, crouched low and backed off about 75 yards away from the river. Then, still keeping low, I walked to a point about 100 yards below the working fish and cautiously eased into the river. I worked my way upstream again to where the fish had moved. To my amazement I saw brown trout breaking the surface in all directions for 100 yards.

The feeding activity had increased when the spent wing was on the water. The fish were feeding in pairs and bobbing their heads – at the surface, under, then to the surface again. When trout stick their noses and months out while feeding, I call them gulpers, and that's exactly what these babies were doing. As they fed into the current they often came within a rod's length of me. In fact, all my prior caution was for naught, as they were virtually impossible to spook during their gulping ritual.

I was down to my last two flies, #18 Greenwell's Glories, and the fish had become choosier even when I made direct presentations. The spent wings on the water seemed smaller, so I began thinning out the hackle and that helped. The fish were feeding so voraciously that one fish I hooked and broke off kept right on feeding with the hook still in its mouth.

I hooked nine fish and of these landed five and kept three. All those landed weighed between four and five-and-a-half pounds. Those three fish I kept represented half of the total I kept to eat out of more than 100 I caught.

In November and December of 1969, I was a guest of the New Zealand Government Tourist Bureau. My wife and I spent six weeks fishing both the North Island and the South Island.

The average temperature in November was 70° F during the day and 55° F at night. We dressed for fishing as we would if we were fishing In Montana or Wyoming in the early summer or early fall.

Getting oriented in a new country is not easy and much valuable time will be wasted if you do not have the proper aid and advice. One place to get it is from the Internet, at Anglers Aid in New Zealand.

We discovered on our trip that when the hotels specify eating times, they meant exactly what they said. If you like to fish early and late as I do, you will have to make special arrangements or go hungry. The Takaro Lodge was the only place that I found back then in all of South Island New Zealand that an angler or hunter could get a meal prepared any time of the day or night, even if one's tastes were for Chateaubriand to Trout Normande.

If you are fortunate you will experience a streamside cookout at some point during your visit. The following recipe shows how it is done, and I can see no reason why it shouldn't work just as well back home as it does on the banks of the Mataura.

Cut and gill one trout. Wrap in brown paper. Wrap this package in seven layers of wet newspapers and place on hot coals. When the newspapers are dried out, the trout is done to a turn and will be almost as wonderful to eat as it was to catch.

CHAPTER

TWENTY

HONDO AND THE

SPINDLEBEAKS'

Pacific Sailfish with a Basketball Super-Star

I woke up, suddenly alert, peering into the soft dawn light that filled the room, my ears cocked like a loaded gun. Something was different. Suddenly the realization came: It was quiet, not a sound. The patter of rain that had been pelting the roof of the lodge for five days was gone. Even the palm fronds were quiet, their incessant rustling ceased. There was no wind.

No rain, no wind. We would be fishing today.

Five days of playing cards and killing time waiting for a break in the weather had given this trip an ominous beginning, especially disappointing to me. Sure, I had experienced my share, or more, of rained-out fishing trips, but on this one I was serving as a field host on a segment intended for "The American Sportsman" television series. We were at a fairly new camp called "Club Pacifico" on the penal island of Cobia, just off the Panama mainland. Sailfish were on the agenda, with bait-casting tackle and fly rod, with basketball super-star John "Hondo" Havlicek, of the Boston Celtics. Like myself and the film crew, John had outlasted the weather delay, his thoughts on a light-tackle angling experience like no other he had ever known.

Club Pacifico was founded and owned by my friend Bob Griffin, a Miami electrical contractor. I had helped Bob find and create the camp through a fortuitist series of events—the same sort of events that had led to my experiences in helping pioneer "The American Sportsman."

After doing the ABC "Wide World of Sports" television show with Joe Brooks and Al McClane in 1962, Producer Roone Arledge decided that the crew had shot so much good footage that the network should do a pilot film for a new series in the works titled ABC's "American Sportsman." They returned to my modest home on Little Torch Key with a much smaller film crew, Joe Brooks and the well-known announcer-personality Curt Gowdy. A new show was born that would set viewing records and achieve numerous awards for many years. "The American Sportsman" mainly portrayed hunting and fishing with celebrities on location literally around the world– Africa, South America, Alaska, wherever creatures with horns, feathers or scales could be found.

The Club Pacifico fishing adventure with John Havlicek in June of 1973 was to be my first show in which I acted as field host. I had been flying into Club Pacifico twice a year for the past two years, so I thought I knew what was ahead.

Before founding Club Pacifico, Bob Griffin had owned another fishing camp on the Panama mainland. There, some years earlier on our last day of a fishing trip with my wife Bernice, Ray and Doro Donnersberger, a big Huey helicopter swooped into the clearing near the camp and hovered for a moment while two heavily armed men wearing military fatigues dropped to the ground. They circled back and forth to secure the area before the helicopter landed. A stately looking gentlemen dressed in a white guayabera shirt stepped out, followed by two more soldiers dressed in fatigues with .45 pistols jutting from their hips. As they walked toward the camp, Bob ambled out to meet them.

It was General Omar Torrijos, the Panamanian dictator who had seized power in a military coup. The General had heard through the grapevine I was at Bob's camp and flew over to greet me. I was honored and a bit awed to have this Head of State going out of his way just to say "Hello." Between his broken English and my semi-Spanish we did pretty well discussing ideas on bringing more American fishing tourists into Panama.

The roots of our conversation had developed six months earlier when I spent five days with Bob and others on a 28-foot Prowler towing a 19-foot Mako. We were exploring for virgin fishing waters, which we ultimately found along the north and west sides of the island of Coiba.

At that time, the General invited me into his helicopter to fly over the areas in that part of Panama to assess the tourist fishing possibilities.

I had a fantastic tour of the Pacific side of Panama from the Costa Rican border to the various out islands in the Pacific, including the Island of Coiba. This is a place where they interned murderers and life-termers and from which no one has ever escaped alive. The few that made a break for it were eaten by sharks or drowned.

A pretty cove with a white sand beach on the east side of the island looked like the perfect place to build a fishing camp. After some discussion, the General said that he could make the area available to Bob on 100-year lease and guarantee security from the prisoners.

This first meeting with the General eighteen months earlier had been instrumental in the government allowing Bob to establish this new camp.

I couldn't wait to give Bob the good news, but instead of heading back to his camp we proceeded south to Rio Hato, the General's Summer Palace, as it was called. He insisted I join him for cocktails, dinner and spend the night before having his limo take me back to my wife and friends.

Bob needed a name for the resort that would be easy for Americans to remember, and I came up with Club Pacifico. And thus a super fishing Lodge was born.

My trip there with "The American Sportsman" crew to film John Havlicek got off to a good start at the Miami airport when my wife Bernice and I met John and his wife Beth. We were to meet Bob Duncan, the show's Producer, a crew of two cameramen and a sound man for our three-hour flight to Tocumen airport in Panama.

John and I had talked at length on the telephone about the type of fishing he had done in the past, and about what I thought we would be able to accomplish on film at Club Pacifico. I found him to be an extremely warm, outgoing individual and we hit it off right from our first handshake.

Depending on the conditions, my first hope was to help John catch his first Pacific sailfish ... on a fly rod. The second choice was to use Garcia Ambassador plug-casting reels, light casting rods and 17-pound-test line for these large Pacific sailfish. But of course I knew the conditions would dictate what equipment we used and how we fished for them with artificial lures or natural bait. John, being a true fisherman, said it did not make any difference to him and he was just excited to be on this trip.

Our Pan Am 747 flight to Panama gave us time for a little round-robin discussion with the whole crew while sitting in the first class upstairs lounge. They wanted to know how they were going to get all the camera and sound equipment to the far-away island of Coiba, where Club Pacifico was located.

I said, "No sweat. I already made arrangements through Bob Griffin with General Omar Trejiios to supply a special military airplane for the camera crew and equipment. The rest of us will fly a twin otter along with our equipment. And, weather permitting, we will have a one-day use of his helicopter for aerial shots."

That immediately put a smile on the face of Bruce Buckley, the lead cameraman. Turns out, Bruce spent a few years in his earlier life as a multi-engine pilot in the U.S. Air Force and figured he had probably flown whatever airplane the Panamanian military was supplying.

I'd already told Bob Duncan about the arrangements made for us to spend our short night in the La Siesta Hotel, a short minibus drive to the small civilian airport where we would be departing from in the morning. A wonderful lunch was served to us in the upstairs lounge, and after all the loose ends were tied together, I went back downstairs to my seat for a nice little nap. I was still soundly sleeping when the captain slipped this big bird onto the runway.

Almost before we knew it, the airplane was on the deplaning tarmac near the terminal. With the engines shut down, the flight attendants quickly had two doors open, when a stern-looking passenger service agent boarded the airplane to ask everyone to remain seated. Two burley sergeants dressed in fatigues with pistols and nightsticks stepped into the first-class section and spoke to a purser for a moment who promptly pointed to where I was sitting.

The men marched to my seat, and one said, "AhStu Aptee?"

I nodded. The meanest looking one with Master Sergeant stripes gruffly said, "Come weeth us, ahora!" Everyone stared and some shook their heads as I stood up. With one on each side of me, placing a firm hand under my arm, I was quickly rushed and half-carried off the airplane.

I could not imagine what could have provoked an encounter like this with the Panamanian Policia Militar. Having heard rumors of their reputation for being rough, if not bloody, when they apprehend someone, I was starting to worry and actually sweat.

It seemed to me that the closer we got to the terminal, the faster and rougher they were walking me. I tried glancing back over my shoulder at the airplane a couple of times to see if the passengers were starting to come off. But each time I did so they jerked me forward. Christ, I wondered, what the hell is going on?

As we entered the terminal building. I noticed half a dozen other Policia Militar just standing by, as though they might be needed. They fell in behind us as I was ushered through a door down a short hallway and into an office with a Private sign on the door.

My mind raced like a tornado trying to figure out what was about to happen and at the same time trying to keep a good posture so I didn't appear to be as frightened as I was becoming. Show no fear, I told myself.

One of the sergeants opened the door beckoning me to enter, which I did. General Torrijos was tilted back in a cushy high-back chair, his feet on the table while puffing on a huge cigar. He gave the two sergeants a slight gesture with his hand. They did a crisp about-face and left the room.

Looking me up-and-down, Torrijos started with a chuckle that turned into a belly laugh, which stopped as quickly as it started. Now standing up and extending his right hand, with a smile he said, "Ah Stu, mi amigo, how you like zis surprise welcome I arrange for you?"

Relieved beyond words, I smiled back. "General, you scared the shit out of me."

This again brought a brief, hearty laugh, ending with him saying, "Eh, tank you for come here. I want you know if you need somesing, I here for you."

A quick thought ran through my head to the effect "with friends like you, I don't need enemies," but wisely held my tongue. Instead I replied, "Thank you very much, General. I am a bit concerned about my wife and the members of my television crew not knowing what has happened to me."

"Ah Stu, don't worry. They told this a joke, eh? They put through customs weeth all, how you say, all their cameras and ekeepment. They now at La Siesta hotel."

He touched something under the edge of the desk and the door immediately opened. The same fierce-looking Master Sergeant stepped into the room. The General rattled something off in Spanish faster than I could understand. Whatever was said brought a big smile to the sergeant's face as he came to attention and saluted smartly. Turning to me, the General said, "Sergeant Rodriguez drive you to hotel. I make sure everysing run bueno for you on Coiba. You call on radio when you need hellycopter." He then switched from Spanglish and said in Spanish, "Buena suerte con la pesca, mi amigo."

With those words wishing me luck fishing, he sat down again, this time picking up some papers that it appeared he was going to sign. I'd obviously been dismissed. Sergeant Rodriguez motioned me to follow, and I did. At the La Siesta's desk, I was told General Torrijos had ordered his personal suite for Bernice and me. It was normally reserved only for him or visiting dignitaries. Wow, I thought, all is well that ends well.

At the General's suite, Bernice told me, "We all got the word about the General's prank before we got off the airplane, and from some of the comments I heard from the crew I'm sure you'll be getting some razzing at dinner this evening."

A double vodka martini and good dinner helped me smile at some of the questions and comments I got from the group. Tomorrow morning we would have an hour and one-half flight to Coiba and a 40-minute boat ride to Club Pacifico. John Havlicek was going to get his sailfish action, and we were going to get a great show for "The American Sportsman." The dinner conversation reflected our excitement and anticipation.

Nobody mentioned rain.

* * *

We gathered in the hotel lobby for coffee at 6 a.m., just as our minibus pulled up. It was just starting to get light, and I could see that the ground was wet with numerous deep puddles from a heavy rain during the night. Such quick showers are common that time of year in Panama. I just hoped it was not one of those subtropical, equatorial stationary fronts that sometimes pushed north from the jungles of South America and can hang around for a week or more.

Good thing there were six of us men to handle all the camera and sound gear. Whenever "American Sportsman" goes to a faraway location, they always carry backup camera equipment for the backup camera equipment. It makes more sense than having to come back and re-shoot something.

I breathed a sigh of relief during our 20-minute drive to the small civil airport. The sun was now above the horizon, and I could see patches of blue sky, which gave me hope that we would have good flying and good fishing weather.

In the small terminal, they weighed each piece of our luggage and checked our passports before letting us go out to board our airplane. The twin-engine military airplane was nearby on the tarmac, with a single Guardia National soldier standing guard. Our three-man film crew walked alongside the baggage cart to make sure none of the delicate camera equipment got banged around.

By 7 a.m., after the captain and co-pilot blessed themselves with the sign of the cross over their chest, we were accelerating down the runway for takeoff. Looking out the window at a bird's-eye view of the city along the coast, I was hoping I had mentioned the possibility of filming this to the crew in the other airplane.

We turned north and west, for the first 30 minutes flying along the coastline; gradually land disappeared behind us, and there was nothing but water around us. Then, almost at once, we were surrounded by clouds and heavy rain.

Our pilot started a gradual descent toward the water, hoping to be out of the clouds. Leveling off at 2,500 feet, it appeared as though we were below the base of the clouds but still in the rain accompanied by sudden downdrafts and updrafts that brought some loud sighs from all of us.

It sounded to me like our pilot and co-pilot were discussing the possibility of whether they should turn back or continue to Coiba. About that time we broke out of the rain and rough air, at least for a while. Because of our lower altitude, we were also beyond the range of receiving the VOR navigation track, which is only line-of-sight navigation. If we had stayed at the higher altitude of 8,500 feet, we would still be able to navigate that way. Now all we had to navigate by was an ADF low-frequency receiver, which was swinging through a 20-degree arc, and the Doppler system that should pick up our cross track drift. This meant that we were basically flying by DR – dead-reckoning navigation – hoping that the Doppler system was able to pick up our cross track drift, and that we would not end up flying beyond Coiba out into the Pacific Ocean, never to be seen or heard from again.

Once out of the rain and the clouds, the pilots decided to climb, if they could, back to the original altitude. We did manage to get to 7,000 feet before leveling off, still below the base of the clouds.

It must have been another 30 minutes of flying, occasionally in and out of rain squalls, accompanied by turbulence, when the co-pilot was so excited he nearly jumped out of his seat and pointed ahead, about 20 degrees to the right side of our aircraft. He pointed at something and I strained to see it, but being restricted by my seat belt all I could view was the back of his head.

The captain, looking back over his right shoulder, quickly said, "There's Coiba, prepare to land." With that he started descending while making a slight turn to the right.

We all breathed a loud sigh of relief. Bernice had been squeezing my hand so hard it was almost numb, and it now felt good to have blood flowing back into it.

The short gravel runway at the prison camp on Coiba was unique, to say the least. No matter what the wind direction, the pilot had to land coming off the water going uphill, and all takeoffs were just the opposite, going downhill toward the water. The runway marking consisted of a line of military helmets painted white, and placed every 100 feet along each side of the runway.

Every landing I ever experienced here turned out to be a rough one, and this one was no exception. As the pilot reached the end of the runway and turned the airplane around, we were greeted by the prison commandant and his entourage of commissioned and non-commissioned officers

John suggested that I get off the airplane first because I had been here a few times before. Stepping out onto the gravel runway, I was greeted warmly by the commandant with a handshake and a pat on the back. Looking back I could see the lieutenant was helping Beth and Bernice off the airplane.

We now had to walk about a quarter of a mile to the shoreline. We were escorted by some of the military prison guards. A bunch of the prisoners offloaded and carried our luggage down to the water, wading out almost knee deep to put the luggage in a small panga. A number of the prisoner trustees were standing about 50 feet back from the path, holding up beads, paintings and various other articles for sale that they and other prison inmates had made. I asked the lieutenant to please tell them that we'll take a look on our way back home.

I had planned this trip over a full moon, which normally has some of the best fishing. It also has the most extreme high and low tides, which in this part of the Pacific can be as much as a 20-foot difference.

We arrived on the island during the extreme low tide condition and instead of boarding our 25-foot Mako from the pier for our run to Club Pacifico, we had to take our shoes off, roll up our pants legs and wade out about 50 feet in soft muck to get aboard the panga. It was obvious that some of the guards were snickering and even laughing at our plight.

Once aboard the panga, we used a bailing can to wash off our feet. They did have a couple of towels for us to dry our feet before putting our shoes back on. While the sea was smooth for our short trip to the far side of Coiba, we could see ominous rain showers in the distance toward the mainland.

I softly said to John, "I sure hope this front passes through quickly, leaving us with some bluebird weather for fishing and filming."

John replied with a big grin, "Stu, I don't care what happens with the weather. This already has been a memorable trip."

"Just wait, my friend, until you hook up with a large Pacific sailfish, longer than your 9-foot fly rod," I replied.

Just as we arrived at Club Pacifico and were deposited on the white, sandy beach, we could see a large rain squall heading toward us. Bob had enough help to swiftly cart all of our bags and fishing gear up to the main lodge just before the big drops of rain driven by gale force winds arrived with crashes of thunder and lightning.

"Holly-molly, we made it without a moment to spare," John exclaimed for all to hear.

Bob added, "The whole island and especially my private vegetable garden can make good use of the rain. It should pass over in an hour or so, and I'll have the boys show you to your rooms while taking your luggage and fishing gear there. You should be quite comfortable; each room has two queen size beds, a dressing room with a full shower and bathroom."

"We have a series of cabins back in the other direction for the captains and mates, and here comes Donald McGinnis, your captain now. Stu has fished with him a few times and thanks highly of his abilities, and he speaks English like the American that he is."

I said, "I don't want to give Donald a big head, but he is one of the most knowledgeable captains I have fished with in all of Latin America."

"Thanks Stu, coming from you that means a lot and I will try and live up to your expectations," said Donald. "Yesterday I located a large amount of sailfish off the Island of Jaicaron, and with this full moon they should remain in that area for at least a week."

"From your mouth to God's ears," I said. "I'm hoping we will have enough sailfish around to introduce John Havlicek to his first Pacific sailfish, up-close and personal, with a fly rod."

"Not a problem, Stu. If he can cast a fly half as good as you had told Bob, he should do well and we'll have many chances to hook up."

Almost as fast as the squall descended upon us, it passed on to wherever squalls go. Bob was now getting a bunch of the mates along with the normal crew to help carry our luggage to our rooms in another group of buildings. Meanwhile he had been on the side-band radio talking to the prison and was informed that the military plane with the camera crew and equipment had arrived half an hour after we left. They had been in safe hands, enjoying a cold beer while waiting for the rain to stop, and were presently en route.

I had been wondering if they had turned back to the airport in Panama, but had not want to bring up the subject for fear of starting something that would have the rest of our group worrying about them.

With only the afternoon left, today would be an in-camp day. After lunch we would have plenty of time to unpack and rig all of our fishing tackle with the help of some of the captains and mates.

While Bernice and I were walking over to the main lodge, I saw one of the other 25-foot Makos coming around the corner. It was a good feeling to know that the camera crew and equipment made it in good shape.

I had forewarned Bob about all of their camera equipment, so he had lots of extra strong hands ready to help with the muscle work.

Bob's chef and crew certainly knew how to feed his guests.

Chunky lobster bisque to start with; then a homegrown fresh vegetable chef salad with three kinds of cheese, ham, salami, fresh shrimp, bologna.

We were finished with our lobster bisque when the film crew, led by the Producer, Bob Duncan, came in for lunch. First words out of his mouth were, "Did you guys fly through that big-ass storm? I thought my life was over. We were being tossed around like a falling leaf in the wind and seemed like one time we were almost upside down, and I really thought we were going to die."

I nodded. "Sounds like you must have flown into one of the towering cumulus clouds, which can actually tear the wings off an airplane. Just as soon as we hit the heavy rain, our pilot descended down below the base of the clouds. Even so, we continued to fly through heavy rain showers that tossed us about."

Trying to lighten up the near-death conversation, I said with a hint of humor in my voice, "Sit down and wrap your mouth around some of this lobster bisque and it may help you forget your harrowing flight."

We spent the following five days playing nickel-dime poker, reading books and playing with our fishing tackle while the torrential rains from the stationary subtropical equatorial front continued to fall day and night, without showing any prospects of letting up. Three days into the poker playing, John and I were both getting a severe case of cabin fever, so I suggested that we put on our rain suits, grab one of the captains, take one of the 22-foot Makos and run the half mile across the small protected bay to fish for some wahoo and snapper near the small island of Ranchoria. Using spinning tackle and 17 pound test line, casting half ounce bucktail jigs we both caught numerous 20- to 30-pound wahoo, giving John a thrill when he hooked his first wahoo speedster, and half a dozen 5- to 10-pound red snappers. We headed back with enough great eating fresh fish to feed the camp for our stay–soaking wet but with broad smiles on our face.

Day Five was a continuation of the pelting rain. Now everyone began catching cabin fever. The poker game changed into sets of gin rummy and hearts. We were starting to wonder if, and how, we were ever going to get out of here.

The sixth morning was the one on which I awoke to the complete quiet. I quickly donned my filming and fishing clothing, making sure that I had a second set of exactly the same shirt and pants neatly folded and stashed in my waterproof carry-on bag—this to maintain continuity in the filming in case a change of clothes was necessary.

Movies or TV segments are generally shot backward. First, you go out and catch the fish, making sure the most important and uncontrollable part is available or as the film crew calls it, "in the can." Next we build the story around the happening, by shooting an opening and a closing for the segment, often right on location, necessitating changing from our already soiled garments in order to look as though we were just starting the trip.

I thought I was getting the jump on everyone else in the crew as I grabbed my gear, almost bolting out of the door. Hondo was way ahead of me with his long strides; he was almost all the way to the dining room. Shouting for him to find a dry spot under the canopy to leave his waterproof bag containing all of his gear, I accelerated my steps, trying to catch up. Our camera crew was already well into their breakfast of hotcakes, bacon and eggs with corn muffins, eating like it was their last meal.

"Looks like we are finally going to do it," Bob said. "Captain McGinnis said we should be into the sailfish about forty-five minutes after we start running. He also said both the camera boat and the fishing boat were fueled, loaded with gear and ready to go when we are."

With those words I started shoveling scrambled eggs with diced pieces of ham and cheese into my mouth, washing it down with swallows of good Costa Rican coffee. In 10 minutes flat, I was pushing back from the table and wagging my finger at John and also Andy Roe, our second cameraman, who were both still enjoying their breakfast.

Grabbing a couple of the mates, I motioned them to follow me to the tackle room where I had stowed my personal fishing equipment, consisting of three fly rods, four 6500c bait-casting reels on rods that most people would use for largemouth bass fishing, and two tackle boxes full of lures and flies for probable on-camera use. I instructed the mates to be sure to put all my equipment on Donald's boat.

As we headed toward the beach we heard "good luck" cried out in unison from our wives, who were on their way to the dining area. With a wave and a "thanks, love you," we continued to the water's edge to board the panga that would transport us out to our 26-foot fishing boat.

As we climbed aboard the boat, I couldn't help but ask John if he was feeling as excited as I was at that moment.

He replied with a grin that lit up his whole face. "Excited and primed ... send me in coach," he said. "I'm glad that this game is finally going to start."

***

Donald had everything stowed in their proper places. The engine was idling, and I could hear conversation on the VHF radio between the lodge and the camera boat, so I assumed the radios were going to work.

The soundman, Joe, wired us with a small battery pack, running a thin wire from it inside of our pants, under our shirt to a very small lavaliere microphone pinned out of sight on a T-shirt under our regular shirts. We quickly performed a sound check so he would have the proper level for each of our voices. It has been often said that my voice projects well, possibly due to making endless PA announcements on airplanes or from the years that I guided anglers backcountry fishing.

The camera crew did bring a set of walkie-talkies with a two-mile range for boat-to-boat conversation. We would have our VHF radios turned off during the filming in the event conversation or static stepped on our on-camera conversation.

Our boat crew consists of Captain Don McGinnis, lead cameraman Bruce Buckley and soundman Joe Mangono – who will spend his day cramped in the little cuddy cabin so as not to be seen on camera – and of course John Havlicek and myself. The camera boat carried producer Bob Duncan, second cameraman Andy Roe, host Bob Griffin, Captain Reito and a mate. They also carried all of the extra batteries, cameras, large tripod, cases of 16mm film and sound equipment.

It was already 7:30 a.m. and we were just pulling anchor for the 45-minute run that Don McGinnis promised for the first sailfish of the day. The wind blew lightly and the seas were relatively calm, but not even a patch of blue sky could be seen – only dark layers of cumulus clouds in all quadrants. At least it was not raining, and Bob Griffin said the weather forecast he received at 5 a.m. showed this stationary front moving back to the south, leaving only broken clouds in this part of Panama.

We were all anxious for the games to begin. Donald slowly eased the throttle forward to get the heavily loaded hull on plane. Before we had traveled 100 yards, John and I wished each other good luck, ending it with a high-five palm slap.

Twenty minutes had passed when we were intercepted by a large school of spinner dolphins. There must have been at least 200 of them cavorting in front of our bow and jumping our wake like water skiers. Then, as quickly as they appeared, they evidently tired of escorting us and vanished.

It seemed like another 20 minutes went by when Donald loudly exclaimed, "Hey, I see a free jumper, and I think they're right on time."

Two 30-pound line-class trolling rods sported a pair of plastic artificial squids that I rigged in tandem without any hooks. These plastic squids should bring sailfish to the surface close enough to the boat for us to try and select the biggest one. For John to fly fish for these big Pacific sailfish, we'd have 40 feet of fly line stripped off the reel into a bucket, placed in the right corner below the boat's transom.

When one or more sailfish attacked the teaser, I would holler "neutral" and Donald would bring the boat out of forward gear. As soon as that happened, John could start false casting his big popping bug fly, dropping it 40 feet straight behind the transom.

I would be handling the teaser rod, bringing the fish closer to the boat. The moment John's fly hits the water, the most important part of my job was to snatch the teaser out of the water, away from the hungry and excited sailfish. At the same time, John, holding his rod tip toward the water, would start stripping line into the boat with an erratic, hard motion, making his fly pop and gurgle to attract the sailfish that instinctively thinks it overran its original prey.

If all went as planned and the sailfish ate John's fly, he had a one-in-five chance of catching his first one. This should be no problem with the amount of sailfish around, providing we'd get two or three days to film the segment.

Since bad weather had claimed five of the six planned days for filming the show, putting our backs up against the proverbial wall, I needed to make a command decision. As field host for this segment of ABC's "American Sportsmen," it was my job to make sure that we produced a completed, exciting show. I called Bob Duncan on our walkie-talkies.

"Bob, with only one full day of filming left, I decided to make sure we're going to get some sailfish action," I told him. "I'm going to rig the four bait-casting outfits with a hooked strip of bait. We'll do a bait and switch, teasing the sailfish close to the boat for the camera before John feeds the strip bait back to one of them. If we get enough action footage quick enough, we can then try having John catch one with a fly rod."

Bob put his blessing on my revised plan, and as Donald started easing the throttle back to trolling speed, John and I each took a teaser rod, free-spooling the tandem-rigged squid about 100 feet behind the boat.

An hour past without raising any sailfish to our teasers, prompting me to wonder aloud about what happened to that first promised sailfish in 45 minutes, as by now two hours had elapsed.

"Don't worry Stu," Donald replied, smiling slyly at my needle. "I know there are plenty of sailfish around here. All we have to do is find the mother lode."

He sounded quite certain, so all eyes remained on the water and

272

mouths shut until a few minutes later he got extremely animated. "There, 11 o'clock, almost on the horizon, looks like a couple of sailfish free jumping," he gushed excitedly. "Or it might just be some more of those spinner dolphin. Let's reel the teasers in and make a run for that area because we're not finding anything here."

As we drew closer it became clear that these were indeed large, free jumping Pacific sailfish. I motioned to Donald with my palm down to slow down to trolling speed before we got into the middle of what appeared to be, as Donald described, the mother lode of sailfish.

"Let's get the teasers out," I hollered to John, so happy and relieved that I could barely speak.

We were both free spooling the squid just like we did an hour ago, but this time we didn't even get the teasers back very far before four sailfish were trying to eat them. The huge spindlebeaks slapped the squid with their bills and grabbed the second squid and the tandem rig in a competition over our teasers.

Donald left the steering wheel long enough to grab two of the bait-casting outfits that were already rigged with a strip of houndfish, a sailfish delicacy.

"Okay John," I cried. "Put your teaser rod in the rod holder and take this rod and free-spool your bait back to where your teaser is holding the sailfish."

It looked like a Chinese fire drill, for while John free-spooled his bait, I did the same on the other side of the boat near my teaser. Six sailfish chased the teasers and baits, slashing those nose swords like dicing knives. Not watching my bait, my concern was making sure John hooked up and landed a nice sailfish on camera. Seeing that the fish were still 15 or more feet behind his bait I told John to free-spool his line back about 20 more feet.

As he did that and not watching my own bait, a sailfish inhaled it and my reflexes inadvertently set the hook. "I've got mine," I yelled, as the startled sailfish took off at about 50 miles per hour, the line screaming off my reel at the same speed. Donald asked if we should chase after my fish.

"No, just keep trolling. I don't care about my fish. I want to make sure John gets hooked up." I instructed John to push the lever to free-spool line and drop it back a little more.

Finally, it happened. "One's got it!" I screamed. "Let him take it for a moment. Okay, now turn your handle to re-engage the spool." John did just as I asked, and when I added for him to strike the fish sharply four times, the hook held steady in the fish's mouth.

Luckily, my fish made a big mistake by swimming back to the rest of the school, allowing me to retrieve most of the line or I would've been standing there with an empty reel. As it was, John's fish was ripping line at breakneck speed in the opposite direction from my fish.

Donald again drew perplexed. "Stu, what should I do?"

"Just go after John's fish, that's the one we have to get. I don't care whether I catch mine or not. This is his first Pacific sailfish ever and he's doing a great job so far."

John's spindlebeak, as Joe Brooks used to call them and many others since then, was doing a spectacular job of tail-walking, using its tail to skip across the surface of the water for a few seconds. It then went deep and came barreling into the air, its hundred-plus pounds of weight about five feet in the air.

John and I were sitting back-to-back in the middle of the open cockpit on the engine box. Our fish headed in opposite directions, the worst scenario when fishing for big fish on light tackle. My fish seemed to have sounded to around 80 feet and was probably resting as we slowly made our way toward John's still-wild fish. He did a sterling job of pumping and reeling, regaining line like he had been doing this type of fishing with light tackle all of his life. This natural instinct of a great professional athlete was showing itself.

Twice Donald put the boat in neutral and came back to grab the 15 feet of 80-pound-monofilament leader. The fish would surge, taking 50 or 60 feet of hard-fought line off John's reel. Like they say, the third time is a charm and in this case it proved true. John pumped the now tired-sailfish back to the boat, and Donald was able to grab the leader and muscle the sailfish close enough to grab its bill. He hoisted it high enough alongside the boat's gunwale and toward the camera so that John could pat the big fish on its cheek.

Easing this beautiful example of nature back into the water, Donald instructed John to get his side cutters out of the sheath on his hip and quickly cut the leader close to the fish's mouth. "Don't worry, the hook will rust out of its mouth in a couple of days," Donald assured.

"Attaway, Johnny baby, catch 'em and put 'em back, that's the name of the game," I said, totally gleeful that we'd accomplished the mission.

High-five congratulations could be heard slapping all around. Meanwhile, my sailfish was acting strange, not fighting the way most sailfish do. It would only swim down, not out and away from the boat, which had me believing it may be tail wrapped. So I increased the amount of drag by a couple more pounds and doubled the pumping pressure I had been applying. This worked, and five minutes later I had a very large sailfish coming to the surface next to the boat, tail first.

Donald grabbed its tail in one hand, the leader in the other, un-wrapping it from around the base of the sailfish's tail. Turning it around head first, he was able to take the bill and remove the hook from the corner of its jaw, lifting its head high enough for me to pat it on the cheek, a ritual I go through for every large fish I release.

After being tail wrapped my sailfish was really tired. We held it in the water facing forward while we put the boat into forward gear, helping it breath, like an athlete inhaling 100-percent oxygen.

About four minutes of this and it was trying to break free from our grasp. Donald once again put the boat into neutral before I released my grip, saying, "Okay, baby, go home, go see Davy Jones and give him my fondest regards."

Not only did John catch the first sailfish he ever hooked, he did so using extremely light tackle and as part of a doubleheader with my fish. And, most importantly, he did it on camera for millions of people to witness on their television screens.

Even though the sky still looked dark and menacing, the temperature had to be close to 95 degrees and we'd both been working hard. It was time to take a 15-minute break, guzzle down some cold water and flex tired fingers and muscles. This also allowed

Bruce to reload his 16mm 400-foot magazines and Joe to do the same with his Nagra sound recorder.

I didn't even have to wave the camera boat to come over. Bob Duncan was as excited as John Havlicek and could hardly wait to come alongside before expounding on how great that doubleheader looked from their vantage point. They believe they filmed a great jumping scene with the sailfish in the foreground and the boat in the background. They were also responsible for shooting what is known as the master scene, a wide shot of the boat with both anglers fighting the fish. Bruce's job was to get all the tight shots and he was pleased with what he felt was in the can. Joe, who had been listening through his earphones the whole time, was sure he had great audio.

"All right!" I exclaimed to no one in particular. "We have the basis of a good segment, now all we have to do is build the scenes by doing some production."

Bob was starting to give Bruce and Joe some instruction on how he thinks the production acting should be filmed. I interrupted him. "Sorry, Bob, but I just saw two more sailfish free jumping a couple hundred yards behind us. With all of the sailfish we have in this area right now, I think we should at least spend another hour getting one more sailfish fish-fighting sequence in the can."

"Good idea, Stu," he replied while nodding. "Should John try and do it with a fly rod?"

"Actually, we probably should use the same equipment, backing up what is already in the can for cutaways, tightening up our scene. That is if John still feels up to it."

John smiled at the challenge. "Hey, if we can handle two, I know we can handle four."

While this conversation went on, the good captain Donald had been re-rigging both of the rods with new leaders, sharp hooks and fresh strip baits. Turning the boat toward the last sighting of free-jumping sailfish, we quickly put our teasers back just beyond the boat's whitewater wake.

There was no wait at all; a couple of big bruiser sailfish were after the teasers before they were trolled 100 yards. Before I could even suggest it, John – being a quick study and true athlete – quickly free-spooled his strip bait back to the marauding sailfish. Almost before he was ready, what looked to be one of the biggest sailfish I'd ever seen inhaled it. As John was setting the hook with three quick jerks of the rod, this monster vaulted eight feet out of the water, confirming my thoughts about its possible world-record size.

Just as quickly, it tail-walked almost completely around our boat before screaming line off John's reel, making a blistering 150-yard run. It started going deeper, either to rest for a moment or to settle down to the fight by spreading its big pectoral fins to create more drag.

After more than an hour and a half of this dogged fighting, John's arms and fingers were starting to cramp. As I'd reminded him previously, the muscles he was using were completely different than he those for playing basketball. While I massaged his forearms and hands, he said, "I feel like I am a shade away from being wiped out – and that's no easy admission for a professional athlete to accept."

As common with light-tackle battles, John fought the fish without a fighting belt or harness to help relieve the strain and the pain of the rod butt grinding into his belly. I asked how he was doing and John admitted changing positions of the butt about 10 times already because, "I can't seem to find a place that isn't bruised and tender."

The gigantic sailfish changed its tactics again. It came to the surface with another high jump, made two greyhound tail walks, and finally charged the boat only to dive underneath about 20 yards before reaching us.

I yelled for Donald to quickly put the boat in reverse and turn the wheel to the right, taking the propeller away from where the fish and line would be going under the boat. As Donald spun the wheel, something happened to the steering cable and the boat did not respond, allowing the boat's propeller to cross over the line, cutting off the grand prize.

Not wanting to end the show with sour grapes, I called Bob on the walkie-talkie for him to come over for a powwow.

He wondered what went wrong. "Man, that looked like one big fish."

"It damn sure was," I replied. "Probably a world record. I'm sure it was more than 200 pounds. John did a fantastic job of almost kicking this big fish's butt, but when it swam directly under the boat, coming up on the other side, it cut his line with the propeller. And that was all she wrote."

"What a shame!" Bob said. "We could have had a grand ending for the show with a world-record catch by a world-class athlete."

"Bob, why don't we do a little production, showing the viewing audience part of what actually happened," I intoned? "Instead of having the line getting cut off under the boat, let's show the steering cable breaking and the fish ending up taking all of John's line because we were unable to follow it."

"Do you think it could be a believable bit of acting for the cameras?" Bob asked.

"I don't know," I replied. "I do know one thing though: We have a saying in the Florida Keys that you don't know if you don't go."

"Okay, let's get set up and reenact this happening," Bob said to the camera crew.

Wanting this to be correct the first time, I asked for everyone's attention for just a moment, while I give a briefing on what my intentions are. "Let's reenact the fish going under the boat and my asking Donald to turn the boat to the right," I said. "Put one of the cameras on Donald spinning the wheel, with nothing happening. Next, have one camera on me and the other on John as I tell Donald with surprise in my voice that the boat is going the wrong way.

"Get a shot of Donald going down below, asking for a moment to see if he can fix the problem. Meanwhile the fish is screaming line from John's reel. This can be simulated by hooking John's line to the camera boat and having it slowly run away from us, until all of the line runs off John's reel."

John did a fantastic, very believable job of acting, Academy Award-style. After all the line was gone from the reel and it broke at the end, he showed genuine anguish and hurt while massaging his wrist and rubbing his stomach, saying, "It was a real gut ache."

This "American Sportsmen" show won a Teddy award for the best television fishing segment filmed in 1973. And you were there.

CHAPTER

TWENTY-ONE

PILOT IN COMMAND

It's Time to Move Into the Left-Hand Seat

In September, 1973, after spending almost three full years as a 747-rated First Officer, I had the opportunity to become a Pan Am Captain on the 727, the racy-looking tri-jet popular with many airlines, mostly for domestic operations.

The amount of additional money I would make as a 727 Captain was negligible. Pan Am had a strange way of breaking down our pay by the hour, calling it increment pay, which included the gross weight of the airplane, the speed of the airplane, one rate for day flying and a slightly higher rate for nights.

As a senior 747 First Officer, the majority of my flying took place at night, giving me a slight amount of additional pay. As a junior 727 Captain I would basically be flying a schedule, something that the more-senior Captains didn't want to do.

I had made the decision early on to never pass up an opportunity to upgrade my position, regardless of how the move affected my finances. Always I hoped the impact on my paycheck would be temporary, and that as I moved ahead in flying time and seniority, so too would my salary improve.

With a proud feeling in my chest and teary eyed, I flew my last 747 flight as a co-pilot from London's Heathrow airport to John F. Kennedy on September 29th.

Now I was scheduled for five weeks of 727 ground school and

simulator training before I could be at the controls of an actual aircraft—and in that coveted left-hand seat. Working from my base at Pan Am's training facility on Northwest 36th Street in Miami during four days spread out over a week, I made 36 takeoffs and landings at TNT, a little training airstrip out in the Everglades.

After getting an "up" from my instructors, I needed to pass a very important pre-command check; which you only have to do one time before becoming a Pan American Captain. My pre-command check consisted of flying to Freeport, Grand Bahama Island on instruments under the hood with Howard Ashcraft, the Chief Pilot in the right seat as the Co-Pilot – and making believe he's just a new, clueless Co-Pilot, but all the while making steely-eyed judgments on everything I did and said. He would put the 727 in a variety of dangerous situations during the ILS approaches, landings and takeoffs, to see if the new Captain in Command had the ability to take the aircraft away from him before letting the situation get out of hand.

Taking command of the situation was never a problem for me, when it came to airplanes or fishing.

Four days later I operated a passenger flight with Art Milo, one of Pan Am's finest check captains in the right-hand seat as my Co-Pilot, going from Miami to St. Thomas to St. Croix, spending the night in St. Croix. The next morning we flew to St. Thomas and back to St. Croix then up to New York's JFK. After spending the night in New York, it was back to St. Thomas, St. Croix and on to Miami, this time with an FAA inspector in the jump seat to hopefully sign me off.

Flying in and out of St. Thomas airport before they lengthened the 4,820-foot runway was truly a test of one's flying skills. It was important to put the airplane on the runway within the first thousand feet, pull your speed brake handle up, place all three engines in reverse and apply heavy braking at the same time. It almost reminded me of my Navy flying days.

There were several other check rides, but finally I was signed off by one of Pan Am's check pilots. The left seat was mine. Another major hurdle in my life as a pilot had been passed..

My first "pay-for-play" flight took me from Miami to Barranquilla, Columbia, to Maracaibo, Venezuela, where spending that night at the Intercontinental Hotel in Maracaibo I bought drinks for the crew to celebrate my first command flight.

As far as I was concerned the Boeing 727 was the biggest fighter plane in the sky and the next two years of flying into Central America, the North coast of South America and all of the Caribbean Islands was some of the most enjoyable flying of my airline career. Not that it was always smooth sledding; I remember one of my early flights in the wintertime from JFK to Montego Bay Jamaica, which was a piece of cake, then Montego Bay to Chicago O'Hare which had me puckering. The flight was close to the "three-holer's", as we affectionately called the 727, maximum range with a severe cold front approaching the Chicago area. I had just barely passed my first hundred hours command which would now allow me to operate to lower minimums on an instrument approach. As we got within one hour of O'Hare we were checking the weather for various possible alternate airports because Chicago was reporting heavy snow flurries that sometimes made landing conditions below minimums and it looked like my best alternate would be Louisville, Kentucky. Keeping a fuel on board score is very important. You can't just pull over to the side when you run out of fuel and call for AAA assistance. The flight plan is predicated on shooting an instrument approach at the destination airport, executing a missed approach, climb out and fly to your alternate airport, shoot an instrument approach and land. That's all well and good, if it works out that way. Chicago Center instructed me to enter a holding pattern, making two circuits before turning us over to Chicago approach control, who gave us a dissent and vectors to the outer marker for an ILS approach to the active runway. Just prior to over heading the outer marker they had a major wind shift, closing the runway. Approach control gave me instructions to execute a missed approach and fly on vectors to the outer marker of another runway. Then just like déjà vu this same scenario happened again, this time because the runway visibility went below minimums, making me wonder why I did not land at Louisville, Kentucky when I passed over it.

I quickly briefed my crew on the new runway, telling them if we execute a missed approach again we are heading to Louisville.

Wind gusts on this approach had us bouncing around and I didn't even have time to make an announcement to our poor passengers who were probably wondering why we were descending and then climbing back out again twice.

Just before minimums which would've had me executing a missed approach again my first officer said "I've got the rabbit!" This is a lead-in-strobe light just prior to the runway.

This big fighter plane performed like a champion and on our way taxiing to the terminal I gave our passengers a brief explanation of what had happened. I remember wondering if this was an omen of future things to come.......

Finally, in 1976, my days and nights in the 727 came to an inevitable end. I would take command of a different airplane—once I had learned to fly it.

I didn't know it at the time, but ferrying a 727 from Berlin to Miami with refueling stops in Keflavik, Iceland, and Boston was to be the last flight I would operate as a 727 Captain. Entering Miami's Flight Operations to turn in the flight's paperwork, I noticed an unusually large group of pilots milling around the glass-encased bulletin board.

"What's up, guys?" I asked of no one in particular.

"The 727s have been excessed out of Miami and the pilots senior enough to fly the 707 in New York have had their last 727 flight this month," someone replied.

Tired from a long flight, I was not in the mood to think about the consequences of probably a month of ground school, eight to 10 days of simulator training, getting a 707 simulator rating, going through a seven-hour FAA oral exam, having a type rating ride in the airplane with the FAA, and an OEC (Original Equipment Check) all over again, just when I was feeling really comfortable and enjoying my job.

The past several months flying as a 727 Captain has been some of the most enjoyable civilian flying I can remember. Hearing other pilots talk about how heavy the 707 controls felt compared to flying the 727 with hydraulic boost was not something I was looking forward to doing. Whenever asked how I like flying the 727, my standard answer was that "… it's the biggest fighter plane in the sky."

Like it or not, I was heading for Boeing 707 training and check rides. At least, I would still have four stripes on the sleeves of my jacket and sit in that left seat.

After a month of ground school training, I spent the first six days flying the simulator with Jack Miller, an ex-Naval Aviator, who flew AD Sky Raiders in VA 175, the dive bomber squadron in my air group. Jack was one of the two ex-Navy pilots I ran into on 36th Street that had just been hired by Pan Am right after tearing up my contract with Eastern Airlines.

Jack was quite a few numbers senior to me because of the month I'd taken off to go fishing before going to work for Pan Am. His reputation as a good pilot and a nice guy preceded him.

The first couple of days in the simulator were pretty routine. Doing all of the normal checklists, engine starts, engine shutdowns, normal takeoffs and instrument landings – basically getting used to the heavy feel of the controls. Jack would be in the Captain's seat for the first two hours with me in the Co-Pilot seat, then after a 15-minute cigarette break we'd reverse seat positions, putting me in the left-hand Captain's seat.

During the third simulator period, we started getting into abnormal procedures. This involved engine-out during takeoffs, engine-out instrument approach and landings, various hydraulic and electrical failures, and some of which created additional problems such as having the yaw dampener become inoperative, putting the airplane into a Dutch roll. The yaw can be severe enough to actually rip the engines from the airplane, making it not a very good day to fly.

The abnormal recovery procedure for getting the airplane out of the Dutch role was not a difficult procedure, but had to be precisely implemented.

Because Jack was senior to me, he was in the left-hand seat first when the training instructor put the simulator into a Dutch roll. It was obvious he was not doing or feeling good, and then he turned to me saying, "You've got it."

Taking the yoke, I responded, "I've got it. Jack. What's wrong? Are you okay?"

Before answering he reached into his briefcase, got out a burp bag and began throwing up. Now Captain Rod Joshlin, the simulator instructor, got into the act, asking Jack if he wanted him to secure the simulator.

Jack said, "Hell no, I'm okay now. I've got the controls now, Stu."

Jack did a good job doing the rest of the two-hour session. During our 15-minute cigarette break, he told us that when he went through flight training as a cadet in the Navy, he had to carry burp bags in all the pockets of his flight suit because he would be sick on every single flight. He said that his instructor told him he was doing too good to wash him out, but he should do himself a favor and turn in a quit chit. He stuck with it because he loved flying, and now at this latter stage of his life only certain things affect his inner ear. We both finished the simulator training with good marks and had our seven-hour FAA oral exam a few days later.

My 3 ½-hour aircraft rating ride with the FAA was from Kennedy to Stuart Field in upstate New York, where I demonstrated my abilities with three takeoffs and landings, one of them simulating an engine out. That check-ride was followed by a seven-hour original equipment check, from JFK to London Heathrow, with Frank Altomari a Check Captain in the Co-Pilot seat and an FAA inspector in the jump seat looking over my shoulder.

The next day I deadheaded as a passenger from London to Paris, then operated the flight from Paris to Philadelphia, as part of my OEC (Original Equipment Check). Still being two landings and takeoffs shy of the four necessary with the FAA on board to complete my OEC, five days later I operated a quick turnaround flight from JFK to Bermuda and back to JFK.

Finally! I had my new rating. I sighed so hard at now being considered a qualified 707 Captain that I practically sucked all the air out of the room. I could also operate anywhere in the world.

The next day had me once again deadheading, this time from JFK to Pittsburgh, to operate my first productive "pay-for-play" flight as a 707 Captain. A charter flight from Pittsburgh to Shannon, Ireland, with an overnight layover in Shannon, then operate a charter to Boston and ferry the airplane to JFK.

The most outstanding thing in my mind from this flight was that someone from the Chief Pilot's office or Flight Administration had ordered and paid for a fantastic Chinese dinner, with bold printing on the top stating, "CAPTAIN'S CHOICE." It was common knowledge in Pan Am that I was a Chinese food buff.

After only three months of flying the line, the 707 was starting to feel a little comfortable, but I still felt like I was driving a Mac truck.

After operating the first leg of Pan Am's 002 eastbound around-the-world flight to London, I was called with only minimum rest at the hotel. Headquarters wanted to know if I would volunteer to operate a United Nation's mercy flight from London to Akrotiri, Cyprus, where there was a raging war between the Turks and the Greeks for control of the island. The British had the island blockaded both air and sea. With the prospect of new adventures and high adrenalin flow, of course I volunteered.

My approach to the airport was from over the water, and I had to be in the slot on that approach within a prearranged five-minute span or be shot down by two British frigates stationed along the approach route to keep any unwanted aircraft from landing. This was a cargo flight carrying blankets, medical supplies and the likes for the ravaged civilian population.

The first thing I noticed when I stepped off the airplane was the sight of all the British soldiers milling around, wearing flak jackets and carrying sub-machine guns. While they were unloading my airplane, I was in Flight Operations doing the necessary paperwork to ferry the airplane to Rome when a United States Brigadier General from the U.S. Embassy introduced himself, asking if I could please take his wife and two children on my ferry flight out of Cyprus.

Explaining that without proper authorization from Pan Am, I was unable to take them on a cargo airplane, as much as I would like to comply with his wishes. My suggestion was that he use the Operations telephone and teletype to call both London and New York, getting the proper clearance to take passengers on this ferry flight.

Unfortunately the clearance did not come through prior to my rushed departure by the British military, and I occasionally wonder what happened with this general's wife and children.

The next year of flying the 707 went by so fast it was hard to believe. I flew all over Europe, Africa, South America and Central America. On one occasion I flew Robert Williams, President of Bell Helicopter, and a team of his pilots and maintenance instructors and their families on a charter flight from JFK to London and then Tehran, the capital of Iran. They were going there to teach the Iranian Air Force how to fly and maintain the large order of helicopters they had purchased, and would probably be in Iran six to eight months.

The next morning as I was checking out of the Tehran Intercontinental Hotel, Mr. Williams walked up and introduced me to a high-ranking Iranian Air Force officer, thanking me again for such a good flight. The Air Force officer presented me with an Iranian Air Force cap and their Air Force wings. Shaking hands and patting me on the shoulder, he informed me I was now an honorary member of the Iranian Air Force.

But the best of Iranian trips was yet to come. While operating a charter flight from Tehran to Paris with an overnight in Paris, then continuing to JFK, my distinguished group of passengers included U.S. Congressmen and Senators, presidents of major universities, the U.S. Ambassador to Iran, and the Iranian Ambassador to the United States. They'd been attending a symposium in Tehran and were now going to Washington, DC, on my airplane.

I had no less than 16 "Attaboy" letters forwarded to me through the Pan Am chain of command from this flight. The truth-in-jest saying among the Pan Am pilots was that ten "Attaboys" could offset one "Oh Shit."

As I gained seniority on the 707, I probably became the only pilot in the whole airline industry to bid flying schedules by the phase of the moon and the tides in order to have the best times off to fish. The long-haul flights in the 707 paid off big time in the long periods off between flights when I could pursue my fishing passion.

A couple times each month, depending on the time the year, Bernice and I would spend a week on the Caribbean side of Costa Rica. We'd snook and tarpon fish at Parismina Tarpon Rancho or on the Pacific side of Panama, at the new Club Pacifico. That is, when it wasn't the optimum time to indulge my main passion, fly fishing for big tarpon on the flats of the Florida Keys. Once again I was blessed by having a wife who was willing to put up with my fishing escapades and even most of the time enjoyed going along.

Bernice finally went on one of my Pilot in Command flights after I had been Captain on the 707 for more than three years. Having gained enough seniority on the 707 to be based flying out of Miami again, it was a five-day flight with good layovers in Rio de Janeiro and Buenos Aires. We were at 39,000 feet during the 8 hour and 45-minute flight from Miami to Rio with an FAA inspector in the jump seat behind me doing a periodic route check. Out of the blue, the outer pane lamination on the window next to my head sounded like a shotgun was fired next to my left ear, as the outer panel was stripped away.

Frank Monoco, the FAA inspector, fearing the possibility of being sucked out of the airplane if the other panels of the window blew out, was out of his seat and headed for the back of the airplane without saying a word. I immediately called for and received descent clearance to 31,000 feet and a little while later for further descent clearance to 28,000 feet, helping to relieve some of the cabin differential pressure in case the window actually blew out. I had quickly hooked my shoulder harness into my seat belt, making sure they were not just snug but tight.

If that window had blown out at 39,000 feet, all four of us would have been sucked out the opening in a matter of seconds, and of course everyone in the airplane would have been dead from anoxia before it reached the ground.

As we descended into Rio de Janeiro, approach control informed us that due to construction there was only one runway in operation and the winds were 40 gusting to 50 mph, almost blowing a direct crosswind. The last four airplanes that tried to land executed missed approaches and gone to their alternate airport. Would we like to try the approach or just go to our alternate airport at this time?

"Standby," I replied.

Checking with the flight engineer to find out if his computations matched mine as to our fuel state for shooting the approach, executing a missed approach, climbing out and flying to our alternate airport. He promptly advised me that we had enough fuel to make three approaches and then climb out and proceed to our alternate airport.

"Rio approach control, Clipper 441 would like to try the approach but wish to file a flight plan at this time to our alternate airport in case we do execute a missed approach."

"Roger, Clipper 441, you are clear to continue your descent to the outer marker and the approach."

The cross winds extreme angle from the outer marker to the airport required my holding a 35 degree crab to the left, into the wind creating an illusion I was going to fly across the runway instead of onto it. This was more than a little disconcerting, to say the least...

Just prior to planting this big beast on the concrete, I took the crab out, dropping my left wing in order to keep the airplane going straight down the runway.

The engines on my left wing were probably only inches from touching the concrete as the airplane traveled the first 2,000 feet down the runway, with only the wheels on the left side touching. After getting all the wheels on the ground, I was still holding full left aileron with my control wheel until I had the airplane going slow enough to take one of the high-speed turnoffs to taxi back to the terminal.

After shutting the engines down, Bill Hooper, the First Officer, and Mike Rossum, the Flight Engineer, excitedly jumped out of their seats. They started pounding me on the back and yelling that they had never seen a 707 flying like that in all of their years flying for the Air Force and Pan Am. I appreciated the accolades, but I silently hoped I'd never again have to land any airplane in that much 90-degree crosswind.

All our passengers knew about the incident was that it had been very bumpy flight. I was thinking that it was too bad our frightened FAA inspector was not sitting in the jump seat where he was supposed to be.

Clearing customs was a piece of cake, as we were the only airplane in more than an hour that actually landed, so no lines at immigration or customs. Once again, I was tired and sweaty but feeling very proud when my First Officer and Engineer were telling my wife and anyone else within earshot what a fantastic job I did. With a smile stretching my face, I said, "Even a blind pig finds an acorn once in a while."

Two nights in Rio at the new, plush Intercontinental Hotel is a great way to spend a couple nights on a layover with your wife. And after the window scare, wild crosswind landing and FAA on board, I was ready for some R&R.

We were scheduled to go from Rio to Asuncion, Paraguay, to Montevideo, Uruguay, to Buenos Aires, Argentina, spending an 18-hour layover in BA. It was plenty long enough to experience a dinner to always remember: a one-kilo baby beef T-bone steak, cooked on a flaming grill for all to see. It was one of the finest steaks I ever had the privilege of sinking my teeth into. For dessert they had humongous vine-ripened strawberries with pure, unwhipped, no-sugar-added heavy cream that was fantastic enough to write home about.

We made our scheduled takeoff from Buenos Aires right on time with a full load of passengers heading nonstop back to Rio de Janeiro. Then it happened. As we were climbing out through 25,000 feet over Montevideo's airspace, everyone's ears suddenly felt like they were coming off their heads

Not knowing what caused the loss of cabin pressure, but knowing that I had to get the airplane down below 10,000 feet or have passengers die from lack of oxygen, I did what we jokingly call, "The Big Dive." I executed an emergency descent, first putting my oxygen mask on, switching it to 100-percent oxygen while rolling into a turn away from the mountains, pulling my throttles all the way off. At the same time, I extended my speed brakes and when my airspeed got slow enough, dropped my landing gear. Everything was to make the airplane drop down to 10,000 feet or lower as fast as possible.

We were squawking 7700 "Emergency" on the transponder, and Bill was talking to Montevideo Center to get us a clearance at 9,000 feet back to Buenos Aires.

After leveling off at 9,000 feet I was able to take my oxygen mask off and take a moment to talk to passengers on the public address system, telling them that I was sorry for the scare but it was a necessary procedure and we are heading back to Buenos Aires.

Back at the terminal, the ground personnel removed all passengers from the airplane into the passenger lounge and I went into operations. Mike, our flight engineer, was busy with the maintenance people describing exactly what happened.

The culprit turned out to be a spring that operates the forward outflow valve, metering the cabin pressure at a pre-designated differential. For some unknown reason it decided to quit working and went full open, dumping all the air out of the cabin.

There was not another one of the springs to be had in anybody's 707 maintenance stash. They said no one has ever had that spring fail. New York maintenance gave them permission to wire the forward outflow valve shut and gave me a QXI to legally operate the flight to Rio.

Walking into the passenger lounge, I could feel all their eyes were on me, so I walked up to the podium, switched the microphone on and asked, "Is everyone okay?"

I can see a lot of up-and-down head bobs along with a lot of yes's and si's, so I inform them that we have the problem fixed and we will be departing for Rio in about 45 minutes. Is there anyone that would not like to continue on my flight? Only one person raised his hand and stood up, saying he would miss his connection from Rio to Cape Town, South Africa, so he would rather spend the night here and take the Pan Am flight tomorrow morning.

Not bad, only one passenger not getting back on the airplane with me after an emergency descent...Not bad indeed.

I can't help wondering now: Can it be Bernice is a jinx on this series of flights? I hope not, because we still have two more legs before getting home.

This time, our nonstop flight back to Rio was easy as falling off a log, and the 30-hour layover at the Intercontinental gave me a little time to go sightseeing with my wife before the long 10-hour flight back to JFK.

Because the flight is more than 8 ½ hours, we do have an extra Co-Pilot and extra Flight Engineer to share in the flying duties, allowing me to spend my rest time sitting in first-class with my wife.

After a long night, we arrived at JFK at 8 o'clock in the morning, cleared customs just in time to get on a National Airlines flight to Miami, giving me one day off at home before operating a cargo flight from Miami to Maracaibo, Venezuela, and back to Miami the same day.

Then I had 11 full days off to go fishing. I fly, and then I fish. That's my life, and it's a good one!

My next scheduled flight was from JFK to Dakar, Senegal, Africa, for a 12-hour layover before flying to Monrovia, Liberia, where I have a two-day layover giving me a good day of fishing near Roberts Field. The next day I paid my dues for any of the easy flying I had previously done in Africa.

It was a night flight from Monrovia to Accra, Ghana, and back to Monrovia for a well-deserved 24-hour rest. We fought our way through severe coastal thunderstorms, with lightning flashes making it almost impossible to see outside the cockpit because our pupils would contract with each lightning flash. The torrential rains made landing out of a non-precision ADF approach into what looked like a black bottomless pit. Touching down into a couple of inches of water on the runway, we kept the big bird from hydro- planning and skidding. When we shut down the engines, we certainly figured we had earned our pay again that night. All this drives home the true saying that airline flying represents hours and hours of utter boredom, interrupted occasionally by moments of sheer terror.

CHAPTER

TWENTY-TWO

HARD-BALL FISHING WITH

DICK BUTKUS

The Greatest Linebacker Goes on Offense!

He was rumored to be the meanest, nastiest, fiercest, most-feared linebacker to ever play the game of football. He had the speed and quickness to make tackles from sideline to sideline and to cover tight ends and running backs on pass plays. He was All-NFL seven times and played in the Pro Bowl eight times.

In 1975 Dick Butkus was a true legendary figure, an icon instantly recognizable to legions of football fans. His playing days were over, ended by a second knee operation. But at 6 feet, 3 inches and 250 solid pounds, he looked and acted like a man ready to take on just about anything.

Also in 1975, Dick Butkus had only been fishing once in his life. Just once! And that had been years before with conventional 30-pound-test trolling tackle. When he told me about it on the phone, he seemed quite proud of the 4-pound snook he had caught—the only fish in his life. And he seemed absolutely eager to respond to the reason I had called him: To be on camera in a segment for ABC's "The American Sportsman" television series. We would be going after sailfish and other assorted denizens of the deep in the fish-rich waters of the Bat Islands off Playa Coco on the Pacific coast of Costa

293

Rica.

As field host for the segment, I would once again be holding the reins on all the logistical aspects of the "shoot," as they are called—just as I had on the segment that had featured basketball superstar John Havlicek. That show had created a lot of interest among viewers and the advertising community and had won a Teddy Award for the best television fishing segment of 1973.

In July, 1975, we began assembling in San Jose, Costa Rica. Our agenda had been arranged and handled by my old friend Carlos Barrantes, who had already made several Costa Rican fishing adventures possible for me.

Dick Butkus brought a linebacker football friend, Jerry Moocha, who recently had the same type of knee operation Dick had received. Once again, we have a fairly large filming crew: two lead cameramen, Bruce Buckley and Andy Roe, with one assistant cameraman, Larry Johnson; one sound man, slight-built, redheaded Jimmy Lynch; and the show's producer, Pat Smith, who was writing the voice-over narration for all of "The American Sportsman" shows.

I also had invited my old friend Flip Pallot to join us and to run the fishing boat that would be on-camera during the shoot. He would be taking time off from his position as Vice President of the International Bank of Miami. [Flip's great presence in the film we would shoot eventually helped launch him from banking into worldwide fame, hosting two outstanding television series, "The Outdoor Life Show" and the "Walker's Cay Chronicles" on ESPN and OLN. To think I played some small part in making great things happen for Flip still gives me a flush of pride to this day.]

Carlos Barrantes had made arrangements for our flight from San Jose, in the center of Costa Rica, out to the Pacific coast in an aging, World War II vintage Lockheed Lodestar. We landed on a grass field near Playa Coco where cows and donkeys were grazing. We boarded an old, beat-up bus for the 1 ½ hour, 30-mile drive on a dirt road filled with holes and ruts. The big decision was whether to close the windows and swelter in the heat or leave the windows open which brought enough dust into the bus to make it difficult to breathe. Someone suggested leaving the windows open and covering our noses and mouths with handkerchiefs.

During the week-long filming, all but the camera crew were scheduled to live on Carlos's cousin's 80-foot, very high-sided, steel-hull ship that seemed almost as ancient as the Bat Islands. We were told each of us had a small stateroom with teak wood floors, an upper and lower bunk bed, small closet and small sink. But the shower and toilet was just down the passageway, around the corner. Flip's and my state room were on the starboard side of the ship and Dick and Jerry's individual state rooms were on the port side The camera crew needed, and had, an air-conditioned vessel... A 54 foot Hatteras anchored easy hailing distance from our aging home away from home. Our fishing boat would be a 24-foot Sportcraft named "Wet Dream" loaned to us by Lance Leonard, a fishing acquaintance.

As Flip and I start descending to our petite staterooms in the lower decks, the strong smell of diesel fuel reminded us that this wasn't the newest boat in the fleet. I quickly opened the four portholes on the bulkhead alongside my bunk bed, leaving the cabin door open and pulling the chain on the small overhead fan. I was hoping the cross-ventilation would clear out the diesel odor. Spreading most of the fishing tackle on the upper bunk, I was unpacking and neatly hanging up the clothes I would wear on camera. Flip walked into the room saying, "Damn Stu, I hope we can get rid of this horrible diesel smell."

"Me too, Flipper, I just hope the ship doesn't have a leak in one of the fuel tanks."

"Not a nice thought, my friend," he quickly replied.

It didn't take long for the two of us to get a couple of spinning outfits rigged for Dick to fish with during the filming and a two large bait-casting rods with Ambassador 7000 reels to use for teasing. We were chomping at the bit to get out on the Wet Dream and stretch some string, as they say, catching a couple of nice big fish.

The other boys wanted to kick back, not ready to fish yet. Butkus did place his order for a nice big, grilled red snapper for dinner.

As Flip and I descended the steep boarding ladder to the Wet Dream, I was thinking, "So be it. This will probably be the only time the two of us can have a relaxed couple of hours of fishing on this whole trip."

We decided to start off trolling a couple of 2-ounce lead-head Japanese feathers rigged with 7/0 hooks. With the rods inserted into a rod holder on each side of the boat, we barely got 200 yards from our anchored home away from home when the rod designated as Flip's bent in an arc, line screaming from the reel.

Flip was running the boat to get used to its operation, which will be his job starting tomorrow while we are filming.

Quickly bringing the throttle back to neutral, he made a beeline for his rod. The fish burned 150 yards of monofilament line, running like an express train with the right of way.

Just as fast, I leaped to the controls, spinning the bow toward this unknown streak of lightning, gradually allowing Flip to retrieve some of the 200 yards back on his reel.

"Hey Flipper, what have you got?" I yelled. "It screamed line like a sailfish, but hasn't jumped yet."

"Don't know, but it's a strong critter," he replied.

Fifteen minutes later we had our first glimpse of the 35-pound striped silver lightning bolt, so aptly named wahoo.

"Fantastic!" I yelled as I impale it with the gaff hook.

"Careful, Stu!" Flip said with concern in his voice. The wahoo's razor-sharp teeth have required many anglers to have their wounds stitched, after they were in the boat.

"Flip, let's head right back to the boat, cut some steaks to grill or deep fry for tonight's dinner, and if the captain has some limes, vinegar, onions and chili peppers I will make the best ceviche anyone here has ever tasted."

"I'm damn sure ready to head back after that fight, and I love ceviche," Flip said while massaging his left arm.

Captain Rodriguez met us at the gangway and, seeing the wahoo, hollered for one of his mates to bring a sharp knife. When I asked about the necessary ingredients for ceviche, he said he did have a large bushel of Key Limes, a small croaker sack of jalapeno chilies, as well as all the rest of the necessary ingredients.

Flip asked the captain where was the best place for him to clean the fish, saying, "I caught it, I'll clean it."

As always, he did an outstanding job of fish cleaning, eliminating all the bones and streaks of red bloodlines in the fillet portions, leaving nothing but firm white meat that will make excellent ceviche. He cut two-inch thick steaks to throw on the charcoal grill with the other half of the wahoo.

Preparations for the ceviche got under way with the use of the captain's lime squeezer to squeeze out a half gallon of Key Lime juice which we mixed with a quart of good white vinegar. I told Butkus, "Ceviche is a dish that will make your taste buds active. It's a South and Central American dish consisting of very fresh, firm, diced up, fingernail-size fish, marinated in lime juice with diced up onions and chili peppers."

Flip cut up the limes, Dick took over squeezing duties, and I started tending bar, making some cocktails.

, I didn't ask what anyone wanted to drink, because I had brought the makings for a special, flavorful, light-afternoon cocktail called a Mohito. It's a Cuban mint julep that I was introduced to in the mid -1950s by Ernest Hemingway on his boat Pilar at Havana Yacht Club harbor.

While I was making the Mohitos, I could hear Flip pleading for the second time, "Dick, please don't squeeze the limes quite so hard. We only want the juice from the limes, not the rinds."

One hour later, probably an hour before the ceviche was fully marinated, everyone was sampling it, showing their enjoyment.

Jorge, our chef, did a great job breading and frying two-inch strips of fillet. Not being much of a fish eater, I had asked him to do the fried wahoo especially for me, knowing how good it will be cold for lunch tomorrow in the boat.

Because Dick had requested grilled red snapper, we decided to let the chef "do his thing," preparing wahoo steaks on the charcoal grill. And it was like watching an artist as he arranged each wahoo steak on top of a bed of thinly sliced tomatoes, lemons and onions on a sheet of aluminum foil, covering it with another layer of tomatoes, onions and sliced lemons. He shook a liberal amount of garlic powder, oregano, salt and pepper, before folding the foil over and crimping the edge.

I actually started thinking that the way it looks, I might even try a taste. Needless to say, dinner was a tremendous success and we toasted the chef with glasses of Chardonnay.

Our Costa Rica fishing adventure with football's greatest linebacker was off to a super start.

The next day dawned early, and when I rolled out of bed, I had the bee-jeezus scared out of me. There was an inch of bilge water over the teak floor. What with the diesel smell of the day before, I just knew this old ship was sinking or about to blow up out here in the Pacific Ocean between Nicaragua and Costa Rica. I flipped the light switch up, nothing happened. Grabbing a flashlight, barefoot and butt naked, I hightailed it down the passageway to Flip's room and swung his door open, shouting, "Get up, get up now, we're sinking!"

"What the fuck are you talking about?" He said in a befuddled voice.

"We already have water over our decking and there's no electrical power for lights or anything else. Grab your flashlight and let's go."

As we reached the top deck, one of the ships diesel engines suddenly started and shortly thereafter the lights came on, along with a couple of additional whirring and clanging sounds.

Flip and I looked at each other and started laughing; two concerned, butt-naked guys breathing sighs of relief, no longer thinking we would have to be doing a half-mile swim to the nearest of the Bat Islands.

Just then, Captain Rodriguez came up on deck and seeing us, immediately started laughing with a strange expression on his face. "Are you going sweeming naked in the dark?" he asked in broken English.

"Hell no, Captain, we thought the ship was sinking and didn't know how fast we would have to swim for the nearest island. When I got up, I had about two inches of water over the floorboards in my cabin."

"My apologies to you both. I always turn the *sheep's* generators off between 11 and 12 o'clock, letting them rest for six or seven hours. When I do thees, the sheep's bilge pumps stop operating. She is a very strong but very old vessel that has water leaking into the bilge. Some of it was probably seeping into your cabins," he almost whispered.

Flip and I looked at each other, understanding the reason everything in our cabins smelled from diesel fuel.

Flip's and my cabin are evidently the only ones with water over the floorboards, creating the strong odor of diesel fuel. No one else in our group mentioned anything about sinking, so neither did we.

My suggestion was to do a commando raid today, taking only Bruce Buckley, our lead cameraman, Jimmy Lynch with his Nagra recorder, Dick, Flip and myself on the Wet Dream. We'd keep everybody else on the big 54 Hatteras nearby, shooting boat-to-boat jumps if we get lucky.

This being Dick Butkus's first time ever using spinning tackle or fishing for big fish, my plan was to give him a crash course on what to expect and what he should do when hooked to one of these 100-pound sailfish. We would troll the same type artificial squids we use as teasers to raise and excite the sailfish, with one major change: This time they would have hooks in them.

Our day went along pretty much according to my expectations. We did have half a dozen sailfish grab Dick's artificial squid without getting hooked, prompting me to explain the proper hooking technique after each one.

After the fifth sailfish swam off unhooked, it was obvious Dick was getting frustrated. I said, "Dick, remember these fish have a very hard, bony mouth. All you have to do for good hook penetration when you come tight is make believe you're hitting someone with a series of sharp jabs. Only instead of punching, you should be jerking with the rod."

Dick went to war on the sixth sailfish, striking it repeatedly, even while it was screaming line from his spinning reel. I said, "Dick, that's enough, looks like you have a good hookup on this one."

He did have a good hookup and fought it for 20 minutes before the hook pulled out, 40 feet from the boat.

"Ah fuck! What did I do wrong this time?" He asked.

"Not a single thing, my friend. That can happen, depending on where the fish is actually hooked. Remember, you're only fishing with 17-pound-test line and your drag can't be tight enough to really impale your sharp hook into hard bone. It does require a certain amount of luck having that hook go into the right place."

This was a successful first day. Dick learned some important techniques on hook setting and the proper way to pump and wind without putting a lot of twist on the line. Bruce Buckley shot close to 1,000 feet of 16mm film, some of which would be used as cutaway inserts.

That evening after supper, Dick and his friend Jerry were up on the sundeck when one of the camera crew remarked they were "... smoking funny cigarettes." Dick and Jerry hollered down to us, wanting to know: "What are all of these fish doing?"

Flip and I raced up the gangway to have a look for ourselves. This old tub had lights every 20 feet, extending out over the water, which attracted a variety of small fish that in turn attracted schools of several varieties of jacks feeding on them.

"Hey. guys, would you like to catch some of those fish?" Flip asked.

"Hell yes, why not?" They replied in unison.

Ten minutes later we handed them each a spinning rod with a half-ounce buck-tail jig attached to a short leader. When I noticed the way Jerry was holding it, I asked, "Did you ever use a spinning outfit before, Jerry?"

"This is the first one I ever had in my hands. Are you going to show me how to use it?"

Briefly explaining how to hold the rod with the stem of the reel between his two center fingers, picking up the line with his first finger, opening the bail with his other hand, I demonstrated a cast as I explained it.

The jig hardly hit the water when a three-pound jack had it. Quickly handing the rod to Jerry, I briefly explained the technique of pumping and reeling. Dick's competitive spirit got the best of him as he quickly cast and hooked up.

Flip and I looked at each other with an up-and-down head shake and a thumbs up. We headed back down to the fantail, where we had been having an after-dinner libation with a cigarette before being interrupted.

During the next half hour we can hear them both whooping and howling with double hookups. Then we heard a tremendous splash right alongside the boat. We both jumped up, fearing the worst. Just then, Dick came out of the water, limping up the boarding gangway and hollering, "Okay, Mooch, that's a fin you owe me."

Jerry Moocha was fighting a nice-size jack when an 8-foot shark made a pass at it. As it circled back for another try at catching the jack, Jerry bet Dick five bucks he wouldn't jump on top of the shark. Without a moment's hesitation, Dick was over the rail leaping the 15 feet to the water on top of the shark with the same reckless abandonment of fear he showed when playing football.

The shark could just as well have turned around, biting a large chunk out of Dick. But as it turned out, Dick probably scared it back across the border.

Our two football players decided they had enough fishing and would call it a night. Dick probably wanted to shower the salt water off his body before going to bed.

Finishing our drinks, putting our cigarettes out, we were not far behind them. Tomorrow should be a very busy day.

Before going to bed, I asked Captain Rodriguez if someone would please start the generators earlier so the bilge pumps can clear the water off of my deck before I get out of bed.

"No problem, Señor *AhStu*," he said with a smile, probably remembering how silly we looked this morning, naked on deck.

Sun was streaming through the portholes when I opened my eyes, looking around and wondering where I was. Then in a blink it came back to me: Stu, get out of bed, you have an important job to do today.

Today's fishing would almost be the same as yesterday, except the two squid teasers would be just that, teasers without hooks. I set Dick up with the same type spinning outfit he used yesterday, with a couple of major, more sporting changes. We would tease each of the sailfish in close enough to the boat for Dick to cast a much smaller squid near them, putting the boat in neutral, requiring him to reel, instilling action to the small squid.

My main reason for doing this was so all of the initial action happens near enough to be very visual to the television audience. Dick cast his squid at seven different sailfish, hooking all of them. Three of them threw the artificial lure during one of the first or second jumps, no fault of Dick's. The hook pulled out during the first two minutes of battle with two of them. Dick remembered everything he learned yesterday and landed the other two, near 100-pound sails, having to fight one of them that made a mistake thinking it was as tough as Dick Butkus for two hours and the other for a little more than an hour.

Each and every one of us in the crew could not have been more pleased with the action and success of this show. Now we have to take the time and set up doing our production work, which sometimes takes a couple of hours, filming close-ups of hands reeling, rods bending, facial expressions showing strain, Flip's hands on the steering wheel and controls, my pointing toward the fish and so on. It's always best to do production as soon as possible, with the same lighting and water conditions.

One line I tried to get Butkus to say – and have it sound spontaneous – was, "Hey, Stu, how did you ever find such a remote, beautiful place as these Bat Islands?"

My response was going to be, "Dick, I always keep my ears to the rail so to speak, during my job as a pilot, flying all over the world for Pan Am." For some reason or another, after more than half a dozen attempts, we never managed to get a good take.

Back on our slowly sinking steel home, we showered before gathering on the fantail for cocktails and debriefing. Pat Smith, the field producer of the show, asked if I brought a fly-fishing outfit suitable for sailfish. I replied, "Patrick, I don't leave home without it. Why do you ask?"

"Our camera crew is convinced we have a bang-up show in the can. So I thought maybe we could put a little icing on the cake tomorrow, seeing if you can catch one of these sailfish with your fly rod while Dick does the teasing for you."

I loved the idea. "Sounds like an excellent plan for tomorrow's filming. You can bet I am up for it, maybe we can even catch a world record on film."

After dinner I excused myself, wanting to spend a couple of hours making sure my 10-weight fly tackle was in perfect operating order. I tied six extra 15-pound-test leader tippets to go along with the 10 I rigged before coming on this trip.

Sleep did not come fast, with visions dancing in my head of all the many ways I could screw up on camera. Tomorrow would be my moment of truth, like so many other important moments I had encountered during my 45 years. When I did fall asleep, it was into a deep sleep until the bright rays of sun once again caught my attention.

The ritual of setting up my clothes, tackle and shaving the night before gets me off and running in a hurry. Waking up that morning, I was feeling especially good, hungry as a bear, ready to take on the world. I started off the day by engulfing a king-size portion of Chef Jorge's fantastic, everything-but-the-kitchen-sink omelet, washing it down with swallows from a large mug of Costa Rican café con leche.

Today, like yesterday we would have a full film crew on board, consisting of Bruce Buckley, Andy Roe, Jimmy Lynch, Dick Butkus, Flip and myself. The rest of the crew would be suffering in the air-conditioned 54-foot Hatteras, filming a master shot and being close by in case we need any of the extra equipment.

We got off to a slow start. We trolled squid teasers from a rod on each side of the transom for more than two hours without anything happening.

Thoughts started running through my mind. "Am I jinxed?" popped into my head. No, I don't believe in that kind of stuff, was the next thought. But then why do I pick up every penny I find if it's heads up, I thought to myself.

Before this charade of thoughts could continue, Flip hollered, "There's a sail on the left teaser."

That brought me back to reality and had me quickly moving to the teaser rod on the other side. I reeled as hard and fast as I could, getting that teaser outfit put away, which will give me room to cast a fly from the right side facing the aft portion of the boat.

Flip urged Dick to slowly reel the teaser the fish was following in closer to the boat. I picked up my fly rod, standing ready to cast at the right moment. "Okay, Dick, reel a little faster," I said with excitement.

"Flip, neutral!" I yelled. Turning my attention to Dick, I urged him to reel faster. Now that the boat was in neutral and not moving forward, the only movement of the squid was by Dick's reeling, and it had to continue looking like real prey to the sailfish.

When Dick had the sailfish and teaser about 50 feet from the boat, I started a false cast, dropping the fly slightly in front of the sailfish. I yelled, "Take it away." Expecting the teaser to come flying out of the water away from the sailfish, I started working the fly.

The sailfish had another idea for the squid, clamping down with all its might. Dick was unable to snatch it away and the sailfish followed the squid right to the transom of the boat before letting go. That happens sometimes; in this case the film crew probably got some interesting close-up footage of the sailfish after the squid.

I knew this was not Dick's fault because it had happened to me more than once, including a time while my wife was teasing for me: The sailfish got bill-wrapped with the 80-pound-test leader and she ended up fighting and landing the fish without a hook.

This kind of bait-and-switch fishing requires as much coordination between the boat captain, fly fishermen and person teasing as it does between the center, running back and the quarterback in a football game.

An hour went by before raising the next sailfish to the teaser. It was déjà vu all over again, with Dick unable to snatch the teaser out of the water at the proper time. Luckily, fish were starting to show up behind the teaser with some regularity. After two more botched teasing attempts, my nerves had gotten a little frayed.

"Damn it, Dick, snatch the fucking teaser out of the water when I say, take it away," I thundered. This prompted a look from Dick telling me I was about to go swimming. I doubt that anyone in his adult years had talked to him in that tone of voice and survived.

Dick kept his cool, thank God, and all went well with the next fish at the teaser. With the boat out of gear, Dick continued keeping the sailfish's interest while bringing it to 40 feet from the transom before snatching the teaser out of the water with such force that it ended up in the water in front of the boat.

Dropping the fly just off the sailfish's left eye with perfect timing as the teaser was pulled from the water; the beautiful billfish engulfed my 9-inch popping bug without hesitation.

Setting the hook three times sharply brought a slow, head-shaking reaction, like it was thinking, "Why is this little goody pricking me?" With the fish's mouth open, on the last head-shake the fly fell free.

Picking the fly up with a long backwards stroke of the rod, I made one false cast changing direction, once again dropping the fly in front of the fish. This time it came to the fly, smacking it with an 18-inch bill and it immediately was feeling this morsel darn sure didn't taste like the goody it had been after. It turned away and swam off, but Flip was pointing. In a very excited voice he hollered, "Stu, over here there's another one!"

Stripping in the excess fly line while moving to the other side of the boat, dodging both of the cameramen, I somehow managed to drop the fly near this still-eager sailfish, who jumped all over it like it was starving.

Anyone that says luck doesn't play an important part in fishing doesn't know what he's talking about. Call it having good luck or being blessed, almost my whole life has been a lucky one. I'll never know what kind of fight the first fish would have put up. It might have been a very tough, dogging fish like the one Dick fought for two hours. But this sailfish did a fantastic job of tail walking, high jumping then tail walking again during the 12-minute battle before Flip reached over the gunwale, grabbing its bill.

After taking the fly out of its jaw, Flip held the sail by its bill long enough for me to do my ritual pat on its cheek before the release.

I noticed Dick looking at me and at the fish, then a strange look back to me again, probably wondering why both of his fish took so long and mine was so quick.

Turning to face him I said, "These fish are all individuals, like people, some are tougher than others. I just had an easy one and you just happened to buy a couple of tough ones."

I could tell he was still thinking about how quick my fight was, and like the great athlete he is, trying to analyze what he could've done different.

As Pat Smith had said the night before, "If I could catch a sailfish on a fly, it would be like putting the icing on the cake."

And the icing, it was. This "American Sportsman" show received the very prestigious Teddy Award for the best fishing film aired on television in 1976.

Another fine memory I have of this adventure is playing a great practical joke on Dick, Mr. Tough Guy. One day during the trip, Flip and I were rigging fishing tackle in my little state room. Dick and Jerry had been sunbathing on the upper deck, when suddenly we heard their boisterous chatter as they made their way down the gangway that passed right past my room's three portholes. I don't know what prompted me to do it, but I grabbed a large can of Right Guard and stood by the porthole. When Dick passed, butt naked, I gave his private parts a full blast.

"Holy shit! What the fuck was that?" Dick screamed.

This prompted Flip to leave my cabin like lightning, and me to get under the covers in my bunk as fast as possible, pretending I was asleep.

Dick never came looking for us. He talked about the incident later, and it was clear he never knew what had hit him.

Now he knows!

CHAPTER

TWENTY-THREE

BACK TO THE BIG BIRD

New Time in the 747—And New Adventures in Living

If the old saying "time flies when you're having fun" is true, I must have really been having a great time during my five years flying the 707 in the captain's seat. If I had not been looking at my flight logbook, I would not believe the time could go by so fast.

We were living in a newly developed area in Southwest Miami called The Village of Kendale, only a short commute to the airport for my flights. I also lived an hour-and-a-half drive to Islamorada in the Florida Keys. We had a large fenced-in backyard from when we had our three adult German Shepherds that had since passed on to their happy hunting grounds.

One morning at breakfast Bernice was thumbing through the Miami Herald and exclaimed, "Hey, honey, here's an ad in the classified section for a year-and-a-half old, half Timber Wolf that's half German Shepherd. I think I'll give them a call."

"Yeah right, a wolf is just what we need in the house," came my sharp reply.

Damned if she didn't call, and 30 minutes later said she was going to take a drive and have a look at it. My parting words as she walked out the door: "Do not under any circumstances bring that wolf home without my having a look first."

Two hours had gone by and I was starting to get a bit concerned, visualizing her buying this critter and having something happen on her driving back home. Finally I heard our station wagon pull into the driveway.

On pins and needles, I greeted her at the door, not knowing what to expect. I sighed with relief when I noticed she was home without the wolf. As she approached the front steps, I said, "For once, you listened to me and did not bring the wolf home with you. What did he look like?"

"He was magnificent! He was fantastic! He was gorgeous!" she gushed. "And I for sure would have brought him home if they would let me. They're going to come by our house later this afternoon to see if our facility would be okay."

I inhaled deeply, letting my breath out slowly before asking, "Why are they selling this critter?"

"It seems that Lobo – that's his name – had a confrontation with their male Doberman stud breeder and ended up killing it. They actually breed guard dogs."

And that's how I ended up with a 130-pound Timber Wolf/German Shepherd, which was by far the most difficult animal I ever undertook to train. Lobo had already been through the Schetsen School of Attack Training, but flunked out because they could never get him to make a direct frontal attack. The wolf in him instinctively made him circle behind the trainer before attacking.

As with most wolves, he became a family/pack-oriented animal, and as soon as he understood I was the Alpha member of the family he readily accepted the number two position. That put Bernice in the number three slot because, evidently in the eyes of Lobo, she was a female.

Of course as a captain with Pan Am I was starting to earn a very good salary, good enough that for the first time in my life, I started looking for investments that would also provide some income tax relief.

Owning rental property in the Florida Keys was very appealing to both my investing and fishing mind. So, in 1977, I purchased a couple of two-bedroom, two-bath condominiums at The Palms on the ocean side in Islamorada, Florida, for preconstruction prices. Bernice enjoyed selecting and furnishing them both.

The Palms was almost next-door to the famous Bud N' Mary's Marina and I was sure they would be appealing rental units to fishermen coming to the Florida Keys. This would enable anglers to come in late from a long day of fishing, take a shower, and have something to eat before hitting the sack until the next morning's fishing. During April, May and June – tarpon time, my addiction to fishing for the silver kings – had me staying in one of these condo units almost entirely between flights.

With Lobo, it was impossible for my wife to spend even one night with me in the condominium because of a restriction in the condo bylaws about having only one dog not exceeding 15 pounds. This prompted Bernice to make some daytime visits to the Keys looking for a house of her liking, with the idea in mind of selling our place in Miami and moving back full-time to the Florida Keys.

The fall of 1978 found us closing on the sale of our place in Miami in the morning, then later the same afternoon signing closing papers for our new house on the bayside of Plantation Key. This made for a bit longer commute to the airport, but I had gained in seniority as a 707 captain, giving me a better opportunity to pick and choose the flights and my time off for fishing.

Having helped my old friend Dr. Lenny Berg make design changes in the Maverick boat, I ended up with the very first Kevlar Maverick. Now living full-time in the Keys, I was able to fish more and also spend more time at night with my wife. It was kind of like having my cake and eating it too.

It was better than I could have envisioned: A year of easy flying to South and Central America without being more than two hours out of my time zone, plus great tarpon fly fishing in the Florida Keys, along with the many trips Bernice and I made to Club Pacifico in Panama and Parismina Tarpon Rancho in Costa Rica. This certainly was a far cry better than my status in 1964, when I gave up my lucrative guiding career in order to go back to flying with Pan Am. For some reason, things with Pan Am seemed to always occur in December – good and bad. My major layoff notifications back in the 1950s always came in December, and now, due to retirement and expansion, Pan Am posted Captain vacancies on the 747 in

New York.

Thus far in my career I had never passed up a chance to upgrade my position, and without giving it a second thought I accepted the position and transfer to New York. On January 2, I began three weeks of intensive ground school and simulator refresher training. Back in December, 1969, I had received my Airline Transport Rating from the FAA, authorizing my flying the 747 as a Captain even though my seniority with Pan Am had me flying it as the First Officer. Now all I had to do was pass a periodic "B" check, operate a flight from JFK to Houston, Texas, to Mexico City and back to JFK in the same routing, with a Check Captain in the Co-pilot seat. Two days later would follow an Original Equipment Check flying from JFK to Nice, France, continuing to Fiumicino airport in Rome, Italy, for an overnight before flying back to JFK, with a Check Captain and an FAA inspector on board to certify my competency.

My first productive flight, without a check captain in the other seat and instead an FAA inspector in the jump seat, was from JFK to London's Heathrow airport, an overnight. It was then back to JFK and I'd be on my own, finishing off my months flying with two more round trips to London and one to Frankfort, Germany.

March proved to be a horse of a different color, as the saying goes. I operated the 002, around-the-world flight, from JFK to London to Frankfort, with a two-day layover in Frankfort. Then the 002 continued on to New Delhi, India, with an overnight before flying to Karachi, Pakistan, and deadheading to Dhahran, Saudi Arabia.

After what seemed to be an all-too-short overnight, I picked up two extra first officers and one extra flight engineer for a total of three copilots, two flight engineers and myself as the captain. This would be my first 747 SP flight. The SP stands for Special Performance and it's a smaller, long-range version of the 747-100 series. The plane has an upper and lower bunk bed in the back part of the cockpit area for the non-operating crew to take rest during the 15-hour nonstop flight to JFK.

Three weeks later I was operating my first nonstop flight from JFK to Narita airport in Tokyo, when shortly after takeoff the flight engineer notified me we had lost all the oil in number four engine and had to shut it down. We immediately notified Kennedy departure control of our plight and asked to be vectored into an area to dump enough fuel to be able to return and land at JFK. It seemed to me whoever was in charge was trying to lead me down the proverbial primrose path, wanting me to dump fuel in a circular holding pattern. Without hesitation, I informed them that there was no way I wanted to fly back through the same 140,000 pounds of fuel I was in the process of dumping. Instead, I was going to commence my dumping procedure now while on straight course vectors. I had quickly figured it would take 28 minutes to dump 140,000 pounds of fuel at an average of 5,000 pounds per minute.

All this was taking place during the 1980 fuel crunch, when we were doing all kinds of procedures to save fuel. I instructed my extra first officer and flight engineer to get into the aircraft manual and quickly find out what my limiting gross landing weight would be. As it turned out, the aircraft flap speed for a given gross weight would be the deciding factor.

After dumping down to a landing gross weight of 485,000 pounds – 30,000 pounds heavier than the certified landing gross weight – Kennedy approach control gave me vectors to land on runway 31 Left, which was not the active duty runway, in case my landing was not a good one and tied up the runway for a while.

My landing was so smooth even I could not feel when the 16 main tires touched the runway. It had been exactly one hour and twenty-five minutes from the time we pushed back from the same departure gate until shutting down the remaining three engines.

What a way to start my first JFK to Tokyo nonstop flight. An hour later, after maintenance did a landing gear inspection for the over gross weight landing, they informed me the aircraft was good to go. I checked with my cockpit crew to see if they would be willing to exceed their contractual duty time limits. They replied almost in unison with, "If you're willing to go, I'm willing to go."

With this information I next went to the flight attendants briefing room, and gathered the 12 flight attendants in a group to ask them if they were willing to exceed their contract duty time. Probably not wanting to be put into the reserve pool for the rest of the month, they did a quick huddle and agreed to stay with the flight if we could leave within the hour.

The balance of the flight went as scheduled, but we were one tired crew arriving in Tokyo after being on duty for 16 hours and 10 minutes. After our 52-hour scheduled legal layover at the Keio Plaza hotel, we were well rested but probably not ready for the 17-hour and 25-minute duty day we would encounter on our trip back. The cold front that was supposed to have come and gone in the New York area before our prognosticated arrival time put on the brakes when it hit the eastern seaboard, dumping snow, sleet and freezing rain, playing havoc with the hundreds of inbound flights to Kennedy airport.

We were still almost two hours from JFK when we were notified by Pan American Operations that many of the inbound flights were diverting to other airports around the country to wait for a weather improvement. They asked, "What was our present fuel state and are we plus or minus with our fuel score? How long will we be able to hold in the Kennedy area before having to divert to an alternate airport?"

I told the First Officer Richard Mitchell to tell Pan Op we would get right back to them with answers. Tailwinds from the jet stream's easterly flow gave us a plus fuel score, providing enough fuel to hold for at least one hour before having to divert to our alternate airport, Washington Dulles.

First Officer Mitchell passed this information on to Pan American Operations, further telling them to keep us advised of the traffic flow and length of holding time to the Kennedy area.

"Hope this isn't going to be another one of those marathon endurance contests," I mumbled to myself. About this time, New York Center gave us a fuel saving, endurance slowdown, saying that we are in a long trailing conga-line of airplanes approaching various holding fixes.

Thirty minutes out we were cleared to descend and maintain 29,000 feet, to enter a holding pattern, with an expected further clearance time of more than an hour. This would be beyond our fuel endurance and I had my extra Co-Pilot, John Maguire, map out a diversion route to Washington.

While starting into my third circuit in this egg-shaped holding pattern, New York Center informed us that an opening at Newark airport was coming available and would we like to divert to that airport. Quickly thinking, if push came to shove, Pan Am could provide buses for our passengers, which wanted to go to New York. My reply to New York Center came without hesitation. "Roger that, sir, Newark airport would be just fine, thanks."

We were given a heading to fly with a clearance to expedite our descent to 12,000 feet. The weather at Newark's airport had intermittent freezing rain and occasional snow flurries, but the runway continued to be above the category II landing minimums of the 747. As I asked for the descent check-list while getting out the approach plates for Newark airport, a surge of adrenaline wiped the fatigue from my mind and body. Next we were switched to Newark Approach Control, which gave us a new heading vector and further descent clearance to 2,000 feet.

"Let's have the approach checklist." I said to Don Schneider, our First Engineer.

Upon reaching 2,000 feet, Newark Approach Control gave us a final vector heading to the outer marker, and cleared us for the ILS, Instrument Landing System Approach.

We broke out of the clouds with a visual sighting of the runway with room to spare before reaching the allowable approach minimums. What was even more important than that: We had plenty of fuel to spare.

We spent exactly one hour on the ground before once again getting airborne for our flight to JFK. This time we were vectored into a 40-minute holding pattern by Kennedy Approach Control before receiving our clearance to execute an ILS approach to runway 22 Left.

We had a total flight time of 13 hours and 57 minutes with an on-duty time for the crew of 17 hours and 23 minutes. A solid days work for sure.

The rest of the year went like clockwork, flying long nonstop trips to Saudi Arabia, Pakistan, India, Japan, Brazil, Argentina,

Venezuela, numerous places in Africa and some short back-to-back trips to England and Germany. These were all flight patterns that would give me the necessary time off to pursue my fishing addiction during the best times of each month.

And then, like a bolt of lightning out of the blue, Pan Am posted some new 747 crew vacancies in Miami. Miami is a much smaller and more senior domicile, but even so, I decided to bite the bullet in order to no longer have to commute to New York. Being more junior meant I would no longer have my first or second choices of flight patterns and particular times off. But on the plus side, the majority of my flying would be to South and Central America; not flying through so many time zones that all I have to do during my layover is take my wristwatch off and turn it upside down, just reading where the hands are pointing.

Not expecting to receive my first choice of a September vacation, I was amazed when the vacation awards were posted and nobody senior to me evidently wanted it.

Bunching my August flying during the first part of the month but still following the Federal Air Regulations for necessary rest time, I returned from my last flight August 16 extending my six-week September vacation to eight weeks, not having to fly again until October 21. Montana, here we come again.

The previous year, while we were spending our six weeks Pan Am vacation in Montana, Bernice decided she would like to have a vacation home in the Bozeman, Montana, area. So we bought a five-acre lot in the newly developed Little Bear Subdivision in Gallatin Gateway from a friend of her friend. I later found out that I paid considerably more than I should have, but it was a piece of property with a fantastic view that Bernice fell in love with.

Maybe the reason I let her pick the house we bought in the Florida Keys was because I felt a bit guilty spending so much time on the water when I was home from my flights. Now, for the same reason, knowing I would either be hunting or fishing with my friends, I let her select the property in Montana where she would be most comfortable living. My absences, no doubt, were a greater hardship on Bernice than in most families because we did not have children. A severe illness a year after we had been married had forced her to undergo a complete hysterectomy. We had considered adoption, but for several reasons—including my financial status as a laid-off Pan Am pilot and fledgling fishing guide—we had decided against it. Life had gone on, without children, with us both coping with that fact.

The past six months Bernice had been drawing a house to scale on graph paper that she wanted to have built out of logs. Our little 2,400-square-foot log cabin in the woods surrounded by Aspen and Fir would back into the Gallatin National Forest, giving us thousands of acres behind our house and would be only the second house in Little Bear.

As a veteran pilot with about 14,000 hours in the sky, I felt I had paid enough dues about then to deserve the rewards now coming my way, among them a beautiful wife; a home in Florida where my beloved tarpon, snook and bonefish swam over the crystal flats; a home in Montana in the big sky country of trout, elk, black bear, pheasant, ducks and grouse; and time for free rides on Pan Am to visit exciting foreign destinations where my passport was always another ticket to adventure.

Truly, life was good. But there were clouds on the horizon, and I didn't see them.

CHAPTER

TWENTY-FOUR

CURT GOWDY: UNFORGETABLE, SIMPLY UNFORGETABLE

I've Never Raised a Fishing Rod or a Glass with a Better Man

As we walked through an overgrown, dank, shadowy jungle path to get to a portion of beach I wanted to wade-fish for snook, Curt Gowdy turned to me with the fearful question: "Hey, Stu, are there any snakes in this part of the jungle?"

"Only fer de lance and bushmasters, so keep your eyes peeled," I replied matter-of-factly.

Curt gulped. "Bushmasters – they stalk a man, don't they? Stu, you've got to be kidding."

I assured him that I was only kidding, but I did offer a frank warning to beware of big nests of fire ants in all the heavy foliage.

It was 1977, and the famed broadcaster/announcer and I were co-hosting an "American Sportsman" show in Costa Rica at Isla de Pesca, a new fishing lodge on the Colorado River on the Atlantic coast in the northeast corner of Costa Rica. This was to be the trip's first morning of fishing.

317

Jason Miller, an academy award nominee from the movie "The Exorcist" and author of the Pulitzer Prize-winning play "Championship Season," was what ABC always termed the "talent in the show." Jason was the young priest who performed the exorcism on Linda Blair and then...[well, I better not spoil the ending, in case you haven't seen the movie and want to check it out on DVD].

We had come to this part of Costa Rica on my say-so with the promise of great fishing for big snook, while wading in the surf from a beautiful dark volcanic sand beach. We also planned to navigate out the river mouth, casting to big schools of giant-size tarpon beyond the surf.

Unfortunately, and unknown to us, a few days before we arrived in Costa Rica a subtropical equatorial front looked unfavorably upon our filming this TV show. While passing through the Caribbean side of Costa Rica, it dumped a tremendous amount of rain, bringing large trees floating out of the river into the now coffee-colored water.

This made fishing for snook extremely difficult, but being the good sport that he was, Curt waded out into the riled water despite large pieces of timber rolling in the surf.

Jason Miller had never fished a single day in his life, so upon reaching the beach, Curt and I gave him a crash course on using spinning tackle. He picked it up quickly. The three of us spent the next two hours wading in the surf and dodging big logs that were flowing toward us in the river current and rolling in the three-foot waves crashing on the beach.

Fishing was very slow, probably because the snook were unable to see our lures in the dark water. Curt thought the key to catching these fish was to visualize one of them coming up behind your lure. Then, if you could hold onto that thought, you would automatically start working the lure just right. The thought must have appealed to the actor's imagination in Jason Miller, because even with the surf beating around his legs and waist, he kept right on believing and working until it paid off.

With beginners luck, Jason hooked and landed a nice snook, catching his first fish ever for all to see on national television. There must have been a school of fish coming by, because a few moments later I got a heavy hit and landed a 15-pound snook.

Curt summed up our success quite adroitly: "We all need to know, sooner or later, two key words – patience and persistence." Even so, Curt and Jason finally decided to take a break from fighting the surf, as it became even heavier from the huge storm system developing in the Caribbean and heading our way. I continued fishing for another half hour before deciding to take a break as well, joining them to sit on a big tree trunk that had washed ashore.

The tranquility of this volcanic beach became quite entertaining, with the surf crashing and seabirds chirping, combined with Curt talking about his thoughts on why some of us diehards fish.

"When I fish, it's a complete release for me, requiring my full concentration," he said. "Some men are compulsive gamblers, some men are compulsive drinkers, but I'm a compulsive fisherman. When I get out there I really forget everything except trying to catch the fish I'm after."

Curt related that his dad taught him how to fish when he was eight years old in his home state of Wyoming. "My dad started teaching me how to fish with love as well as care for the fish and the ecology around me. Back in those days there were only 200,000 people in the whole big state of Wyoming."

A flight of pelicans gave us a clue that the snook were probably lying farther out where the surf could not bounce them around so much. Their precise formation prompted me to tell Curt it reminded me of my Navy flying days. I knew I'd played the perfect straight man to Curt when he retorted, "Stu, if you could fly like that, you'd be all right."

The surf continued building, and I suggested that we ask our guide, Renaldo, if we had time enough left in the day to walk back to his aluminum skiff. It was a 40-minute run to Sámi Lagoon, one of my favorite tarpon fishing spots in this part of Costa Rica. Without any hesitation, he started gathering our extra gear while I told the camera crew to pack up as quickly as they can to change locations and fish species. I explained that we would be visiting a beautiful lagoon, surrounded by coconut and big mahogany trees, laced with air and orchid plants seemingly sprouting from their branches.

Prepared for this next phase of our fishing, I had stashed three 12-pound-test spinning outfits fully rigged, including the lures, in Renaldo's 17-foot aluminum john boat.

As we motored to the lagoon, I heard Curt briefing Jason on what to expect when hooked to a 50- or 60-pound tarpon. He mentioned about how important it is to bow to the Silver King each time it shows its face, and how dangerous it can be if one happens to jump into the boat.

Upon entering the mouth of Sámi Lagoon, Renaldo shut off the 40-horsepower engine. He used the transom-mounted electric trolling motor and his paddle to get us within casting range of the many tarpon we could see slowly rolling about 100 yards away.

As we approached, the slowly rolling tarpon, I explained to Curt and Jason that it looked as if the fish were in a relaxed mood, but they could still be difficult to tease into striking a lure. I described exactly how to work the Rapala plugs I'd attached to their lines ahead of two feet of 60-pound-test monofilament leader. By using a double-twitching motion of the rod tip, it makes the lure dart to the side, and that really excites the fish, even when they're not feeding.

For the better part of an hour, we cast in the direction of the rolling tarpon without any success. Then I felt a slight tap, almost like somebody gently tapping me with their forefinger. Quickly reeling any slack out of my line, I reared back once, twice and three times, sharply setting the hooks.

I hollered for Jason to quickly take my rod. He did so just before the tarpon came up for its first spectacular head-shaking jump. Now Curt and I were starting to count the jumps. "Number two, number three number... ah he's off!" we said in unison.

I explained to Jason he didn't do anything wrong, as tarpon have a very hard, bony mouth. Even with my extra sharp hooks, there are only a few places they can sink deeply enough to avoid flying out on one of its head-shaking jumps.

After giving Jason back his rod, I cut off four inches of the scuffed leader, quickly retying the orange-and-yellow lure. Before

Jason's next cast, I checked the hooks to make sure they were sharp enough to dig into my thumbnail with no effort.

Maybe I could have been a good actor, because I always visualize a fish coming toward my lure as I give it action. My cast was almost halfway back when the lure just plain stopped. Not leaving any slack in my line, I immediately set the hook sharply three times, feeling a solid hookup. Jason's lure was still out about 50 feet from the boat when I reached across to hand him my rod while snatching the other rod from his fingers.

While I rapidly wound his line in to get it out of the way, Jason's fish screamed 75 yards of line from the reel before making its first wild, high jump.

Renaldo used his paddle to keep the boat heading toward the tarpon. But the fish changed tactics by rapidly swimming back to the boat, creating lots of slack line.

"Wind it, Jason, wind as hard and fast as you can!" I yelled, wanting to know exactly where his fish was while our camera boat remained somewhere in between. Just as Jason's line came tight on the reel, this gill-rattling silver king burst out of the water only 20 feet from the boat, the colorful lure dangling from its jaws.

As the fish turned tail and raced away again, line once more melted off Jason's reel, but not quite as rapidly as the last long run. Now it would be a case of pump and reel, a technique Jason had never experienced. I explained to him how he must slowly lift the rod tip without any line coming off the reel, and then wind line while bringing the rod tip back down, each phase bringing Mr. Poon a little closer.

Twenty minutes went by before a tired Jason was able to bring the equally exhausted tarpon alongside the boat, close enough for me to put a release gaff in its lower jaw. Curt picked three silver dollar-size scales from the side of the tarpon, exclaiming that we'll dry them out and all three of us will sign each scale as a keepsake of our trip.

After only a few minutes of artificial respiration, this beautiful, hard-fighting animal was on its way, swimming back to join up with the school and not tethered by either line or lure.

Curt Gowdy's closing words to end the show summed up how we all felt: "I'm sure the three of us will always remember that graceful, fantastic leap in the air. For Jason Miller, the amateur, that was quite a beginning."

"The American Sportsman" TV show was the longest-running and most-viewed outdoor hunting and fishing show ever. And Curt became known as *The American Sportsman*. His recognizable voice was not only on the shows he produced, but also for "Wide World of Sports," voice of the Red Sox's, Super Bowls and many other sporting events.

Everyone who knew Curt could see how much he truly loved to fish and enjoyed the company of skilled anglers and well-known fishing areas like Islamorada in the Florida Keys. During the last couple of years of his life, when his back was hurting so bad, it was difficult for him to spend much time standing in the boat. Still, he went fishing, standing only to cast when a fish was spotted. Anglers would pay a premium for the honor of spending time in the boat with Curt, as he helped promote fund-raising tournaments that stand for conservation such as Bonefish and Tarpon Unlimited's Backbone Tournament, The Chuck LaMar Pediatric Cancer Research Tournament, The Redbone Tournament Series for Cystic Fibrosis research, and of course his friend Ted Williams' favorite, The Jimmy Fund.

I first met Curt Gowdy in 1962, as I described back in Chapter Five. He was doing the introduction to an ABC's "Wide World of Sports" show that involved a fly-fishing tarpon competition between Al McClane, the Angling Editor of *Field and Stream* magazine, and Joe Brooks, Angling Editor of *Outdoor Life* magazine. The show opened with a very young-looking Curt standing in front of a large banner stretched between two coconut palms, with the old humpback Bahia Honda Bridge in the background.

Forty-two years later in March, 2004, Curt asked me to help do an hour and a half program about the early years of fishing in the Florida Keys at the prestigious Ocean Reef Club in North Key Largo. There was standing room only in the 350-seat theater, typical for any event with Curt on the program.

Without Curt's knowledge, I gave my copy of the 1962 show to the film projectionist. With a prearranged signal at the end of the program, the lights dimmed and on a theater-size screen appeared Curt in front of the "Wide World of Sports" banner as he introduced the show. The audience went wild.

As we walked out of the theater to a room set up with cocktails and hors d'oeuvres, Curt put his arm around my shoulder, giving me a hug. With tears running down his cheeks, he said, "Stu, I didn't even know you had that footage. Thank you so much for bringing it. But Stu, look what has happened to me."

I smiled at him. "My friend, age has snuck up on us both. That's what is called life."

Two years later, on February 20th 2006, Curt went to that place in Heaven where all good American Sportsmen hope to go.

As a footnote, let me add that Curt Gowdy probably is the only person who has been inducted into 20 Halls of Fame, including broadcasting, sports, conservation and fishing.

It was my extreme honor to be inducted into The International Game Fish Association's Fishing Hall of Fame two years after Curt's induction.

CHAPTER

TWENTY-FIVE

TOP GUIDES, MONSTER FISH

Epic Battles on the Tarpon Flats

It is early afternoon, late May, 1980, in Homosassa, Florida. Captain Hal Chittum and his client, "Mad Dog" Marvin Levine, scan the clear saltwater at the daisy-chain circle of big spawning tarpon. They cannot believe their eyes. The armored monster in the center looks more than eight feet long. Circling are a dozen 100-pound companions looking like drones attending their queen bee. Chittum slowly shifts his push-pole and sucks in his breath. He has to have that fish. Levine, an expert with a fly rod, will try for it on 15-pound-test tippet. He takes careful aim with a false cast, and presents his fly perfectly.

The big fish lunges, throwing up a bow wave that splashes the tiny blue streamer fly away. "Awesome," Hal gasps. Again the fish lunges, and misses. "Breathtaking." His pulse is racing. The tarpon wheels for a third try, and Levine begins stripping in line, moving the fly in quick jerks. But Chittum yells sharply at him, "Stop! Stop the fly! Stop stripping! Let her take it. That's the biggest goddamn tarpon I've ever seen!"

The "biggest goddamn tarpon" comes on, unafraid, and closes its bucket-size mouth on the fly. Hal can no longer control himself. "Hit it," he yells. "Hit it! Hit it! Hit it!"

Levine strikes it, two, three, four times. The fish shakes its huge head and takes off like a rocket. In an instant, it burns 250 yards of backing from the big Emery fly reel.

Hal guns the engine in pursuit, shouting, "I've never seen anything like this. I'm running 3,500 RPM just to keep up. That tarpon is Goliath." Visions of the legendary 200-pound-plus tarpon on fly floods his mind. This one will go 250, even 300, and hang up the tarpon record forever.

It is a record Hal Chittum, super guide, wants more than any other: the first 200-pound tarpon on fly. Although records themselves are nothing new to this big, affable young man, this one will be his measure of immortality as a Florida Keys fishing guide. He is already in a class by himself. To date, Hal's clients own every major record for tarpon on fly rod. It is a distinction no other guide can claim. Any expert angler will admit that guides were responsible for at least half the angler's fishing accomplishments.

With Hal, big tarpon are his specialty. No, more than that. They are an obsession, a personal goal driving him stronger than anything else in his life. In a business where a few hundred men make their living, his big-tarpon fever has made him rise to the top and be acclaimed and sought by some of the most accomplished anglers in the world.

Yet, Hal Chittum is only 28 years old. He has been guiding as a professional for less than six years. "It may be a short time as guiding goes," he observes, "but it wasn't always easy."

As a former guide myself, I know he's right. Going fishing every day in the paradise of the Keys for a $165 daily fee in the 1970s may sound like an ideal way to make a living, but it isn't easy. It's a game of expensive equipment and very specialized know-how. It's rigging tackle and tying leaders every night, rolling out of bed at 4 a.m., and poling a boat for hours at a time – damn hard labor. It's fighting and gaffing fish plenty big enough to hurt you. And it's a world of psychology, catering to clients who can be very demanding. And the bottom line is knowing where the fish are and what they are hitting, every day. It's 200 days of fishing a year just to break even. This is not a job for anyone out of shape or not passionate about fishing.

Like every trade, guiding has its experts and its also-rans, and a few, like Hal, who do everything well. His trademarks are the best in equipment, an intelligent approach to fishing, the physical strength to do the job, and a charming enthusiasm for his work. Ask him how he's doing and he'll invariably come back with, "Excellent!"

Today his expertise, however, is a sharp contrast to the days back when Hal was a beginner. A big, raw kid, 6 feet, 3 inches, 225 pounds, with only a little skill but a lot of burning desire, he was just out of college and in pre-law. Hal was accused of "wasting people's time and money," by other guides and anglers. "The bumbler," some called him.

But Hal was ambitious and determined. He spent a couple of years fishing on his own and learning from others about the fish, the tides, and the techniques. Eventually, some of his teachers began to value his services as a guide over all other guides, especially for saltwater fly rodding for tarpon.

In the rarified atmosphere of top-notch saltwater angling, the pinnacle of man against fish is the light-tackle, big-game fish match up, where 10-to-one odds are only the beginning, even when the fly-rod expert is considered to have the highest level of skill. These are the men who eventually became Hal Chittum's clients, and he guided some to world records. Now Hal's clients include me with a fly rod tarpon record of 82 1/2-pounds on 6-pound class leader tippet and a 1071/2-pounder using a bait-casting outfit, with a Texas rigged plastic worm on 6-pound class line. Others include Lenny Berg with a 128-pound tarpon on 10-pound tippet, Billy Pate with a 155-pound tarpon on 12-pound tippet, and Billy's 182-pound tarpon on 15-pound tippet.

It is the 15-pound record that Marvin Levine is now shooting for. But it is much more than that firing up Hal: It's that 200-pound poon, something he has wanted more than any other fish in his life.

For six long hours Marvin and Hal fight the tarpon. In the shallows, through the channels, up the Chassahowirzka River until, with night falling, Hal gets them close enough for a shot with the eight-foot kill gaff.

But the fish is not through. When the steel strikes, its huge body shakes violently, launching the 225-pound guide as if he is a pole-vaulter into the water eight feet away, the gaff still in his hands. For two minutes the fish tows him, scraping and bumping along the bottom. Finally, he knows he has to let go or drown He comes up sputtering, "I'm sorry. I lost the fish."

But he hasn't. The hook holds, and the fish jumps for the first time since they hooked it six hours ago. They see it is indeed the all-time tarpon record on fly. The magnificent body crashes down, and the gaff falls free. They recover it and fight for another 20 minutes before the fish stops in the shallows. Hal stretches out with the gaff. The fish veers, and the point plunges into its head, between the eyes.

At that instant, the 15-pound tippet parts, and the fish is free.

According to the rules, the fight is over. Stunned, speechless, Chittum withdraws the gaff, with one palm-size scale still impaled on the point. They almost took the world's largest tarpon on fly. But not quite. They had beaten the fish, and lost.

There have been other fights only slightly less dramatic that he's won. Almost every spring, big tarpon gather at Homosassa Springs, Florida, just north of Tampa, to spawn. They are followed by the big-time tarpon anglers, hot rod personalities who want most of all to measure themselves against big fish on fly fishing tackle.

For the Homosassa season, the top guides are booked as long as a year in advance, some for 30 straight days of fishing by the same angler. The guides trailer their fishing skiffs up from the Keys. In the early 1980s, these skiffs represent specialized boats for flats fishing – 18-foot open runabouts costing an average of $12,000 with 140- to 225-hp outboards plus electric trolling motors, two special platforms, one on the bow for the angler to fish from and one at the stern for the guide to stand on while looking for the fish as he poles the boat.

Because these anglers are experts, they furnish most of their own equipment. This is the big league of light-tackle fishing. The guide leaves at home his 30 or 40 top-quality rods and reels, a further investment of perhaps $5,000. His job there is to follow the mating tarpon, pole the boat long and strong enough to head off cruising fish, follow them after they're hooked, and sink the gaff with the kind of authority to subdue a fish that could weigh more than either the guide or fisherman.

It is a demanding place to fish, with deep water, strong winds and currents that make the boat hard to handle. It takes an extremely strong guide to pole the boat in these conditions. It also takes a guide who knows where the fish will be, and who is capable of landing and gaffing a giant tarpon.

In May 1979, angler Doctor Lenny Berg hires Captain Hal Chittum. Fishing 10-pound tippet, Berg has broken off several big fish when he gets another good shot. A strong fish, Hal doesn't want to lose it. He advises Berg to go easy on the pressure, since 10-pound breaks a lot easier than the 15-pound he is accustomed to. The fish makes a couple of jumps early, then settles into a pattern, rolling just out of range of the gaff. He leads them to deep water where a number of big sharks often lurk. Hal notices that about every five minutes the fish is coming up for a breath, as big tarpon must, using their rudimentary lung mechanism. He eases the boat forward, anticipating a roll, and when it comes up, Hal hits it with the gaff.

The fish hauls him right over the bow and out of the boat.

"The water is deep," he says, "twelve feet or more." As he hangs onto the gaff, he realizes that he's halfway between the surface and the bottom, with no leverage, and being pummeled by the fish's tail. He needs a breath, but the fish will not yield. Finally, he inches himself forward on the gaff handle, and grabs the tarpons jaw. Using the gaff handle as a lever, he steers the fish and rides the tarpon to the surface to get a breath.

What lasts about four minutes feels like an hour to him. Hal calls the boat over; the fish has dragged him 100 yards by then. He climbs aboard and lands the fish. "I was seeing blue spots, about to black out," he admits. It turns out to be Berg's 128-pound record on 10-pound tippet.

Only a few other guides I know have been determined enough to hold onto the gaff after being dragged overboard. Steve Huff is notable, having been launched more than once. Jimmie Albright is another, going overboard more than once. And I, too, as a guide, was snatched out of the boat twice by Joe Brooks' 148 1/2-pound tarpon record, but landed the fish. According to Marvin Levine, Hal was once pulled in with a ravenous bunch of sharks and, "Came back in so fast he didn't get his deck shoes wet."

Not all fish are that tough or dangerous. Some big ones are comparatively easy. Billy Pate's big tarpon on 15-pound tippet took only 19 minutes to land. It gave in so easily after being pressured, both Pate and Hal thought it was a smaller fish. They intended to break it off and go after larger prey. But, a tape measure convinced them they probably had a record beater. When weighed, the tarpon went 182 pounds, beating Joe Robinson's 180-pound record.

Pate, an angler who has taken tarpon, sailfish, and marlin on fly, says of Chittum, "He's outstanding in his positive attitude and possesses great strength. And he's such a pleasant guy to be with, it's a great combination."

Most all Hal Chittum's fishing involves expert anglers, or records. Of course, even when the record-busting tarpon migration is over, a guide still has to work. He gets bookings by word of mouth or through previous clients. These he takes out for tarpon, bonefish or permit on the flats, and the whole idea of guiding takes on a different role. He is tolerant of duffers, and enjoys showing them how.

For the "sometime" fisherman, Hal furnishes the rods and reels as well as the boat and the expertise. He has some advice for tourist anglers: One thing they need to do is practice before they come down. They wait a whole year for this week but haven't learned how to cast accurately. The time to learn tackle and to practice casting is *before* a trip, not when a big tarpon is in front of you.

Seeing fish in the clear waters can also be a problem for a visitor. You have to scan, continuously, watching for something moving against the ripples, a bluish shadow that has shape and form, and moves. That's a tarpon.

Recognizing the speed of fish is important, too. "Trout fishermen, for example," Hal says, "don't have to think about speed, but on the flats the fish move with astounding speed. You have to be able to put your lure where the fish is going to be."

If you're picking a guide by a visit to the docks, look for the guide with top-notch tackle. A guide with scruffy equipment might just do a sloppy job of finding fish for the unsuspecting angler. With beginner or expert alike, the good guide gives his customary charged enthusiasm. He will yell encouragement when a big fish is on, as anxious to land it as the angler is. But almost immediately after a big fish is landed, the obsession returns to find a bigger one. Though fishing is usually a mixed bag of the unexpected, he also enjoys that rare day when everything goes exactly as planned, as it did for us a couple of times.

One night Hal and I sat up half the night tying leaders for 6-pound fly and rigging 6-pound casting gear, with the intention of going after both records in one day. It is late in the season, but we hope some large fish are still around.

Next morning, a beautiful, clear day with water almost flat calm, we leave Islamorada before daybreak and run to the wide flats at Flamingo in Florida Bay. Just at dawn, with Hal poling and tarpon rolling all around us, I cast my orange and yellow streamer fly to a good tarpon. It quickly gulps down the goody and after a 61-minute melee, without making a single jump, we haul the fish into the boat. Throughout the fight we knew it was bigger than my friend Flip Pallot's 32 1/2 pound record prompting us to run it into the Flamingo Marina for a weighing, where we confirm it is a new record for tarpon on fly with 6-pound-class tippet, 82 1/2 pounds.

Two hours later we are back in the same area trying for a tarpon on 6-pound-class casting tackle. Again Hal poles while I stand guard from the bow casting platform, and we soon spot another target. I cast an orange 7 inch long plastic worm, rigged like they do in Texas for largemouth bass; the fish engulfs it and takes off. This fish is stronger than the first, and Hal has to pole like the bionic guide if he is to keep up. The idea is to keep as little line in the water as possible, since flimsy 6-pound will break off from the slightest touch by a weed or snag.

We close in. Ten yards away the fish jumps in a spectacular display of aerobatics, gills rattling, and tail walks across our bow. But the exertion tires it quickly; in less than half an hour the tarpon is lying exhausted at the surface. Hal poles over and spikes the fish with the eight-foot kill gaff. Hauling it into the boat, we run back to Bud & Mary's Marina in Islamorada where we left our vehicle. Our second fish of the day weighs in at 107 1/2 pounds, the result of team effort and planning executed perfectly. It is a very satisfying day, the kind even Captain Hal Chittum judges as, "Excellent."

"I came down here years ago because I loved fishing so much," he admits. "I wanted to get it out of my system. It took a couple of years to learn the territory, even with the help of my mentor, Stu, before I could start guiding. I was driven by it as a personal challenge. Now, every year that drive gets worse instead of going away. After I catch that 200-pounder, I want to expand my fishing horizons to cover the world. I guess that can't be all bad."

Not half bad indeed. In fact, I'd say, "Excellent."

* * *

It's May 11, 1982, and my good friend Captain Ralph Delph of Key West and I decide to celebrate my birthday fly fishing for the Big Momoo … the 200-pound tarpon at Homosassa, Florida. Just to sweeten the pot, a new TV film producer has heard about the five days we're going to spend searching for big tarpon. He asks if he could follow along in a second boat, staying out of our way but shooting the happenings.

The plan involves having the producer and his cameraman meet Ralph and me for dinner on May 10 at the Riverside Villas, right on the Homosassa River. But they experience difficulties renting some of the sound equipment and can't join us until May 13. They will miss the first two days of fishing.

You can probably guess what happens.

The morning starts off in a normal way, with the two of us taking turns. I lead off by catching a pretty nice fish about 110 pounds, then Ralph nails one that looked to be around 130 pounds. At that point a non-fishing boat runs right down the center of tarpon Mecca, forcing us to clench our jaws and fists in anger. This prompts me to suggest that we get away from the boats and run north for about five miles to another area I knew.

We shut down the big engine and start using the electric trolling motors and push-pole to maneuver us into the proper depth of water where tarpon should be coming through.

Ralph sees a fish roll around 300 yards away, and we head toward it. Seventy-five yards off to my right at 3 o'clock, a school rolls and goes into a daisy chain. A daisy chain involves a doughnut-shaped school of tarpon to ball up baitfish, when frightened by a predator – sort of like circling the wagons – and when mating.

It's amazing when you're fishing in six to eight feet of water, and fish aren't rolling, how close you can be to them without knowing they're there.

Ralph poles me to the daisy chain and we see a very big female in the center of the doughnut. Females are the prizes when loaded with roe because they can weigh 30 pounds or more than normal.

I must cast perfectly in order to get the fly across the other tarpon in the daisy chain without disturbing them. Using a 12-foot leader, most often I can put the leader across some fish without disturbing them. This time my cast is pinpoint perfect, and as I strip the fly in front of the big female, another smaller tarpon makes a quick move taking the fly. I guess its weight at about 140 pounds. Not the one that I wanted, so I try not to come tight setting the hook. It still comes out with a little head shaker and gets rid of the fly. But that's just enough commotion to break up the daisy chain, and the school slowly swims away.

Luck stays with us, and about 100 yards away they stop and chain up again. Ralph once again uses the electrics and the push-pole and maneuvers me into position for a second try at "Madame Big."

The positioning and my cast go as they did the first time. The difference now is that she's not about to let some upstart 140-pounder take that goody away from her.

I'll never forget that jump when I set the hook. She blasts out of the water like a Polaris missile. Fully eight feet long with a big, thick body. We know that this is a monster, the quintessential legend of Homosassa.

All hell breaks loose in the boat. Ralph stows the push-pole and begins to lower the big outboard. Normally we'd never crank the outboard with another boat nearby, but we knew this to be an exceptional fish and she's screaming line off my reel like there's no tomorrow. Already, 200 yards melts off the reel. Only one other boat is nearby with my friend Captain Steve Huff, another outstanding Florida Keys guide in Homosassa for the same reasons we were. We radio him and say we've got on the line the fish we've all been looking for, talking about and imagining. Steve immediately says not to worry, and to go ahead and fire up the engine.

This fish quickly develops a constant rhythm with its tail, and doesn't even seem to be exerting a lot of energy. Ralph manages to keep me within 30 to 40 feet of this big lady, allowing me to put maximum pressure on her all the time. During the first 20 minutes of the fight she rolls periodically, gulping oxygen before heading back toward the bottom. Each time she starts elevating I put about two feet of my fly rod into the water, making her work hard to come to the surface for air.

Fifteen minutes of this and she's set up a rhythm in her rolling. Now I'm beginning to predict when she's coming up for air. My theory of sticking the rod tip underwater and pulling down and back toward her tail is what I nicknamed "down and dirty." This technique makes it difficult for her to get the oxygen, and it begins to take its toll. I want this fish to feel that she has to fight her way to the top – a bit of psychology that generally pays off handsomely.

Forty-five minutes into the fight, the nail knot reaches the rod tip and slides past the first stripping guide as the fish nears the boat. I tell Ralph that the next time she comes up, I'll hold her there and he can hit her with the gaff. He moves from the console and gets in front of me in the cockpit. I pressure the fish and it wallows like a drunken sailor.

Ralph braces his knees on the gunwale and sinks the gaff home. In a split-second I glimpse a view of the bottom of Ralph's shoes as he's vaulted over the gunwale into the water beside the fish, having gaffed it just in front of the dorsal fin. He hands the gaff handle to me and starts climbing back into the boat when the gaff comes out of the tarpon's back.

Miraculously, I still have the fish hooked and the fight is on again. Fifteen minutes later we get the giant tarpon and boat together once more, programmed the same way. This time, however, I ask Ralph to please use my large barbed gaff that I made especially for great big tarpon like this one and not his smaller gaff, which I firmly believed didn't possess a big enough bite in the hook. Ralph being Ralph, elects to ignore my plea and instead used his smaller gaff yet again.

It's the same scenario all over again, except this time when Ralph strikes the fish with his gaff, it jerks his butt clean out of the boat again, but now it charges more than 50 yards away with Ralph hanging on like a hitchhiker. I don't realize it at the time, but the boat is still in slow-idle forward gear.

This has become no laughing matter. Ralph appears to be in trouble while literally wrestling with a beast far bigger than he – and in its element. Both of Ralph's arms and legs wrap around her. [Later tells me that he tried to put one hand and arm up through its gill plate in order to secure it while at the same time trying to hold that little gaff hook in place.]

At one point this monster fish comes up half out of the water with a head-shaking jump, and damned if Ralph isn't still wrapped around it. I drop the fly rod and dash back to the console quickly advancing the throttle while at the same time swinging the bow toward friend and fish. We're in eight feet of water and Ralph definitely looks like he's not having fun.

I grab a very large release gaff as the boat approaches the pair. Ralph's console is different than mine, and I somewhat fumble with the controls as I approach them. At what I figure is the right moment, I put his engine in reverse to stop the boat's forward motion, and back into neutral. I charge to the bow, aiming to hook that big tarpon under its lower jaw with my release gaff.

I immediately realize that the boat isn't in neutral, but instead is still in gear and idling forward. I run back to the console, throw the boat in hard reverse and switch the ignition key off.

Too little and too late! I've got Ralph bore-sighted, and he has to take one arm off the tarpon to keep the stem of the boat from running over him, which rolls both him and the fish under, forcing him to release his grip.

The legend of Homosassa gets off the gaff and swims away.

Disappointment. Utter disappointment. And I'm upset at Ralph being stubborn in not using my gaff either time.

Ralph climbs into the boat dejectedly. "Why did you run me over?" he asks.

I explain that I thought he was in serious trouble, and not being familiar with his throttle quadrant believed we were in neutral rather than idle forward.

Ralph is so full of tarpon slime from being wrapped around that big poon that he got everything in the boat coated in that heavy, grease-like film. Actually the ignominious leavings of that tarpon has put an exclamation mark on the gloom we feel at the moment.

Yes, we fish some more and catch two tarpon that day, and as the hours tick on Ralph smells like a very ripe tarpon – and I treasure the moments when he stands downwind of me.

We do not mention that fish even once during the rest of the day or that night in the motel, or for that matter the next day out fishing. But the next evening at dinner Ralph turns to me and asks, "What do you think that fish really weighed, Stu?"

I say, "Ralph, let's not influence each other as to the weight." I tear a paper napkin in half, hand him half, and ask him to write down how much he thinks the fish weighed while I do the same.

Ralph jots down "230+" and from my side of the table I write "230 plus." At that time, the largest tarpon ever landed weighed 188 pounds on 16-pound tippet, so this fish even on 12-pound-class tippet would have smashed it. Another irony: Fate has dealt an unfortunate hand to that camera crew, which otherwise would have captured this epic battle on film.

Nineteen years later to the day, May 11, 2001, my young friend Jimmy Holland caught the first 200-pound tarpon on a fly ever. It weighed 202 ½ pounds and became the International Game Fish Association's 20-pound-class tippet world record. Of course we can talk "maybes" until the cows fly home, but that gargantuan poon that Ralph and I lost would have probably set an unbeatable benchmark.

CHAPTER

TWENTY-SIX

EMERGENCY AT 35,000 FEET

A 747 Flight Anything But Routine

Our Pan-Am 747 flight from New York's Kennedy Airport to Tokyo, Japan's, Narita Airport in September, 1984, was a non-stop long haul, scheduled for 13 hours. On flights of this length we carried two first officers, each with a type-rating in the airplane, and two flight engineers. We had an upper and lower bunk bed in the back part of the cockpit area so the crewmembers not on duty could relax, read or grab some shuteye. At approximately 10 hours into the flight, I was in my customary left seat as Captain, and we were right on our flight plan, at 35,000 feet and picking up Russia's Kamchatka Peninsula on our radar, showing about 100 miles ahead. There we were scheduled to climb to 39,000.

We had left JFK on time at 11:30 a.m. and crossed Canada at our original assigned altitude of 33,000 feet. Approaching Anchorage, Alaska, we received climb clearance and climbed on up to 35,000. The higher the airplane can fly at a given gross weight, the most efficient is its fuel consumption, and the higher altitudes are obtained through a series of careful calculations of fuel burned and weight reductions. We were flying at an indicated .85 Mock which is 85% of the speed of sound, making good a true airspeed of 495 knots at 35,000, and once we reached 39,000 we would be burning less fuel while maintaining the same true airspeed. Our positions were calculated by three Inertial Guidance System Computers, the same type the astronauts had used going to the moon. Basically, we were flying the same route as the Korean 747 Flight that had come to grief two years before by straying off course and being shot down by Soviet fighter jets. Something had gone wrong with the Korean flight's Guidance System programming—rumor had it they had probably inserted an incorrect number into their Inertial Guidance System; a tragic mistake I was determined would never happen on my watch.

With Kamchatka just ahead, I was thinking that once we had climbed to our new altitude, I would take a break and go back to business class to chat with an old friend who was on this flight, Leon Chandler, Vice President of Cortland Tackle and affectionately known by many as the "Fly Fishing Ambassador to the World." Hours earlier I had already taken advantage of the Captain's first choice for a break by going back into the cabin to have lunch with Leon. And now, once again it was getting to be time for me to take a break and let one of the first officers have some left-seat time. The instruments and gauges that gleamed back at the me and the Co-Pilot were pegged where they belonged. The flight couldn't have been going smoother.

Directly behind the Co-Pilot and me, however, facing his own side panel of instruments, was the Flight Engineer, Dennis Grevuli. The instruments he was reading were not so benign. Suddenly his voice lashed out: "Holy shit! We have a wing overheat light on the port wing."

This was a serious warning—a death threat! A broken high-temperature high-pressure duct from one of the engines on that left-wing could possibly cause enough structural damage to have our left wing collapsed… making it a bad day to fly. Immediate and correct action was required.

While Dennis was getting out the abnormal procedures portion of the aircraft manual, I had already started retarding the throttle for the number one engine, the first step in the abnormal procedures for a wing overheat light. Dennis had quickly isolated the engine bleeds, from both engines on our left wing. These bleeds have many important functions within the airplane, the air-conditioning and pressurization just to name two.

By now the cockpit flight deck was crowded. The other First Officer and the Second Engineer were now out of the bunk beds and wanting to know what was happening.

Meanwhile the on-duty Flight Engineer was reading the abnormal procedures out loud. "Slowly retard either throttle on the overheat wing, and if the overheat light goes out, continue to operate the engine at that power setting."

That was exactly what I was doing. Unfortunately, the light did not go out until I had the No. 1 engine throttle all the way back to idle power, which hardly contributes any thrust. Now that the light had been extinguished, our next step, reading from the abnormal procedures, was to reintroduce the bleeds from No. 2 engine into the system.

For some unknown reason, when Dennis opened the bleed valves, the number two engine stalled, silently, without a *boom* like a backfire. The first indication was a bouncing EPR gauge and an erratic N1 tachometer gauge, then number two engine fire warning light came on, with the bell ringing loudly.

Now I recited the emergency engine fire drill verbatim, while the Engineer and First Officer did each of the procedures I called out, shutting down number two engine and shooting both fire bottles into the engine area, extinguishing the flames.

We are now 50 miles off the Kamchatka Peninsula, and I quickly told Vince Miller who was currently the on-duty First Officer in the co-pilot seat, "If we have anything else happen, I don't care what it is, immediately start broadcasting a Mayday on HF long-range radio guard frequency to the world, telling them what has transpired and that we are turning north to fly into the Kamchatka Peninsula of Russia to make an emergency landing at the Russian Air Force fighter base. It's where the fighter plane shot down the Air Korean 747 two years ago because it flew into their airspace."

I knew two things for sure: One, even if nothing else happened, our work to make this flight have a happy ending was cut out for us. Two, I did not intend putting our airplane and passengers in the North Pacific Ocean.

Now began four and a half hours with me literally glued to my seat flying the 747 on two engines. At a much slower airspeed, we were burning more fuel and could not climb to our programmed fuel saving higher altitude. Our fuel computations, however, kept showing the numbers we needed: We could make Tokyo, shoot a missed approach, if necessary, and still go on to our alternate, Yokota on the northern coast of Japan.

We were in VHF radio contact with Tokyo Control when we were 150 miles out. We knew then that the Tokyo weather was not going to do us any favors. On the contrary, it would add difficulties to our plight.

It was storming in Tokyo with low clouds, heavy rain and gusting winds creating a landing problem due to the low visibility. A precise instrument landing system (ILS) approach would be needed.

When made aware of our engines-out situation, Tokyo immediately wanted to know if we needed to declare an emergency, clearing the airspace of other aircraft as we got closer to the airport, giving me priority to land.

"Tokyo control, Clipper 801 affirmative," we called, "we are declaring an emergency and I would appreciate clearance from my present position, INS direct to the Narita airport outer marker beacon, for an immediate ILS approach."

"Roger, Clipper 801, squawk Ident on transponder code 0423, I have you in radar contact Clipper 801, you are cleared from your present position, direct to the Narita outer marker beacon for the ILS approach to runway three four left. You are clear to descend to 15,000 feet at your discretion, call leaving level 350. Be advised; landing conditions at Narita are reported to be occasionally below landing minimums by the last aircraft making a missed approach."

Not wanting to prematurely go to a lower altitude where we would burn fuel more rapidly, I decided to wait until I was about 75 miles from the airport before starting my descent.

After informing the other four members of the crew what my intentions were, I called for a pre-descent check and briefed everyone on the ILS approach procedures for runway 34 Left. I made an announcement on the PA to the passengers, telling them that we were starting our descent, and should be landing in about 25 minutes; also telling them about the poor weather conditions at the airport. I told the co-pilot to call Tokyo Control, informing them that we were leaving flight level 350.

The in-flight service director and the purser working in first-class were the only members of our cabin crew aware that we were having any problems whatsoever. As long as I was continuing the flight to our original destination, there was no need to create unnecessary anxieties among the passengers or crew. I could imagine my friend, Leon Chandler, back there in business class wondering why his old friend Stu had not come back to chat with him, as promised. When I had left Leon after our lunch, I had promised to return later into the flight.

Our meeting on this trip was entirely by happenstance. Leon had hailed me as I walked through the crowded passenger waiting area, and he was pleasantly surprised to find that his fishing buddy was Captain of the flight. [Another surprise for Leon came after the plane's doors were closed and I was able to have the purser move him from one of the worst seats on the plane in the very rear up to business class.]

As we began our descent, my thoughts focused on the challenge ahead: An instrument approach on two engines with the weather right on the minimums. Pilots train constantly in simulators for this sort of emergency, but this was for real.

"Clipper 801, switch to Narita Approach Control on 126.1. Happy landings."

"Roger, Tokyo Control, thanks."

On calling Narita Approach Control, we are further cleared to descend at our discretion for the approach to runway 34 Left, and they had us in radar contact.

Because of the yaw created by only having thrust from engines No. 3 and 4 on the right wing of the airplane, I was forced to hold a considerable amount of right rudder-pedal pressure to keep us flying straight ahead and not skidding off to one side of the ILS track. With my heart pumping a fast cadence and my mind speeding along as my eyes scanned the flight instruments, I was able to keep the crosshairs on the ILS instrument centered, indicating I was right on track and on glide path.

The minimum descent altitude is the point where the pilot must have some visual reference to the runway or execute a missed approach and fly to the alternate airport. As I approached the minimums, the rain was coming down in heavy sheets, pushed by gusting winds. This would be a difficult enough approach to make even with all four engines operating. I made a split-second decision to continue the approach slightly lower than the published minimum as long as I had the ILS centered, showing me I was exactly where I should be.

The first officer yelled out, "I've got the rabbit!" The flashing strobe light leading to the runway strobe light is known as a rabbit. "You're right on center line for the runway ... fucking fantastic."

Still working extra hard to plant this big bird on the center of the runway, I slowly eased the pressure off my now-shaking right foot, releasing most of the rudder pedal pressure, as I brought the throttles into idle power. I quickly slid my feet onto the upper portion of the rudder petals, applying the brakes on all 18 wheels, and brought the Number 3 engine throttle up into idle reverse. We are hydroplaning down the runway because of all the rainwater, and if I applied more reverse thrust from my two operating engines, we would have been torqued off the runway by the asymmetrical thrust.

Actually, I was surprised at how well we stopped, still having a few thousand feet of runway ahead of us. After being in a hushed quiet during the approach and landing, the cockpit came alive with everyone at the same time shutting out yahoos.

Turning off the duty runway onto a taxiway, I looked back over my right shoulder at Dennis, the Flight Engineer who first noted the wing overheat light. I said with a chuckle, "You weren't kidding a few hours ago when you said, 'Oh Shit!"

I saw Leon Chandler in Customs, while we are waiting to retrieve our bags. He was all smiles with his right hand out, saying, "Great flight, fantastic landing, we didn't even feel it touchdown. Did you hear everybody in the whole airplane applauding? But, my friend, you said that you were going to come back and visit with me before we got to Tokyo. What happened?"

Putting my arm around his shoulder, I slowly walked him toward a slit window where you can see our airplane, parked facing us. Giving him a slight pat on his back I said, "Leon, old buddy, I was not able to get out of my seat to even go to the toilet for the last four half hours of the flight. We had two engines on the left wing inoperative, one because of a major engine fire and the other because of a ruptured high-temperature pressure duct. You might say that I was a little busy."

Looking out the window, he was rapidly turning pale. Slowly, as my words sank in, he replied, "Stu, nobody told us anything."

I explained that as long as I'm still taking the airplane to its original destination, there is no reason to create unneeded anxieties among the passengers or crew. None of the flight attendants even had knowledge of our problems

"We don't get paid the big bucks for just getting the airplane from point A to point B," I joked with him, trying to stem his anxiety even though he was safely on the ground. "It's for getting the passengers safely to their destination when things have turned into a can of worms."

The special crew bus that was taking us to the Kino Plaza Hotel was buzzing with Pan Am flight 801's 20 crewmembers talking about not knowing of the engine problems. I asked John, the in-flight service director, to see if he could get everyone to quiet down for a moment, I wanted to make an announcement.

After the buzz stopped, I said, "You are an outstanding crew and after we check into the hotel and get cleaned up, I would like to buy everyone a cocktail, say six o'clock local time." The bus was silent for a moment and then the buzz of conversation started again. They'd never heard of a captain buying drinks or anything else for the whole crew.

That was one of the most satisfying rounds of drinks I've ever plunked down for in my life. We had been tested, and we had not failed.

Of Wind and Tides

CHAPTER

TWENTY-SEVEN

A RED STAR FOR SALMON

Pioneer Fishing in Russia's Atlantic Salmon Paradise

I know I'm being watched.

I sense the intruder's eyes on me. But, after all, this is Russia, north of what is now St. Petersburg above the Arctic Circle, and it is natural, I suppose, that somebody is keeping track of an "*Amerikanitz.*"

The Umba River is cold, and I have dressed for it with Blue Johns fleece bib overalls and a set of warm Simms chest-high waders. I know that I will be wading, sometimes quite deep. The fish are here, too – Atlantic salmon, bigger and more plentiful than I have ever found before. I can see them broach, the flash of their broad bodies as they cross a ripple going upstream and drop to rest in the calm holding pools. I ready my line to cast, then turn quickly and see him behind me in the thick tree cover. Silent. The watcher.

I roll-cast the line in front, and make a long looping back-cast, then ease the fly in just above the pool where the water swirls out of the rapids. It curves, floating past my target, and I twitch the line. Instantly, the big salmon takes and I come tight on it. The big body arches out of the water, flashing silver, shakes twice, and is off. I slowly strip in my line, and behind me I hear a voice say, "Amerikanitz! Nyet! Nyet! Nyet!"

The man comes out of the birch forest, dressed in rough peasant clothes, short, stocky, so I am pretty sure he's not KGB secret police.

He ambles over to me with a big concerned smile on his face. He is looking at my rod, a graceful 9½-foot, 8-weight, Loomis IMX model. He shakes his head, thinking, "Too small." He wags his finger at the tiny fly and breaks into a grin, almost an embarrassed laugh, and repeats, "Nyet."

The year is 1988, and few Americans have ever fished in Russia for Atlantic salmon. Our party numbers eight of the first outsiders to be allowed in that region. But now, with Glasnost, new attitudes are shaking Communism to its very foundations. They have also opened up new frontiers for American fishermen to these virgin waters.

We are here on a fishing exchange, a specially arranged trip allowing a handful of Americans to travel to the southeastern coast of the Kola Peninsula to fish a Russian River for Atlantic salmon. At this time very few Americans have ever fly fished in Russia, and very few Russians have ever seen a fly rod. My "stalker" is named Nikolai, and as near as I can make out, he is an avid salmon fisherman. But obviously he thinks what I am doing is tantamount to trying to catch a bear with a switch.

On the other hand, I think the sort of old-fashioned spin tackle Nikolai has been using such heavy monofilament is like using an elephant gun to hunt quail. He persists. Almost shyly, he draws out of his pocket what he thinks is surefire to catch a 15- to 20-pound salmon in this Soviet river. He wants me to try it.

It's a spoon that weighs the better part of an ounce. He doesn't understand that in fly fishing you cast only the weight of your line, and any heft at the end of your leader stops the rhythm of your cast. I gave him the old American trademark grin, and said, "Wait a minute, I'll show you how it's done, Western style." His eyes brighten, puzzled. He understands as much English as I do Russian – not a word. But he's intrigued.

I strip in my line and show him that the fly is very small. Salmon flies are historically from Europe, with catchy names like Black Bear-Green Butt or Black Dose. I try a Monroe Killer, and finally settle on a size 8 Rusty Rat. He runs his thick fingers over my leader, about 8-pound test, and his eyes take on a mischievous glint.

Surely this *Amerikanitz* is crazy. To him the leader is like the thread from a spider. He nods, as though watching an indulgent child, and backs away while I cast, working my way down river. It is wide, maybe 200 feet, and somewhat rocky.

It takes about 20 minutes, but then a big fish flashes in, and this time I hook it solidly in about four feet of water. In a fairly short fight, I bring the salmon to a shallow, mossy cove and swing it up by the tail. It is probably a 15-pounder.

Suddenly the man is back, watching over my shoulder. He's so excited, his mouth drops open and he jumps up and down as if he has just witnessed a miracle. Then he stops, stunned, as I release the fish. With the legal exchange rate of $1.60 for one ruble, and 3.63 rubles per pound, that fish would have brought around $87. At the village of Umba, where a high salary might be the equivalent of $200 to $300 dollars a month, salmon is one of their main sources of income. I can see the wonder in his face as he examines me, a strange alien who has come a very long way just to release a prize fish. He thinks I'm crazy without doubt.

They say a journey of a thousand miles begins with just one step, and this fishing odyssey behind the Iron Curtain began when Gary Loomis, the G. Loomis rod maker, called me and said, "Stu, are you ready to go to Russia?" He had met with Bill Davies, then President of a Trout Unlimited Chapter in Arizona, and Bill's Russian wife Tanya from Moscow, who felt there could be an opportunity under Glasnost to do this. They asked me to help assemble a group of fly fishermen to represent America.

This group certainly does just that. It includes Sandy Moret, who runs the Florida Keys Fly Fishing School, and his brother Randy, who skillfully fishes big tarpon and bonefish in the Florida Keys. The Minneapolis twins, Bud and Ted Burger, who have fished Atlantic salmon in Canada for many years; Dave Robinson, of Montana, and senior vice president of Simms Waders; David Beshara, contractor from New Hampshire, who had brought Scientific Angler fly lines to leave as gifts for the Russians; and Steve Zuckerman, a California angler noted for his record catches of black marlin and blue marlin in Australia and Hawaii.

Planning such an ambitious excursion isn't that easy. There are some important logistics to work out, but as a result of this trip, Russian rivers, where the fish have never seen a fly, may be in the future for American anglers.

The important part is that we eventually find ourselves face to face with the Russian people, and enjoy some of the finest Atlantic salmon fishing any of us ever experienced. Perhaps the world's best. The Russians turn out to be … just like us. In the cities, men are in dark blue suits with briefcases, the women in stylish dresses and high heels, all in a hurry, clicking away to some meeting. In the country, the folks are laid back, wanting to talk, and meet you with a smile. The kids are all giggly and beautiful.

In mid-September while we are here, the rivers run cold and fast, 46 to 48 degrees, but are full of big, brutish fish that, if you're not careful, will go charging off with all your fly line and backing.

It's tough just getting to the village of Umba. The eight of us fly Finn Air to Helsinki on the first leg, then Aeroflot to one of Russia's greatest cities, Leningrad (St. Petersburg). There, we have our first fishing experience in Russia, fishing for landlocked salmon, brown trout and grayling in the River Voix, a mere two hours drive from Leningrad. We then take Aeroflot to Murmansk on the Barents Sea, and head southward to Umba on the White Sea, just north of the Arctic Circle. The Umba River flows south from the Kola Peninsula, emptying into the White Sea.

In fish geography, it is a place unique. The river boasts of not only migrating Atlantic salmon, but also spawning "humpies," Pacific salmon, as well a numerous Arctic grayling and sea-run brown trout.

St. Petersburg, formerly known as Leningrad, has been capital of Russia for two centuries and the pivotal city in three historical revolutions. It housed the Winter Palace of the Czars as well as the Academy of Sciences and Arts, and provided Peter the Great with the strategic positioning and stronghold from which to defeat King Charles XII of Sweden.

Today it is a vibrant, cosmopolitan city, rushing, noisy, yet much different from New York, where everything is plentiful. It was also the sight of Russia's most devastating and heroic role in WWII, when, during a three-year siege, as many as two and a half million people were buried in mass graves. The evidence of that struggle remains in the soil, releasing bacteria called "giardia," which made it impossible for us to drink the water. Nevertheless, there are plenty of other liquids to slake one's thirst.

The Russians roll out the red carpet for us. The Hotel Pribaliyskaya, where we stay in Leningrad, is equal to any five-star hotel I've seen. A banquet reception given for us by the Hunters and Fisher Club features smoked salmon and an impressive Russian champagne, short and witty speeches by its director Alexay Kojaev, a retired KGB Colonel, cognacs so smooth they slid down neat, and Stolichnaya vodka, which some in our group made liberal use of to [ahem] balance the lack of potable water.

Our first fishing venture outside Leningrad in the River Voix is only an appetizer, a limbering up exercise. All of us catch loads of grayling and some brown trout. Dave Robinson takes a brown that weighs 10¾ pounds. When I ask Andrey, our interpreter and a state ichthyologist, about it, he insists they are lake trout. There are so many two- to three-pound grayling they become a nuisance. We take one land-locked salmon, but this is not what we came for as we are all itching to get at the virgin river far to the north.

Aeroflot jets us to Murmansk, where 11 of us – fishermen, interpreters and officials – are transferred to an ancient biplane of WWII vintage with fabric covered wings and a big four-blade prop. Its huge engine, at least 3,000 horsepower, thunders away and we get off the ground quickly, lumbering along at about 80 knots. In less than two hours, we mush down on the short gravel strip in Umba, which is the name of a town, a village and a river full of salmon, nestled in beautiful birch forests.

We think the trip in has been rugged, as most of us have been without sleep for more than 48 hours. But five days later when we leave to come home, we can't fly due to low ceilings so we have to make the trip back to Murmansk by bus. The first two hours of the six-hour ride are a tooth-jarring journey over a corduroy road chockfull of holes, yet covering only 40 miles.

Finally, though, we are on the river, ready to fish for Atlantic salmon holding the first fly rods that the people of Umba have ever seen. Unfortunately the local people are no help in finding the salmon. Not one of us knows the first thing about fishing this river, and they only fish commercially with a net stretching across the Umba about four miles up river. They have little idea about fish habits, what a holding pool is or why we should be wading the rocky shores and shallows waving our willow-like rods.

We decide to separate into pairs, dropped off along the river at varying intervals, transported by the only outboard-powered boat in the area. After all, this is an exploratory fishing trip.

At various times throughout our stay, this boat is to be the cause of both frustration and anxiety. Frustration on the one hand in not being able to get from one area to another when we want to, and anxiety on the other while drifting down river toward fast waters as our boatman once again pulls the cowling to clean the sparkplugs.

Even though our first day on the Umba is a typical case of the blind leading the blind, our unique group of fly fishermen, half of whom had never fished for Atlantic salmon before this trip, hook 22 salmon, certainly a tribute to this fantastic fishery.

Bud and Ted Burger are the most experienced Atlantic salmon fishermen on our team. So, we all listen with interest that evening as Bud describes how he waded into the head of a run that has a large rock creating a break in the current rip.

"Salmon were jumping," he remembers. "I tried some Labrador tactics. I cast at the end of the riff to let the fly drift parallel to the shoreline, then let the line mend right and left, sweeping the fly in the current. I jugged the rod tip. Zap! The salmon struck right then. So it told me salmon in the deeper part of the run were following the fly into the shallows, and watching curiously. The twitch of the rod tip triggered the strike."

Normally, the salmon take when the belly of the fly line makes its swing, accelerating and bringing the fly toward the surface. Bud says he tried a #4 Black Dose, but it was a little too large, and went back to a #6 for the proper velocity. He quickly had six hookups, landing three. Atlantic salmon can be extremely sensitive to either size or color.

Ted Burger used a 12-foot leader, a 12-pound tippet tied to a No. 6 Rusty Rat, then a Monroe Killer with a black body and a green-and-orange hair wing, on a floating line. "In 25 minutes," he reports, "I hooked three fish and landed two. Dave Beshara and I landed one at the same time. I noticed fish rolling. In five more minutes, I landed another one."

"It was getting late, and we were in a place where the fish came up a narrow alley, about 70 feet wide, "Beshara recalls. "I was using a 9-weight IMX rod, weight-forward floating line, with a 12-foot leader tapered to a 12-pound tippet, and after I saw Ted hook up, I changed from a jig fly to a Rusty Rat. Within four or five casts, I got a 20-pound-class salmon. With that concentration of fish, and a little more time, we could have more than doubled the catch. Absolutely fabulous."

"All the fish cared about," Dave Robinson deduces, "was proper drift, patterning the area thoroughly. I found that systematically working the fly six to 10 inches further out every presentation, letting the current do it, got these rolling fish to take. It would be tougher with jumping fish."

We find that the fish are fresh run, just in from the ocean. They still have marks from sea lice on them, some marks as big as pencil erasures. If they'd been there longer, the marks would have faded. They have come to spawn in this cold northern river under overcast, gray skies. They are fresh and feisty.

The next day, everyone catches salmon. We are beginning to learn some of the holding areas of the Umba River. In only six hours of fishing, 47 salmon are hooked and fought, with 30 being tailed. All but two of these are released. One is Bud Burger's 26-pound salmon, the largest actually weighed on this trip.

That night, Viktor Didenko, the Mayor of Umba, has a banquet for us, and a vodka-toasting contest with Dave Robinson, our designated toastmaster. Dave certainly understands that old saying about discretion being the better part of valor. They serve tasty, clear salmon broth, potatoes, vegetables and very fresh, succulent poached salmon steaks. Their whole grain breads are so rich and heavy that a loaf could weigh, I'm afraid, about six pounds. Throughout the visit they offer us complete and hearty meals, not gourmet foods with delicate sauces, but rip-roaring portions, wonderful in texture and taste.

After dinner, the Mayor assigns us into teams of four anglers. He says he has invited all the townsfolk to have a day in our honor, to come and watch. We are to fish a stretch of river that runs through the Village of Umba, closer to its mouth. Each team would work one side of the river. The Russians like competition and the team that catches the most and the biggest salmon wins their little tournament.

Since the people take a living out of this river, Viktor asks us to keep only our largest fish of the day. But how can you know which one that will be? We decide to release everything and just tape them for size. He doesn't explain whether the best team will win prizes or money – turns out to be neither – but it works anyway. We all get separate areas to start and the river is easily waded.

The first salmon I hook that day gets away without me ever seeing it. The fish takes and goes running down through the rapids. I have to get out of the river and run down the bank after it. I carry 230 yards of 20-pound backing on my STH Elisio reel. About the time the backing gets within a couple of turns to the end, the fish grounds my fly line on a rock, zooms back into the rapids, and goes off. Truly a wild fish.

We are all using weight forward No. 8, 9 or 10 fly lines. Some use a sink tip but most of us diehards stay with a floating line. I caught almost all of my fish on a 9½-ft., 8-weight IMX, G. Loomis rod, and a No. 8 weight-forward floating line. I use a 13-foot leader with an 8-pound-test tippet. You can use a 15- or 20-pound leader tippet because these fish aren't shy. They have never seen a leader before. But, oh, they are strong.

Dave Robinson, using a No. 9 sink tip, has a big salmon in that same area actually spool him. It just chugs away, right down to the end of the backing, while he sloshes after it. He finally has to grab the line and break it off or it will have taken his whole rig.

A 10-salmon total actually turns out to be our poorest day

of fishing. But, we did have some great encounters with the local people, as well as the fish. Steve Zuckerman will never forget his encounter with each. He has just landed a whopping 24-pound salmon when a village elder stops by to marvel. Getting around the language barrier, Steve gives the villager a present, a few of his lures. The man is so grateful he leads Steve back to his cabin and insists he, too, accepts a present. It was a hand-carved model of a Russian church he has worked on for three years. Steve refuses the gift a dozen times, but finally feels he has to take it, the man's most prized possession. That night, Steve makes a special trip back to the village, and hands the villager a package containing a spinning reel, lures and lines, and a kit of toilet articles that you just can't get in Russia. Even then, he has to almost force the man to accept it.

It's certainly not necessary, and in some conditions not even possible, to bring your fish or even the skin back to a taxidermist. Knowing this, we each use two lengths of monofilament, one for the length and the other for the girth of our biggest fish. All we have to do is clip off and measure, take a picture or two and turn them loose. By using the formula of the girth squared times the length divided by 800, you can find out approximately what your fish weighs. For example, for a fish that is 20 inches in the girth and 49 inches long, the calculation goes like this: 20 x 20 = 400 x length of 49 = 19,600, divided by 800 = 24.5 pounds. It's a quick calculation, and easy to do with a hand calculator.

All a good taxidermist really needs is the length, girth, approximate weight and a good photograph – you don't need to kill the fish.

Because Ted and Bud Burger own a number of sporting goods stores specializing in hunting, fishing and outdoor equipment, we naturally asked them to do some research on taxidermists for us. They came up with Viktor Birontas at Artistic Anglers in Nissua, Minnesota. All eight of us have him do a graphite mount of one of the largest salmon each of us caught to further immortalize our first Russian Atlantic salmon trip.

"There are so many trophy-size salmon over 15 pounds in this river," Bud says. "And the great thing about this river is its unusual ability to have a number of fish in the 10- to 12-pound class, and also trophy sizes 15 pounds and up. In Iceland, it's unusual to have a fish go to 15 pounds. Here, 20 percent or more are in the trophy range, and this is a commercially fished river."

I see fish here, lying on the line between the ripple and current, about five feet from shore that will weigh 35 pounds, even though the villagers set gill nets in the river from June to October during the spawning run. The nets are open three days and closed one for conservation. Yet the recorded catch during the heaviest part of September has run as high as 6,000 fish some years. They figure that is 1 percent of the run.

If we had another week on this water, we could double or triple our catch, because we now know where most of the likely holding pools are. In our honor, the Mayor named the newly registered holding pools after each of us. So anglers in the future may fish the Dave Beshara Pool, the Sandy or Randy Moret pool and on and on. Who could believe that this could happen in an area in which Americans have never been allowed to visit?

The future could mean trips for Americans to this fishy place. A joint venture between the Russians and Americans currently in the works involves placing a first-class fishing lodge right on the Umba River, within a one-mile walk to at least five holding pools. They expect to accommodate eight anglers and have two or three new outboard-powered boats. In my opinion, this river could easily handle 10 to 12 fly fishermen at a time.

The Mayor of Umba, in one of his innumerable toasts to us, expresses his hopes that the Iron Curtain melts even more than it has, and that the exchange between our two countries becomes friendlier than ever before. "The Military cannot create such a friendship, but hunters and fisherman can," he says.

As it is, in four days on the Umba River we have 110 salmon hooked and fought, with 67 landed. Considering that we fish only an average of six hours a day, our total fishing time is less than 23 hours. We certainly improve as we get to know the territory.

On the last morning, we have 29 on, 24 landed. We manage to miss breakfast so we can spend another three hours on the river before it's time to depart. I am very glad we do. The fish is in the wrong position when I see it roll, just above the rocks where I am wading. The flash of its sides as it broached makes it one of the biggest fish I'd seen all week. If it was upstream another 20 feet I would have had a much better shot at it. I have to make the presentation slightly upstream, directly in front of its face.

The chances of an Atlantic salmon taking under these circumstances are almost nil. But suddenly, it takes. I see the flash under the water, and I come tight on it. The fish explodes, thrashing spray, and is into my backing on the first jump. That's 86 feet of fly line gone, but I have more than 200 yards of 20-pound Dacron backing. The fish jumps five more times, charging through the rapids around rocks, twisting, head shaking, but I know this will be my last chance. I ease it toward the shallows, and eventually it comes to me, exhausted. Ted scoops it up by the tail, the biggest fish of the trip.

Taped, it measures close to 30 pounds. I am glad to let it go to fight another day. Atlantic salmon don't die after spawning. Next year, it'll be even bigger. And I plan on being back.

CHAPTER

TWENTY-EIGHT

THE PEOPLE YOU MEET

Never a Dull Moment

During my years of guiding with my flats-fishing skiff Mom's Worry, I had a great variety of people in my boat, ranging from everyday folks to visiting dignitaries to sports luminaries. In addition, my activities in the fishing community led to many enduring and pleasant associations. I have written about many of the characters I've know and fished with, but there are others that are noteworthy to me. At the risk of being called a "name-dropper," I intend to make this a chapter of "sketches," if you will, glimpses of some memorable days fishing and visiting with a cast of characters whose names you will recognize.

President Harry S. Truman

John Spotswood had been Monroe County's Sheriff for more than a decade, and by January 1959 I had become his fair-haired boy when it came to taking dignitaries visiting Key West on fishing trips. During that time I guided on bonefishing trips of a day or more with the U.S. Secretary of State, a Commandant of the Marine Corps, head of the Florida Highway Patrol, a visiting U.S. Congressman, and Senator Estes Kefauver.

Because of Sheriff Spotswood, I found a long-term client in Bill Reynolds, President of Reynolds Aluminum Corporation, who would tie his 130-foot yacht *Intrepid* at Munson Island, locally known as Sheriff's Island. This was just off Little Torch Key, where I lived across U.S. 1 Highway on the northwest end.

If somebody had told me when I was a young Naval fighter pilot that one day I'd take an ex-President and First Lady out fishing, I'd have wondered what they'd been drinking. But it happened, and I found myself worrying about proper protocol as the day began. That uneasiness went away the moment I picked up the President and Bess at the *Intrepid* with my 15 ½-foot skiff and we started our run to the Content Keys. This was one of my favorite haunts and a spot that seemed to be home for schools of wily bonefish.

The weather was storybook perfect, and with great anticipation I brought the skiff to a stop, tilted up my 35-horsepower Johnson Outboard, and tied the boat to a 16-foot-long wooden push-pole I easily jammed into the soft mud bottom.

Now it was time for a little instruction on how to cast accurately with a spinning outfit. After a couple of "Excuse me, sir" comments on his technique, I showed President Truman how to coordinate releasing the line from his first finger a fraction of time later so his shrimp would fling outward instead of straight up in the air. President Truman quickly picked up the rudiments and was casting good enough for me to start polling the boat against the incoming tide toward Content Passage. In short order it seemed like we were almost surrounded by feeding bonefish mudding and tailing in the incoming tide.

The President's third cast was perfect, slightly up-current in front of a small feeding group of 6- to 7-pound bonefish. Like magic he was hooked up to a wild fish that took off like it was shot out of cannon, screaming 100 yards of 8-pound-test monofilament from his spinning reel. I quickly pushed toward the fleeing silver bullet of a fish, but to no avail. On one of its lightning-like darts, the line got wrapped around a large loggerhead sponge, creating enough additional resistance to break the line, setting the magnificent drag-racer free.

"! &#%" President Truman uttered under his breath as he turn toward me, asking what happened.

Twenty minutes later this same scenario was repeated like déjà vu. When Mrs. Truman softly, almost shyly looked toward me, she asked, "Captain, what does a lady do when a lady, er, has to go?"

"Well, ma'am, I could put you on that little beach on West Content Key," I replied, pointing to that area, "but the mosquitoes, deer flies and no see-ums would certainly try feasting on your tender flesh. Or, I could run you back to my house on Little Torch Key, but we would lose about two hours of this prime bonefish tide."

President Truman quickly interjected, "Oh no, those two fish hooked me and I want to catch at least one bonefish today."

Walking by Mrs. Truman, I lifted the lid on my live-bait tank in the back of the boat, just behind the cockpit exposing the live shrimp and holes in the bottom of the boat, and politely said, "Well ma'am, I have had other ladies ..."

Without any other words she looked me right in the eye, saying, "I understand, Captain. Both of you gentlemen go to the front of the boat, whistle, sing or splash water ... just make noise."

President Truman hooked four more bonefish, landing two of them before the tide changed and we ran back to the *Intrepid*, ending a fantastic few hours of fishing for a great President. It had been a dream-like great honor for me that ended with a hearty handshake.

* * *

Papa Hemingway's Mojitos

The year was 1958, and I was in Havana visiting an American friend, Mike Brandon, whose wealthy parents owned a clothing manufacturing business and a chain of Mini Max Supermarkets throughout Cuba. Their beautiful home was in a gated community called Country Club Palace, situated in an exclusive residential part of Havana. They were members of the Havana Yacht Club, and Mike enjoyed taking visitors from the U.S. there to look over the big yachts, large fancy fishing boats and to partake in an expensive lunch.

After having lunch with him one day at the club, Mike was invited to go somewhere with a very pretty young lady. He asked if I would mind fending for myself for an hour or so. I told him no problem, and that I'd spend a couple of hours strolling along the docks looking at the boats, the big tarpon rolling in the harbor and the multitude of fish alongside the docks looking for handouts.

"See you later." Mike said, looking back over his shoulder as he and his lady friend briskly walked off holding hands.

I've had good reason to believe that most things in my life seem to happen for a good reason, and once again I was about to experience one of those happenings. It was around 2 o'clock, there was very little activity on the boats that were tied up at the dock, and I was thoroughly enjoying my walk while reading their interesting names and admiring all the fish swimming alongside them.

Walking up to a boat with a name that seemed vaguely familiar – *El Pilar* – I politely asked the gentleman sitting on the lone fighting chair if he had been out fishing lately. I was speaking to Ernest Hemingway.

"You're an American, huh? And you like to fish," he said whimsically.

"Yes sir, I'm a part-time fishing guide in the Florida Keys and a part-time pilot for Pan-American World Airways," I answered.

"Well, Mr. Fishing guide … pilot… come aboard and join me for a Mojito." He gestured for me to come aboard.

Taking my shoes off before stepping onto the gunwale and into the cockpit area, I asked, "Thank you for inviting me on board for a, uh, Mo, Mo … what did you call that drink?"

"You're welcome, young man, it's merely a Cuban mint julep and it's pronounced Moe-HEE-toe," he said.

Cuban mint julep indeed, I thought, what will they think of

next? Truthfully, I don't know how many Mojitos we polished off while talking fishing and fully agreeing on fish-fighting techniques during the next few hours. It was hard for me to believe when he said he knew my name and guiding reputation from reading some of the numerous Sunday columns of Vic Dunaway, the outdoor editor of the *Miami Herald* who wrote about my successful guiding out of Little Torch Key.

After Mike Brandon came walking along the dock looking for me and my doing a slurred introduction, I required a little dockside help to leave *El Pilar*.

I later found out Ernest Hemingway would make the Cuban Mojito almost as famous as the running of the bulls in Pamplona.

This is how Papa Hemingway made them: Put four to12 mint leaves with stems in a highball glass, one teaspoon powdered sugar and about two ounces of club soda. Slightly crush the mint leaves until you get the mint aroma. Add two ounces of good white rum, two ounces fresh squeezed key lime juice fill the glass with crushed ice and stir in club soda to taste. Use a sprig of mint as garnish.

Sit back with a fishing friend and discuss the pros and cons of the various ways to land big fish quickly. The only thing you won't have is the one and only Ernest Hemingway mixing them for you.

* * *

Stormin' Norman's First Tarpon

A few years ago I fished with Captain Sean O'Keefe out of Key West, a guide I previously heard good things about. Indeed, I had a great day of shallow-water backcountry sight-fishing for big tarpon. I only hooked and landed the smallest one of about 50 or 60 pounds, but had at least 12 opportunities to cast at big fish.

The following December, Sean called to invite me to fish with him again on open dates in April. During that same time, the tournament director of a sailfish event going on at the same time got in touch to say that General Norman Schwarzkopf had asked him to find out if I would be available to take him out fly fishing for tarpon this year. He added that the General needed left-handed fly reels.

"Certainly the pleasure would be all mine, and I'll make sure to have left-handed wind fly reels for him," I eagerly responded.

I got in touch with General Schwarzkopf at a private cocktail party before the tournament, and we formulated a game plan for the next day's tarpon trip. We arranged for a second skiff to include General Ellis, run by Sergeant Robert Allen, the Port Security Director.

All was going according to plan, and Sean had a good plan for starting off the morning not far from the marina, saying there has been many tarpon in the Boca Chica channel on this early morning in-coming tide.

Fifteen minutes later we were idling up to a shallow edge of the channel and we could see three different schools of tarpon rolling farther out, looking like they are coming our way. Shutting the engine off and using his push-pole to hold the boat in position with the bow pointed towards the incoming tide and the tarpon, Sean said, "Looks like they are right on schedule, better get the rod with the intermediate ghost tip out and be ready." A slight northeasterly breeze was coming offshore, giving us this close to the shoreline some protection – a good set up.

Making a cast to see how much distance that was actually set up for the General, I passed the 11-weight fly rod over and backed out of his way. I casually asked him to make a few practice casts to get used to the rod.

It was immediately obvious that this was the first time he ever had a fly rod this big in his hand. After a little instruction and half a dozen practice casts, he was able to cast all of the 55 feet of line I had out of the rod tip, certainly more than enough for this type fishing situation.

Turning to face me, he said, "Stu, thanks for the instruction, you certainly have a good way of presenting what has to be done."

"Thank you, sir." I replied, adding that he wasn't the first four-star I've had in my boat.

"Oh yeah, who else?" he asked, looking directly at me.

"Well sir, back in 1960 when I was laid off from Pan Am making a full-time living as a backcountry guide here in the Florida Keys, I guided General Cates, the ex-Commandant of the Marine Corps during the Korean war, for three days of bonefishing."

"Humph, only a Marine General," he said with a twinkle in his eyes and a chuckle.

All of this time I could see the schools of tarpon getting closer. Then, as if by magic, two slow-rolled, coming up from the deep part of the channel angling toward us.

"Hurry, General" I exclaimed in a somewhat hushed voice, "drop the fly right at 11 o'clock…good…let it sink for a moment… now strip in some line to get the slack out. That was okay, now pick up and cast right back to the same place; I think they're still lying out there."

He cast again, and my advice continued, "Perfect…start a slow strip…twitch the line at the end of each strip." The words were barely out of my mouth when I saw his fly line stop. "I think he's got it," I exclaimed. "Hurry, strip the slack out and set the hook."

No sooner said than done; the next sound we all heard was the fly line, then the backing screaming from the General's reel and 50 yards out a 75-pound silver king came out in a flashy, high-flying jump. Almost as quickly Sean had his engine trimmed all the way down and started, pulled his push pole out of the bottom, put the boat in forward gear, seemingly all in one motion. and turned the steering wheel directly toward the fish. Now 150 yards out, this feisty tarpon was once again jumping.

Standing slightly behind and on the left side of General Schwarzkopf, I suggested he lift as much line out of the water as he could, winding line quickly while Sean moved the boat toward his fish.

The General appeared to be having somewhat of a problem cranking the reel with his left hand, but in all fairness, he did manage to pickup line as we got closer to this young adult tarpon. About 20 minutes into the fight, we were within 30 feet of Mr. Poon, when for some reason not known to either the General or me, instead of winding the reel handle forward he wound in the opposite direction, creating a serious amount of slack line within the reel. Of course the tarpon chose just this moment to surge and start another short run, creating a backlash in the reel, breaking the 20-pound-test tippet with the surge.

"Close, but no cigar, General," I laughingly said.

"Sure, close only works with horseshoes and hand grenades," he replied while flexing his arms.

His face stern, he said, "Stu, I don't like what you have done to me ... don't like to lose."

"This was just the first battle, sir, not the war," I replied.

While Sean was running his boat the half a mile we had traveled fighting the fish, back to the edge of the channel I was already stripping fly line off Sean's left-hand-wind reel in order to wind it back onto my right-hand-wind reel. If the good General was going to fight another tarpon, I wanted him to wind with what I now knew was his dominant right hand. By the time we were back in position, I had selected a new leader with the same type fly from my leader stretcher case, and was tying it onto the butt section of the leader coming from the fly line. One thing I had learned a long time ago about fly fishing for tarpon is you have to be ready or you'll miss good some opportunities.

As I was stripping fly line off the reel to get the General set up, I heard a big splash and both Sean and the General asked if I'd seen that one jump.

"No, I was too busy getting things set up," I said looking up and seeing three fish roll just out of our 55-foot range. Quickly stripping more line off the reel, I roll-cast the fly out of my fingers forward, shooting line on the back-cast and laying out 75 feet of line. Letting it sink for the count of four, I started my normal easy tarpon strip with a twitch on the end of each strip when the line came tight in mid strip. Setting the hook smartly, I quickly turned to the General, pushing the rod into his hands and saying, "Take it, this is really your fish."

Sean had everything secured with the engine running in less

than 30 seconds, except on her first jump it was obvious to all of us she was a full-blown adult of more than 100 pounds. This time I got my left-hand cotton fish fighting glove out of my case and waited for the right moment when the fish was not screaming line or coming toward us to put it onto the General's left hand.

It was immediately obvious that I made a wise decision having General Schwarzkopf fight the fish with a right-hand-retrieving fly reel. He was winding three times faster with his right hand then he had on the other fish using his left hand.

Getting a better look at this handsome fish on its next two jumps, I now estimated its weight at 120 pounds. A true adult for sure....

One hour and fifteen minutes into the fight after, a tour of two different marinas, the mooring harborage of two dozen sailboats, into a shallow mangrove-lined bay, General Schwarzkopf had the leader's nail knot in through the tiptop of the fly rod, which is the criteria in all release tournaments that signifies a caught fish.

I could tell the General's back was creating an enormous amount of pain on top of the muscle and stomach pain he was feeling from a long hard fight with a tremendous fish. I've always said that I never caught a big fish using light tackle without hurting during the fight and again the following day.

Mission accomplished, I thought, let's not have a successful operation and have the patient die. Reaching around with my right hand, I gently but firmly took the fly rod out of the General's hands.

"Damn good job, sir on one helluva big poon," I said.

Sean was patting him on the shoulder with congratulations too. That evening at the tournament party, the three of us, Jeannine, Sean and I, were invited to sit at the General's table for dinner. And as you could well imagine, much of the conversation had to do with fly fishing for tarpon and looking forward to the next time.

* * *

Jazzing It Up with Yaz

It was November 1961. My soon-to-be wife and I were spending the first of many Thanksgiving dinners with Ted Williams at his new home in Islamorada in the Florida Keys. His last home, a ground-level structure on the ocean side of Islamorada, was gutted and almost completely destroyed on September 9 the previous year by Hurricane Donna.

Ted had a new bride of two months named Lee Howard, and while she was preparing a fantastic turkey dinner with all the trimmings, Ted was telling me about a new left fielder the Boston Red Sox had signed.

"Stu, you won't be able to pronounce his name but you will dam sure remember it. Carl Yastrzemski will no doubt be a good replacement for Teddy Ballgame."

Ted certainly knew what he was talking about. Yaz, as he was affectionately called, became a solid player his first two years and then emerged as a rising star in 1963, winning the American League batting championship with a batting average of .321 and leading the league in doubles and walks. He enjoyed his best season in 1967 by capturing the American League Triple Crown with a .326 batting average, 44 home runs and 121 RBIs. He was the last hitter in 1967 to win the Triple Crown and was voted the American League's Most Valuable Player almost unanimously.

In 1969, Yaz hit the first of two consecutive 40 home-run seasons, as he led the Red Sox to third-place finishes. Yaz got four hits and won the All Star Game MVP award in 1970, even though the American League lost. His .329 batting average that season was his career-high.

For the past three years, I had been working as a fishing consultant for the DuPont Company, helping develop and promote their new Stren Monofilament Fishing Line. Part of my job was performing at various sportsmen shows around the country, which included the New England Sportsmen's Show; where I was doing three 40-minute casting demonstrations on center stage in front of approximate 12,000 people. Whenever possible I would team up with a local hero on stage and then spend time as a guest answering questions and signing autographs in booths.

My performance on center stage with Carl Yastrzemski brought a standing-room-only crowd of more than 12,000 because of the promotion on radio, TV, in newspapers and large billboards throughout the War Memorial Coliseum. This time, I would instruct Yaz on the best way to cast for accuracy and distance with an open-face Ted Williams 400 spinning reel.

Using a 1/4-ounce rubber Skish lure made for practice casting, he was casting it with bull's-eye accuracy right off the bat – pun intended. He picked it up so fast that in order for me to be on stage the prescribed 40 minutes, I had to come up with some trick ways of casting to teach him, like the bow-and-arrow cast and stepping-on-the-lure cast for extremely confined areas. Yaz was a quick study on each of the different ways to cast, making it difficult for me to stretch the time on stage. The audience would go wild after each demonstration and it was obvious that Yaz was really enjoying the program.

Then it happened. When I bent over to pick up an ultra-light spinning outfit for a slightly different demonstration, the black Sharpie permanent marker in the top pocket of my shirt fell at my feet. I had been using it to autograph caps while spending time between shows in various booths. It came to me like a bolt out of the blue: A unique way to close this performance would be having Carl Yastrzemski sign Yaz on the small 1/8-ounce Skish lure attached to the ultra-light, 2-pound-test spinning outfit, and dangle it in front of him with the bail open and have him knock it into the upper tier for a "home run."

We were wearing small wireless microphones so the entire audience heard me ask Yaz if he would autograph and hit the little lure into the upper deck – I just needed to get someone to run a baseball bat up to the stage. The audience started a deafening chant of YAZ-YAZ-YAZ that was the most unbelievable thing I had ever heard.

This was no sooner said than a Louisville Slugger from a nearby booth was passed up to me. Handing it to Yaz, I quickly stepped back, giving him room to take a few practice swings the way he would before stepping up to the plate. Quickly I explained to him how I would be out of the way while dangling the small lure, with the line resting on my forefinger, bail open as though I was going to cast. Instead, when the bat made contact, one of two things will happen – the lure will fly, streaming fishing line behind it or the shock will be so great that the 2-pound-test line will break as the lure flies into the upper deck.

Yaz stepped into position, tapping the bat on the stage as though it were home plate. The audience fell quiet. Taking a deep breath and holding it to make sure I did not move the lure, I waited.

There was a SWISH but no SPLAT as Yaz had a swing and a miss. The audience went wild with cheers. Yaz turned to me, forgetting he had a microphone on, and said, "Stu, why did you move it?"

"Honest, Yaz, I did not move anything. Remember it's only an inch-and-a-half long and you're used to hitting something considerably larger."

The audience started the YAZ chant again as I stepped back once again, dangling the small lure. This time he connected with a home run, knocking it into the very top row, to the complete jubilation of the spectators.

This was the only performance we were allowed to end by hitting the lure into the audience for fear of someone being injured.

* * *

Finding Good Luck with Wade Boggs

Wade Boggs was a base hit machine, racking up 200 hits in seven consecutive seasons with his Jedi-like approach to his craft. It's been said that his methodical approach to hitting was an extension of his methodical personality. He was called quirky by some sports writers because of his superstitions. They say he awoke at the same time every morning, ate chicken before every game, and took exactly 150 ground balls during infield practice. For night games, Boggs stepped into the batting cage at 5:17 and ran wind sprints at 7:17. Before each at-bat Boggs would draw the Hebrew word "Chai" in the batter's box, and his route to and from the playing field was so precise that by late summer his footprints were often clearly visible in the grass in front of his home dugout.

It's a fact that Wade batted left handed and threw with his right hand. While fishing together I observed him casting a spinning outfit with precision using either hand.

I never had the pleasure of watching Wade play baseball, but I have had the pleasure of spending time with him during more than half a dozen Pediatric Cancer Research Tournaments in St. Petersburg Florida, of which he is now the Celebrity Host; numerous Redbone Tournaments for Cystic Fibrosis Research; and recently fishing with him in a TV show while participating in a one day fishing tournament in Tampa Bay. This tournament was for snook, redfish and trout. It was a team event with both anglers on the boat able to score. The rules stated you measure and photograph the largest of each of these three species before they are released. In order to be in the Winner's Circle at the end of the day, you must have caught and photographed all three species. The team with the most total inches from the largest of these three species is declared the winner.

Robert Stewart, Executive Producer of Southwest Florida Outdoors TV show, suggested we start filming on the warm-up day before the tournament. That sounded good to me, as I always liked fishing for snook and redfish and an extra day on the water with Wade while getting to know our guide at the same time. I had never met the very accomplished Captain Tom Larkin.

Captain Tom dipped a handful of sardine like white bait from his live well and threw them as far out as he could, slightly up current and abeam of where we were anchored. Explaining that this was an area of deep crevices in the bottom, he found some years ago. During the months of April, May and June, depending on the water temperatures, it played host to a large amount of gag and Nassau groupers. It only took a few moments before the water was erupting with swirls and explosions of feeding fish. Captain Tom quickly handed Wade a spinning outfit rigged with a circle hook tied to three feet of 40-pound Fluorocarbon leader and a four-inch-long live white bait. I had previously made my decision to use a five-inch Berkeley Powerbait Swimming Mullet instead of live bait. Before I could cast into the area of busting fish, Wade was hooked to a hard-fighting grouper that was trying its best to get back home into the crevice.

This was not the way I expected to start the morning filming our warm-up day for the tournament. I thought we should have been scouting for concentrations of snook and red fish…certainly not grouper which was not one of the tournament specie.

As he generally did, I found out later, Robert Stewart knew exactly what he was doing; in little more than an hour of this fast, exciting fishing Robert knew no matter what else happened he had a good TV show.

Thirty minutes later found us near the mouth of a mangrove-lined creek where Tom eased out the anchor and quickly threw a handful of white bait on the up current side of a mangrove point. As we drifted into position, Tom handed us a lighter spinning rod rigged with a circle hook and live white bait. Almost déjà vu of the grouper spot we just left, swirls and an occasional pop signifying snook feeding told us we were in the right spot at the right time. Wade and I cast at the same time to almost the same spot and we both hooked up at almost the same moment.

Landing a pair of 22-inch snook that looked like peas out of the same pod, we quickly baited up and cast toward the mangroves again. This time Wade hooked and landed a 26-inch snook as my white bait went untouched. This prompted Tom, to explain, it would require a bit of time resting the balance of the snook before they would feed again. And now that we know the *where* and *when* of this particular spot, he wanted to see if we could find some schools of redfish and trout. "After all this is just a scouting mission for tomorrow's tournament." He quipped.

We spend the rest of the day running to various hidey-holes in and around Tampa Bay without finding any redfish and only one undersized trout before calling it quits for the day and heading back to the Tortuga Inn, the beautiful spot Robert Stewart had arranged for us to stay during the filming.

The next day we worked on filming a good TV show. Wade caught a 38-inch snook, I landed a legal-size redfish, and both of us caught numerous trout to round out the three fish necessary for being a contender in the Winner's Circle. The filming highlight of the day for me was autographing and swapping trading cards with Wade and finding out the card he gave me was his rookie year card.(Boy did I get the best of that trade.)

That evening at the tournament banquet we found out that we had won second-place out of 43 boats, missing being the grand champion by only half an inch.

CHAPTER

TWENTY-NINE

BREAKUP!

My Marriage of 33 Years Crashes and Burns

It happens to every professional airline pilot: A final flight. A time when you taxi to the gate and shut the engines down for the last time. A final time when you slide out of that coveted left seat, and become…well, just like everybody else. No longer a Pilot in Command. Of commercial flights anyway. You can still fly your private airplane all you want.

For professional pilots, retirement is mandatory at age 60, although medical issues can force an earlier age. When the time comes for the final run, many retiring pilots take their wife along, and has a celebration with the crew once the trip is over.

For me, the chance to make a big deal out of a final flight was not meant to be.

On April 5, 1985, while on a layover in Tokyo, I had been out to dinner with both of my copilots and flight engineers. We were just leaving the restaurant to walk back to the hotel when I started getting the aura that preceded the cluster migraine headaches I had been experiencing off and on for the past two years. This aura was so severe and totally incapacitating that I could not see or speak clearly. My mind seemed to work okay but my speech would come out like gibberish and my vision was so befuddled it was even difficult to walk. Thank God, it had never happened in the airplane or even anywhere near the airport, but now I had to make a big decision, one of turning myself in to the Pan Am medical department. The very thought of the possibility of being stricken while I was making a tight instrument approach was horrifying.

The next day I felt perfectly fine and operated the nonstop flight from Tokyo back to New York. Upon my arrival, I promptly went to Pan Am's medical department and told them about the occurrence. I was immediately grounded and the Medical Director said he would make an appointment for me to go to the world-renowned Diamond Headache Clinic in Chicago.

That trip to Chicago proved to be the end of my flying career. After spending 10 days at their hospital-like clinic, going through multitudes of tests daily, Dr. Seymour Diamond wrote a letter to the Pan American Medical Director, copying the FAA informing them of his opinion that I should not fly airplanes any more.

So that trip back to New York from Tokyo on April 6, 1985 had turned out to be the last time I would ever be at the controls of an airplane. Four years as a fighter pilot on active duty and five years flying fighters in the reserves; thirty four years as a commercial pilot on Pan Am's seniority list; More than 14,000 hours in the cockpit, in all weathers, in all seasons, all over the globe. It was all over.

Like that old saying goes, "It was better than a poke in the eye with a sharp stick." Contractually I had a full sick bank giving me seven months of full pay, then I was put on disability receiving half pay until my retirement date of June 1990.

Bernice and I continued our wonderful life of living in both Montana and the Florida Keys until 1989. That was the year I was jolted—big time!—when Bernice suddenly announced she no longer wanted to live in the Florida Keys and instead desired to live full time in Montana. She said she would go along with renting a place in the Keys for two or three months during tarpon time to appease me.

All this prompted us to put our house up for a quick sale. [Some many months later, I heard rumors of Bernice having a falling out with some of the local garden club ladies.]

Bernice had already drawn plans to add on a 1,100-square-foot great room to the Montana house, large enough to accommodate a lot of her beautiful antique furniture. However, turning 60 years old May 11, 1990, I no longer would be receiving the nice disability check of $65,000 a year from Pan Am. Instead, I'd be getting my Pan Am A-fund retirement check monthly. I rolled my B-fund 401[k] into an IRA and received my C-fund's 22,000 shares of ESOP Pan Am stock. Not bad, considering I only had two years before starting to collect Social Security.

By December 1990, Bear Creek Log Homes had completed this two-story open cathedral addition, and we decided to have a new, hot-water radiant form of central heating installed throughout the whole house, with four individual heating zones. Now we were really ready for the tough Montana winters.

We were able to build and enlarge our Little Bear home without taking a mortgage. I had planned well enough to maintain our lifestyle as long as I kept consulting and doing occasional fishing seminars. I had already decided that when I turned 60 it would be time to hang up my push pole and no longer guide, I realized those long 12-hour days on the water were not as much fun anymore, and were starting to take its toll. Once again, I wanted to do the fishing, not the guiding.

In February 1991, I was at the Worcester Massachusetts Sportsmen Show, doing one of the many fly-fishing seminars I do around the country for the G. Loomis Rod Company. After each of my seminars I'd spend the next few hours in the G. Loomis booth showing rods, answering questions and occasionally taking some of the interested people to one of the casting pools, letting them try one or more rods of their choice.

It was late Saturday afternoon that a young man and his dad came into the booth and were looking at some of the top of the line fly rods. Being free for the moment I walked up to them and asked if I could show them anything in particular. The dad turned to his son asking, "Is there any special rod you would like to see, Joel?"

Directing his reply to me, the young man looked me in the eyes and asked, "Do you have a nine for a five?"

Surprised by his reply, I located a 9-foot, two-piece, five-weight fly rod that had a fly reel with the fly line on it, already set up for interested customers to cast. Handing it over to this young man, I was again surprised at the way he flexed the rod to feel its action. Very few adults that have been fly fishing for many years are aware of the proper motion to flex a fly rod.

With my interest aroused, I asked them both if they would like to go over to the casting pool to give it a try. With a positive nod they agreed. As we walked toward the casting area, the father casually asked if I was still living in the Florida Keys. Not wearing a nametag and not knowing that he even knew who I was, I answered, "No, I'm living full time in Montana."

Watching this youngster cast 50 feet with apparent ease did my heart good. In between casts I asked him who taught him to cast and how long he'd been at it. Standing up straight, almost at attention, he pointed to his dad and said, "My dad taught me how to cast when I was five years old."

"How old are you now?" I asked.

"I'm 11," he softly replied. He was big enough that I guessed him to be 13 years old.

I spent the next 30 minutes giving him some casting pointers, which lengthened his casts to 70 feet and farther than most experienced adult anglers can cast. Most young people have good timing and coordination, and that's all it takes to be a good fly caster.

While practicing his casts, his dad introduced himself as Ray Plante, saying his son's name was Joel and he was a cabinetmaker carpenter in New Hampshire. He went on to say that things had turned to worms in the construction business and he'd been offered a good job in both Bozeman and Ennis, Montana.

Normally I don't give my business card to people not in the fishing industry at these shows, but I was so impressed with this young man's abilities that I gave Ray my card, telling him to give me a call when he got situated in Montana. I added that I'd like to take Joel fishing and he could come along too.

December 1991, Pan Am went into Chapter 6 bankruptcy, making my 22,000 shares of Pan Am stock worthless. I later found out that I could not even take a tax loss on my income tax because ESOP came out of my salary before taxes. Shortly thereafter, I was notified by the Pension Benefit Guarantee Corporation that Pan Am only had 45 percent of the A-fund in an annuity with Prudential Insurance, and the rest was in worthless Pan Am stock. PBGC decided to only pay 75 percent of the 55 percent they took over. I was supposed to continue the same medical coverage with Travelers Insurance for the rest of my life, paying just a small premium. Then Travelers notified me that both the $150,000 insurance policy Pan Am issued me on my retirement that stated was paid in full, and the medical coverage, became invalid after Pan Am's demise because they were making term payments on both of the policies.

Even after retirement, my wife and I were supposed to have some pretty good travel privileges for the rest of our lives on other airlines, and they, too were no longer valid as those were receptacle agreements ... and Pan Am could no longer reciprocate.

My retirement took a hit, and I faced the fact that was no longer the fat cat I had anticipated being. On the plus side, I was healthy with a loving wife, a great house on the side of a mountain in Montana, and I still have the means of making a supplemental living doing fishing things I like.

In July, 1992, Ray Plante called, saying he had been working for a cabinet shop in Ennis, Montana since the first of the year. Because Joel was visiting him during his summer school break, could they possibly take me up on my fishing offer?

Without hesitation I asked him if he could meet me at 10 o'clock the next morning at a Conoco gas station on the south side of Four Corners, a place almost midway to where I plan to take them fishing in one of my favorite hidey holes on the Gallatin River. They both experienced a great day of dry fly fishing to rising trout in an area seldom fished.

After explaining to Ray that I consider the best fishing in this part of Montana to be when most of the tourists leave in September, he told me he was divorced and Joel was only visiting him for the summer, but that he was trying to get full custody.

I took them fishing at least half a dozen more times, introducing them to about six new places within a 2 ½-hour drive from Ennis before Joel had to go back to school in New Hampshire.

In November, I took Ray hunting with me as well as my dear friend Freddie Anderson, who was visiting from Florida. We all had deer and antelope tags to fill, and I knew just the place to get that done: just south of the Snowy Mountain Range at a 22,000-acre ranch owned by Tom and Sheena Glennie, long-time acquaintances of mine in Judith Gap, Montana.

The numerous times each year I camped on their ranch with my little 15-foot travel trailer had become a ritual over the past 10 years. I hunted pheasant, sharp tail grouse and Hungarian partridge along with some of the finest grain fed antelope and whitetail deer I ever sunk my teeth into.

Tom planted many acres of wheat, barley, oats and rye, but also kept hundreds of acres uncultivated in order to receive conservation tax credits. This was a habitat oasis for game birds and animals alike.

After a highly successful two-day hunt, filling my two antelope tags, I decided to save my whitetail buck tag with almost a month left in hunting season. Both Fred and Ray filled their one-each antelope tags and each of their whitetail deer tags.

Tom Glennie drove over to our campsite to tell us about a weather forecast of a strong early winter storm that was about 24 hours away. Discretion being the better part of valor, we decided to head back to Bozeman before it reached us, making travel difficult.

During the last week of November the deer were in full rut and still having my whitetail buck tag to fill, I asked my neighbor if he would like to take the two-hour drive to Judith Gap with me. Dick had also been saving his whitetail buck tag for this exciting time when the big mature bucks lose their stealth, coming out of hiding during daylight hours and stalking does.

After making a call to Tom Glennie and getting permission to hunt his ranch, we left early enough the next morning to arrive about an hour before daylight, giving us enough time to get into our hunting gear and make a plan.

I had a good feel for where the big bucks should be coming down the side of a steep hill and heading toward the creek bottom, and put Dick on the main trail to wait. I walked slowly in the dark around the other side of a rocky ridge, sitting on a deadfall with sufficient foliage behind me so I would not be easily seen.

Both with hunting and fishing, local knowledge is very important, and I have been hunting this area for the past 10 years.

I love it when a plan comes together….

We both filled our tags with big mature, grain-fed bucks and were on our way back to Gallatin Gateway by 10 o'clock, a little tired but extremely pleased with our success. After hanging both deer at Dick's place, the sky opened up with large soft flakes of snow gently drifting down, as if a reminder that Christmas was just around the corner.

At home Bernice was just putting the finishing touches on the 16-foot blue spruce Christmas tree in front of the back picture window in our great room. Ginger, my golden retriever, lovingly met me at the door. All seemed well in the Apte household.

For some reason holidays, especially Thanksgiving and Christmas, were always a downer, difficult for Bernice to cope with. She explained it was because of her not having any close immediate family, and I can only assume she was correct. During the past five years, whenever she would have major periods of being unhappy about our life in general, I tried to get her to go to a psychiatrist, just to see if there might be a chemical or physical reason for her deep depressions. Each time she would come back at me saying I was the one that should see a psychiatrist, and I would generally make the matter worse by telling her that I was happy and extremely satisfied with my life.

Because of her depression syndrome, getting through these holidays were sometimes a chore. I tried to help cheer her up with gifts and telling her how lucky we are, which unfortunately did not always work.

It seemed like no matter where we traveled in the world, there wasn't anything or anywhere that lived up to her expectations, from what she had read in books or seen in the movies. She never seemed to remember any good or happy times, but kept the unhappy moments in her life handy, like in an alphabetical file.

One thing that gave her happiness, at least on a temporary

basis, were new clothes, furniture or changing things in the house she loved. We had been living in our enlarged log cabin for 11 years when Bernice decided she really wanted to have all-new, built-in kitchen cabinets and replace our pinewood kitchen floor with the same kind of oak hardwood floor we had in the added-on great room.

After receiving what I thought were high estimates from two different Bozeman area cabinet shops, I suggested giving Ray Plante a call in Ennis, only 50 miles away, inviting him to an early dinner and to see what kind of an estimate he would come up with.

Ray was extremely busy, sometimes working seven days a week in the cabinet making trade, and would not be able to come by for dinner and to give an estimate until after we got back from spending our annual March, April and May in the Florida Keys. I'd rented a nice place, on Lower Matecumbe in Islamorada with two bedrooms and two baths upstairs and one bedroom one bath downstairs. It was situated on the water, only a 20-minute run by boat to some of my favorite tarpon fishing grounds.

Bernice made use of these months in the Keys visiting numerous homes and cabinet shops, getting ideas and making sketches of various types of cabinets. Less than a week passed after we returned to Montana in mid-June, before she was on the phone trying to set up a date with Ray for dinner and a look-see estimate. During this conversation, Ray told her he had received full custody of Joel, and would it be okay to bring him along?

Of course it was all right, and as planned Ray and Joel showed up Sunday afternoon for one of Bernice's fantastic roast leg of antelope dinners with all the trimmings, including a pineapple chiffon pie for desert.

After dinner Ray took measurements, looked at Bernice's sketches and pictures of the type of cabinets she wanted to have built and installed, and promised to do some research and get back to us by Wednesday. He also suggested we drive to Ennis and have a look at some of his work. His estimate was 35 percent less than the lowest estimate from either of the cabinet shops in Bozeman, making it worth the drive.

To say he did good work would be a gross understatement. Ray is truly a superb finished cabinetmaker and after our visit, without any hesitation we decided on having Ray do the work. Times had been tough for Ray and he needed one-third in advance before he was able to order the necessary equipment and lumber. I would not be as quick to do this sort of deal if I didn't know Ray, who at that point was a friend.

By August things were well on the way. While waiting for some of the cabinets' specialized items, Ray started replacing the knotty pine kitchen floor with tongue and groove hard wood. Rather than have Ray wasting at least two hours each day driving back and forth to Ennis, Bernice suggested that both Ray and Joel move into our downstairs sub basement, guest bedroom and private bath, while he was working upstairs. Joel won't be starting school in Ennis until the second week in September, and hopefully he'll be finished by then. But as it turned out, some of the items Ray ordered ended up being on backorder, slowing some of the intricate cabinet installation.

I had to be in Denver September 15 at the Fly Tackle Dealer Show, working in the G. Loomis booth and the Mackenzie Fly booth, talking to fly shop and tackle shop dealers. The show closed on the 19th but one of the major tackle manufacturers had previously invited me to fish some excellent private waters with him on the 20th. I didn't want to refuse for two reasons: I really wanted to fish this renowned Spring Creek, and I wanted to spend some time with this gentleman, with the prospect of become a consultant for his company.

As always, I called home every evening while away doing seminars or working at shows. Everything sounded great the first two nights and Bernice was very excited about how nice the new cabinets were starting to look. Then the third night she sounded a bit strained, almost distant, like something was really bothering her.

"Is everything all right?" I asked.

"Yes, fine," she answered after a slight hesitation.

"Okay sweetheart, I'll call you tomorrow evening." But an unnerving thought crept into my head. Could she be having an affair with Ray? After all, he is very good-looking, gregarious, always smiling and in the house with her alone for almost a week. "Yeah," I calmed myself, "but he's also at least 20 years her junior."

Bernice picked me up at the Bozeman airport Tuesday afternoon, saying how pleased she was with the new kitchen cabinets, and now the only thing left to do was polish and stain the hardwood floor. She was full of chitchat, almost rambling on nonstop, during our 30-minute drive home. The hardwood floor presented a striking change as I entered the kitchen area, even before being polished and stained, as did the new kitchen cabinets.

Telling her what a good team they made, with her doing the design work and Ray doing the rest. I thought to myself that maybe this will help her get through Thanksgiving and Christmas without going into a depressive funk this year.

After clinking wine glasses in a toast to her newly designed kitchen, we sat down to one of my favorite dinners. She had prepared a beef brisket pot roast from one of my mother's many recipes. That night we made love – in a quiet, subdued manner. The next morning, Bernice was up fussing around the kitchen before I rolled out of bed.

The aroma of bacon cooking and fresh coffee perking filled my nostrils as I descended down the flight of stairs to our living area, leaving me with the feeling of well-being and that it was great to be home again.

Halfway through breakfast, out of nowhere, Bernice, sitting across the table from me and looking very serious, said, "Stu, I want a long-term separation."

At first thinking this was some sort of sick joke, I said, "And what constitutes a long-term separation?"

Still very serious she answered, "Around a year, so I can go out and do my thing, whatever it takes to make me feel happy."

"You're serious, aren't you?"

"Yes, I've been giving it lots of thought for some time now," she replied, almost in a whisper.

Dumbfounded for the moment, not quite believing what I just heard her say, I got up from the table and went into the living room. I was willing to do almost anything possible to finally make her feel as content and happy as I had been with my life. Walking back into the kitchen, I said, "Bernice, if this is what it will take to make you truly happy, we'll have to have an attorney write some legal separation papers pertaining to our finances. You'll probably need a set amount to live on during this period of separation. Other than that, all of our resources, checking accounts, savings accounts, securities and the likes that are setup for either one of our signatures will have to be changed, requiring both signatures."

Turning around to face me with a look of anger on her face, she replied, "I just don't understand why we would have to change any of our financial accounts! What if I refused to do that?"

"What you have been saying sounds to me like you don't want a separation, you want a divorce."

Without a word of reply, she turned, walked down the steps and out of the house to the garage.

When I looked out the dining room picture window, I could see her car driving down the hill at a breakneck, dangerous speed. This was September 22, 1993, and by early October she had filed for divorce, requiring me to move from our master bedroom upstairs to the guestroom in the subbasement. Living under the same roof was almost emotionally more than I could bear, especially during the nights when she did not come home.

She would tell me that it was none of my damn business whenever I broached the subject of where she had spent the night. I was sincerely worried about her welfare each time I sat up all night watching out the picture window for her car to turn the corner and climb our hill. Foolishly, I suppose, I was still hanging to a thread of hope that our marriage might somehow come back into shape; that we might have a fresh start.

Finally one day when she came home to do laundry, seeming reasonably calm, wanting to talk about her lawyer's proposal, just at a time I wasn't feeling well. I said that I'm going upstairs to the toilet and to take a shower and we can talk when I come down.

Only a few minutes later, following me up the stairs into the toilet, she threatened me with our wedding picture she took off the hall wall, then threw it against the wall shattering the glass and frame. Screaming and crying at the same time, she did the same thing with some other pictures, including her favorite grandfather's picture.

I tried to salvage the frame and wedding picture by putting them on the side, but she came back and ripped them both to pieces. All this time she was in a rage, crying and screaming at me that I was trying to destroy her by telling friends about our problems in this divorce. She said Ray did not want her staying there anymore, not while she was still married to me, even though she was sleeping on the couch in the living room while Ray and Joel slept together on the double-size bed.

She had truly lost it this time, and I realized that the toll of her psychological meltdowns over the years had come to a head. And finally, I had to face the truth I could not bear to admit: Now she had fallen in love with another man, a man I had befriended and made one of my hunting and fishing companions, invited into my home with his son when they needed a helping hand.

It was at this point that I fell into the deepest, darkest sense of betrayal and despair I had ever known. The failure of my marriage seemed to leave my life empty, devoid of hope, eternally dark and bitter. I seriously began to consider taking my own life. Then, one day, I almost did

CHAPTER

THIRTY

STARTING OVER

Quitting Is Not an Option!

It's hard for me to believe or even remember how I felt on that almost-fatal afternoon in September 1993, when I came within a heartbeat of putting an end to my life.

As our marriage crumbled toward a divorce, I had been forced to visualize what life would be like without Bernice, after spending more than half my life with her. The very thought was unbearable, devastating beyond any crisis I had ever experienced. Finally, I reached a point where I felt I could not go on. The future I was facing seemed impossible to bear.

Sitting on the edge of the bed I had shared with Bernice, I put my Colt Trooper Mark IV .357 Magnum in my mouth. I cocked the hammer and my forefinger rested on the hair trigger.

To this day, I don't know what it was that stopped me from ending it all. Could it be survivor instincts deep within me? Whatever, something – call it fate – decided it just wasn't my time yet.

With both hands on the big, deadly revolver, I removed it from my mouth as if in slow motion. The stainless steel taste is still a memory. With tears distorting my vision, I just as slowly omitted deep sobs. Placing the gun on my bed, I tried to get a grip on myself.

I could hear the telephone next to the bed ringing, but it was difficult to focus neither eyes nor mind. It must have rung at least seven times before I managed to negotiate the two steps to answer it.

My dear friend Freddie Anderson was calling from the airport in Seattle, Washington. His wife, Anita, had left an emergency message for him with United Airlines Flight Operations. An hour earlier I had called Fred's house, needing someone to talk to during the absolute pit of my emotional crisis.

The distraught sound of my voice had prompted Anita to try to contact her husband. Fred was a 767 Captain on a 2 ½-hour layover in Seattle. While we were talking, he persuaded me to immediately drive to the Bozeman airport and wait for him to arrive on the first available flight from Seattle.

Thank God, I had regained enough composure to do exactly as Fred had ordered. At that moment, he was more than a friend—he was a savoir.

Fred had called in sick, necessitating a replacement captain to operate his flight, which would now be delayed. Arriving in Bozeman where I was still waiting a few hours after his call, Fred remained with me for the next three days before having to head out for his next scheduled flight. The therapy of his friendship steadied my nerves, made me able to cope. When Fred left, I once more was feeling like a Pilot in Command of my own life.

Negotiations moved along slowly, as they sometimes do, with some divorce lawyers wanting to keep both parties as adversaries in order to increase their total fees. My attorney, Kent Kasting, said I was the first divorce client to ever come into his office telling him what I wanted to do *for* the wife who had left me, instead of what I *did not* want to do. I was still in love, although extremely emotionally distraught, and wanted to make sure Bernice would be financially taken care of for the rest of her life.

Kent is one of the nicest, most helpful people I have ever met, and given his way, this divorce would have been finished and over four months earlier. Not so with Bernice's attorney, who seemed to want this divorce to continue on and on. I just wanted to put all of the breakup behind me, pick up the pieces of my life, and try to continue with what was left.

Returning to the Florida Keys the second week of March, I spent the first four days at the house of friends Dick and Ginny Campiola until the place I made arrangements to rent for the three months was available. The day after moving into my new place on the Gulf side of Islamorada in an area aptly named Safety Harbor, I received a new Tournament Edition Bonefisher backcountry skiff from the manufacturer to use during the three months I would be in the Keys.

John Philips, the young man who trailered the skiff four-hours from Fort Pierce Florida, was insisting on driving home that same evening. I was equally adamant about him staying for an early dinner at the landmark Papa Joe's Restaurant in Islamorada, which was the least I could do to repay his kindness. He finally conceded to join Steve Thomas, a fishing guide friend and me, for an early dinner of prime rib.

Even at 6 p.m., the restaurant was jam-packed with early-bird diners and we had an hour wait before we could be seated. Convincing John that the prime rib was worth waiting for, we went to the bar. Steve and John opted to sip beers while I still felt the need of tossing down a couple of vodka Apte-tinis on the rocks.

When a table on the far side of the room became available, the maitre d' tapped my shoulder with a motion to follow him. Not having eaten since an early breakfast, I began to feel those two good-size vodkas and my eyes lit up when a very attractive blonde waitress appeared. Wearing short-shorts and a Papa Joe's t-shirt swished up to our table with menus. She asked if we'd like to order a cocktail first.

Without hesitation I said, "Sure, lovely lady, I'll have vodka on the rocks, some olives and olive juice on the side. I like to dirty my own martinis. And my two friends are drinking Heineken's with frosted mugs, please."

"I'll get your drinks first, then tell you what tonight's specials are, if you're interested." As she spoke, a very pretty smiled lightened up her face.

"I would be very interested, if you're one of the specials." The phrase rolled off my lips before even realizing what I had said.

Appearing annoyed, she turned with a pronounced jerk, moving rapidly to the bar to get our drink order.

"Hey, Steve, I mused, "she looks as good walking away as she did coming toward us."

"You know, Stu, I met her at a party a couple weeks ago, and I'll be happy to make an introduction if you like," Steve said with a knowing wink.

"Thanks, buddy, I think I can take care of my own introduction." Steve nodded at my air of confidence. And, I did just that, giving her one of my old business cards with my new phone number on its flipside just before dessert arrived. I quickly told her to check with Frank, Papa Joe's owner, about me. I boldly asked for her phone number, and she quickly stated that she did not give that to strangers. Her nametag stating she is Mary from New York revealed all I knew about her.

Evidently Frank's good report card must have been flattering, because three days later Mary called to invite me as her date for the annual Papa Joe's one-for-all birthday party. This was the beginning of a four-and-a-half-year relationship that was sometimes on, sometimes off. During most of the three months I was renting, Mary would leave work at around 11 o'clock, drive the three miles to my place, spending the night before driving the 14 miles north to her house in Tavernier.

My divorce was final May 13, two days after my 64th birthday. [A year after our divorce, Bernice would go on to marry my old "friend" Ray Plante.]

Knowing I would need a place to permanently hang my hat, I had previously made a small down payment on a three-bedroom, 2 ½ bath townhouse in a newly developed area on the west side of Bozeman. It was necessary to fly back to Bozeman, clearing all of my stuff out of the ill-fated Gallatin Gateway log home before the May 30 sale closing.

My hunting and fishing friend Curt Stovall, Public Relations Director for the Coca-Cola Bottling Company in Bozeman, and two of his friends helped me move all of my heavy stuff from Gallatin Gateway to my new townhouse. It looked like I would be parking on the curb until I got things sorted out and put away because we damn near filled up the two-car garage.

Life felt empty and lonely, not knowing anybody in the immediate area; then a nice young man bought the other side of the townhouse. Dennis Thomison, a letter carrier in Bozeman and a hard-core outdoorsman, was almost walking in the same shoes I was, being newly divorced, except he was in his mid-30s. Dennis's two-bedroom townhouse had a one-car garage that was filled with his toys–a full set of exercise equipment including barbells, motorcycle, bicycle, camping equipment and no telling what else.

My backyard neighbor Ken Eiden had a similar townhouse on the next street, his backyard butting into mine. He had been a 285-pound offensive tackle and captain of the Montana State University football team his last two years before graduating with honors in an accounting degree, and was in the process of becoming a CPA with a large accounting firm in town. Ken had just separated from his wife of only two years and was in the throngs of divorce, but he also was an outdoor person who liked to hunt and fish.

What a threesome my neighbors and I made.

Even spending most of June and July fishing some lakes, the Gallatin River, Madison River and occasionally driving over to Livingston fishing the Yellowstone River, my nights were lonely, prompting me to spend endless hours on the telephone with Mary and running up an exorbitant long distance phone bill. Knowing August and September were extremely slow months for her waitress job at Papa Joe's restaurant, and that Mary had never been to Montana, I invited her to come out for a seven-week visit to see if she liked it out here. Of course I would make reservations and send a round-trip airline ticket with an open return date so she wouldn't feel locked in to staying.

August and September came and went and so did Mary. My life had settled down to the fall hunting routine with some trout fishing on occasional nice days. Christmas and New Years Eve were lonesome but also came and went with my thoughts turning more and more to fly fishing for big tarpon in the Florida Keys. Continuing to burn up the phone lines and having a long-distance romance with Mary, we made a plan for my moving into her two-bedroom prefabricated double-wide, on a bayside canal for March, April, May and part of June, at which time I would return to Montana for the summer and fall.

This plan seemed to be working and my life was slowly heading in the right direction. The following August, Mary drove her new Honda sports car the 2,700 miles from Key Largo to Bozeman in two and a half days. As you can imagine, she was exhausted after such a Herculean trip, and I knew it would take her a few days to recuperate.

A month went by, seemingly too fast, the two of us spending some quality time fishing and relaxing. Then came a phone call with her daughter in New York telling her that her 12-year-old grandson had been hit by train while skateboarding. They had to put a stint in his head, casts on his left arm, left hip and leg and he was stable but expected to be in the hospital for a long time. Mary was packed and on the road in an hour. She did not want to fly, figuring she would be there almost as fast driving and have her car with her.

I flew to New York 10 days later, spending the next three weeks there to give whatever moral support I could. Mary never came back to Montana, but the following spring on my next trip to Florida, I convinced her to attend school and obtain a real estate license so she could leave the waitress job. About a year after she became a realtor, we broke up for good and she went back to Long Island, New York. I was once again living the life of a bachelor.

I've said it before; life works in strange ways. If I had not helped Mary get her real estate license I would have never found my fantastic house on Plantation Key. She actually found it while doing an open house walk around with a group of realtors from her office. When she returned home later that afternoon she told me about it, explaining it was far more than I intend to spend. After hearing her description, it sounded like everything I could hope for and more, so I suggested that she take me there for a look. She was right when she said it was more than I thought I could pay but the owner, a gentleman farmer from Georgia who only spent two months each year in the wintertime in his hideaway house in the Keys, struck up a friendly conversation with me. I told him how much I liked his property but his asking price was beyond my means. His reply was for me to make him an offer and if I did not want all the furniture maybe we could work something out. Actually I did not need any of the furniture. Mary, acting very indignant, broke up our conversation saying I have to go through the proper realtor chain of command when making an offer. The next day in a telephone conversation with the listing agent I made an offer of 20% under his asking price. When I hung up Mary went into a tirade saying I had never intended buying that house but was just wasting everyone's time. Not 30 seconds after her outburst the telephone rang and the listing realtor said he accepted my offer.

There was one snag though, coming up with $100,000 at closing would necessitate my cashing a CD before it was due. One day while casually discussing it with my new friend Paul Wingrove, an ex student of mine in the Florida Keys Fly Fishing School; without hesitation he said, "I'll write you a check Stu, how soon do you want it?" Thankfully the way it turned out I didn't need his help but it was a gesture I'll never forget.

One afternoon the first week of January, 1999, I stopped in to visit my next-door neighbor Captain Larry Greenwell, a local backcountry fishing guide, to share some fishing information. Now that I no longer had a significant other, I asked if he knew anything about the pretty lady who had bought the house across the street from me almost a year ago.

He said that he thought she was dating the dock master at a local marina. While we were talking, a big dude looking like a football player knocked on the door and came inside. Larry made a quick introduction of Terry Adams, saying he was married to Cindy, the daughter of the lady neighbor I had been asking Larry about.

The introduction gave me an immediate entree to asking Terry if he thought it was all right to ask his mother-in-law out to dinner, as I was batching it, eating out by myself three or four nights each week. His matter-of-fact, unconcerned answer was, "I don't know, you'll have to ask her."

I learned my pretty, across-the-street neighbor's name was

Jeannine. I had waved a hi-neighbor greeting a few times while I was playing "Farmer Brown," as Mary called it, working in the yard. But we had never actually met on the same side of the street anytime during the past year. I had not wanted to get too friendly, even as a neighbor, because Mary was an extremely jealous person. [Unknown to me, at the same time Jeannine had thought that I was married, because on occasions when she had tried to have a friendly conversation with Mary, she had felt snubbed.]

On March 15, while looking out the kitchen window, I noticed my neighbor digging in her yard, transplanting a small tree of sorts.

Bernice was gone…Mary was gone…I was alone.

I went downstairs, opened the front door, and started across the street. The walk was to change my life forever.

CHAPTER

THIRTY-ONE

JEANNINE

My Luckiest "Catch" Ever!

Jeannine tells our friends that when she saw me coming, she said to herself, " Oh no, not today."

She had been working hard and it was a very hot day, causing her to perspire profusely, and had given up the idea of my ever coming across to meet her, much less invite her for a date. After all, almost two months had gone by since Terry told her of my interest, and she said she had noticed a variety of cars parked in my driveway overnight at different times.

"Hi, I'm Stu Apte, your neighbor across the street," I politely said while extending my right hand.

"My name is Jeannine Smethers, but everyone calls me Granny. Nice to finally meet you, neighbor," she said, looking right into my eyes.

"I'm a bachelor, eating out a lot by myself and wondered if you'd like to go to dinner with me one night?" I asked, straight away, still gazing into her almond colored eyes.

Hesitating for a brief moment, tilting her head slightly to one side to look me up and down, she replied, "Maybe we should do lunch first sometime."

She definitely was not taking any chances on her first date with this Stu Apte guy. She suggested we meet at noon the next day at the Captain's Table, a restaurant not far from where she had a part-time job and two and half hours off for lunch. I told her that that worked for me. It was easy enough to find the restaurant, but I got there 15 minutes early just to make sure I would not be late.

We had a very pleasant seafood lunch with both of us enjoying the casual conversation. She still had more than an hour left before going back to work, so I suggested we have a glass of wine at Coconuts, an open-air restaurant and bar on the water not far from where she worked.

I followed her there, we parked and found a table right on the water's edge. Ordering a glass of white wine for Jeannine and a Bud Light draft for myself, I was suddenly taken back by her beauty and sexuality. I guess it was showing the way I was looking at her, because she gave me the same kind of look when she had suggested we do lunch before a dinner date. Suddenly, she said, "Stu, I'll be right up front with you: I'm too old for you."

"I don't think so," I said with a slightly bewildered look.

"Hey, I'm 67 years old," she added with a slight smile.

"That's okay, I'm 68," I said.

"No you're not, you're only saying that."

Wow I thought, as I retrieved the wallet from my back pocket, I can't remember the last time I was carded. Probably quicker than I had intended, I was showing Jeannine my driver's license, proof positive of my age.

Now, when relating this happening, she chimes in to friends that she responded with, "You know how it is here in the Florida Keys; most older men you see have a much younger lady at their side."

And this was the beginning of the best part of my life.

Late the next afternoon there was a knock at my door and there stood Jeannine with a key lime pie she had made using the limes from her own key lime tree. After lunch the day before, when our waitress had asked if I would like a slice of key lime pie for dessert, I casually mentioned, "Normally that's what I would have, but I'm too full, thanks." That's when Jeannine told me she makes the best key lime pie ever.

"Yeah, right," I had said, with a gleam in my eyes.

Now here she was standing at my front door, being invited in, with a freshly made key lime pie in her hands.

It flashed through my mind that perhaps now I would have a newfound occasional dinner companion. After sitting in the living room and chatting for the better part of an hour, I thought I should find out if this was to be the case.

"Now that we have had lunch first, how about going to dinner with me this weekend?" I said.

Without too much hesitation, she said, "I don't have to work Sunday, so how about Saturday night?"

"Great, Saturday night it is. Have you ever been to Bentley's Restaurant?" I blurted out. "They have the best seafood in this part of the Florida Keys and an appetizer that will knock your socks off called Best of the Weird Oysters." The thought of more than just her socks coming off flashed in my mind as well.

"Sorry, but I never eat oysters," she replied, making a face.

"That's okay, they prepare fish, shrimp and lobster more than 15 different ways and I'm sure you'll find something on the menu that will light your appetite," I said. "Should I make a reservation for seven o'clock?"

"Whatever time works for you, works for me," she replied.

Now when the conversation of our first date comes up with our friends, she tells them that the next day when two of her co-workers asked what her plans were for the weekend, she started to reply with, "Well, this guy named Stu Apte…" that was as far as she got. They both cut-in almost in unison saying, "Stu Apte!" Making the thought flash through her mind, "Maybe she should reconsider going on this date. Was Stu Apte notorious?"

Then the one co-worker laughingly said, "You don't know who he is do you?"

"Only that he lives across the street from me and seemed like a reasonably nice person," she answered, to which they said with excitement, "Across the street! Wow, aren't you the lucky one."

Not a fishing person, Jeannine had never even heard of fly-fishing guru Lefty Kreh, although she lived 30 minutes from him in Maryland for many years before moving to the Florida Keys.

[Today, Lefty calls her his Maryland girl.]

Dialing Jeannine's phone number Saturday evening a half hour before our seven o'clock reservation, I was mildly surprised and very pleased when she informed for me she was ready and would be right over. What a fantastic change it was from my ex-girlfriend of more than four years, who required hours of preparation before going out to dinner.

This was March 20, still high tourist season in the Florida Keys, and when I finally found a parking place near Bentley's at least 20 people were waiting outside for a table. We were still five minutes earlier than my seven o'clock reservation and when we went inside, Pam, the hostess, gave me a big hug and a little kiss saying, "I have your favorite booth ready for you Stu. Who's your lovely lady friend?"

"Jeannine, say hello to Pam, my Tennessee gal. You sure are busy tonight, what are you giving away?" I asked, having a problem looking serious. While following her to our table, I scanned the posted specials and appetizers menu on the wall and was pleased to see they had my favorite appetizer tonight, Best of the Weird Oysters. I was going to try and get my new dinner friend to try one even though she said she would never eat an oyster.

We ordered cocktails, a glass of white wine for her and Kettle One vodka on the rocks with a little olive juice and olives on the side for me. Jeannine said she would pass on the appetizer but I ordered the oysters, explaining that they don't always have this yummy appetizer and when they do I always have an order. For my main course I ordered my favorite dish, Florida lobster Out-Of-Hand, a 1 ½ pound lobster split in half, placed on a bed of Florentine spinach, with a lemon butter caper sauce enhanced with mushrooms, crisp cashews, shrimp and scallops. When it was explained to Jeannine, she thought that sounded pretty good but decided not to be too adventurous and opted for Dolphin in the Weeds – mahi-mahi lightly breaded and baked over creamed spinach, shrimp, crab and artichoke hearts stuffing.

We were just finishing our cocktail when the Best of the Weird Oysters showed up fresh out of the oven, looking good. When I explained that the oysters on the half shell were prepared with diced up shrimp, crab meat, diced red, yellow and green sweet peppers topped off with two kinds of cheese before it's baked, she said, "Okay, I'll be a good sport and try one."

And good sport she was. During the next week and a half we went out to dinner four more evenings, spoke on the telephone at least twice a day and sat in either her house or mine getting to know more about each other. The more I learned about Jeannine, the more enamored I became. One evening I invited her over for a dinner to share a special thick-cut New York strip steak, my specialty on the charcoal grill, with baked potato and Caesar salad. I wanted this evening to be special and as it turned out it most certainly was.

We sat on the couch listening to soft music from the '40s and '50s, drinking one of my specialty cocktails, rum-dumb-boogie punch, while still learning more about each other. This concoction of orange juice, pineapple juice and banana juice laced with a heavy hand of Myers's rum served on the rocks in a tall glass is a real sneaky drink, and by the time I had the medium-rare steaks off the grill we were just finishing our second drink and both in need of some food to tame the glow from the rum.

I opened a special bottle of South African Merlot to complement the steak's flavor, which it did while at the same time enhancing our feeling of well-being. As we finished our dinner I stood up from the table, I took Jeannine's hand and asked her if she would dance with me to the slow romantic music streaming out of the speakers, all the while knowing I wanted to hold her in my arms more than anything else at that moment.

"Of course Stu, I would love to dance with you," she said with a smile and a sparkle in her eyes.

I'm not a good dancer, but the way she melted into my arms we seemed to float across the floor as we danced; it was as though we had been dancing together for years. She felt so perfect in my arms and the bouquet from her perfume made me hold her even tighter. The music for a super-slow dance was being played, the kind that I always called "why dance." I held her tightly, bending her back slightly with a deliciously long kiss. I could feel the pressure as she was pressing her body up against mine. No longer able to dance, we embraced with long kisses that were almost making me dizzy with passion.

Slightly pulling away from our embrace for a moment, she said, "What are we going to do now?"

With a tender kiss I picked her up in my arms, carrying her down the wide hallway to the master bedroom where I gently eased her on to my king-size bed where we continued to hold each other with passionate kisses. This was the first night of the rest of my life with Jeannine.

It took me a little while, but I finally convinced her to start spending the whole night with me, setting an alarm to get up before daylight to sneak back across the street without her daughter or son-in-law knowing she had been out all night. This continued for more than a week, when I managed to talk her into going to Tropic Star Lodge in Panama with me to celebrate her 68th birthday. A week away from home without the normal hustle and bustle happenings really solidified my feelings toward her.

Back home in the Keys, we continued our daily charade of Jeannine sneaking across the street before daylight until one morning her son-in-law, Terry, who was up and out much earlier than usual, bumped into her before she managed to get up her stairs.

"What are you doing out this early, Granny?" he asked.

"I'm just going to put the garbage out for pick-up this morning," she shyly replied.

"Come on now, Granny, you know this is not a garbage pick-up morning," he said with a knowing smile.

"Okay Terry, I guess I'm busted. I'll tell you about it later," she said as she headed up the steps.

The following week in early June, I convinced Jeannine to pack up and move everything across the street to what was to be converted from *my* house to *our* house.

I had been intending to sell the 24-foot Tracker motor home I had only used on one trip, that being with my ex-girlfriend Mary. The three weeks on that trip were probably the most miserable three weeks vacation I can ever recall, prompting my wanting to sell the

Tracker. But Jeannine had other ideas, saying she loved to camp and why don't we give it a fair trial before selling.

We headed for Montana in early July, returning to the Keys the first week of September after one of the most enjoyable times of my life. I now knew for sure that this lady was going to be my wife. We had both said to each other in all honesty that neither of us wanted to ever get married again, and we would be very content living together in sin. But thoughts of marriage had begun stirring within me.

A couple days after we got back, we had Cindy and Terry over for dinner to tell them about our Western camping trip. I'll never forget it. Jeannine had made the best lasagna you could ever imagine eating. While we were enjoying this delicacy I casually out of the clear blue sky, said, "Sinful (my nickname for Cindy), what would you say if someday I asked your mother to marry me?"

Nobody even stopped eating when she answered laughing loudly, "Oh wow, that's even better than my asking you to adopt me." Of course they all thought this was a joke, since we did not make any bones about our never getting married again.

The last week on our camping trip I started having severe pains in my chest when I would lie on my left side, and sometimes just lying on my back. The only relief would be to stand up straight. Of course, the first thought was my heart, so I went to my doctor who immediately gave me an EKG which was fine, but he made an appointment with a cardiologist who put me through a nuclear stress test. He told me that if I was an outboard motor red-lined at 5,500 rpm, he just ran me up past 7,000 rpm, and my heart was like a young man in his 30s.

Next my family physician made an appointment for me with a gastroenterologist, who during the first visit decided I should spend the next morning in the hospital having a camera called an Endoscope put down my throat into my chest cavity, doing biopsies if necessary. The procedure was basically a piece of cake compared to what was to follow. The next morning the good doctor called from his cell phone on his way to work, explaining he hated to be the bearer of bad news but the sooner I started doing something about my condition, the better.

He informed me that I had a non-Hodgkin's type lymphoma, but I would need more extensive biopsies to find out exactly which type. This procedure took place on Friday morning and I was scheduled to fly to Alaska Sunday morning to shoot three TV shows during the next 10 days.

Wild thoughts were screaming through my head. How long do I have to live, one month, six months, a year? The doctor had no idea nor would he make a guess. I explained that the film production company had already spent a lot of money setting this trip up and my big question to him was, would 10 days make a major life or death difference in having the biopsy performed? His answer was an indecisive "probably not."

I got an extra supply of pain pills and flew to Alaska after making an appointment with Dr. Stephen Smith, a vascular surgeon, to have a biopsy performed the morning after I returned. During my consultation exam, he asked which armpit I would prefer to have him take the lymph nodes from.

"Dr. Smith, I do a lot of fishing. Actually fishing is my whole life; I cast with my right arm and fight the fish with my left arm." I explained. "Isn't there anywhere else on my body you could get the lymph nodes for the biopsy?"

"I felt some swollen lymph nodes on the left side of your neck and if you'd like to take a chance that I can get enough for the pathologist, I'll do it," he replied.

Eighteen stitches in my neck later, Dr. Smith sent the pathology report to my oncologist, Dr. Citron at the Baptist Medical Center in Miami, who did not believe the pathology report. He said that neither he nor the pathologist at the Center ever encountered anyone with both lymphoma and leukemia at the same time. He would have to perform a bone marrow biopsy as a confirmation.

Leukemia *and* lymphoma? At first I felt vulnerable, but then gave myself a lecture to suck it up and not feel sorry for myself.

Bone marrow biopsy is not a fun happening, but a necessary one. Shortly thereafter I started the first of 7 1/2 months of a very aggressive chemo treatment. Dr. Citron politely informed me that I might lose my hair. Trying to keep it on the light side, I responded, "What, both of them?"

Back at the Mariner's Hospital in the Keys, only half a mile from where I live, Dr. Smith surgically inserted a port-a-cath in the left side of my chest–a device where I would be intravenously receiving my chemo treatment, eliminating the possibility of destroying my veins.

Jeannine would drive me the 65 miles to the Baptist Medical Center in Miami Monday through Friday, for five days of chemo treatment, then I'd have 25 days off. She always carried my booking calendar on the Friday treatment in order to make my next appointment coincide with my schedule of seminars, TV shows, speaking engagements and teaching trips to Costa Rica or Panama. I did not miss a single scheduled function during the 7 1/2 months of treatment. Dr. Citron could not believe I was able to function this way because of the aggressive type of chemo. I told him I would not let cancer get the best of me, and if it did I was going to go down fighting.

Four months went by slowly, and then one evening in early February after we had just returned from a trip to Costa Rica, we were in the shower when Jeannine asked me to see if I could feel a hard little lump in her left breast. "It feels like a little marble," I said. "I'll make some calls and find out who is considered the best doctor for breast cancer in the South."

The hand's-down opinion from both local doctors and nurses was Dr. Robert DerHagopian, an Oncologic surgery specialist in Miami. When I called for an appointment, the first time he could see Jeannine was in six weeks. I put Jeannine on the phone to give the receptionist all of the information and book the appointment, then I got back on the telephone, telling the receptionist if there were any cancellations even on short notice we would be there.

I called his office every day to find out if there was a cancellation and to reiterate the fact that we would be there when there was one. Eight days later the phone rang and there had been a cancellation, asking if we could be there this afternoon. Jeannine said "No," she couldn't make it today, and I said "Yes, let's go," and we went. Three o'clock that afternoon Dr. D., as we found everyone called him, did a painful needle biopsy in his office.

The next afternoon he called to say that it was malignant and she would have to make a decision on how to proceed. With either a mastectomy, removing the entire breast, or a lumpectomy, removing only the malignant tumor, some of the surrounding area would have a series of radiation treatments.

While waiting for her surgery date six weeks away, Jeannine spent many hours on the computer, researching the survival rate between the two procedures, and decided on the lumpectomy. Meantime, I continued my daily call to Dr. D.'s office, inquiring about a surgery cancellation. One morning 12 days later, the doctor's office called with a surgery cancellation for the next day. Jeannine had answered the phone, and I could tell by the conversation it was the doctor's office. So I picked up the other phone and listened. She hesitated for a brief moment and said she could not make it to the hospital today to be operated on tomorrow, at which time I interrupted the conversation asking what time we should be at the hospital. And we were there. I have always been tenacious, and this was further proof that perseverance pays off. Jeannine had her surgery the next morning, weeks before she was even scheduled for her first visit to the doctor's office.

She was only in the hospital a total of a day and a half, and the latter part of the following week she accompanied me back to Miami for my chemo treatment on the same day they removed her stitches. A very dear friend, Bette Beshara, accompanied us for my chemo treatment because we didn't think Jeannine would be able to drive me home yet, and of course I would not be in any condition to drive. After lunch at the New York-New York delicatessen in a shopping center, while walking back toward the car we stopped to look in the window of a jewelry store. I pointed at some rings and made an offhanded comment, "Someday, I may have to think about something like this."

With an expression of disbelief, Jeannine responded, "Yeah right!"

More than a month before, we planned a big dinner party at

our house, sending invitations to 48 friends for what now turns out to be the evening after her stitches are removed. Believing it was to celebrate our first year of blissful living together, she said she wasn't feeling up to it and wanted to just cancel the whole thing. What she didn't know was my plan to propose to her in front of our large group of dinner guests. I had been waking up in the middle of the night for the better part of a month, planning my speech. Only five of the dinner guests were aware of my intentions to propose. One of them, Jose Wejebe (host of "The Spanish Fly" TV show), had to drive 180 miles to be there and did so only because I told him my intentions.

Of course the Beshara's, Bette and Dave' and the Campiola's, Dick and Ginny, knew what I was up to. They had spent many hours preparing some fantastic Lebanese dishes and Italian specialty dishes to go along with the 25 pounds of jumbo shrimp cocktail, 40 pounds of stone crab claws, shrimp scampi over rice and a variety of other appetizers. Almost all the guests thought the appetizers were dinner until my friends started bringing out their specialty dishes.

Four large coolers were filled with iced-down beer, wine and soft drinks, and I had a full bar set up with all kinds of mixed drinks including a two-gallon punch bowl with a gallon of rum-dumb-boogie punch laced with a 1.75 liter of Meyers's rum that had to be refilled twice. Dick, being in the wholesale diamond business, had a perfect 2 3/4 ct. engagement ring made for me many weeks in advance of this happening. I just been waiting for the right moment to ask her to marry me.

More than halfway through dinner, everyone seemed to be extremely well oiled and happy, so I said to Jeannine, "Let's walk halfway up the steps, get everyone's attention and tell them really why they are here this evening." Still thinking it was to celebrate our first wonderful year living together, she said, "Okay, good idea." I took her hand as we walked up the steps to the first landing. Projecting my voice, I said "excuse me," which apparently was not heard. Once again, this time loudly, I hollered, "Excuse me!"

Still to no avail. Cupping my hands around my mouth, I bellowed, "Hey everyone, *quiet!*" And that worked.

With Jeannine standing on my right, I started my planned speech, telling everyone how we had met and the traumas we experienced. Six minutes into my dissertation, one of my friends that had over-imbibed started yelling out catcalls at me, making my mind go completely blank for the moment.

Taking a deep breath, I turned to Jeannine and loud enough for all to hear said, "Sweetheart, will you marry me?"

She responded with a gasp, a yelp and tears when Dave Beshara, standing off to the side, yelled, "She hasn't answered you yet."

Jeannine did respond: "Yes, YES, YES."

By now I had managed to get the ring box out of my pocket and I was trying to put the ring on her proper finger, but on the wrong hand. I had nursed one drink all evening, being a good host, and I was sober as a judge.

Bedlam broke out with cheers of "Congratulations, atta-boy Stu, it's about time you joined the club!" and other such comments. It was March 18, 2000 … a happening and an evening I'll never forget.

Between March 18 and May 16, Jeannine continued with radiation treatments Monday through Friday and I continued with chemotherapy, working these treatments in between my shooting a TV show May 1 through May 4 in Tampa with Frank Sargeant; taking Jeannine to Panama May 19 to May 27 while teaching fly fishing for sailfish school and doing another TV show at the same time.

I had committed to shooting two more TV shows, this time with Trevor Gowdy, Curt's son, May 30 through June 9 and fishing for striped bass at Woods Hole, Massachusetts, and Block Island off the coast of Rhode Island. You might say I had a busy month.

My chemo treatments and Jeannine's radiation treatments were finally over, hopefully leaving us in full remission. Now all we had to do was blood workups every month, visit the doctor every three months, and in my case have a CAT-scan every six months. Thank the good Lord and the U.S. Government for Medicare.

The following month on July 10, I flew to northern Saskatchewan, Canada, spending nine days at Wollaston Lake lodge shooting an

Outdoor World TV show on great northern pike. Then my bride-to-be and I left the Florida Keys August 2 with our 24-foot motor home, heading to Montana and two months of dearly needed camping and trout fishing tranquility.

We returned home in early October just in time for me to put on seminars at the Shallow Water Fishing Expo in North Carolina, then do fly fishing exhibitions at the Fort Lauderdale Boat Show later in October.

November 6 found us on an American Airlines 777 nonstop flight from Miami to Buenos Aires, Argentina, where I was to address the Sixth Argentine Congress of Trout and Salmon fishing and put on a saltwater fly fishing seminar. We returned to Miami the early morning of November 15 after an all-night flight, drove directly to the Baptist Medical Center Hospital to get my port-a-cath flushed – a procedure that had to be performed every 27 to 32 days or face the possibility of dying.

This convinced me to have serious words with Dr. Citron about having the cath surgically removed from my chest. My travels take me to too many places both inside and outside the U.S. where the hospitals do not know how to flush the port; this was brought home to me in September by the only person at the Deaconess Hospital in Bozeman Montana who—after a fashion–knew how to perform this procedure.

In January 2001 we were counting the weeks until the big day. Jeannine was busy cutting 175 tarpon out of heavy silver poster board as part of the place settings with each guest's name on each tarpon. I was doing a Shallow Water fishing Expo in Charleston, South Carolina, then we both flew to Mazatlan, Mexico, with some friends for a week, where she completed addressing the wedding invitations.

After that I was thankful my busy schedule continued, keeping my mind off the slowly-approaching day I was looking forward to so much. I had fishing schools, seminars and TV-show filming sessions in Costa Rica, Atlanta, Sarasota, Guatemala, Ft. Lauderdale, Maine and Mazatlan.

Finally the day arrived, May 2, 2001, our wedding day. The

wedding was being held at Islamorada's famous Checca Lodge–
"Keys casual" attire, barefoot on the beach–with 168 of our family
and friends attending. But Mother Nature did not comply with our
wishes. Two hours before the wedding ceremony was to take place,
sheets of rain were still coming down being pushed by wind gusting
to 35 miles an hour. Unfortunately this constituted bringing the
wedding party indoors.

The wedding ceremony was performed by a fishing friend,
attorney, photographer and great orator, Pat Ford. During the
marriage ceremony he kept the audience in the palm of his hand,
sometimes smiling, sometimes crying, sometimes applauding and
laughing with gusto. That included Jeannine and me. Everyone who
was there or had heard about the wedding said it was the best party
Islamorada had seen in 25 years. For Jeannine and me, it was one
fantastic happening, a dream come true.

Not only did I gain someone who is the light of my life, I also
acquired a fantastic ready-made family consisting of two daughters,
two sons-in-law, five grandchildren and five great-grandchildren (so
far), that have made me feel like I was always there with them.

Now I'm walking with Jeannine by my side, into the sunset of a
life well spent, carrying this thought in my heart:

Jeannine:

Inside my old carcass a young man still dwells,
And now and again my battered heart still swells.
I can still remember the joys; I can still remember the pain.
And I'm living and loving my life with you, all over again.....

THE END